NE능률 영어교과서

대한민국 고등학생 **10**명 중
4.7 명이 보는 교과서

영어 고등 교과서 점유율 1위
(7차, 2007 개정, 2009 개정, 2015 개정)

리딩튜터

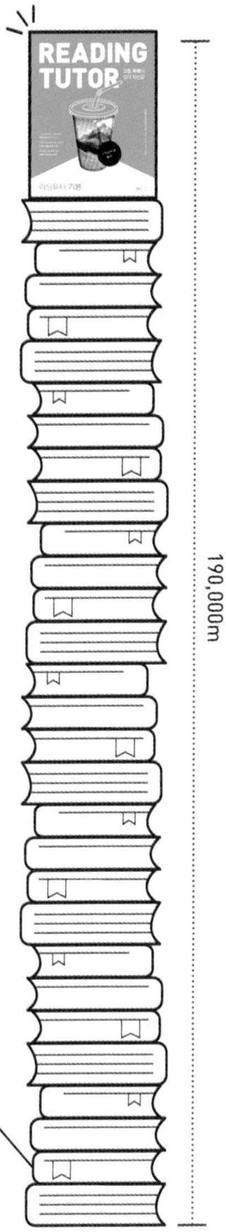

그동안 판매된
리딩튜터 1,900만 부
차곡차곡 쌓으면 19만 미터

에베레스트
21 배 높이

에베레스트 8,848m

능률보카

그동안 판매된
능률VOCA 1,100만 부

대한민국 박스오피스
천만명을 넘은 영화
단 28개

그래머존

그동안 판매된 400만 부의 그래머존을 바닥에 쭉 ~
1000km 서울-부산 왕

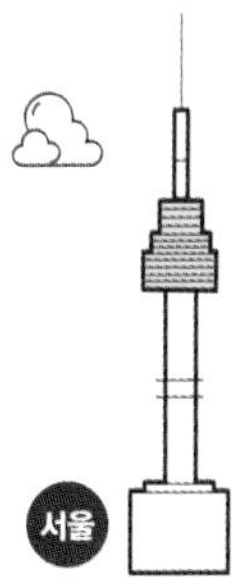

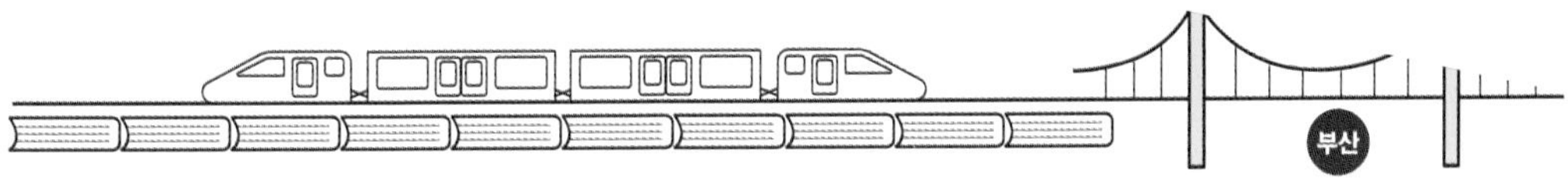

능률 VOCA 고난도

지은이	NE능률 영어교육연구소, 홍성수
선임연구원	김진홍, 신유승
영문 교열	Joan M. Dawson, Colm Barker
표지 디자인	민유화, 안훈정
내지 디자인	여백
맥편집	윤욱현
영업	한기영, 이경구, 박인규, 정철교, 하진수, 김남준, 이우현
마케팅	박혜선, 남경진, 이지원, 김여진

교재 개발에 도움을 주신 선생님

· **원고 구성** Moraig Macgillivray

· **기획자문** 류화정 선생님, 김호성 선생님

· 상위권을 위한 고난도 독해 필수 어휘 ·

능률 VOCA

고난도

Introduction

Who is this book for?

본 교재는 능률 VOCA 어원편보다 난이도가 한 단계 높은 어휘들 중에서 토익 · 토플에 공통적으로 자주 등장하는 어휘들을 수록하였다. 따라서 특목고 준비생이나, 토익 · 토플 시험을 준비하는 중고생, 그리고 능률 VOCA 어원편 이상의 어휘 실력을 키우길 원하는 상위권 학생들을 위한 교재이다.

How were the words in this book selected?

본 교재는 Part I의 essential words 900여 개와 Part II의 테마별 어휘 800여 개를 합친 1700여 개의 표제어 이외에 파생어와 동 · 반의어, 관련 어휘까지 포함하여 총 7800~8000여 개의 단어를 수록하고 있다.

오른쪽 도표에서 볼 수 있듯, Part I의 어휘는 능률 영어교육 연구소에서 분석한 토플 빈출 어휘와 토익 빈출 어휘에 공통적으로 포함된 1,300여 개의 어휘 중에서 능률 VOCA 어원편과 겹치는 400여 개의 어휘를 탈락시킨 후 900여 개의 핵심 단어를 선정하였다. 처음 추출한 1,300여 개의 어휘는 두 시험에 공통적으로 출현하는 단어인 만큼 중요도가 높으며, 능률 VOCA 어원편과 겹치는 400여 개의 어휘를 탈락시킴으로써 고등학교 평균 수준의 단어는 제외시켜 상위권 학생들에게 필요한 핵심 고난도 어휘만을 수록하였다.

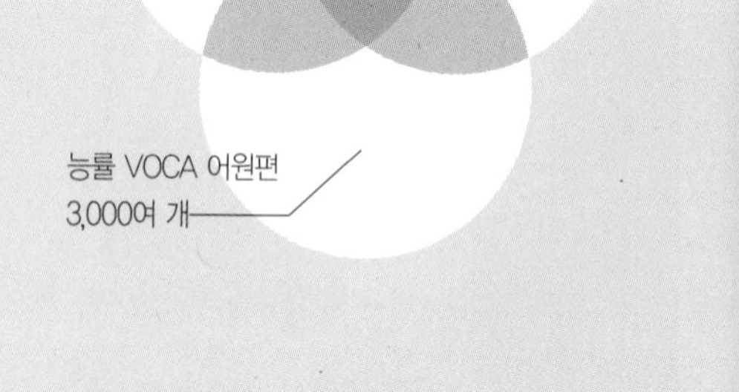

Part II에서는 고난도 독해 시 자주 등장하는 20개의 테마를 선정하고, 각 테마별로 평균 40여 개의 어휘들을 찾아내어 총 800여 개의 테마별 어휘를 선정하였다. 이렇게 선정된 어휘들을 오른쪽 그림과 같이 마인드맵 형태로 제시함으로써 보다 효율적으로 암기할 수 있도록 하였다.

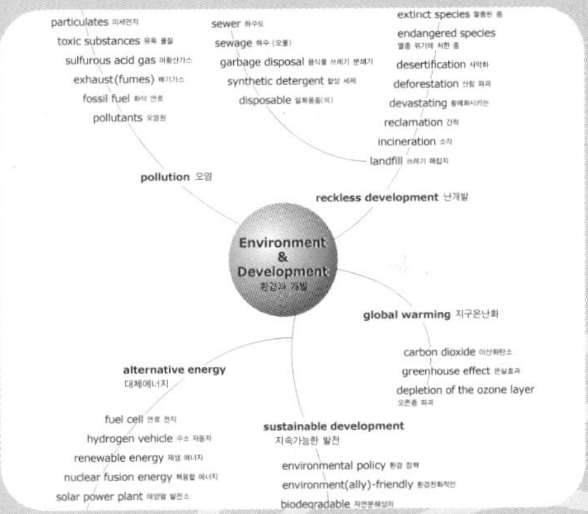

How to use this book

본 교재는 핵심 어휘들로 고난도 어휘의 기본기를 닦은 다음 특정 주제에 관한 독해력을 높일 수 있도록 essential words를 Part I에, 테마별 어휘를 Part II에 배치하였다. 하지만 반드시 이러한 순서대로 학습할 필요는 없으며 개인의 학습 목적과 스타일에 맞게 얼마든지 바꿀 수 있다. 만약 단시간에 고난도 독해 실력을 높이고 싶다면 Part II를 먼저 학습할 것을 권장한다. 그리고 개인에 따라서는 Part I만 학습하면 다소 지루할 수 있기 때문에 Part I과 Part II를 번갈아 가면서 학습하는 방법(예를 들면, 5일 단위로 계획하여 3일은 Part I을, 2일은 Part II를 학습)도 효과적일 수 있다.

Legend

v. 동사(verb)	**n.** 명사(noun)
a. 형용사(adjective)	**ad.** 부사(adverb)
syn. 동의어, 유의어(synonym)	**ant.** 반의어(antonym)
sb somebody	**sth** something
AmE. 미국 영어	***BrE.*** 영국 영어
to-v to부정사	**v-ing** 동명사
( ) 생략 가능 어구, 보충설명	[ ] 대체 가능 어구

Contents

Part Ⅰ essential words

Part Ⅱ 주제별 어휘

Part I
essential words

| 권장 학습법 |

◉ 하루에 30개의 어휘를 30일에 걸쳐서 학습하자.

◉ 단어의 기본적인 뜻뿐만 아니라 파생어 및 유의어, 반의어를 함께 학습하고, 다양한 예문 속에서 단어의 쓰임을 살펴보자.

◉ 우리말 뜻이 애매한 경우, 영영정의를 참고해서 단어의 정확한 의미를 이해하도록 하자.

◉ voca+의 추가 어휘 정보를 알아두자.

◉ 비슷한 의미를 가진 단어들 간의 뉘앙스 차이를 알아보자.

◉ 고급 이디엄(idiom)을 살펴보자.

◉ 학습한 어휘들을 연습문제(exercise)에서 복습하자.

◉ MP3 파일을 들으면서 암기하자.

affirm
[əfə́ːrm]

n. affirmation 확언, 단언
affirmative n. 긍정, 찬성
a. 긍정적인

v. 1. 공언하다, 긍정하다 syn. assert, confirm
2. (믿음 · 생각 등을) 지지하다

1 My boss has ***affirmed*** that he is resigning.
2 He claims that historical facts ***affirm*** his belief in God.

breakthrough
[bréikθrùː]

n. 획기적 발전, 중요한 성과[발견]

3 The discovery of penicillin was an important ***breakthrough*** in medicine.

voca+ make a breakthrough 획기적인 성과를 이루다

clamor
[klǽmər]

a. clamorous

v. 1. 시끄럽게 요구[불평]하다
2. 외치다, 떠들다

4 Members of the board started to ***clamor*** for his resignation.
5 Children ***clamored*** excitedly.

n. 아우성, 소란, 항의

coordinate
[kouɔ́ːrdənèit]

n. coordination
1. 조정, 조화 2. (근육의) 작용
coordinator 조정자

v. 1. 조정하다, 통합하다
2. (의상 · 가구 등을) 조화시키다

6 Martin will ***coordinate*** the entire advertising program.
7 Choose a tie that ***coordinates*** with your shirt.

n. [kouɔ́ːrdənit] 1. 좌표 2. (의상 · 가구 등의) 조화

8 the x, y ***coordinates*** of any point on a line

distort
[distɔ́ːrt]

n. distortion
a. distorted

v. 1. (형태 · 소리 등을) 일그러지게 하다
2. (진실 · 사실 등을) 왜곡하다 syn. twist, falsify

9 The curved screens can ***distort*** the picture.
10 The paper was accused of ***distorting*** the truth.

1 사장은 사임하겠다고 공식 발표했다. 2 그는 역사적 사실이 신에 대한 그의 믿음을 뒷받침한다고 주장한다. 3 페니실린의 발견은 의학계의 획기적 사건이었다. 4 이사회 임원들은 그의 사퇴를 소리 높여 요구하기 시작했다. 5 아이들이 흥분해서 떠들어댔다. 6 Martin이 전체 광고 일정을 조정할 것이다. 7 네 셔츠와 어울리는 넥타이를 선택해라. 8 직선 위 한 점의 x, y 좌표 9 휘어진 스크린이 화면을 일그러뜨릴 수 있다. 10 그 신문은 왜곡 보도로 고소당했다.

fidelity
[fidéləti]

n. 1. 정절, 충성 syn. faithfulness, loyalty ant. infidelity
2. (원본 · 원작에) 충실함 syn. closeness

1 His *fidelity* to his wife is very strong.
2 the *fidelity* of the movie version to the original book

voca+ hi-fi(high-fidelity) 음질이 깨끗한

inauguration
[inɔ̀ːgjəréiʃən]

v. inaugurate
inaugural n. 취임사
a. 취임식의, 개회의

n. 1. 취임(식)
2. 개시, 개업[준공]식 syn. initiation

3 the president's *inauguration* speech
4 The *inauguration* of the new stadium took place last week.

voca+ Inauguration Day 미국 대통령 취임일 (1월 20일)

mourn
[mɔːrn]

n. mourning 1. 상(喪) 2. 상복
mourner 조문객, 문상객
a. mournful

v. (죽음 등을) 슬퍼하다, 애도하다 syn. lament, grieve for

5 John *mourned* the death of his grandfather.

voca+ mourning period 애도 기간
in mourning 상(喪) 중인

novice
[nɑ́vis]

n. 신참, 초심자 syn. beginner

6 He is a *novice* at skiing.

retreat
[ritríːt]

v. 1. 후퇴하다, 물러나다 syn. withdraw, recede ant. advance
2. (결정 등을) 철회하다 syn. back off

7 The police didn't *retreat* in the face of the angry crowd.
8 The politician *retreated from* his campaign promises.

n. 1. 후퇴, 퇴각, 물러남
2. 휴식처, 휴양지, 은신처

9 They spent a romantic weekend at a mountain *retreat*.

voca+ beat a (hasty) retreat 서둘러 떠나다

1 아내에 대한 그의 정절은 매우 강하다. 2 원작에 대한 영화의 충실도 3 대통령 취임 연설 4 새 경기장의 준공식이 지난 주에 열렸다. 5 John은 할아버지의 죽음을 애도했다. 6 그는 스키 초보자이다. 7 경찰은 분노한 군중을 마주 대하고 후퇴하지 않았다. 8 그 정치가는 자신의 선거 공약을 철회했다. 9 그들은 산 속의 휴양지에서 낭만적인 주말을 보냈다.

subtle
[sʌ́tl]

n. subtlety

a. 1. 미묘한, 포착하기 어려운 ant. obvious, noticeable
2. 교묘한 syn. crafty
3. 민감한, 예민한 syn. delicate

1 I felt a ***subtle*** change in her attitude.
2 She is ***subtle*** in giving her opinion.
3 The job required a ***subtle*** mind.

anonymous
[ənɑ́ːniməs]

n. anonymity

a. 1. 익명의 syn. unnamed
2. 눈에 띄지 않는, 개성이 없는

4 This book was written by an ***anonymous*** author.
5 She has a rather ***anonymous*** face.

ephemeral
[ifémərəl]

n. ephemera
일시적으로 사용하는 제품군

a. 수명이 짧은, 순간적인, 덧없는 syn. short-lived, transitory

6 Physical beauty is rather an ***ephemeral*** concept.

appraise
[əpréiz]

n. appraisal

v. 값을 매기다, 감정[평가]하다

7 The real estate agent ***appraised*** the house at $200,000.

| Nuance | "평가하다/감정하다" 관련 어휘 뉘앙스 차이

appraise 평가하다, 감정하다	| 전문가의 판단에 의해 가치를 감정하다. 8 appraise works of art
estimate 추산하다, 어림잡다	| 크기 · 수량 · 가격에 대해 주관적이거나 다소 부정확한 판단을 하다. 9 They estimated the crowd at 50,000.
evaluate 평가하다	| 신중한 판단 후에 평가하다. 10 The new drug is being evaluated in clinical trials.
rate 평가하다, 등급을 매기다	| 등급을 결정하기 위한 평가를 하다. 11 rate the restaurant higher than any other
assess 평가하다, 사정하다	| 주로 금전적인 가치를 평가하는 판단을 하다. 12 assess real estate for investors

1 나는 그녀의 태도에서 미묘한 변화를 느꼈다. 2 그녀는 교묘하게 자기 의견을 제시한다. 3 그 일은 섬세한 사고력을 요구했다. 4 이 책은 익명의 작가에 의해 쓰여졌다. 5 그녀는 다소 개성없는 얼굴이다. 6 육체의 아름다움은 그저 순간적인 개념이다. 7 부동산 중개업자는 그 집의 가격을 20만 달러로 매겼다. 8 예술 작품을 감정하다 9 그들은 군중 수를 5만 정도로 추정했다. 10 그 새로운 약은 임상 실험 판정 중이다. 11 그 식당의 등급을 다른 어느 식당보다도 더 높게 매기다 12 투자자들을 위해 부동산의 가치를 사정하다

deride
[diráid]

n. derision
a. derisive (=derisory)

v. 비웃다, 조롱하다 syn. mock, ridicule

1 His most recent movies have been ***derided*** as being too commercial.

foster
[fɔ́(:)stər]

v. 1. (성장 · 발달을) 촉진하다, 육성하다 syn. promote, encourage
2. (남의 아이를) 양육하다, 돌보다

2 The president's aim is to ***foster*** better ties with neighboring countries.

3 The couple had never had their own children but helped to raise others through ***fostering***.

a. 양육하는

voca+ foster parent[child] 수양 부모[자녀]

complexion
[kəmplékʃən]

n. 1. 안색, 혈색, 얼굴빛
2. 성향, 기질

4 Too much sun is bad for your ***complexion***.

5 the political ***complexion*** of the government

voca+ put a new[different] complexion on ~에 새로운 국면을 부여하다
fair-complexioned 피부가 흰[뽀얀]

intrinsic
[intrínsik]

a. 본질적인, 내재된 syn. inherent ant. extrinsic

6 Praying to God is an ***intrinsic*** characteristic of most Christians' behavior.

voca+ intrinsic value 진가

overt
[óuvəːrt]

a. 공공연한, 노골적인 ant. covert

7 The shopkeeper displayed ***overt*** prejudice against all foreign customers.

voca+ a market overt 공개 시장

1 그의 최근 영화들은 너무 상업적이라는 이유로 비웃음을 샀다. 2 대통령의 목적은 이웃 국가들과 더 나은 유대 관계를 구축하는 것이다. 3 그 부부는 자녀가 없었지만 대신 다른 아이들을 맡아 돌보면서 양육을 도왔다. 4 햇볕을 너무 많이 쬐면 얼굴빛이 나빠진다. 5 정부의 정치적 성향 6 신에게 기도하는 것은 대부분의 기독교인들이 가진 고유한 행동 특성이다. 7 그 가게 주인은 모든 외국인 고객들에 대한 노골적인 편견을 드러냈다.

provoke
[prəvóuk]

n. provocation
a. provocative

v. 1. (부정적인 반응을) 일으키다, 유발하다 syn. cause, evoke
2. (고의적으로) 화나게 하다, 도발하다

1 The CEO's decision to cut jobs ***provoked*** a strike.
2 He is just trying to ***provoke*** us.
3 The US warned North Korea against their ***provocative*** missile launch.

voca+ thought-provoking 시사하는 점이 많은

conjure
[kándʒər]

n. conjurer 마술사 (=conjuror)

v. 마술을 부리다, 마술로 ~을 만들어내다

4 The magician loved to ***conjure*** rabbits from hats.

voca+ a name to conjure with 유력한 사람(의 이름)
conjure up 1. (믿기지 않는 일을) 해내다 2. ~을 상기시키다

tacit
[tǽsit]

a. 암묵적인, 무언의 syn. implicit

5 Her gestures suggested a ***tacit*** approval of his suggestion.

voca+ tacit agreement[approval/support] 암묵적 동의[승인/지지]

accrue
[əkrúː]

n. accrual 증가(액)

v. (이자 · 이익이) 발생하다, 누적되다[시키다] syn. accumulate

6 My savings account has ***accrued*** $75.

voca+ accrue to ~에게 이익이 되다, 혜택을 주다

cryptography
[kriptágrəfi]

n. cryptographer 암호 작성가
a. cryptic 암호같은

n. 암호(문), 암호 작성[해독]

7 Today, ***cryptography*** is a tool used within computer and network security.

---

1 일자리를 줄이겠다는 CEO의 결정 때문에 파업이 시작됐다. 2 그는 단지 우리를 화나게 하려는 것이다. 3 미국은 북한의 도발적인 미사일 발사에 대해 북한에게 경고했다. 4 마술사는 모자에서 토끼를 만들어 내는 마술을 무척 좋아했다. 5 그녀의 몸짓은 그의 제안에 대한 암묵적인 승인을 나타냈다. 6 내 예금 계좌에 75달러의 이자가 붙었다. 7 오늘날 암호는 컴퓨터와 네트워크 보안에 이용되는 도구이다.

filibuster
[fílibʌ̀stər]

v. (긴 연설로) 의사 진행을 방해하다

1 The senators *filibustered* for two days by making long speeches.

n. 의사 진행 방해

palatable
[pǽlətəbl]

n. palate 1. 입천장 2. 미각

a. 1. 입에 맞는, 맛 좋은
2. 마음에 드는 ant. unpalatable

2 The wine in this restaurant is always *palatable*.
3 That option is not very *palatable*.

unlettered
[ʌ̀nlétərd]

a. 문맹의, 교육받지 못한 syn. illiterate ant. literate, lettered

4 He remained *unlettered* well into adulthood.

impending
[impéndiŋ]

a. (재난 · 위기 등이) 임박한, 눈앞에 닥친 syn. imminent

5 The coastguards prepared for the *impending* typhoon.

voca+ impending danger[doom/disaster] 임박한 위험[종말/재앙]

IDIOMS

cost an arm and a leg 매우 비싸다 (to be very expensive)

6 His new car *cost an arm and a leg*.

crunch time 결정적 순간 (a time when an important or difficult decision has to be made)

7 At *crunch time* the team really pulled together.

1 상원의원들은 긴 연설로 이틀 동안 의사 진행을 방해했다. 2 이 레스토랑의 포도주는 언제나 맛이 좋다. 3 그 선택 사항은 별로 마음에 들지 않는다. 4 그는 성인이 되어서도 한참 동안 문맹이었다. 5 해안 경비대는 곧 닥칠 태풍에 대비했다. 6 그의 새 차는 엄청나게 비쌌다. 7 결정적 순간에 그 팀은 정말 잘 뭉쳤다.

day **01** exercise

A Match the words in the left column to the sentences in the right column.

ⓐ **coordinate**: to organize or put together

ⓑ **intrinsic**: naturally occurring or being characteristic of

ⓒ **tacit**: unspoken but implied

ⓓ **accrue**: to build up or add to

ⓔ **impending**: going to happen soon

1. Greed is a(n) ___________ quality of capitalism.
2. The news bulletin made people aware of the ___________ disaster.
3. I will let the interest ___________ in my savings account.
4. She will ___________ every aspect of the workshop.
5. He gave his ___________ approval to the plan.

B Choose the word or phrase that best explains the underlined word.

1. If you ***affirm*** something, you _______________ it.
   ⓐ respect ⓑ agree with ⓒ misunderstand ⓓ dispense with

2. If you ***retreat***, you _______________.
   ⓐ run away ⓑ come along ⓒ regret ⓓ struggle

3. If you ***deride*** people, you _______________ them.
   ⓐ fire ⓑ pressure ⓒ ridicule ⓓ applaud

4. If you are ***provoked***, you are likely to _______________.
   ⓐ fight ⓑ joke ⓒ hide ⓓ laugh

5. If you don't have ***fidelity***, you are _______________.
   ⓐ lonely ⓑ unkind ⓒ unfaithful ⓓ defensive

정답 및 해설 p.370

C Choose the option that is closest in meaning to the underlined word.

1. a scientific ***breakthrough***
ⓐ setback ⓑ discovery ⓒ accident ⓓ experiment

2. a ***novice*** driver
ⓐ drunken ⓑ beginner ⓒ careless ⓓ veteran

3. ***distort*** the truth
ⓐ declare ⓑ discover ⓒ request ⓓ twist

D Choose the option that is the opposite of the underlined word.

1. all that ***clamor***
ⓐ labor ⓑ peace ⓒ waste ⓓ mess

2. ***overt*** hostility
ⓐ violent ⓑ apparent ⓒ unfounded ⓓ hidden

3. ***subtle*** differences
ⓐ obvious ⓑ minor ⓒ problematic ⓓ fundamental

E Choose the best word or phrase.

1. Who is the most important person at an ***inauguration***?
ⓐ the master of ceremonies ⓑ the president-elect
ⓒ the lead singer ⓓ the would-be bride

2. Which of the following would be most likely to be ***anonymous***?
ⓐ a television appearance ⓑ an award acceptance
ⓒ a charitable donation ⓓ a bill payment

3. Which of the following would you have ***appraised***?
ⓐ a proposal ⓑ a conversation ⓒ a viewpoint ⓓ an antique

4. You ***mourn*** when somebody close to you ________________.
ⓐ gets fired ⓑ has a baby ⓒ has died ⓓ visits you

compliment
[kámpləmənt]

a. complimentary
1. 칭찬하는 2. 공짜인

n. 칭찬, 찬사 syn. praise

■1 She kept paying Matt ***compliments*** on his appearance.

voca+ return the compliment 받은 만큼 돌려주다, 되갚아 주다
back-handed[left-handed] compliment 빈정대는[마음에 없는] 칭찬

v. [kámpləmènt] 칭찬하다

delegate
[déligit]

n. delegation 대표단, 사절단

n. 대표, 사절, 파견위원

■2 The convention was attended by 150 ***delegates***.

v. [déligèit] 1. (일 · 권한을) 맡기다, 위임하다
2. (~할 사람으로) 지정하다, 임명하다

■3 He always ***delegates*** and never helps.
■4 I was ***delegated*** to train the new employees.
■5 He is a member of the Brazilian ***delegation*** to the U.S.

epoch
[épək]

n. (역사상 중요한) 시대, 시기 syn. era

■6 the beginning of a new ***epoch*** of peace and cooperation

voca+ epoch-making 새 시대를 여는, 획기적인

bereaved
[biríːvd]

n. bereavement

a. 가족 · 친구를 잃은, 사별한

■7 His ***bereaved*** relatives were crying at the funeral.

voca+ the bereaved 유가족

anatomy
[ənǽtəmi]

n. anatomist 해부학자
a. anatomical

n. 1. 해부학, 해부학적 구조 2. 신체

■8 Basic knowledge of ***anatomy*** is used to draw a human body.
■9 Which part of his ***anatomy*** has been tattooed?
■10 ***Anatomists*** study the form and structure of animals' bodies.

■1 그녀는 Matt에게 계속 그의 외모에 대한 찬사를 늘어놓았다. ■2 그 총회에는 150명의 대표들이 참석했다. ■3 그는 언제나 일을 맡기기만 하고 절대로 돕지 않는다. ■4 나는 신입사원 교육 담당자로 임명되었다. ■5 그는 대미(對美) 브라질 대표단의 일원이다. ■6 평화와 협력의 새로운 시대의 시작 ■7 그의 유가족들이 장례식에서 울고 있었다. ■8 기초적인 해부학 지식은 인체를 그리는 데 활용된다. ■9 그의 신체 어디에 문신을 했어? ■10 해부학자들은 동물 신체의 형태와 구조를 연구한다.

parallel

[pǽrəlèl]

n. parallelism 1. 유사점 2. 병행

a. 1. 평행의, 병렬의 2. 동시에 발생하는, 매우 비슷한

1 The road runs *parallel to* the river.

2 *Parallel* decisions were reached in Tokyo and Beijing.

n. 유사[대등]한 것, 필적하는 것 syn. equivalent

voca+ draw a parallel between (두 가지를) 비교하다
have no parallel 비할 데 없다, 최고[최악]이다

v. ~와 유사하다, ~에 필적하다

percipient

[pərsípiənt]

n. percipience

a. 이해력이 뛰어난, 눈치가 빠른 syn. perceptive

3 a *percipient* observer

guild

[gild]

n. 동업 조합, 연맹, (중세의) 길드

4 the Publishers *Guild* chairperson

sober

[sóubər]

n. sobriety

a. 1. 술에 취하지 않은 ant. drunk
2. 진지한, 침착한
3. (색이) 수수한, 어두운

5 I must stay *sober* tonight – I have to drive.

6 We need a more *sober* approach to these scandals.

7 He dressed in a *sober* grey suit.

voca+ stone-cold sober/as sober as a judge 정신이 말짱한, 전혀 취하지 않은

v. 진지[냉정]해지다, 진지하게 하다

voca+ sober up 술이 깨다[깨게 하다]

indigenous

[indídʒənəs]

a. 토착의, 지역 고유의 syn. native

8 Cranberries are *indigenous to* America.

1 그 도로는 강변을 따라 있다. 2 도쿄와 베이징에서 같은 결정이 내려졌다. 3 눈치가 빠른 관찰자 4 출판 조합장 5 오늘밤에 난 취하면 안 돼. 운전해야 되거든. 6 우리는 이 추문들에 대해 더 침착한 대응을 해야 한다. 7 그는 수수한 회색 정장을 입었다. 8 크랜베리는 미국 토종 식물이다.

affiliate
[əfílièit]

n. affiliation
a. affiliated

v. (더 큰 조직 · 단체와) 연합[제휴]하다, 결연을 맺다

1 Our college is ***affiliated with*** a university in Tokyo.

n. [əfíliət] 계열사, 지부

realm
[relm]

n. 1. (지식 · 활동 등의) 영역, 범위 syn. field, domain
2. 왕국 syn. kingdom

2 The idea belongs in the ***realm*** of religion.
3 the rise and fall of the ***realm***

voca+ within[beyond] the realms of possibility 가능한[불가능한]

converge
[kənvə́ːrdʒ]

n. convergence
a. convergent

v. 1. (한 곳으로) 모이다, 만나다
2. (생각 · 목표가) 모아지다, 일치하다 ant. diverge

4 The demonstrators ***converged*** in front of the city hall.
5 Their feelings on social issues seldom ***converged***.

appease
[əpíːz]

n. appeasement

v. 달래다, 진정시키다

6 The leader tried to ***appease*** the angry people.

| N u a n c e | "달래다" 관련 어휘 뉘앙스 차이

appease 달래다	적 또는 반대 진영이 원하는 것을 주어 달래다. 7 a move to appease critics of the regime
pacify 진정시키다	화난 사람을 진정시키거나 분쟁을 종식시켜 평화를 정착시키다. 8 The mayor is trying to pacify the street protestors.
placate 누그러지게 하다	화난 사람을 달래 진정시키다. 9 an attempt to placate the angry farmers
conciliate 조정하다	어떤 조치를 취해 분쟁을 끝내다. 10 conciliate the union on strike

1 우리 대학은 도쿄의 한 대학과 결연을 맺었다. 2 그 관념은 종교의 영역에 속한다. 3 왕국의 흥망성쇠 4 시위대가 시청 앞에 모였다. 5 사회적 쟁점들에 대한 그들의 생각은 일치하는 일이 거의 없었다. 6 그 지도자는 분노한 사람들을 달래려고 노력했다. 7 정권을 비판하는 사람들을 달래려는 조치 8 시장은 거리의 시위대를 진정시키려 애쓰고 있다. 9 분노한 농민들을 달래려는 시도 10 노조의 파업을 조정하다

distill
[distíl]

n. distillation
distiller 증류주 제조업자[업체]

v. 1. 증류하다, 증류하여 만들다(to make a liquid pure by heating it until it becomes a gas and cooling it so that it becomes a liquid again)
2. (요점을) 뽑아내다

1 Whisky is made by a process called *distilling*.
2 The research findings will be *distilled into* a summary.

feudal
[fjú:dl]

n. feudalism 봉건제 (=feudal system)

a. (중세) 봉건제의 (relating to a social system in which people were given land by a nobleman and had to work and fight for him in return)

3 *feudal* society
4 *Feudalism* existed in Europe from the ninth century to the fifteenth century.

transplant
[trǽnsplæ̀nt]

n. transplantation

n. 1. 이식 (수술) (an operation in which a damaged organ is replaced with one from another person)
2. 이식된 장기

5 She is on a waiting list for a liver *transplant*.
6 Her body rejected the *transplant*.

voca+ heart[kidney] transplant 심장[신장] 이식

v. [trænsplǽnt] (장기 · 식물을) 이식하다, 이전하다 syn. implant

meager
[mí:gər]

a. 빈약한, 적은, 불충분한 syn. scanty ant. ample

7 Many poor countries have *meager* natural resources.

pliable
[pláiəbəl]

n. pliability

a. 1. 유연한, 잘 휘어지는 syn. flexible ant. rigid
2. 영향을 받기 쉬운, 융통성 있는 syn. compliant

8 The *pliable* material has been developed to reduce injuries in crashes.
9 Children have very *pliable* minds.

1 위스키는 증류 과정을 거쳐 만들어진다. 2 연구 결과는 요약되어 정리될 것이다. 3 봉건 사회 4 봉건제는 9세기부터 15세기까지 유럽에서 존속했다. 5 그녀는 간 이식 수술 대기자 명단에 올라 있다. 6 그녀의 몸이 이식된 장기에 대해 거부반응을 보였다. 7 여러 가난한 나라들은 천연 자원이 적다. 8 그 유연한 소재는 충돌시 부상을 줄이기 위해 개발되었다. 9 아이들은 (다른 사람에게) 아주 쉽게 영향을 받는다.

repel
[ripél]

repellent
n. 1. 방충제 2. 방수제
a. 혐오스러운

v. 1. 물리치다, 쫓아버리다 syn. drive off
2. 불쾌감을 주다 syn. repulse
3. (자석이 같은 극끼리) 밀어내다 ant. attract

1 a lotion that ***repels*** insects
2 His constant winking ***repels*** many women.
3 Like poles ***repel*** each other, and opposite poles attract.

sporadic
[spərǽdik]

a. 간헐적인, 불규칙적으로 발생하는 syn. intermittent

4 ***Sporadic*** clashes broke out between gunmen and police.

unanimous
[juːnǽniməs]

n. unanimity

a. 만장일치의, 전원 합의의

5 The student won the essay contest by a ***unanimous*** decision.
6 To go forward, the board needs to reach a degree of ***unanimity***.

voca+ be unanimous in v-ing 만장일치로 ~하다

periphery
[pəríːfəri]

peripheral
n. 컴퓨터 주변기기
a. 1. 지엽적인, 중요하지 않은 2. 주변의

n. 외곽, 외부, 변두리 syn. outer boundary

7 the development plans for the ***periphery*** of Seoul

voca+ on[at] the periphery of (장소 · 모임 등의) 주변에 있는, 비주류인

luminescence
[lùːminésəns]

a. luminescent

n. 발광(發光), 냉광, 은은한 빛

8 In scientific terms, ***luminescence*** means 'light produced without heat.'

1 벌레 퇴치용 로션 2 그의 끊임없는 윙크는 많은 여성들을 불쾌하게 한다. 3 같은 극끼리는 서로 밀어내고 다른 극끼리는 끌어당긴다. 4 총기를 소지한 자들과 경찰 사이에 간헐적인 충돌이 발생했다. 5 그 학생은 심사위원 만장일치로 글짓기 대회에서 대상을 받았다. 6 계속 진행하기 위해서는 이사회가 전원 합의에 이르러야 한다. 7 서울 외곽 지역 개발 계획 8 과학 용어로 '냉광'은 '열 없이 발생하는 빛'을 뜻한다.

incumbent
[inkʌ́mbənt]

n. incumbency
1. 현직 2. 재직기간

n. 재직자, 현직자, 현직 의원

1 The *incumbent* was reelected by nearly 60 percent of the vote.

a. 현직의, 재직 중인

2 The *incumbent* mayor faces a tough challenge from his young opponent.

voca+ be incumbent on[upon] ~의 의무이다, ~가 해야 한다

prosaic
[prouzéiik]

a. 지루한, 진부한, 재미없는 syn. mundane

3 He is described as an intelligent but *prosaic* man.

flagrant
[fléigrənt]

a. 뻔뻔스러운, 극악한 syn. blatant

4 His *flagrant* disregard for the law led to his arrest.

pervade
[pərvéid]

n. pervasiveness
a. pervasive

v. ~에 널리 퍼지다[가득 차다], 충만하다 syn. permeate

5 Sweet smells of flowers *pervaded* the garden.
6 Fear of earthquakes is *pervasive* in this area.

IDIOMS

slip one's mind 깜박 잊어버리다 (to be forgotten)

7 Mom told me to buy some eggs, but it totally *slipped my mind*.

take a rain check 다음 기회로 미루다 (to say you will do something in the future, but not now)

8 How about dinner tonight? – Sorry, can I *take a rain check* on that?

1 현 재직자는 거의 60%에 이르는 표를 얻고 재임되었다. 2 현직 시장은 젊은 상대의 거센 도전을 받고 있다. 3 그는 똑똑하지만 지루한 사람으로 묘사된다. 4 그는 법을 악의적으로 무시하여 체포되었다. 5 정원에는 달콤한 꽃 향기가 가득했다. 6 지진에 대한 공포가 이 지역에 널리 퍼져 있다. 7 엄마가 나한테 달걀 좀 사오라고 했지만 나는 까맣게 잊었다. 8 오늘밤 저녁식사 어때? – 미안해, 다음에 하면 안 될까?

exercise

A Match the words in the left column to the sentences in the right column.

ⓐ **transplant**: to take an organ from one person's body and put it into another's

ⓑ **appease**: to calm or soothe

ⓒ **periphery**: the outer area or edge of a place

ⓓ **incumbent**: holding an official post

ⓔ **pervade**: to be present throughout

1. The doctor will ____________ the dying man's heart to the man with the heart condition.
2. The ____________ mayor lost the election.
3. The same theme ____________(e)s the author's many works.
4. The mother ____________(e)d the crying child with kind words.
5. The ____________ of the property is outlined by a fence.

B Choose the word or phrase that best explains the underlined word.

1. If a decision is ***unanimous***, everyone ____________.
ⓐ votes ⓑ gathers ⓒ agrees ⓓ argues

2. If a group is ***affiliated*** with a larger one, it ____________ it.
ⓐ is next to ⓑ works for ⓒ seeks help from ⓓ is connected with

3. If you ***delegate*** tasks, you ____________.
ⓐ appoint others to do them ⓑ do them yourself
ⓒ refuse to take part in them ⓓ fail to finish them

4. If roads ***converge***, they ____________.
ⓐ become one ⓑ are paved
ⓒ are separated ⓓ are under construction

5. A ***sober*** person hasn't ____________.
ⓐ been to college ⓑ gotten enough sleep
ⓒ had a drink ⓓ met a deadline

정답 및 해설 p.370

C Choose the option that is closest in meaning to the underlined word.

1. *flagrant* disregard
   ⓐ subtle ⓑ obvious ⓒ flavory ⓓ unintentional

2. *indigenous* people
   ⓐ agricultural ⓑ adventurous ⓒ industrious ⓓ native

3. the *realm* of science
   ⓐ field ⓑ purpose ⓒ conclusion ⓓ experiment

D Choose the option that is the opposite of the underlined word.

1. *pliable* material
   ⓐ smooth ⓑ durable ⓒ rigid ⓓ large

2. *compliment* an outfit
   ⓐ put on ⓑ insult ⓒ soil ⓓ purchase

3. *sporadic* events
   ⓐ entertaining ⓑ popular ⓒ brief ⓓ regular

E Choose the best word or phrase.

1. Which of the following would you try to ***repel***?
   ⓐ insects ⓑ sweets ⓒ trees ⓓ horses

2. Who would be most likely to be referred to as "the ***bereaved***"?
   ⓐ a gambler ⓑ a graduate ⓒ a widow ⓓ a bride

3. Which of the following might be ***distilled***?
   ⓐ water ⓑ wheat ⓒ soil ⓓ coal

4. If you earned a ***meager*** salary, you might ________________.
   ⓐ buy expensive things ⓑ have many degrees
   ⓒ ask for a raise ⓓ retire early

abhor
[əbhɔ́ːr]
n. abhorrence
a. abhorrent

v. 몹시 싫어하다, 혐오하다 syn. hate, loathe, detest

1 The woman *abhorred* all forms of violence.

banquet
[bǽŋkwit]

n. 1. 연회, 향연 syn. feast
2. 진수성찬

2 a list of food items served during the wedding *banquet*
3 a *banquet* cooked by a first-rate chef

confide
[kənfáid]
n. confidence
1. 비밀 2. 자신감 3. 신용
a. confident
1. 자신 있는 2. 확신하는

v. 1. (비밀을) 털어놓다
2. 신임하다, 신뢰하다 syn. trust
3. 맡기다, 위탁하다 syn. entrust, commit

4 I often *confide* my feelings to her.
5 My father is the only person I can *confide in*.
6 He *confided* his laptop to his friend's safekeeping.

designate
[dézignèit]
n. designation

v. 1. 지명[지정]하다, 임명하다 syn. assign, delegate
2. 가리키다, 나타내다 syn. indicate, represent

7 She was *designated* as the spokesperson.
8 Red crosses *designate* hospitals.

hygiene
[háidʒiːn]
a. hygienic

n. 위생, 청결 syn. sanitation, cleanliness

9 Restaurants need to ensure good *hygiene* in kitchen areas.

1 그 여자는 모든 형태의 폭력을 혐오했다. 2 결혼식 연회 때 제공되는 음식 목록 3 일류 요리사가 요리한 진수성찬 4 나는 내 감정을 그녀에게 자주 털어놓는다. 5 아버지는 내가 신뢰할 수 있는 유일한 사람이다. 6 그는 자신의 노트북 컴퓨터를 친구에게 맡겨 보관시켰다. 7 그녀는 대변인으로 임명되었다. 8 빨간 십자가는 병원을 가리킨다. 9 식당에서는 반드시 주방 주변의 청결을 유지해야 한다.

linger
[líŋgər]

a. lingering

v. 1. (떠나지 않고) 꾸물거리다 syn. loiter
2. 좀처럼 사라지지 않다, 계속 남아 있다

❶ Many students *lingered* after the exam.
❷ Doubts about the truth of the episode still *linger on*.

perish
[périʃ]

a. perishable

v. 1. 죽다, 소멸하다, 붕괴되다
2. *BrE.* 썩다, (썩어서) 못쓰게 되다 syn. decay, rot

❸ Thousands *perished* when the plane crashed.
❹ Sunlight can cause the rubber to *perish*.

redundant
[ridʌ́ndənt]

n. redundancy

a. 1. 불필요한, 중복되는, 남아도는 syn. superfluous
2. *BrE.* 해고된 syn. dismissed

❺ *Redundant* information should be removed.
❻ The factory is closing and making staff *redundant*.

staple
[stéipl]

n. stapler 스테이플러 (호치키스: 상표명)

n. 1. (주로 복수로) 주요 산물, 중요 상품
2. 주요소, 주성분
3. 호치키스심, 제책못

❼ Rice and wheat are *staples* for most of the world's population.
❽ Investment is a *staple* of business.
❾ Use *staples*, not paperclips, to keep the papers together.

a. 주요한, 중요한, 기본적인 syn. principal, chief

❿ Prices of *staple* foods have been increasing.

v. 꺾쇠[호치키스]로 묶다

transfusion
[trænsfjúːʒən]

n. 수혈

⓫ Every six months she needs a blood *transfusion*.

---

❶ 많은 학생들이 시험이 끝난 뒤에도 가지 않고 있었다. ❷ 그 사건의 진실에 대한 의혹은 아직도 사라지지 않고 있다. ❸ 비행기가 추락했을 때 수천 명이 죽었다. ❹ 햇빛은 고무를 부식시킬 수 있다. ❺ 중복되는 정보는 삭제되어야 한다. ❻ 공장은 문을 닫으면서 직원들을 해고할 예정이다. ❼ 쌀과 밀은 전세계 인구 대부분의 주식이다. ❽ 투자는 사업의 주요소이다. ❾ 클립 말고 호치키스를 사용해서 서류를 한데 묶어라. ❿ 주요 식품들의 가격이 오르고 있다. ⓫ 그녀는 6개월마다 수혈이 필요하다.

uneven
[ʌníːvən]

n. unevenness

a. 1. 평탄하지 않은, 울퉁불퉁한 syn. rough, bumpy
2. 불규칙한 syn. irregular
3. 공정하지 않은 syn. unequal, lopsided

1 The ground was rough and *uneven*.
2 Her pulse had become *uneven*.
3 an *uneven* income distribution

algae
[ǽldʒiː]

a. algal

n. 조류, 해조 (단수형 alga)

4 *Algae* are types of plants with no stems or leaves that grow in water or on damp surfaces.

cardiac
[kɑ́ːrdiæ̀k]

a. 심장(병)의

5 The patient needs to undergo *cardiac* surgery.

voca+ cardiac arrest[failure] 심장(박동) 정지

loathe
[louð]

n. loathing
a. loath

v. 몹시 싫어하다, 질색하다

6 I *loathed* singing in front of others.

| Nuance | "혐오하다 / 증오하다" 관련 어휘 뉘앙스 차이

loathe 질색하다	생리적인 역겨움과 구역질이 느껴질 정도로 강하게 싫어하다. 7 I loathe snakes.
detest 혐오하다	감정적 악의 없이 혐오하거나 경멸하다. 8 I detest dishonest people.
hate 미워하다	감정적 악의를 지닌 채 증오하다. 9 Why do you hate me so much?
abhor 몹시 싫어하다	도덕적으로 옳지 못한 것에 대해 반감을 가지다. 10 I abhor cruelty to animals.

1 땅은 거칠고 울퉁불퉁했다. 2 그녀의 맥박이 불규칙해졌다. 3 불공평한 수입 분배 4 해조류는 물 속이나 축축한 지면에서 자라는 줄기도 잎도 없는 식물의 일종이다. 5 그 환자는 심장 수술을 받아야 한다. 6 나는 다른 사람들 앞에서 노래하는 것을 무척 싫어했다. 7 나는 뱀이 질색이다. 8 나는 정직하지 않은 사람을 몹시 싫어한다. 9 넌 왜 그렇게 나를 싫어하니? 10 나는 동물 학대를 싫어한다.

dubious
[djúːbiəs]

n. dubiousness

a. 1. 수상쩍은, 미덥지 않은 (not completely honest, safe, or reliable)
2. 의심하는, 확신하지 못하는 (not sure whether something is true or good)
syn. doubtful

1 Their claims are *dubious* and not scientifically proven.
2 I'm *dubious* about his intention.

forgo
[fɔːrgóu]

v. ~하지 않다, ~없이 지내다 syn. abstain from, give up

3 The workers agreed to *forgo* any bonuses.

intercept
[ìntərsépt]

n. interception
interceptor [군사 무기] 요격기

v. 가로채다, 가로막다

4 The police *intercepted* the message from the kidnapper.
5 Cyber crime can be committed by communication *interception*.

muffle
[mʌ́fl]

n. muffler
1. 목도리 2. (자동차의) 소음기
a. muffled (소리가) 희미한

v. 1. (싸거나 덮어서) 소리를 줄이다
2. (보호 · 보온을 위해) 감싸다 syn. wrap up

6 The city sounds *muffle* the birds' singing.
7 My ears were *muffled* against the cold.

mural
[mjúərəl]

n. 벽화

8 She painted *murals* on the church walls.

a. 벽 (위)의, 벽에 그린

9 *mural* art[paintings]

1 그들의 주장은 미덥지 않고 과학적으로도 증명되지 않았다. 2 나는 그의 의도가 의심스럽다. 3 직원들은 보너스를 받지 않는 데에 동의했다. 4 경찰은 유괴범으로부터 온 메시지를 가로챘다. 5 사이버 범죄는 통신도청으로 인해 일어날 수 있다. 6 도시의 소음에 가려 새들의 노랫소리가 잘 들리지 않는다. 7 내 귀는 추위를 막기 위해 감싸져 있었다. 8 그녀는 교회의 벽에 벽화를 그렸다. 9 벽화

preclude
[priklúːd]

n. preclusion

v. 방해하다, 불가능하게 하다 syn. prevent

1 Lack of witnesses may *preclude* a prosecution.

voca+ preclude A from v-ing A가 ~하지 못하도록 막다[방해하다]

stringent
[stríndʒənt]

n. stringency

a. 1. 엄격한, 엄중한 syn. strict, rigid
2. (금융시장 등이) 절박한, 자금이 부족한

2 *stringent* air safety regulations
3 *Stringent* spending constraints are in place during an economic downturn.

versatile
[və́ːrsətl]

n. versatility

a. 1. 다재다능한, 재주가 많은 syn. all-(a)round
2. 다목적의, 다용도의 syn. all-purpose

4 He's so *versatile*! He's good at both soccer and boxing.
5 The lemon is an extremely *versatile* fruit.

wretched
[rétʃid]

n. wretchedness

a. 1. 불쌍한, 비참한 syn. pitiable, miserable
2. (지독하게) 나쁜, 열등의
3. 불쾌한, 고약한

6 a lonely and *wretched* old man
7 *wretched* living conditions for the poor
8 I feel *wretched* with this flu.

clan
[klæn]

a. clannish
1. 씨족의 2. 파벌[배타]적인

n. 1. 씨족, 일족
2. 당파, 일당 syn. faction

9 The whole *clan* will gather on Easter.
10 There are opposing *clans* within the party.

1 목격자가 없어서 기소가 불가능할지도 모른다. 2 엄격한 항공 안전 법규 3 경기 침체기에는 자금 부족으로 인한 소비 위축 심리가 생긴다. 4 그는 정말 다재다능해! 그는 축구와 권투를 다 잘해. 5 레몬은 용도가 아주 다양한 과일이다. 6 외롭고 불쌍한 노인 7 빈곤층의 열악한 생활 조건 8 나는 이 유행성 감기 때문에 몸이 너무 안 좋다. 9 온 가족이 부활절에 모일 것이다. 10 당 내부에는 서로 대립하는 당파들이 있다.

exorbitant
[igzɔ́ːrbətənt]

n. exorbitance

a. 너무 비싼, 과도한 syn. astronomical

1 It was a nice restaurant, but the prices were *exorbitant*.

stoic
[stóuik]

n. stoicism 극기(심), 냉정함

a. 1. 냉정한, 극기의
2. 스토아 철학(파)의

2 We knew she was in trouble despite her *stoic* response.

n. 1. 극기[금욕]주의자 2. 스토아 철학자

recluse
[reklúːs]

a. reclusive

n. 은둔자, 속세를 떠난 사람 syn. hermit, solitary

3 He became a *recluse* after his wife died.

refute
[rifjúːt]

n. refutation
a. refutable 논박할 수 있는

v. 1. 논박하다, 반박하다 syn. rebut, disprove
2. (남의 발언을) 부인하다, 부정하다 syn. deny

4 Several professors have tried to *refute* his theories.
5 He *refuted* the accusations that he took a bribe.

IDIOMS

a bird's-eye view 전체 모습, 조감도, 개관 (a wide overall view)

6 I had *a bird's-eye view* of the scenery from the top of the tower.

a basket case 1. 정신병자, 폐인 2. 사회 · 경제적으로 문제가 있는 나라나 조직 (someone or something that is hopelessly broken down)

7 By the end of the test, she was *a* total *basket case*.
8 Ten years ago the country was *a* military *basket case*.

1 그곳은 좋은 식당이었지만, 가격이 터무니없이 비쌌다. 2 우리는 그녀의 냉정한 대답에도 불구하고 그녀가 곤란한 상황이라는 것을 알았다. 3 그는 아내가 죽은 뒤에 세상을 등지고 살았다. 4 몇몇 교수들이 그의 이론을 논박하려는 시도를 했다. 5 그는 뇌물을 받았다는 혐의를 부인했다. 6 나는 탑 꼭대기에서 주변 전체의 전망을 바라보았다. 7 시험이 끝날 즈음 그녀는 완전히 폐인이 되어 있었다. 8 10년 전 그 나라는 심각한 군사적 문제를 안고 있던 곳이었다.

exercise

A Match the words in the left column to the sentences in the right column.

ⓐ **dubious**: uncertain or doubtful; arousing suspicion

ⓑ **recluse**: a person who withdraws from society

ⓒ **stringent**: strict or inflexible, as in rules or time limits

ⓓ **transfusion**: the transfer of blood from one person to another

ⓔ **preclude**: to prevent something from happening

1. The patient has bled a lot. He will require a ___________ to survive.
2. The city has ___________ laws on jay-walking.
3. The thunderstorm will surely ___________ their plans to play baseball.
4. The girl's father questioned her boyfriend's ___________ past.
5. The ___________ lived alone in the woods.

B Choose the word that best explains the underlined word.

1. A person who is ***stoic*** is _______________.
   ⓐ nervous ⓑ passionate ⓒ unemotional ⓓ overweight

2. If you ***abhor*** someone, you _______________ him or her.
   ⓐ respect ⓑ frighten ⓒ await ⓓ detest

3. A person who is concerned with ***hygiene*** pays attention to _______________.
   ⓐ cleanliness ⓑ morals ⓒ genetics ⓓ sports

4. If something is ***redundant***, it is _______________.
   ⓐ annoying ⓑ unnecessary ⓒ original ⓓ inaccurate

5. If you ***refute*** an argument, you _______________ it.
   ⓐ avoid ⓑ contradict ⓒ confirm ⓓ shape

정답 및 해설 p.371

C Choose the option that is closest in meaning to the underlined word.

1. a ***lingering*** question
   ⓐ pressing ⓑ confusing ⓒ remaining ⓓ embarrassing

2. a ***designated*** driver
   ⓐ intoxicated ⓑ appointed ⓒ dangerous ⓓ expert

3. an ***exorbitant*** price
   ⓐ cheap ⓑ negotiable ⓒ reasonable ⓓ expensive

D Choose the option that is the opposite of the underlined word.

1. ***loathe*** camping in the woods
   ⓐ delight in ⓑ cancel ⓒ be afraid of ⓓ organize

2. an ***uneven*** haircut
   ⓐ crooked ⓑ unusual ⓒ awful ⓓ straight

3. ***perish*** in the fire
   ⓐ cook ⓑ extinguish ⓒ survive ⓓ disappear

E Choose the best word or phrase.

1. Who would you be most likely to ***confide*** in?
   ⓐ an acquaintance ⓑ a criminal ⓒ a dentist ⓓ a friend

2. Which of the following is a ***staple*** food?
   ⓐ chocolate ⓑ rice ⓒ grape ⓓ yogurt

3. People who study ***cardiac*** science are interested in the ____________.
   ⓐ lungs ⓑ brain ⓒ heart ⓓ kidneys

4. He decided to ***forgo*** having wine with his meal because he ____________.
   ⓐ enjoyed it ⓑ had to drive
   ⓒ had enough money ⓓ was well-treated

barren
[bǽrən]
n. barrenness

a. 1. 불모의, 메마른 syn. infertile, sterile, arid
2. 불임의
3. 열매를 맺지 못하는
4. 보잘것없는, 시시한

1 For many years, the landscape was *barren*.
2 a *barren* couple
3 a *barren* flower
4 a pointless and *barren* discussion

depose
[dipóuz]
n. deposition

v. 1. (높은 지위에서) 물러나게 하다 syn. dethrone, oust
2. (법정에서) 증언하다 syn. testify

5 King Charles I was *deposed from* the English throne in 1646.
6 He has decided to *depose* at the trial.

desolate
[désələt]
n. desolation

a. 1. 황량한, 황폐한 syn. bleak, dreary
2. 쓸쓸한, 고독한, 우울한 syn. lonely, forlorn

7 The old house was empty and *desolate*.
8 She felt *desolate* without him.

v. [desəléit] 1. 황폐하게 하다 syn. devastate 2. 쓸쓸하게 하다

exert
[igzə́ːrt]
n. exertion
a. exertive

v. (영향 · 힘 · 압력을) 가하다, 발휘하다

9 He *exerted* much influence within the company.

voca+ exert oneself 노력하다

hypocrite
[hípəkrìt]
n. hypocrisy 위선
a. hypocritical 위선적인

n. 위선자 syn. phony

10 Most people believe politicians are *hypocrites*.

voca+ play the hypocrite 위선적인 태도를 취하다

1 여러 해 동안 그 지역은 불모지대였다. 2 불임 부부 3 열매를 맺지 못하는 꽃 4 요점 없고 내용 없는 토론 5 Charles 1세는 1646년 영국 왕위에서 폐위되었다. 6 그는 재판에서 증언하기로 결정했다. 7 그 낡은 집은 비어 있었고 황량했다. 8 그가 곁에 없게 되자 그녀는 쓸쓸해했다. 9 그는 회사 안에서 큰 영향력을 발휘했다. 10 대부분의 사람들은 정치인들을 위선자로 여긴다.

ponderous
[pándərəs]

n. ponderousness

a. 1. 묵직한, 무거워서 다루기 힘든
2. (문제 · 말투가) 장황한, 지루하고 답답한 syn. long-winded

1 His movement was awkward and *ponderous*.
2 a *ponderous* and complicated movie

refer
[rifə́ːr]

n. reference
a. referable 관련있는

v. 1. 언급하다
2. 가리키다, 관련되다
3. 참조하다, 조회하다
4. (사건 · 문제 등을) 위탁하다, 맡기다

3 She said she wouldn't *refer to* the scandal again.
4 The figures *refer to* the company's sales.
5 Please *refer to* the memo for specific information.
6 I decided to *refer* the matter *to* the police.

stationary
[stéiʃəneri]

a. 움직이지 않는, 정지된 syn. motionless, static

7 The stars appear *stationary* because they are so far away.

unprecedented
[ʌnprésədentid]

a. 선례가 없는

8 *unprecedented* economic growth

voca+ on an unprecedented scale 전례 없는 규모로

alienate
[éiliənèit]

n. alienation
alien n. 1. 외국인 2. 외계인
a. 1. 이질적인 2. 외국의

v. 1. ~의 반발을 부르다, ~의 지지를 잃다 syn. estrange
2. 소외시키다, 이질감을 느끼게 만들다
3. [법률] 양도하다

9 The interest rate increases will *alienate* many business owners.
10 She felt that her reputation had *alienated* her *from* her family.
11 *alienate* real estate

voca+ alienate A from B A를 B에서 소외시키다

1 그의 동작은 어색하고 무거웠다. 2 장황하고 복잡한 영화 3 그녀는 그 추문을 다시는 언급하지 않겠다고 말했다. 4 그 수치는 회사의 매출액을 가리킨다. 5 구체적인 정보는 회람을 참조하시오. 6 나는 그 일을 경찰에게 맡기기로 결심했다. 7 별들은 너무 멀리 떨어져 있기 때문에 움직이지 않는 것처럼 보인다. 8 전례가 없는 경제 성장 9 이자율 인상은 많은 사업주들의 반발을 살 것이다. 10 그녀는 자신의 유명세가 자신을 가족으로부터 소외시켰다고 느꼈다. 11 부동산을 양도하다

cascade
[kæskéid]

n. (작은) 폭포 syn. waterfall

1 He swam in the pool at the bottom of the *cascade*.

voca+ cascade of 연속적인, 늘어뜨린

v. (폭포처럼) 한꺼번에 떨어지다[흐르다]

2 The water *cascaded* down the hillside.

influx
[ínflʌ̀ks]

n. 유입, 도래, 쇄도 syn. inflow, inrush ant. outflow

3 a large *influx* of refugees after the war

mutiny
[mjúːtəni]

a. mutinous

n. (함선 · 군대 등에서의) 폭동, 반란, 항명

4 There was a *mutiny* against the ship's captain.

v. 반란을 일으키다, (상관에게) 반항하다 syn. rebel, disobey

beguile
[bigáil]

n. beguilement
a. beguiling

v. 1. 현혹하다, 속이다
2. 즐거운 시간을 보내다, 무료함을 달래다

5 He was *beguiled into* investing all his money in the project.
6 They *beguiled* their time away on the lake.

voca+ beguile A into B A를 속여서 B하게 하다

| Nuance | "속이다 / 현혹하다" 관련 어휘 뉘앙스 차이

beguile 현혹하다, 속이다	매력적이거나 유혹적인 것으로 속이다. 7 beguile people by flattery
deceive 속이다	고의로 거짓을 말하여 속이다. 8 The company deceives customers by using exaggerated advertisements.
delude 기만하다	판단이나 생각을 흐리게 하여 착각하게 하다. 9 delude people with empty promises
mislead 호도하다	잘못되었거나 불완전한 정보를 주어 사실이 아닌 것을 믿게 하다. 10 He misled me into thinking he was rich.

1 그는 폭포 밑에 있는 웅덩이에서 헤엄을 쳤다. 2 물이 언덕 아래로 떨어져내렸다. 3 전후 피난민들의 대량 유입 4 선장에 대항하는 반란이 있었다. 5 그는 꼬임에 넘어가서 가진 돈 전부를 그 프로젝트에 투자했다. 6 그들은 호수에서 즐거운 시간을 보냈다. 7 감언이설로 사람들을 속이다 8 그 회사는 과대 광고로 소비자들을 속인다. 9 말뿐인 약속으로 사람들을 기만하다 10 그는 나를 호도하여 자신이 부자라고 생각하게 했다.

formidable
[fɔ́ːrmidəbl]

a. 1. 만만찮은, 얕잡아 볼 수 없는
2. 강력한, 가공할만한

1 The chess player faced a *formidable* opponent.
2 The building has a *formidable* security system.

daunt
[dɔːnt]

a. daunting 두려운, 겁먹게 하는
dauntless 겁없는

v. 위압하다, 기세를 꺾다

3 She was not *daunted* by his reputation for winning.
4 a *dauntless* hero

voca+ nothing daunted 조금도 굽히지 않는, 두려울 것이 없는

dyslexia
[disléksiə]

dyslexic
n. 난독증 환자
a. 난독증의

n. 난독증, 독서 장애

5 *Dyslexia* is a reading problem that affects about 20% of young children.

predicament
[pridíkəmənt]

n. 곤경, 궁지 syn. dilemma, quandary, plight

6 Without her credit card, Janice was in a difficult *predicament* traveling abroad.

retard
[ritáːrd]

a. retarded 지능 지체의

v. (성장 · 발달을) 저해하다, 지체시키다 syn. slow down ant. accelerate

7 A rise in interest rates would *retard* house sales.

n. [ríːtaːrd] 정신박약자

1 그 체스 선수는 강력한 적수를 만났다. 2 그 건물의 보안 시스템은 강력하다. 3 그녀는 그의 화려한 승리 성적에도 기가 꺾이지 않았다. 4 용감한 영웅 5 난독증은 약 20%의 어린이들이 겪고 있는 독서 장애이다. 6 Janice는 해외여행 당시 신용카드가 없어서 곤경에 빠져 있었다. 7 이자율의 인상은 주택 매매를 정체시킬 것이다.

sublime
[səbláim]

n. sublimity

a. 1. 장엄한, 숭고한, 고상한 syn. noble, splendid
2. 최고의, 탁월한

1 the *sublime* views from the mountaintop
2 This cheese cake is absolutely *sublime*.

n. 장엄, 절정

vex
[veks]

a. vexed
vexing

v. 화나게 하다, 걱정하게 하다 syn. annoy, irritate, bother

3 It *vexed* me to hear people criticize him.
4 Professors have to deal with the *vexed* problem of cheating.

coalesce
[kòuəlés]

n. coalescence
a. coalescent

v. 합병하다, 연합하다 syn. merge, amalgamate

5 Small companies often *coalesce* to form big organizations.

voca+ coalesce into 합쳐져서 ~이 되다

expedient
[ikspíːdiənt]

n. expedience
(=expediency)

a. (도덕적으로 옳지 않더라도) 도움이 되는, 정략적인, 편리한

6 His decision was more *expedient* than honorable.

n. 방편, 편법

7 Our military measures are temporary *expedients*.

matrimony
[mǽtrəmòuni]

a. matrimonial

n. 결혼, 결혼 생활 syn. marriage, wedlock

8 They were united in *matrimony*.

voca+ be joined in holy matrimony 결혼하다
out of matrimony (이혼 · 동거 등) 결혼하지 않은 상태의

---

1 산 정상에서 보이는 장엄한 광경 2 이 치즈케이크는 정말 최고다. 3 나는 사람들이 그를 비난하는 것을 들으면 언짢았다. 4 교수들은 부정행위라는 성가신 문제를 처리해야만 한다. 5 작은 회사들이 합병하여 큰 조직을 형성하는 경우가 자주 있다. 6 그의 결정은 명예를 지키기보다는 정략적인 것이었다. 7 우리의 군사적 조치는 임시 방편이다. 8 그들은 결혼으로 하나가 되었다.

rejuvenate
[ridʒúːvənèit]

n. rejuvenation

v. 1. 다시 젊어지다, 원기를 회복하다 syn. refresh, revitalize
2. (조직 · 체계를) 개선하다, 개편하다

1 I went to a seaside resort to feel *rejuvenated*.
2 The company is making an effort to *rejuvenate* its computer business.

belie
[bilái]

v. 1. ~이 거짓임을 드러내다, ~와 다르다 syn. contradict
2. (감정 등을) 숨기다, 잘못 전하다 syn. misrepresent

3 The reality of events *belies* his descriptions.
4 Kate's calm face *belied* her anxiety.

egocentric
[ìːgouséntrik]

n. egocentricity

a. 자기 중심의, 이기적인 syn. egoistic, self-centered, selfish

5 Her personality was *egocentric* to the extreme.

placebo
[pləsíːbou]

n. 1. 위약, 플라시보, (유효 성분이 없는) 가짜 약
2. 일시적인 위안[안심]

6 Jack was only given a *placebo*, but he claimed he got better—that's the placebo effect.

voca+ placebo effect 위약[플라시보] 효과

IDIOMS

a blessing in disguise 불행으로 보이나 사실은 잘된 일, 전화위복
(something that seems to cause problems, but in reality is a good thing)

7 A crisis can be *a blessing in disguise*.

cutting-edge 최첨단의 (extremely modern and advanced)

8 She works in a *cutting-edge* environment.

1 나는 원기를 회복하려고 해변 휴양지에 갔다. 2 그 회사는 컴퓨터 사업을 개편하기 위해 노력하고 있다. 3 돌아가는 현실은 그의 설명이 거짓임을 보여준다. 4 Kate의 침착한 듯한 모습은 그녀의 불안감을 감추었다. 5 그녀의 성격은 극히 자기 중심적이었다. 6 Jack은 위약을 받았을 뿐인데 상태가 호전됐다고 말했다. 이것이 바로 위약 효과이다. 7 위기는 결국엔 잘된 일일 수도 있다. 8 그녀는 최첨단 환경에서 일한다.

exercise

A Match the words in the left column to the sentences in the right column.

ⓐ **sublime**: majestic or awe-inspiring

ⓑ **influx**: an incoming or arrival of large proportions

ⓒ **predicament**: a problem or dilemma

ⓓ **placebo**: a pill or treatment that contains no medicine, used in control groups in testing new drugs

ⓔ **rejuvenate**: to restore youthfulness

1. __________ music filled the church.
2. The boys didn't know what to do about their __________.
3. This new cream will really __________ your skin.
4. The new amusement park is expected to generate a(n) __________ of visitors to the city.
5. The medication was no more effective than the __________.

B Choose the word or phrase that best explains the underlined word.

1. A ***formidable*** opponent is ______________.
   ⓐ humble ⓑ impossible ⓒ cheerful ⓓ challenging

2. When you ***exert*** your skills, you ______________ them.
   ⓐ improve ⓑ forget ⓒ utilize ⓓ announce

3. ***Egocentric*** people think mainly about ______________.
   ⓐ the environment ⓑ themselves ⓒ properties ⓓ their families

4. When you ***alienate*** someone, you ______________ them.
   ⓐ reward ⓑ exclude ⓒ attack ⓓ accuse

5. Something that is ***unprecedented*** has ______________.
   ⓐ never happened ⓑ not been finished ⓒ been tried before ⓓ not been legalized

C Choose the word that is closest in meaning to the underlined word.

1. a ***deposed*** king
ⓐ respected ⓑ elected ⓒ assassinated ⓓ removed

2. a ***daunting*** task
ⓐ interesting ⓑ challenging ⓒ illegal ⓓ ridiculous

3. join in holy ***matrimony***
ⓐ marriage ⓑ contract ⓒ motherhood ⓓ discord

D Choose the word that is the opposite of the underlined word.

1. a ***barren*** field
ⓐ sandy ⓑ fertile ⓒ flat ⓓ plowed

2. a ***stationary*** bicycle
ⓐ broken ⓑ folded ⓒ mobile ⓓ fast

3. ***belie*** current assumptions
ⓐ affirm ⓑ contradict ⓒ question ⓓ impede

E Choose the best word or phrase.

1. Who would be most likely to lead a ***mutiny***?
ⓐ bankers ⓑ couples ⓒ soldiers ⓓ teachers

2. Which of the following is affected by ***dyslexia***?
ⓐ reading skills ⓑ listening skills ⓒ math ability ⓓ athletic ability

3. When writing a research paper, you might ***refer*** to a(n) ______________.
ⓐ lawyer ⓑ recipe ⓒ soap opera ⓓ journal

4. A ***hypocrite*** ______________ to have certain beliefs that they don't really have.
ⓐ tries ⓑ pretends ⓒ wants ⓓ needs

calamity
[kəlǽməti]

a. calamitous

n. 재난, 재해, 참사 syn. disaster, catastrophe

1 It is no doubt that the earthquake was a devastating *calamity*.

voca+ man-made calamity 인재(人災)

accentuate
[æksént∫uèit]

n. accentuation

v. 강조하다, 눈에 띄게 하다 syn. emphasize, accent

2 The crowd used drums to ***accentuate*** the excitement.

refinement
[rifáinmənt]

v. refine

a. refined
1. 정제된 2. 세련된 3. 정교한

n. 1. (일부분의) 개선, 진보 syn. improvement, enhancement
2. 정제, 정련, 순화 syn. purification
3. 세련됨, 고상함 syn. gentility, sophistication

3 The game will undergo some ***refinements*** before its release.
4 the ***refinement*** of oil
5 a person of considerable ***refinement***

deface
[diféis]

n. defacement

v. (외관을) 더럽히다, 손상시키다 syn. disfigure, mar

6 He was fined for ***defacing*** public property.

detach
[ditǽt∫]

n. detachment

a. detached
detachable

v. 1. 분리하다, 떼어놓다 syn. separate, disconnect ant. attach
2. (군대 · 군함을) 파견하다

7 I will ***detach*** the trailer *from* the car.
8 They will be ***detaching*** police to the stadium.

voca+ detach oneself from ~에서 이탈하다, 벗어나다

1 그 지진은 분명 엄청난 참사였다. 2 군중은 흥분감을 강조하기 위해 북을 이용했다. 3 그 게임은 출시 전에 약간의 개선(작업)을 거칠 것이다. 4 석유 정제 5 상당히 세련된 사람 6 그는 공공 기물을 훼손하여 벌금형을 받았다. 7 나는 차에서 트레일러를 분리할 것이다. 8 그들은 경기장에 경찰을 배치할 것이다.

exile
[égzail]

n. (정치적 이유의) 국외 추방, 망명(자)

1 After his attempt to overthrow the king, he *went into exile*.

voca+ in exile 망명 중인
tax exile 세금을 덜 내려고 외국에서 사는 사람

v. 추방하다, 망명시키다

longitude
[lάndʒətjùːd]

a. longitudinal

n. 경도, 경선

2 All points on the same meridian have the same *longitude*.

oblique
[əblíːk]

a. 1. (목적 · 표현 등이) 간접적인, 완곡한 syn. indirect
2. (방향 등이) 비스듬한, 기울어진 syn. sloping, slanting

3 an *oblique* comment on the president's weaknesses
4 The roof of that house is *oblique*.

consensus
[kənsénsəs]

v. consent 동의[승낙]하다

n. (의견 등의) 일치, 합의 syn. accord, unanimity

5 Could we reach a *consensus* on this matter?

sterile
[stérəl]

v. sterilize 살균[소독]하다
n. sterility
1. 불모, 불임 2. 상상력 부족

a. 1. 불임의, 생산을 못하는, (땅이) 메마른 syn. infertile, barren ant. fertile
2. 살균한, 무균의 syn. germ-free ant. contaminated
3. 독창성[개성]이 부족한 syn. unimaginative

6 The couple adopted a baby because they are *sterile*.
7 The surgery must be done in *sterile* conditions.
8 His writing was too *sterile* to print in a magazine.

1 그는 왕을 축출하려고 했다가 해외로 망명했다. 2 같은 자오선상에 있는 모든 지점의 경도는 같다. 3 대통령의 약점에 대한 간접적인 언급 4 저 집의 지붕은 비스듬히 기울어져 있다. 5 우리가 이 문제에 의견 일치를 볼 수 있을까요? 6 그 부부는 불임이라서 아기를 입양했다. 7 수술은 무균 상태에서 이루어져야 한다. 8 그의 글은 잡지에 싣기에는 너무 독창성이 부족했다.

unruly
[ʌnrúːli]

n. unruliness

a. 1. (사람이) 다루기 힘든, 제멋대로인 syn. uncontrollable
2. (머리카락이) 잘 흐트러지는

1 An *unruly* mob attacked the police.
2 *Unruly* hair makes you look untidy.

allegiance
[əlíːdʒəns]

n. 충성, 충실 syn. loyalty

3 To become a citizen, an immigrant must swear *allegiance to* the U.S.

voca+ the Pledge of Allegiance (미) 국기에 대한 맹세

chivalry
[ʃívəlri]

a. chivalrous

n. 1. 기사도 (정신)
2. (중세의) 기사도 제도

4 *Chivalry* is honorable and polite behavior that is not so common nowadays.

confer
[kənfə́ːr]

n. conference 회의, 협의
conferment 수여

v. 1. 의논하다, 협의하다 syn. consult
2. 수여하다, 주다

5 We should *confer* about this before the meeting.
6 An honorary degree was *conferred on* her by the university.

| Nuance | "주다/수여하다" 관련 어휘 뉘앙스 차이

confer 수여하다	공식적으로 학위 · 칭호 등을 수여하다. 7 confer a medal
award 주다	상이나 상금을 보상으로 주다. 8 award a scholarship
bestow 증여하다	가치 있는 것을 무상으로 주다. 9 bestow a knighthood
concede 양도하다	권력 · 권리 등을 마지못해 넘겨주다. 10 concede further powers to Parliament

1 난폭한 패거리들이 경찰을 공격했다. 2 헝클어진 머리는 너를 단정치 못한 사람으로 보이게 한다. 3 미국 국민이 되기 위해서 이민자는 미국에 대한 충성을 맹세해야 한다. 4 기사도는 요즘에는 흔치 않은 명예롭고 공손한 행동이다. 5 우리는 회의 전에 이것에 대해 의논해야 한다. 6 그 대학은 그녀에게 명예 학위를 수여했다. 7 메달을 수여하다 8 장학금을 주다 9 기사 작위를 수여하다 10 의회에 더 많은 권력을 넘겨주다

ellipse
[ilíps]

a. elliptical

n. 타원(형) syn. oval

1 The Earth's orbit is an *ellipse*.

fortitude
[fɔ́ːrtitjùːd]

n. 꿋꿋함, 불굴의 정신, 강인함 syn. courage, strength

2 He showed *fortitude* in his quest to survive.

voca+ intestinal fortitude 담력, 배짱

infusion
[infjúːʒən]

v. infuse

n. 1. 주입, 투입, 고취
2. (풀을 달인) 약재, 우려낸 물

3 An *infusion* of funds into the company is necessary.

4 A herbal oil is an *infusion* of herbs in a vegetable oil.

negate
[nigéit]

n. negation

v. 1. 무효로 하다, 취소하다 syn. invalidate, nullify
2. (존재 · 진실을) 부정하다, 부인하다 syn. deny

5 The outcome of the experiment *negates* the theory.

6 She *negated* the testimony of the witness.

preempt
[priémpt]

n. preemption
a. preemptive 선제의, 예방의

v. 1. (상대보다 먼저 행동함으로써) 피하다, 예방하다
2. *AmE.* (정규 방송 프로그램을) ~로 대체하다

7 His claims were intended to *preempt* criticism.

8 Regular scheduling was *preempted* by a special news broadcast.

9 *preemptive* strike against the rebels

1 지구의 궤도는 타원형이다. 2 그는 생존하고자 하는 불굴의 의지를 보였다. 3 그 회사에 자금 투입이 필요하다. 4 허브 오일은 약초를 식물성 기름에 담가 우려낸 것이다. 5 실험 결과는 그 이론을 뒤집었다. 6 그녀는 증인의 증언을 부인했다. 7 그의 주장은 비판을 원천봉쇄하려는 의도였다. 8 정규 방송이 특별 뉴스방송으로 대체되었다. 9 반란군에 대한 선제 공격

posthumous
[pɑ́stʃuməs]

a. 사후(死後)에 생긴, 저자의 사후에 출판된

1 The *posthumous* publication of his last novel aroused a lot of interest.

submerge
[səbmə́ːrdʒ]

n. submergence (=submersion)

v. 1. 물 속에 잠기게 하다, 잠수하다 syn. immerse
2. (감정 · 생각 등을) 숨기다, 감추다 syn. suppress

2 The river burst its banks, *submerging* an entire village.
3 He felt his personality was being *submerged* by work.

voca+ submerge oneself in ~에 몰두하다

viable
[váiəbl]

n. viability

a. 1. 실행 가능한, 실용적인 syn. feasible, practicable
2. 생존 가능한

4 I think your proposals are *viable*.
5 Doctors attempted to rescue a *viable* fetus from the dead woman.

commensurate
[kəménʃərit]

a. (자질 · 기간 등이) 같은 정도의, (액수 등이) 상응하는

6 Salary will be *commensurate with* experience.

exponent
[ikspóunənt]

a. exponential 급격한, 기하급수적인

n. 1. 주창자, 옹호자 syn. advocate, proponent
2. 대표적 인물, (~의) 전형
3. [수학] 지수, 승 syn. power

7 Adam Smith is an *exponent* of free trade.
8 the leading *exponent* of this style of architecture
9 In 6^4 and y^n, 4 and n are the *exponents*.

1 그의 마지막 소설이 사후에 출판되자 많은 관심을 불러일으켰다. 2 강이 둑을 무너뜨려 마을 전체를 물에 잠기게 했다. 3 그는 자신의 개성이 일 때문에 묻힌다고 생각했다. 4 나는 너의 제안이 실행 가능하다고 생각한다. 5 의사들은 사망한 여성에게서 생존시킬 수 있는 태아를 구해내려고 노력했다. 6 급여는 경력에 따라 책정될 것입니다. 7 Adam Smith는 자유무역의 주창자이다. 8 이러한 건축 유형의 대표적인 인물 9 6^4과 y^n에서 4와 n은 지수이다.

mediocre
[mìːdióukər]

n. mediocrity

a. 그저그런, 평범한, 2류의 syn. second-rate

1 He got a *mediocre* job after college.

quiescent
[kwiésənt]

n. quiescence

a. (일시적으로) 정지한, 조용한

2 The civil unrest had become *quiescent*.

auspicious
[ɔːspíʃəs]

a. 길조의, 전망이 밝은 syn. promising ant. ominous, inauspicious

3 They won their first match of the season, 5-2, which was an *auspicious* start.

laudable
[lɔ́ːdəbl]

a. laudatory 찬양하는, 기리는

a. 칭찬할 만한, 기특한, 훌륭한 syn. praiseworthy, commendable

4 The campaign against landmines is highly *laudable*.

IDIOMS

a bumpy[rough] ride 힘든 시간 (a difficult time)

5 She's had *a bumpy ride* at work over the last few months.

a fig leaf 치부를 가리는 것, 미사여구 (something that is used to hide an embarrassing fact)

6 Many fallen executives are still allowed *the fig leaf* of "resignation."

1 그는 대학 졸업 후 그저그런 직장을 얻었다. 2 내란이 잠시 잠잠해졌다. 3 그들은 시즌 첫 경기를 5대 2로 이기며 순조로운 출발을 했다. 4 지뢰 반대운동은 칭찬할 만한 것이다. 5 그녀는 지난 몇 달 동안 직장에서 힘든 시간을 보냈다. 6 도태된 많은 임원들이 아직도 '사임'이라는 말로 치장된다.

exercise

A Match the words in the left column to the sentences in the right column.

ⓐ **quiescent**: still or unmoving

ⓑ **detach**: to remove something that was attached

ⓒ **calamity**: an event with a terrible or catastrophic outcome

ⓓ **negate**: to cancel or make invalid

ⓔ **exponent**: one who advocates or supports something

1. Allowing them to hunt will __________ our efforts in conservation.
2. The sea was __________ before the storm.
3. I'm going to __________ my daughter's training wheels from her bike.
4. I've always been a(n) __________ of animal rights.
5. A tidal wave could lead to a(n) __________.

B Choose the word or phrase that best explains the underlined word.

1. A ***mediocre*** musician is ______________.
   ⓐ brilliant ⓑ original ⓒ second-rate ⓓ famous

2. ***Sterile*** instruments have been ______________.
   ⓐ productive ⓑ disinfected ⓒ inspiring ⓓ tidy

3. When you have ***allegiance*** to a cause, you ______________ it.
   ⓐ support ⓑ should study
   ⓒ are undecided about ⓓ are curious about

4. When people come to a ***consensus***, they ______________.
   ⓐ meet to discuss a matter ⓑ take part in a survey
   ⓒ all agree ⓓ cannot decide

5. When a news report ***preempts*** a TV show, it ______________.
   ⓐ bumps it to another day ⓑ criticizes it
   ⓒ advertises it ⓓ is on TV instead of it

정답 및 해설 p.372

C Choose the option that is closest in meaning to the underlined word.

1. ***deface*** a monument
ⓐ construct ⓑ dedicate ⓒ damage ⓓ laugh at

2. ***submerge*** anger
ⓐ feel ⓑ submit ⓒ suppress ⓓ express

3. ***unruly*** children
ⓐ wild ⓑ poor ⓒ attentive ⓓ enthusiastic

D Choose the option that is the opposite of the underlined word.

1. show great ***fortitude***
ⓐ strength ⓑ generosity ⓒ cowardice ⓓ stupidity

2. a ***viable*** plan
ⓐ unrealistic ⓑ unexpected ⓒ wise ⓓ affordable

3. an ***oblique*** question
ⓐ awkward ⓑ difficult ⓒ direct ⓓ important

E Choose the best word or phrase.

1. Who would be likely to engage in ***chivalry***?
ⓐ a princess ⓑ a knight ⓒ a monster ⓓ a peasant

2. Which of the following is a sign of ***refinement***?
ⓐ a criminal record ⓑ a large family ⓒ beauty ⓓ good manners

3. Which of the following might be ***laudable***?
ⓐ a performance ⓑ a truck ⓒ a mistake ⓓ gossip

4. If it is an ***auspicious*** time to take a vacation, you should ________________ it.
ⓐ take ⓑ extend ⓒ postpone ⓓ cancel

acclaim
[əkléim]

n. acclamation
a. acclaimed 호평을 받은

v. 갈채를 보내다, 환호하다 syn. hail

1 The movie was ***acclaimed*** as a masterpiece.

n. 갈채, 환호

2 Despite her newfound ***acclaim***, the actress remains modest.

voca+ (win) critical acclaim 비평가들의 호평(을 받다)

belated
[biléitid]

a. 뒤늦은 syn. overdue

3 Mike was given a ***belated*** birthday cake.

consequent
[kánsikwənt]

n. consequence
ad. consequently 따라서

a. 결과로서 생기는, 결과적인 syn. ensuing, resultant

4 The warming of the earth and the ***consequent*** climatic changes affect us all.

5 That building is well constructed and, ***consequently***, hard to knock down.

duplicity
[dju:plísəti]

a. duplicitous

n. 표리부동, 기만, 이중성 syn. double-dealing, insincerity

6 I will not accept any more of your ***duplicity***.

expedition
[èkspədíʃən]

v. expedite 빨리 하다, 촉진하다
a. expeditionary 원정의

n. 1. 탐험(대), 원정(대)
2. 신속함

7 manned ***expedition*** to Mars

8 We have increased staff to ***expedite*** deliveries to customers.

voca+ make[go on] an expedition to ~로의 탐험을 하다

1 그 영화는 걸작이라는 찬사를 받았다. 2 그 여배우는 최근에 받은 찬사에도 불구하고 겸손함을 잃지 않는다. 3 Mike는 뒤늦은 생일 케이크를 받았다. 4 지구 온난화와 그로 인한 기후 변화는 우리 모두에게 영향을 미친다. 5 저 건물은 매우 튼튼하게 지어졌기 때문에 부수기가 어렵다. 6 나는 너의 기만적인 행동을 더 이상 두고 보지 않겠다. 7 화성 유인 탐사 8 우리는 고객에게 더 빨리 배송하기 위해 직원을 늘렸다.

inordinate
[inɔ́ːrdinət]

a. 과도한, 생각보다 훨씬 많은, 상당한 syn. excessive, immoderate

1 She spends an *inordinate* amount of time planning her vacation.

manifold
[mǽnifòuld]

a. 다양한, 다방면의 syn. diverse, varied

2 Her new duties were *manifold*.

persistent
[pəːrsístənt]

v. persist
1. 고집하다 2. 지속되다
n. persistence

a. 1. 끊임없는, 계속적인 syn. continuous, perpetual
2. 끈질긴, 고집 센 syn. determined, stubborn

3 Parking has been a *persistent* problem in many cities.
4 He is the most *persistent* man I've ever met.
5 He *persisted with* the game in spite of his knee injury.

voca+ persist with 고집을 부려 ~을 계속하다

precocious
[prikóuʃəs]

n. precociousness (=precocity)

a. 조숙한, (신체 · 지능의) 발달이 빠른 syn. mature

6 My son is *precocious* compared to other kids.

reinforce
[rìːinfɔ́ːrs]

n. reinforcement
1. 강화 2. (복수로) 지원군

v. 1. (감정 · 의견 등을) 강화하다 syn. strengthen, support
2. (건물 · 구조 등을) 보강하다
3. 지원군을 보내다, 증원하다

7 Her actions *reinforced* my belief in her.
8 The wall was *reinforced* with concrete.
9 The UN is *reinforcing* its military presence in the country.
10 The riot police called for *reinforcements*.

1 그녀는 휴가 계획을 세우는 데 너무 많은 시간을 보낸다. 2 그녀의 새 임무들은 다양했다. 3 많은 도시에서 주차는 고질적인 문제이다. 4 그는 내가 만난 사람들 중 가장 고집이 센 사람이다. 5 그는 무릎 부상에도 불구하고 경기를 계속하겠다고 고집을 부렸다. 6 내 아들은 다른 아이들에 비해 조숙하다. 7 그녀의 행동은 그녀에 대한 내 신뢰를 더 굳혀 주었다. 8 그 벽은 콘크리트로 보강되었다. 9 UN은 그 국가에 UN군 병력을 증원하고 있다. 10 전경 부대는 지원 병력을 요청했다.

uproot
[ʌprúːt]

v. 1. 뿌리째 뽑다 syn. pull up
2. (토지 · 집 등에서) 몰아내다 syn. displace

1 Many structures were *uprooted* because of the storm.
2 50,000 refugees have been *uprooted* by the war.

alleviate
[əlíːvièit]

n. alleviation

v. (고통 · 문제 등을) 덜다, 경감하다, 완화시키다 syn. ease, relieve, soothe

3 The doctor couldn't *alleviate* her pain.

decipher
[disáifər]

n. decipherment
a. decipherable 판독할 수 있는

v. 1. (필체 등을) 알아내다, 이해하다
2. (암호를) 풀다, 해독하다 syn. decode

4 The detective spent hours trying to *decipher* the handwriting on the paper.
5 The secret agent failed to *decipher* the coded message.

defame
[diféim]

n. defamation
a. defamatory

v. 비방하다, 중상하다 (to say negative or untrue things about someone)

6 Christians say the movie *defames* Jesus.

voca+ defamation of character 명예 훼손

| Nuance | "비방하다/중상하다" 관련 어휘 뉘앙스 차이

defame 비방하다, 중상하다	명예를 훼손하기 위해 단점이나 거짓을 말하다. 7 defame a reputation
malign 헐뜯다, 중상하다	허위 사실로 중상모략하다. 8 a maligned politician
smear 비방하다	공인을 허위 사실 · 거짓말 등으로 기만하거나 비방하다. 9 smear the opposition party leader
slander 중상하다	말로 중상하여 명예 등을 훼손하다. 10 He slandered his political opponent.

1 많은 구조물들이 폭풍 때문에 통째로 날아갔다. 2 5만 명의 피난민이 전쟁으로 인해 삶의 터전을 잃었다. 3 의사는 그녀의 고통을 덜어줄 수 없었다. 4 형사는 그 문서의 글씨를 알아보느라 몇 시간을 보냈다. 5 첩보원은 암호화된 메시지를 해독하지 못했다. 6 기독교인들은 그 영화가 예수를 모독하고 있다고 말한다. 7 명예를 훼손하다 8 중상모략을 당한 정치인 9 야당 지도자를 비방하다 10 그는 그의 정적을 비방했다.

frivolous
[frívələs]

n. frivolousness

a. 1. 경박한, 진지하지 못한 ant. serious
2. 시시한, 하찮은 syn. trivial, petty, trifling

1 Don't be so *frivolous*.
2 He wastes his wages on *frivolous* things.

hermetic
[həːrmétik]

n. hermit 은둔자

a. 1. 밀봉한, 밀폐한 syn. airtight
2. 은둔하는, 사람들과 떨어져 사는

3 Store cookies in a *hermetic* container.
4 He led a *hermetic* life in a temple until he died.

ingenuous
[indʒénjuːəs]

n. ingenuousness

a. 순진한, 천진난만한 syn. naive

5 Jane is so *ingenuous* that she believes everything people tell her.

neural
[njúərəl]

n. neurology 신경학
neuron 신경 세포

a. 신경(계)의 syn. nervous

6 He suffered severe *neural* damage.

voca+ neural과 nervous의 사전적 의미는 유사하지만 neural이 보다 전문적인 용어이다.
neural network 신경망 nervous system 신경계(통)

probation
[proubéiʃən]

n. probationer
1. 집행유예 중인 죄인
2. 수습사원, 견습사원
a. probationary

n. 1. [법률] 집행유예, 보호 관찰
2. 수습[견습] 기간, 가채용
3. AmE. (처벌 학생의) 근신 (기간)

7 The judge put him *on probation* for two years.
8 a three-month *probation* period
9 Joan is *on probation* for two terms.
10 *probationary* employees

1 그렇게 경박하게 행동하지 마. 2 그는 번 돈을 하찮은 것들에 낭비한다. 3 쿠키를 밀폐 용기에 보관하라. 4 그는 죽을 때까지 절에서 은둔 생활을 했다. 5 Jane은 너무 순진해서 사람들이 하는 말을 죄다 믿는다. 6 그는 심각한 신경계 손상을 입었다. 7 판사는 그에게 집행유예 2년을 선고했다. 8 3개월의 수습 기간 9 Joan은 두 학기 동안 근신이다. 10 수습 사원

subside
[səbsáid]

n. subsidence 침강, 함몰

v. 1. (상태가) 가라앉다, 진정되다 syn. abate, wane, die down
2. (땅 · 건물이) 꺼지다, 내려앉다 syn. sink

1 Her high fever has ***subsided***.
2 After the typhoon, part of the building ***subsided***.

substantial
[səbstǽnʃəl]

ad. substantially
1. 실질적으로 2. 견고하게

a. 1. 상당한, 꽤 많은 syn. considerable
2. 실질적인, 실속[내용] 있는 syn. substantive

3 The survey showed ***substantial*** differences between men and women.
4 He became a ***substantial*** leader of the party.
5 The stadium was built very ***substantially***.

volatile
[vɑ́lətl]

n. volatility

a. 1. 변동이 심한, 불안정한 syn. unstable
2. 변덕스러운, 화를 잘 내는 syn. fickle
3. 휘발성의

6 a ***volatile*** stock market
7 She had a ***volatile*** personality and was difficult to deal with.
8 Petrol is a ***volatile*** substance.

extraneous
[ikstréiniəs]

a. 1. 이질적인, 관계없는 syn. irrelevant
2. 외부로부터의 syn. external

9 We don't have to consider details ***extraneous to*** the problem.
10 Prevent ***extraneous*** light from entering your camera lens.

metamorphosis
[mètəmɔ́ːrfəsis]

(복수형) metamorphoses
v. metamorphose

n. 1. (완전히 다른 것으로) 변모, 변화 syn. transformation
2. (곤충 등의) 변태

11 The company has undergone a true ***metamorphosis***.
12 the ***metamorphosis*** of a caterpillar into a butterfly

1 그녀의 고열이 가라앉았다. 2 태풍이 온 뒤, 그 건물의 일부가 내려앉았다. 3 조사 결과는 남녀간의 상당한 차이점들을 보여주었다. 4 그는 당의 실질적인 지도자가 되었다. 5 경기장은 매우 튼튼하게 지어졌다. 6 요동치는 주식 시장 7 그녀는 변덕이 심해서 다루기가 어려웠다. 8 휘발유는 휘발성 물질이다. 9 우리는 그 문제와 관계없는 세부사항들은 고려할 필요가 없다. 10 외부의 빛이 카메라 렌즈로 들어오는 것을 막아라. 11 그 회사는 진정한 변화를 이루었다. 12 애벌레에서 나비로의 변태

rendition
[rendíʃən]

v. render

n. 1. 연주, 공연, 연출 syn. performance
2. 번역(판) syn. rendering, translation, version

1 My *rendition* of *White Christmas* was warmly received.
2 The Korean *rendition* of the musical *Cats* will play soon.

outlandish
[autlǽndiʃ]

a. 기이한, 이상한 syn. bizarre

3 Julie appeared at parties in *outlandish* clothes.

blithe
[blaið]

ad. blithely
태평스럽게, 무분별하게

a. 문제의 심각성을 모르는, 마냥 행복한, 태평스런
syn. heedless, inattentive

4 He shows a *blithe* disregard for economic problems.
5 The little kid *blithely* followed a man without suspecting who he was.

dejected
[didʒéktid]

n. dejection

a. 낙심한, 낙담한, 풀죽은 syn. downhearted ant. elated

6 Trevor looked *dejected* after his defeat.

IDIOMS

a dead end 막다른 곳, 교착 상태, 궁지 (a situation in which no more progress is possible)

7 Diplomatic relations between the two countries came to ***a dead end***.

a pipe dream 환상, 몽상, 망상 (something you wish for that can never really happen)

8 His plans are not realistic – they'll never be more than ***a pipe dream***.

1 나의 'White Christmas' 연주는 좋은 반응을 얻었다. 2 뮤지컬 'Cats'의 한국어판이 곧 상영될 것이다. 3 Julie는 이상한 옷을 입고 파티에 나타났다. 4 그는 경제 문제에 무심하다. 5 꼬마는 누구인지 의심하지도 않고 마냥 즐거워하며 어떤 남자를 따라갔다. 6 Trevor는 패배한 뒤 풀죽은 모습이었다. 7 두 나라 간의 외교 관계가 막다른 상태에 봉착했다. 8 그의 계획은 현실적이지 않다. 그것들은 다만 망상에 지나지 않을 것이다.

exercise

A Match the words in the left column to the sentences in the right column.

ⓐ **rendition**: a performance

ⓑ **frivolous**: trivial or unnecessary

ⓒ **extraneous**: not relating to the topic

ⓓ **inordinate**: excessive

ⓔ **dejected**: depressed or discouraged

1. The task took a(n) __________ amount of time.
2. She felt __________ when she failed the college entrance exam.
3. She wasted her money on __________ purchases.
4. Delete any __________ information that could mislead readers.
5. That was the best __________ of *Hamlet* I have ever seen.

B Choose the word or phrase that best explains the underlined word.

1. If you are ***hermetic***, you __________.
   ⓐ do unfair things ⓑ stay away from people
   ⓒ feel excited easily ⓓ have a lot of energy

2. Something that is ***outlandish*** is __________.
   ⓐ ordinary ⓑ annoying ⓒ unacceptable ⓓ bizarre

3. A ***volatile*** person is __________.
   ⓐ humorous ⓑ diseased ⓒ unpredictable ⓓ nervous

4. If you are ***defamed***, your __________.
   ⓐ reputation is ruined ⓑ belongings are stolen
   ⓒ boss fires you ⓓ marriage is over

5. If you ***reinforce*** something, you __________.
   ⓐ prepare for it ⓑ make it stronger
   ⓒ allow it to change ⓓ ask it to stop

C Choose the option that is closest in meaning to the underlined word.

1. a ***belated*** birthday party
ⓐ heartfelt ⓑ boring ⓒ unexpected ⓓ overdue

2. a ***persistent*** cough
ⓐ occasional ⓑ nervous ⓒ continuing ⓓ serious

3. the ***metamorphosis*** of a tadpole into a frog
ⓐ coloration ⓑ struggle ⓒ lifespan ⓓ transformation

D Choose the option that is the opposite of the underlined word.

1. a ***blithe*** young man
ⓐ charming ⓑ miserable ⓒ clever ⓓ healthy

2. an ***ingenuous*** manner
ⓐ generous ⓑ hostile ⓒ truthful ⓓ dishonest

3. ***substantial*** changes
ⓐ sudden ⓑ small ⓒ dramatic ⓓ enormous

E Choose the best word or phrase.

1. This sandwich will help ***alleviate*** your ________________.
ⓐ health ⓑ energy ⓒ hunger ⓓ weight

2. Who would most likely be on ***probation***?
ⓐ a retiree ⓑ a judge ⓒ a beggar ⓓ a criminal

3. Which of the following needs to be ***deciphered***?
ⓐ a phone number ⓑ a map ⓒ a code ⓓ an address

4. If a film is ***acclaimed***, it will probably ________________.
ⓐ be boring ⓑ win awards ⓒ be banned ⓓ lose money

acronym
[ǽkrənìm]

n. 두문자어 (a word formed from the initial letters of the words in a name)

1 AIDS is an *acronym* for Acquired Immune Deficiency Syndrome.

beneficent
[bənéfisənt]

n. beneficence

a. 선행을 하는, 인정 많은 syn. charitable, benevolent

2 In 1909 nuns were running more than 1,000 *beneficent* institutions.

conservative
[kənsə́ːrvətiv]

n. conservatism 보수주의

a. 1. 보수적인, 보수주의의 syn. right-wing ant. liberal
2. (C~) 영국 보수당의
3. (옷차림 등이) 수수한, 전통적인 syn. traditional
4. (수치 · 평가 등을) 낮게 잡은, 어림잡은

3 a very *conservative* approach to women's rights
4 the *Conservative* Party
5 He's a very *conservative* dresser.
6 a *conservative* estimate[guess]

n. 1. 보수주의자 2. (C~) 영국 보수당원 syn. Tory

digress
[daigrés]

n. digression

v. (주제에서) 벗어나다, 빗나가다 syn. wander

7 Don't *digress*. Stick to the topic.

expel
[ikspél]

n. expulsion

v. 1. (장소 · 조직에서) 내쫓다, 추방하다 syn. drive out, banish
2. 방출하다, 배출하다

8 They were *expelled from* school for unruly behavior.
9 The volcano *expels* smoke.

1 AIDS는 '후천성 면역 결핍증'의 약어이다. 2 1909년에 수녀들이 1천여 곳 이상의 자선 기관을 운영하고 있었다. 3 여성의 권리에 대한 매우 보수적인 접근 4 영국 보수당 5 그는 옷을 매우 수수하게 입는다. 6 낮게 잡은 추정치 7 상관없는 이야기는 하지 말고 주제에 충실해라. 8 그들은 규칙에 어긋난 행동으로 인해 퇴학당했다. 9 화산은 연기를 내뿜는다.

glib
[glib]

n. glibness

a. 입심 좋은, 겉발림의, 말뿐인 (speaking in a confident and persuasive way but without honesty or careful consideration) syn. slick

1 You make too many *glib* remarks.

manipulate
[mənípjəlèit]

n. manipulation
a. manipulative

v. 1. (사람 · 여론 등을) 교묘하게 조종하다 syn. control, pull strings[wires]
2. (기계 · 정보 등을) 잘 다루다, 조작하다 syn. operate, handle

2 He loves to *manipulate* people.
3 A pilot *manipulates* the controls of a plane.

perspiration
[pə̀ːrspəréiʃən]

v. perspire

n. 땀, 발한 (작용) syn. sweat

4 As I jogged, the *perspiration* ran down my forehead.

voca+ antiperspirant 지한제(의)
beads of perspiration 구슬땀, 땀방울

reluctant
[rilʌ́ktənt]

n. reluctance

a. 내키지 않는, 마지못해 하는 (unwilling to do something and therefore slow to do it) syn. disinclined, loath

5 John was *reluctant to* accept my apology.

stifle
[stáifl]

a. stifling

v. 1. 억누르다, 억제하다 syn. suppress, repress
ant. stimulate, encourage
2. 숨을 막다, 질식시키다 syn. choke, suffocate

6 Regulations *stifle* creativity.
7 The demonstrators were *stifled* by the tear gas.

voca+ stifle a yawn[cough/sneeze] 하품[기침/재채기]를 참다

1 너는 입에 발린 말을 너무 많이 한다. 2 그는 사람들을 교묘하게 조종하기를 좋아한다. 3 비행기 조종사는 비행기의 조종 장치를 잘 다룬다. 4 조깅하면서 땀이 이마로 흘러내렸다. 5 John은 마지못해 내 사과를 받아들였다. 6 규제는 창의성을 억누른다. 7 시위대는 최루 가스에 숨이 막혔다.

usher
[ʌ́ʃər]

n. 안내원, 접수원 syn. attendant

1 He got a job as an *usher* at the new cinema.

v. 안내하다, 인도하다 syn. guide, escort

2 She *ushered* the guests to their seats.

voca+ usher in ~의 시작을 알리다

allude
[əlúːd]

n. allusion

v. 넌지시 말하다, 암시하다 syn. hint, imply

3 He *alluded to* the scandal to see her reaction.

clandestine
[klændéstin]

a. 은밀한, 비밀의, 불법적인 syn. secret, stealthy

4 He had several *clandestine* meetings with the Chinese spy.

deter
[ditə́ːr]

deterrent
n. 억제물
a. 억제하는

v. 그만두게 하다, 단념시키다, 막다

5 Inflation is *deterring* many people *from* spending.

voca+ nuclear deterrent 핵 억지력(다른 나라의 공격을 막기 위해 보유하는 핵무기)

| Nuance | "방해하다/막다" 관련 어휘 뉘앙스 차이

deter 단념시키다, 방해하다	어렵고 위험한 것으로 인식시켜 하지 못하도록 하다. 6 The new alarm system should deter car thieves.
prevent 방해하다, 막다	사건 등의 발생 및 진행을 방해하다. 7 prevent cancer from developing
preclude 배제하다	사건 등의 발생 가능성을 미리 배제하여 불가능하게 만들다. 8 preclude the possibility
avert 피하다, 막다	사전조치를 통해 발생을 막다. 9 avert a crisis

1 그는 새로 생긴 영화관에 안내원으로 취직했다. 2 그녀는 손님들을 좌석으로 안내했다. 3 그는 그녀의 반응을 보려고 그 추문에 대해 슬쩍 언급했다. 4 그는 중국 스파이와 몇 번의 은밀한 만남을 가졌다. 5 인플레이션이 많은 사람들의 소비를 막고 있다. 6 새 경보 시스템이 차량 도난을 막아줄 것이다. 7 암의 진행을 막다 8 가능성을 배제하다 9 위기를 막다

deduce
[didjúːs]

n. deduction
a. deducible 추론할 수 있는
deductive 추론적인

v. 연역하다, 추론하다 (to reach a conclusion by reasoning from the general to the specific) syn. infer ant. induce 귀납하다

1 We could *deduce from* his actions that he disapproved.

elude
[ilúːd]

n. elusion 도피, 회피

v. 1. 모면하다, 피해가다 syn. evade, dodge
2. ~에게 생각나지[이해되지] 않다

2 He *eluded* the police for 13 years.
3 I can see his face but his name *eludes* me.

frugal
[frúːgəl]

n. frugality

a. 1. 절약하는, 검소한 syn. thrifty, economical ant. extravagant
2. (식사 등이) 간소한, 간단한 syn. meager, plain

4 In my youth I was taught to be *frugal* and honest.
5 a *frugal* meal of bread and soup

inquisitive
[inkwízətiv]

n. inquisitiveness
inquisition 조사, 심리

a. 1. 캐묻기 좋아하는
2. 탐구적인, 알고 싶어 하는 syn. inquiring

6 She was too *inquisitive* about my financial situation.
7 The children were *inquisitive* of the magician's tricks.

nascent
[nǽsnt]

a. 발생하려 하는, 태동기의

8 Kenya's *nascent* democracy was threatened by conflict.

1 우리는 그의 행동에서 그가 찬성하지 않았다는 것을 추론할 수 있었다. 2 그는 13년 동안 경찰을 피해 다녔다. 3 나는 그의 얼굴은 알아볼 수 있지만 이름은 생각나지 않는다. 4 나는 청소년 시절에 검소하고 정직하라고 배웠다. 5 빵과 수프로 이루어진 간단한 식사 6 그녀는 내 재정 상황에 대해 너무 꼬치꼬치 캐물었다. 7 아이들은 마술사의 속임수에 대해 무척 궁금해했다. 8 막 움트기 시작한 케냐의 민주주의가 분쟁에 의해 위협을 받았다.

nullify
[nʌ́ləfài]

v. 1. (법적으로) 무효로 하다, 파기[취소]하다 syn. invalidate, void
2. 수포로 돌리다, 헛되게 하다 syn. negate

1 We agreed to *nullify* the contract for reasons of fairness.
2 All my efforts were *nullified* when the company collapsed.

procure
[prəkjúər]

n. procurement 획득, 조달
a. procurable 따낼 수 있는

v. 어렵게 손에 넣다, 획득하다 syn. obtain

3 Jim managed to *procure* an interview with the reclusive celebrity.
4 the *procurement* of military supplies

retract
[ritrǽkt]

n. retraction
a. retractable 접어 넣을 수 있는, 쑥 들어가는

v. 1. (약속 · 말 등을) 취소하다, 철회하다 syn. recant, withdraw
2. 쑥 들어가게 하다, 움츠리다

5 I was forced to *retract* my testimony.
6 The turtle *retracted* its head into its shell.
7 The stadium has a *retractable* roof.

volition
[vəlíʃən]

n. 의지(력), 결단(력) syn. free will

8 He quit the team *of his own volition*.

voca+ of one's own volition 자의로, 스스로의 결정으로

meticulous
[mətíkjuləs]

a. 꼼꼼한, 세심한 syn. thorough, fastidious

9 The designer was famous for his *meticulous* attention to details.

1 우리는 공정성의 문제 때문에 그 계약을 파기하는 데 동의했다. 2 회사가 망하자 내 모든 노력은 수포로 돌아갔다. 3 Jim은 은둔하고 있는 유명인사와 어렵사리 인터뷰를 했다. 4 군사 보급품 확보 5 나는 내 증언을 철회하라는 강요를 받았다. 6 거북이는 등껍질 속으로 머리를 쑥 집어넣었다. 7 그 경기장에는 접이식 지붕이 있다. 8 그는 자신의 의사로 팀을 그만두었다. 9 그 디자이너는 세부적인 것에 꼼꼼하게 신경 쓰기로 유명했다.

affable
[ǽfəbl]

n. affability

a. 상냥한, 붙임성 있는, 친절한 syn. amiable, genial

1 Brook is an *affable* and courteous gentleman.

verity
[vérəti]

n. 진실, 진리 ant. falsity

2 Beauty, love, and honor are the eternal *verities*.

voca+ in verity 정말로, 참으로

quandary
[kwάndəri]

n. 진퇴양난, 곤경 syn. dilemma, predicament

3 I was *in a quandary* – should I tell her or shouldn't I?

voca+ in a quandary 진퇴양난에 빠진, 당혹스러운

reprobate
[réprəbèit]

n. 무뢰한, 난봉꾼

4 Don Giovanni was an infamous *reprobate*.

IDIOMS

a long face 우울한 얼굴, 시무룩한 얼굴 (a sad or disappointed expression)

5 A: Why *the long face*?
B: I just got terrible results on the finals.

be on cloud nine 매우 행복하다 (to be very happy about something)

6 Adam *was on cloud nine* after the birth of his son.

1 Brook은 붙임성 있고 예의 바른 신사이다. 2 아름다움, 사랑, 명예는 영원한 진리이다. 3 나는 그녀에게 말해야 하나 말아야 하나 난감했다. 4 Don Giovanni는 악명 높은 난봉꾼이었다. 5 A: 왜 그리 시무룩해? B: 방금 형편없는 기말고사 성적을 받았거든. 6 Adam은 그의 아들이 태어난 후 무척 행복해 했다.

exercise

A Match the words in the left column to the sentences in the right column.

ⓐ **meticulous**: extremely careful; paying close attention to details

ⓑ **reprobate**: a person lacking principles or morals

ⓒ **stifle**: to prevent something from happening

ⓓ **allude**: to refer to something indirectly

ⓔ **manipulate**: to influence with ill intentions

1. I don't want you to associate with that ___________. He sets a bad example.
2. He didn't mention the deal specifically, but he ___________(e)d to it.
3. He tried to ___________ me into signing the agreement.
4. Scientists must be ___________ when they do experiments.
5. Linda managed to ___________ a yawn.

B Choose the word or phrase that best explains the underlined word.

1. If you are ***inquisitive***, you ______________.
   ⓐ go to jail ⓑ work hard ⓒ fail a test ⓓ ask questions

2. A ***reluctant*** person is ______________ to do something.
   ⓐ unwilling ⓑ likely ⓒ doomed ⓓ afraid

3. If you are ***conservative***, you are probably ______________.
   ⓐ rebellious ⓑ wealthy ⓒ traditional ⓓ intelligent

4. If you ***digress***, you ______________.
   ⓐ go off the topic ⓑ give an example
   ⓒ make a point ⓓ summarize your argument

5. If you ***deduce*** the answer, you ______________.
   ⓐ doubt its accuracy ⓑ need help
   ⓒ figure it out ⓓ double-check it

정답 및 해설 p.373

C Choose the option that is closest in meaning to the underlined word.

1. an ***affable*** boy
ⓐ naughty ⓑ funny ⓒ friendly ⓓ rude

2. in a ***quandary***
ⓐ deliberation ⓑ investigation
ⓒ open area ⓓ problematic situation

3. of your own ***volition***
ⓐ fault ⓑ best ⓒ opposition ⓓ free will

D Choose the option that is the opposite of the underlined word.

1. ***frugal*** with money
ⓐ careful ⓑ wasteful ⓒ stingy ⓓ wealthy

2. a ***nascent*** flower
ⓐ budding ⓑ fragrant ⓒ dying ⓓ pretty

3. ***nullify*** a contract
ⓐ modify ⓑ reject ⓒ validate ⓓ break

E Choose the best word or phrase.

1. Which of the following results in ***perspiration***?
ⓐ brief showers ⓑ physical activity ⓒ cold temperatures ⓓ high winds

2. Which of the following would you ***retract***?
ⓐ a book ⓑ a mistake ⓒ a memory ⓓ a statement

3. A ***clandestine*** operation is probably ______________.
ⓐ overt ⓑ illegal ⓒ urgent ⓓ unnecessary

4. The criminal ***eluded*** ______________.
ⓐ the money ⓑ authorities ⓒ criminal activity ⓓ the witness

coerce
[kouə́ːrs]

n. coercion
a. coercive

v. 강제로 ~하게 하다, 협박하여 ~하게 하다

1 They *coerced* him *into* carrying out a robbery.
2 *coercive* measures

voca+ coerce A into v-ing A로 하여금 강제로 ~하게 하다

ardent
[ɑ́ːrdənt]

a. 열렬한, 열정적인 syn. passionate, fervent

3 He's an *ardent* supporter of the Kia Tigers.

conceit
[kənsíːt]

a. conceited 자만에 찬

n. 1. 자만, 오만 syn. vanity
2. (기발한) 비유, 은유 syn. metaphor

4 The smaller the mind, the greater the *conceit*.
5 The poem is full of romantic *conceits*.
6 She was so *conceited* I couldn't stand listening to her.

evade
[ivéid]

n. evasion
a. evasive

v. (교묘하게) 피하다, 회피하다 syn. dodge

7 Don't try to *evade* responsibility for your behavior.
8 His answers are always vague and *evasive*.

transient
[trǽnʃənt]

n. transience

a. 일시적인, 잠깐 동안의, 단기 체류의 syn. transitory, fleeting

9 *transient* fashion trends

n. 떠돌이, 단기 체류객

10 *Transients* often gather around the train station at night.
11 the *transience* of human existence

1 그들은 그에게 강제로 강도짓을 시켰다. 2 강제 조치 3 그는 기아 타이거즈의 열렬한 팬이다. 4 속이 좁을수록 자만심이 강하다. 5 그 시는 낭만적인 비유로 가득하다. 6 그녀는 너무 자만에 차 있어서 나는 그녀의 말을 참고 들어줄 수가 없었다. 7 네 행동에 대한 책임을 회피하려 하지 마라. 8 그의 대답은 늘 모호하고 얼버무리는 듯하다. 9 일시적인 패션 경향 10 노숙자들은 밤에 기차역 근처에 자주 모인다. 11 인간 존재의 덧없음

legacy
[légəsi]

n. 유산, 유물, 물려받은 것

1 They each received a *legacy* of $80,000.

pathetic
[pəθétik]

a. 1. 형편없는, 쓸모없는, 서툰
2. 애처로운, 불쌍한 syn. pitiful

2 She made a *pathetic* attempt to fix the broken chair.
3 Bandaged from head to toe, he looked *pathetic*.

recline
[rikláin]

n. recliner
등받이 각도가 조절되는 의자

v. 1. 기대어 앉다[눕다]
2. 등받이가 기울다, 등받이를 기울이다

4 He was *reclining* on a couch.
5 The seat will *recline* 45 degrees.

replica
[réplikə]

v. replicate 복제[반복]하다
n. replication

n. 모조(품), 복제(품) syn. duplicate

6 It was an exact *replica* of the Mona Lisa.
7 The researcher tried to *replicate* the success of his earlier work.

trigger
[trígər]

n. 1. 방아쇠
2. (사건의) 계기, 도화선

8 pull the *trigger*
9 The hijacking was a *trigger* for the war.

v. (사건 등을) 일으키다, 유발하다 syn. set off

10 Certain foods *trigger* allergies.

voca+ trigger-happy 매우 호전적인, 걸핏하면 총을 쏘는

1 그들은 각자 8만 달러의 유산을 받았다. 2 그녀는 부서진 의자를 고치려는 소용없는 시도를 했다. 3 그는 머리에서 발끝까지 붕대가 감긴 채 애처롭게 보였다. 4 그는 소파에 기대어 앉아 있었다. 5 그 좌석은 45도까지 기울어진다. 6 그것은 모나리자를 똑같이 복제한 것이었다. 7 그 연구원은 이전 연구의 성공을 재현하려 애썼다. 8 방아쇠를 당기다 9 비행기 납치 사건이 그 전쟁의 도화선이었다. 10 어떤 음식은 알레르기를 일으킨다.

aggregate
[ǽgrigət]

n. 총합, 총계 syn. total

1 The party got an *aggregate* of 5,398 votes.

voca+ in (the) aggregate 총, 모두 합쳐서 (=in total)

a. 모두 합한, 총계의

2 *aggregate* demand[supply]

v. [ǽgrigèit] 합치다, 취합하다, 통합하다

3 This system is used to *aggregate* and analyze data.

bilateral
[bailǽtərəl]

a. 쌍방의, 양자[양국]의

4 *bilateral* negotiations between North and South Korea

counterpart
[káuntərpὰːrt]

n. (동등한 역할 · 위치의) 상대방, 대응물 syn. opposite number

5 The prime minister discussed recent events with his Chinese *counterpart*.

divulge
[divʌ́ldʒ]

v. 누설하다, 폭로하다

6 Counselors are not supposed to *divulge* information about their clients.

| N u a n c e | "누설하다" 관련 어휘 뉘앙스 차이

divulge 누설하다 | 비밀로 해야 하는 매우 중요한 정보를 누설하다.
7 Banks must not divulge account details of customers.

disclose 공개하다 | 감춰 왔던 사실을 공개적으로 알리다.
8 The interviewees requested that their identity not be disclosed.

expose 폭로하다 | 개인 또는 조직의 부도덕한 행위를 폭로하다.
9 His criminal activities were exposed by a journalist.

leak 누설하다 | 기밀을 고의적으로 언론 등에 흘리다.
10 A civil servant was suspected of leaking official secrets.

1 그 정당은 총 5,398표를 얻었다. 2 총수요[총공급] 3 이 시스템은 자료를 취합하고 분석하는 데 사용된다. 4 남북한 양자 협상 5 수상은 중국 측과 최근의 일들을 논의했다. 6 상담사는 고객의 정보를 누설하면 안 된다. 7 은행은 고객들의 계좌 내역을 누설해서는 안 된다. 8 인터뷰 대상자들은 그들의 신원을 밝히지 말 것을 요구했다. 9 그의 범죄행위는 한 언론인에 의해 폭로되었다. 10 한 공무원이 정부 기밀을 누설했다는 의심을 받았다.

indigny

[indígnəti]

n. 치욕, 모욕 syn. humiliation

1 The *indignity of* the scandal scarred him deeply.

opaque

[oupéik]

n. opacity

a. 1. 불투명한, 탁한 ant. transparent
2. 난해한

2 *opaque* glass[liquid/clouds]
3 Her poetry is completely *opaque* to me.
4 You can adjust the *opacity* of an image with Photoshop.

flank

[flæŋk]

n. 측면, 옆구리

5 The vet examined the horse's *flank*.

v. 옆쪽에 서다[위치하다]

6 The actor was *flanked* by bodyguards as he came outside.

stagnant

[stǽgnənt]

v. stagnate
n. stagnation

a. 1. (물 · 공기가) 흐르지 않는, 고여 있는
2. 성장이 없는, 정체[침체]된

7 a *stagnant* pool of water swarming with mosquitoes
8 Measures have been taken to revive the *stagnant* economy.
9 the *stagnation* of the electronic industry

polarize

[póulərὰiz]

n. polarization
a. polar 양극의

v. (의견 등이) 정반대로 갈라지다, 분열하다[시키다], 대립하다

10 Korea was *polarized* by the issue of stem cell research.
11 the *polarization* of society into rich and poor
12 The scientists explore the environment of the *polar* regions.

1 그 추문으로 인한 치욕이 그에게 깊은 상처를 남겼다. 2 불투명 유리[불투명 액체/먹구름] 3 그녀의 시는 내게 너무 난해하다. 4 포토샵으로 이미지의 불투명도를 조정할 수 있다. 5 수의사는 말의 옆구리를 검사했다. 6 그 배우는 양쪽에 경호원들을 거느린 채 밖으로 나왔다. 7 모기들이 우글거리는 고인 물웅덩이 8 침체된 경제를 되살리기 위한 조치들이 취해져 왔다. 9 전자제품 업계의 침체 10 한국은 줄기 세포 연구 문제를 두고 여론이 분열되었다. 11 사회 빈부의 양극화 12 과학자들은 극지방의 환경을 탐사한다.

repute
[ripjúːt]

a. reputed ~라고 알려진
ad. reputedly 알려진 바로는

n. 평판 syn. reputation

1 He's a surgeon of good *repute*.
2 He is the *reputed* leader of the gang.
3 He is *reputedly* connected to the criminal underworld.

voca+ of (some) repute 평판이 좋은

molecule
[mɑ́ləkjùːl]

a. molecular

n. [과학] 분자

4 A *molecule* of oxygen gas contains two atoms.
5 *molecular* biology

unravel
[ʌ̀nrǽvəl]

v. 1. (얽힌 실 등을) 풀다, (실 등이) 풀리다
2. 규명하다, 이해하다
3. (계획 · 체제 등이) 무산되다, 실패하다, 와해되다

6 *unravel* the whole sweater
7 The detective *unraveled* the mystery of the murder.
8 Politicians are concerned the peace talks will *unravel*.

cataract
[kǽtərӕ̀kt]

n. 1. 백내장
2. 큰 폭포

9 A *cataract* is a medical condition in which your eyes look cloudy and you slowly lose your sight.
10 Niagara Falls is one of the world's largest *cataracts*.

pathos
[péiθɑs]

n. [예술] 비애, 연민을 자아내는 것, 페이소스

11 The opera is a mixture of comedy and *pathos*.

---

1 그는 평판이 좋은 외과의사이다. 2 그가 그 폭력 조직의 두목이라고 한다. 3 알려진 바에 의하면, 그는 지하 범죄조직과 연계되어 있다. 4 산소 기체 분자 한 개에는 두 개의 원자가 포함되어 있다. 5 분자 생물학 6 스웨터의 실을 모두 풀다 7 그 탐정은 살해 사건의 미스터리를 풀었다. 8 정치인들은 평화 회담이 무산될 것을 우려하고 있다. 9 백내장은 시야가 흐려지면서 점차 시력을 잃게 되는 질환이다. 10 나이아가라 폭포는 세계에서 가장 큰 폭포 중 하나이다. 11 그 오페라는 희극과 비애의 혼합체이다.

levy
[lévi]

n. 세금, 징수액, 부과금

1 raise a *levy* on cigarettes

v. (세금 등을) 부과하다

2 A new tax has been *levied on* foreign goods.

voca+ levy a tax[charge/fine] on ~에 세금[요금/벌금]을 부과하다

proviso
[prəváizou]

n. 전제 조건 syn. provision

3 He left money to her in his will *with the proviso that* she can't use it until she is 21.

voca+ with the proviso that ~라는 조건하에

euphemism
[jú:fəmìzəm]

a. euphemistic
ad. euphemistically

n. 완곡어법, 완곡한 표현

4 "Getting let go" is a *euphemism* for "being fired."
5 Used clothing is *euphemistically* called vintage clothing.

acrimonious
[ӕ̀krəmóuniəs]

n. acrimony

a. 악감정으로 가득한, 신랄한 syn. bitter

6 Their relationship ended in an *acrimonious* split.
7 The talks broke up in *acrimony*.

IDIOMS

within striking distance 아주 가까이 있는, ~을 달성하기 직전인 (very close to achieving something)

8 The golfer is *within striking distance* of winning a major tournament.

to the letter 지시대로 정확히 (doing exactly what you have been told to do)

9 I followed his instructions *to the letter*.

1 담배에 부과되는 세금을 인상하다 2 외국산 제품에 대해 새로운 세금이 부과되었다. 3 그는 그녀가 21세가 되었을 때부터 그 돈을 쓸 수 있다는 조건하에 유언장을 통해 그녀에게 돈을 물려주었다. 4 '떠나게 되다'는 '해고되다'의 완곡한 표현이다. 5 중고 의상을 완곡하게 표현해서 빈티지 의상이라고 한다. 6 그들의 관계는 서로 좋지 못한 감정을 남긴 채 끝났다. 7 그 회담은 악감정을 남긴 채 결렬되었다. 8 그 골프 선수는 메이저 대회 우승을 눈 앞에 두고 있다. 9 나는 정확히 그의 지시대로 했다.

exercise

A Match the words in the left column to the sentences in the right column.

ⓐ **stagnant**: motionless

ⓑ **euphemism**: an inoffensive and indirect expression to refer to something embarrassing

ⓒ **proviso**: a condition or requirement term

ⓓ **bilateral**: involving or affecting both sides

ⓔ **polarize**: to divide into two conflicting positions

1. He was obligated by a(n) __________ in the contract.
2. The two parties made a(n) __________ agreement.
3. I wish he would speak frankly instead of using all of those __________(e)s.
4. The issue will __________ the public.
5. __________ ponds have a lot of bacteria in them.

B Choose the word or phrase that best explains the underlined word.

1. If you ***evade*** the police, you __________ them.
   ⓐ blame ⓑ aid ⓒ attack ⓓ avoid

2. If you make a ***replica*** of something, you __________ it.
   ⓐ remember ⓑ copy ⓒ improve ⓓ display

3. If the government were to ***levy*** a tax, it would __________ it.
   ⓐ remove ⓑ impose ⓒ refund ⓓ decrease

4. If a dispute is ***acrimonious***, it is __________.
   ⓐ legal ⓑ ongoing ⓒ bitter ⓓ friendly

5. If a woman is your ***counterpart***, she __________ you.
   ⓐ serves a similar function as ⓑ is superior to
   ⓒ used to work for ⓓ is in competition with

정답 및 해설 p.373

C Choose the option that is closest in meaning to the underlined word.

1. an ***ardent*** painter
ⓐ talented ⓑ passionate ⓒ successful ⓓ unique

2. ***trigger*** an event
ⓐ attend ⓑ cancel ⓒ cause ⓓ plan

3. ***aggregate*** profit
ⓐ lost ⓑ projected ⓒ total ⓓ possible

D Choose the option that is the opposite of the underlined word.

1. show ***conceit***
ⓐ interest ⓑ sadness ⓒ grace ⓓ modesty

2. a ***pathetic*** attempt
ⓐ failed ⓑ admirable ⓒ pointless ⓓ hopeless

3. ***divulge*** information
ⓐ hide ⓑ analyze ⓒ gather ⓓ ignore

E Choose the best word or phrase.

1. Which of the following might you ***recline***?
ⓐ a fishing rod ⓑ a plastic bottle ⓒ a round table ⓓ an easy chair

2. Which of the following would you ***unravel***?
ⓐ a knot ⓑ a boat ⓒ a book ⓓ a shoe

3. Who will carry on your ***legacy***?
ⓐ your boss ⓑ your uncle ⓒ your parents ⓓ your children

4. A person with a ***cataract*** has a problem with their ____________.
ⓐ skin ⓑ tooth ⓒ eye ⓓ ear

adhere

[ədhíər]

n. adhesion 부착, 접착
adherence 고수, 준수
adherent
n. 추종자, 지지자
a. 접착성의

v. 1. 들러붙다, 부착하다 syn. cling, stick
2. 따르다, 지지하다

1 Strong paste helps the wallpaper *adhere to* the wall.
2 Car drivers must *adhere to* the rules of driving.

voca+ adhere to ~을 고수하다, 지지하다

bestow

[bistóu]

n. bestowal

v. (명예 · 선물 등을) 주다, 수여하다 syn. confer, grant

3 The president *bestowed* a medal *on* the soldier.

voca+ bestow sth on[upon] sb ~에게 …를 수여하다

discern

[disə́:rn]

n. discernment
a. discernible 식별할 수 있는
discerning 통찰력[식별력] 있는

v. 알아보다, 식별[인식]하다 syn. perceive

4 He *discerned* that she was lying.

voca+ the discerning eye[ear] 미술[음악]에 안목이 있는 사람

explicit

[iksplísit]

n. explicitness

a. 1. 명확한, 뚜렷한 syn. obvious, clear ant. implicit, ambiguous
2. (성 · 폭력 묘사가) 노골적인, 숨김없는

5 The essay was concise and *explicit*.
6 sexually *explicit* scenes

impair

[impέər]

n. impairment
a. impaired 손상된

v. 해치다, 손상시키다, 악화시키다 syn. worsen, damage

7 An infection *impaired* her eyesight.

voca+ impair efficiency 능률을 떨어뜨리다
hearing-impaired 귀가 잘 들리지 않는, 난청의

1 강력 접착제는 벽지가 벽에 붙어 있게 해준다. 2 자동차 운전자들은 운전 법규를 지켜야 한다. 3 대통령은 그 병사에게 훈장을 수여했다. 4 그는 그녀가 거짓말하고 있다는 것을 눈치챘다. 5 그 에세이는 간단 명료했다. 6 노골적으로 성을 묘사하는 장면 7 병균 감염이 그녀의 시력을 손상시켰다.

maritime
[mǽrətàim]

a. 1. 바다의, 해운의 syn. marine
2. 해변의, 연해의, 바다에 접한 syn. coastal, seaside

1 The Ministry of *Maritime* Affairs and Fisheries
2 a *maritime* province

phase
[feiz]

n. 1. (발달 · 변화의) 단계, 양상 syn. stage
2. (달 · 행성의) 상(相)

3 There are three *phases* in the life cycle of a butterfly.
4 We studied the *phases* of the moon in school.

voca+ in[out of] phase with ~와 조화를 이루어[이루지 못하여]

v. (단계적으로) 실행하다

5 Existing bank notes will be *phased out* over the next year.

voca+ phase in[out] 단계적으로 도입[폐지]하다

render
[réndər]

n. rendering
1. 연주, 공연 2. 번역

v. 1. (어떤 상태가) 되게 하다
2. (서비스 · 도움을) 제공하다 syn. supply, furnish
3. (해석하여) 표현하다, 묘사하다
4. 번역하다

6 The defect *rendered* the CD player useless.
7 *render* good service
8 The power of nature was subtly *rendered* in the poem.
9 *render* a French book into English

amass
[əmǽs]

n. amassment

v. 모으다, 축적하다, 쌓다 syn. accumulate, gather

10 Mr. Plummer *amassed* a fortune through banking.

vanish
[vǽniʃ]

a. vanished
vanishing

v. (갑자기) 사라지다, 없어지다 syn. disappear, go away

11 The man *vanished* from sight.

voca+ vanish into thin air 온데간데없이 사라지다
vanishing point (투시화법의) 소실점(물체의 연장선들끼리 만나는 점)

1 해양 수산부 2 해안 지방 3 나비의 생애에는 세 가지 단계가 있다. 4 우리는 학교에서 달의 상(相)을 공부했다. 5 기존 지폐는 내년에 단계적으로 폐기될 것이다. 6 그 결함 때문에 CD플레이어가 쓸모없게 되었다. 7 좋은 서비스를 제공하다 8 그 시에는 자연의 힘이 섬세하게 표현되어 있었다. 9 불어판 책을 영어로 번역하다 10 Plummer씨는 금융업을 통해 큰 재산을 모았다. 11 그 남자는 시야에서 갑자기 사라졌다.

stoop
[stuːp]

a. stooped

v. (상체를) 굽히다, (자세가) 구부정하다 syn. bend, crouch

1 The old man *stooped* down to pick up the paper.

n. 1. 구부정한 자세, 굽은 등 2. *AmE.* 작은 현관[계단]

amorous
[ǽmərəs]

a. 호색적인, 사랑의, 연애의

2 Claire tried to ignore his *amorous* comments.

voca+ amorous glances[looks] 추파

cleave
[kliːv]

n. cleaver 큰 칼, 클리버

v. 1. 쪼개다, 나누다
2. 헤치고 나가다

3 The wooden door had been *cleft* in two.
4 He watched the boat *cleaving* through the bay.

voca+ cleave to ~에 달라붙다, ~을 고수하다

sluggish
[slʌ́giʃ]

n. sluggishness

a. 둔한, 느린, 부진한

5 He expressed disappointment over *sluggish* sales.

| Nuance | "게으른/나태한" 관련 어휘 뉘앙스 차이

sluggish 둔한, 느린	행동이나 상황이 평소에 비해 느리거나 활기를 잃은 6 sluggish after lunch
lazy 게으른, 느린	게으르고 열의가 없으며 일하기를 싫어하는 7 He's so lazy that he avoids any kind of work.
idle 일하지 않는, 게으른	필요에 의해 쉬거나 일을 하지 않고 빈둥거리는 8 Most of the factory stood idle during the strike.
indolent 나태한	일에 대해 흥미도 없고 노력도 하지 않으면서 귀찮아하는 9 The indolent girl refused to do her homework.

1 그 노인은 신문을 집으려고 몸을 굽혔다. 2 Claire는 그의 치근대는 말을 무시하려고 애썼다. 3 그 나무 문은 두 조각으로 쪼개져 있었다. 4 그는 배가 물살을 가르며 만을 통과하는 것을 보았다. 5 그는 부진한 매출에 대해 실망감을 드러냈다. 6 점심 식사 후 나른해진 7 그는 너무 게을러서 어떤 일이든 회피한다. 8 공장 대부분이 파업 기간 동안 가동되지 않았다. 9 게으른 그 소녀는 숙제하기를 거부했다.

defraud
[difrɔ́:d]
n. defraudation

v. 속여서 빼앗다, 횡령하다 syn. swindle

1 He was convicted of ***defrauding*** the government ***of*** $14 m.

voca+ defraud A of B A를 속여 B를 뜯어내다

trepidation
[trèpidéiʃən]

n. 불안, 공포 syn. anxiety, dread, fright

2 I used to go to the dentist with some ***trepidation***.

gaunt
[gɔ:nt]
n. gauntness

a. 1. 수척한, 몹시 여윈 syn. haggard, bony
2. 적막한, 황량한

3 The survivors appeared ***gaunt*** after weeks without food.
4 The castle looked ***gaunt*** and threatening.

insolent
[ínsələnt]
n. insolence

a. 무례한, 건방진, 오만한 syn. rude, impudent

5 The child was scolded for her ***insolent*** manner.

ripple
[rípl]

v. 1. 잔물결이 일다, 약하게 흔들리다
2. (소리 · 감정 등이) 파문처럼 퍼지다

6 The water ***rippled*** when the fish jumped.
7 Whispers ***rippled*** around the tables as the winner's name was announced.

n. 1. 잔물결
2. 일었다 사라지는 소리, 웅성거리는 소리
3. 파문, 반향

8 a ***ripple*** of applause[laughter]
9 News of the woman's suicide hardly caused a ***ripple***.

voca+ ripple effect 파급 효과

1 그는 정부 기금 1400만 달러를 횡령한 혐의로 유죄 판결을 받았다. 2 나는 약간의 공포심을 갖고 치과에 가곤 했다. 3 생존자들은 몇 주 동안 먹을 것 없이 지내서 몹시 여위어 보였다. 4 그 성은 적막하고 으스스해 보였다. 5 그 아이는 무례한 태도 때문에 꾸지람을 들었다. 6 물고기가 뛰어오르자 수면에 잔물결이 일었다. 7 우승자가 발표되자 수근거리는 소리가 테이블 주위로 퍼져나갔다. 8 박수[웃음]의 물결 9 그 여자의 자살 소식은 거의 아무런 반향도 일으키지 않았다.

superfluous
[suːpə́ːrfluəs]

n. superfluity

a. 여분의, 과잉의, 불필요한 syn. redundant, unnecessary

1 I had already decided, so her opinion was *superfluous*.

embark
[imbɑ́ːrk]

n. embarkation

v. 승선하다, 탑승하다, 싣다 ant. disembark

2 Passengers check in at the airport before they *embark*.
3 We *embarked on* our new business plan with great hope.
4 You will receive further information on the sailing two weeks before *embarkation*.

voca+ embark on[upon] (새로운 일에) 착수하다

whimsical
[hwímzikəl]

n. whim 변덕, 즉흥, 충동
whimsy 별난 행동[생각]

a. 별난, 색다른, 기발한 syn. unusual

5 Fred is known for his *whimsical* sense of humor.
6 Social policy should not be changed at the *whim* of a government.

voca+ on a whim 일시적 기분으로

connoisseur
[kɑ̀nəsə́ːr]

n. (예술 · 음식 등의) 감정가, 전문가 (someone who knows a lot about a particular thing, enjoys it, and can judge its quality)

7 He is a *connoisseur* of ancient art.

malediction
[mæ̀lədíkʃən]

n. 저주, 악담 syn. curse ant. benediction

8 When he fell off the horse, he shouted *maledictions* at the animal.

1 나는 이미 결정을 내린 상태였기 때문에 그녀의 의견은 불필요했다. 2 승객들은 탑승하기 전에 공항에서 탑승 수속을 한다. 3 우리는 큰 기대에 부풀어 새 사업에 착수했다. 4 승선하기 2주 전에 항해에 관한 상세한 정보를 받게 될 것입니다. 5 Fred는 독특한 유머 감각으로 유명하다. 6 사회정책이 정부의 일시적인 생각에 따라 변동되어서는 안 된다. 7 그는 고미술 감정가이다. 8 그는 말에서 떨어지자 말에게 악담을 퍼부었다.

neologism
[niːɑ́lədʒìzəm]

n. 신조어, 새로운 의미를 갖게 된 단어 syn. coined word

1 With each new technology, ***neologisms*** must be invented.

salient
[séiliənt]

n. salience

a. 현저한, 두드러진 syn. prominent, conspicuous

2 The following are the ***salient*** features of the proposal.

voca+ salient features[points] 특징, 눈에 띄는 점

ingrate
[íngreit]

n. 은혜를 모르는 자, 배은망덕한 사람

3 You are an *ingrate* in the way you react to your parents' kindness.

benediction
[bènədíkʃən]

a. benedictional

n. 축복, 기도 syn. blessing ant. malediction

4 The priest gave the *benediction* on Sunday morning.

IDIOMS

bark up the wrong tree 잘못 짚다 (to have the wrong idea about how to get or achieve something)

5 You're *barking up the wrong tree* if you think I'm going to change my mind.

blow up in someone's face 실패하다 (to go wrong suddenly and cause a lot of problems)

6 One of his deals has just *blown up in his face*.

1 새로운 기술이 나오는 것과 함께 신조어가 만들어져야 한다. 2 다음은 그 제안에서 눈에 띄는 특징들입니다. 3 너는 부모님의 은혜를 저버리는 배은망덕한 인간이야. 4 목사는 일요일 아침에 축복 기도를 올렸다. 5 내가 마음을 바꿀 거라고 생각했다면 잘못 짚은 거야. 6 그의 거래들 중 하나가 방금 실패했다.

exercise

A Match the words in the left column to the sentences in the right column.

ⓐ **connoisseur**: a person with specialized knowledge and tastes

ⓑ **whimsical**: unpredictable or unusual

ⓒ **impair**: to damage or make something less effective

ⓓ **maritime**: relating to the sea

ⓔ **explicit**: clearly expressed

1. Years of working in loud bars will ___________ your hearing.
2. He's a(n) ___________ of fine wines.
3. According to ___________ law, these are international waters.
4. We never knew what the ___________ young man would do next.
5. Please make your intentions ___________.

B Choose the word or phrase that best explains the underlined word.

1. If you are ***amorous***, you are _______________.
   ⓐ humiliated ⓑ in love ⓒ friendly ⓓ broken-hearted

2. If you ***render*** assistance, you _______________ help.
   ⓐ need ⓑ refuse ⓒ provide ⓓ request

3. If you ***amass*** funds, you _______________ money.
   ⓐ raise ⓑ spend ⓒ lose ⓓ borrow

4. If you ***defraud*** someone, you _______________.
   ⓐ reveal their secret ⓑ repay their kindness
   ⓒ earn their trust ⓓ cheat them out of money

5. If you ***cleave*** something, you _______________ it.
   ⓐ catch ⓑ steal ⓒ split ⓓ desire

정답 및 해설 p. 374

C Choose the option that is closest in meaning to the underlined word.

1. the most ***salient*** feature
   ⓐ subtle ⓑ noticeable ⓒ ordinary ⓓ disturbing

2. ***bestow*** privileges
   ⓐ deserve ⓑ thrive on ⓒ deny ⓓ grant

3. ***superfluous*** information
   ⓐ secretive ⓑ valuable ⓒ organized ⓓ unnecessary

D Choose the option that is the opposite of the underlined word.

1. ***vanish*** into thin air
   ⓐ flee ⓑ evaporate ⓒ appear ⓓ pollute

2. a ***gaunt*** physique
   ⓐ chubby ⓑ slender ⓒ short ⓓ awkward

3. an ***insolent*** child
   ⓐ spoiled ⓑ brilliant ⓒ bold ⓓ respectful

E Choose the best word or phrase.

1. Who would be most likely to ***adhere*** to the rules?
   ⓐ a rebel ⓑ a criminal ⓒ a conformist ⓓ a radical

2. What would you be likely to ***embark*** on?
   ⓐ a journey ⓑ an antenna ⓒ a post office ⓓ an understanding

3. Which of the following is likely to ***ripple***?
   ⓐ a statue ⓑ an ice cube ⓒ a flagpole ⓓ a pond

4. If you feel ***sluggish***, you are most likely to ________________.
   ⓐ go to a party ⓑ play a sport ⓒ stay in bed ⓓ clean your room

impartial
[impɑ́ːrʃəl]

n. impartiality

a. 공정한, 치우치지 않은 syn. fair, neutral ant. biased, prejudiced

1 A trial must be fair and *impartial*.

beware
[biwɛ́ər]

v. 조심하다, 주의하다 syn. be cautious

2 Always *beware of* strangers.

discharge
[distʃɑ́ːrdʒ]

v. 1. (군대 · 병원 · 감옥 등에서) 나가게 하다
2. (액체 · 가스 등을) 방출하다, (배터리 등이) 방전되다
3. (의무를) 이행하다, (빚을) 상환하다
4. 발사하다, 쏘다

3 Patrick was *discharged from* the army last year.
4 Sewage is *discharged* directly into the sea.
5 *discharge* your duties / *discharge* a debt
6 A soldier *discharged* his weapon by accident.

n. 1. 제대, 퇴원, 석방 2. 방출, 방전 3. 의무 이행, 상환 4. 발사

voca+ conditional discharge 조건부 석방
honorable[dishonorable] discharge 명예[불명예] 제대

extravagant
[ikstrǽvəgənt]

n. extravagance

a. 1. 낭비하는, 사치스러운 syn. wasteful, prodigal
2. 지나친, 터무니없는 syn. excessive

7 He is too *extravagant* with his clothes.
8 I'm not willing to meet his *extravagant* demands.

adjacent
[ədʒéisənt]

a. 근처의, 인접한 syn. adjoining, neighboring

9 The bank is *adjacent to* the church.

1 재판은 공정하고 공평해야 한다. 2 낯선 사람들을 항상 경계해라. 3 Patrick은 작년에 군에서 제대했다. 4 하수는 곧바로 바다로 방출된다. 5 의무를 이행하다 / 빚을 상환하다 6 한 병사가 오발 사고를 냈다. 7 그는 옷을 사는 데 과도한 돈을 쓴다. 8 나는 그의 터무니없는 요구를 들어줄 마음이 없다. 9 그 은행은 교회 바로 옆에 있다.

maternity
[mətə́ːrnəti]

a. maternal

a. 임산부의, 임신[출산]의 syn. pregnant

1 *maternity* benefits[pay]

voca+ maternity leave 출산 휴가
maternity ward 산부인과 병동

n. 어머니임, 모성 syn. motherhood ant. paternity

2 *Maternity* is the state of being a mother.

philanthropy
[filǽnθrəpi]

n. philanthropist 자선가
a. philanthropic

n. 자선(행위), 박애주의(the belief that you should help people especially by giving money)

3 His legendary *philanthropy* has benefited millions.
4 *philanthropic*[charitable] organization

repent
[ripént]

n. repentance
a. repentant

v. 후회하다, 뉘우치다, 회개하다 syn. regret

5 *Repent of* your sins and beg God's forgiveness.

strife
[straif]

n. 분쟁, 불화, 투쟁 syn. conflict, discord

6 After 20 years of *strife*, the opposing forces signed a peace agreement.

voca+ labor strife 노동 쟁의
religious[ethnic] strife 종교[민족] 분쟁

vendor
[véndər]

v. vend 판매하다

n. 행상인, 노점 상인

7 The park was full of food *vendors*.

voca+ vending machine 자동판매기

1 출산 수당 2 모성은 어머니가 되는 상태를 뜻한다. 3 그의 전설적인 박애정신은 수백만 명에게 혜택을 주었다. 4 자선 단체 5 네 죄를 회개하고 신의 용서를 구하라. 6 20년 간의 분쟁 끝에 대치 세력들은 평화 협정을 맺었다. 7 공원은 음식을 파는 노점상들로 가득했다.

clout
[klaut]

n. 1. (정치 · 경제적) 영향력, 권력 syn. influence, authority
2. (손으로) 강타, 타격 syn. blow

1 We have no political *clout*.
2 Jimmy gave him a *clout* on the head.

v. (손으로) 때리다, 강타하다

degenerate
[didʒénərèit]

n. degeneration
a. degenerative [질병] 퇴행성의

v. 나빠지다, 퇴보하다 syn. worsen, deteriorate

3 The blog *degenerated into* a forum of name-calling and bullying.

a. [didʒénərət] 타락한 syn. immoral, corrupt

n. [didʒénərət] 타락한 자

embed
[imbéd]

a. embedded

v. 1. (물건을) 단단히 끼워 넣다, 깊숙이 박다
2. (생각 · 감정 등을) 깊이 새겨두다

4 A piece of metal was *embedded* in the factory worker's hand.
5 A sense of regret was *embedded* in my heart.

eminent
[éminənt]

n. eminence

a. 저명한, 탁월한

6 She is *eminent* in the field of linguistics.

| Nuance | "유명한/저명한" 관련 어휘 뉘앙스 차이

eminent 저명한, 유명한	l 전문직(의사 · 변호사 · 과학자 등)에서 성공하여 유명해진 7 an eminent psychiatrist
prominent 중요한, 저명한	l 주로 정치 · 사업 · 교육계에서 특출하여 중요한 역할을 하는 8 a prominent business leader
distinguished 두드러진, 뛰어난	l 같은 부류의 사람들 사이에서 업적 · 학식 등이 우월하여 돋보이는 9 a long and distinguished career
celebrated 유명한, 저명한	l 성공이나 성취로 인해 유명 인사가 되어 사람들 입에 자주 오르는 10 Van Gogh, Holland's most celebrated artist

1 우리에게는 정치적 영향력이 없다. 2 Jimmy는 그의 머리를 손으로 세게 때렸다. 3 블로그는 조롱과 따돌림의 장으로 변질되었다. 4 그 공장 노동자의 손에 금속 조각이 박혔다. 5 마음 속 깊이 후회가 일었다. 6 그녀는 언어학 분야에서 명성이 높다. 7 유명한 정신과 의사 8 저명한 기업가 9 장기간의 돋보이는 경력 10 네덜란드에서 가장 유명한 화가인 반 고흐

gland
[glænd]

n. [생리] 선(腺), 분비기관

❶ A *gland* is an organ of the body which produces substances that the body needs, such as hormones or sweat.

voca+ salivary[sweat] gland 침샘[땀샘]
thyroid gland 갑상선

insular
[ínsələr]

n. insularity

a. 1. 자기 지역에만 관심있는, 국수주의적인, 폐쇄적인 syn. parochial
2. 섬의, 섬과 관련한, 섬나라의

❷ An *insular* community would exclude foreigners.
❸ Climate changes might seriously affect the *insular* region.

obstinate
[ábstinət]

n. obstinacy

a. 1. 완고한, 고집센 syn. stubborn
2. *BrE.* 처리하기 힘든, 없애기 어려운

❹ He is *obstinate* in his refusal to follow others' suggestions.
❺ the *obstinate* problem of unemployment

proliferate
[prəlífərèit]

n. proliferation

v. 급증하다, 확산되다 syn. multiply

❻ Books on soccer have *proliferated* in Korea since the 2002 World Cup.

voca+ NPT/NNPT(Nuclear Non-Proliferation Treaty) 핵 확산 금지 조약

robust
[roubʌ́st]

n. robustness

a. 1. 튼튼한, 견고한 syn. sturdy ant. frail
2. (신념 · 의지가) 확고한, 단호한
3. (음식 · 술이) 감칠맛이 도는

❼ He looks *robust* and healthy.
❽ The police need to take a *robust* approach to robberies.
❾ This *robust* soup will warm you up on a cold winter morning.

❶ 분비기관은 호르몬이나 땀과 같이 몸이 필요로 하는 물질을 만들어내는 신체 기관이다. ❷ 폐쇄적인 지역 사회는 외국인을 배척하기 마련이다. ❸ 기후 변화가 섬 지역에 심각한 영향을 미칠지도 모른다. ❹ 그는 다른 사람들의 제안에 따르는 것을 완강하게 거절한다. ❺ 해결하기 어려운 실업 문제 ❻ 2002년 월드컵 이후 한국에서는 축구에 관한 책들이 쏟아져 나왔다. ❼ 그는 튼튼하고 건강해 보인다. ❽ 경찰은 강도 사건에 대해 단호하게 접근해야 한다. ❾ 이 맛있는 수프가 추운 겨울 아침에 몸을 덥혀 줄 것이다.

surmount
[səːrmáunt]

a. surmountable 극복 가능한

v. 1. 극복하다, 이겨내다 syn. overcome
2. (주로 수동태로) ~위에 놓다

1 She had to ***surmount*** many barriers to succeed in the legal profession.
2 The dome is ***surmounted*** by a statue of an eagle.

wince
[wins]

v. (고통 · 당황스러움 등으로) 얼굴을 찌푸리다, 움찔하다 syn. cringe, shrink

3 She ***winced*** as she watched the boy falling.

n. 움츠림, 찌푸림

conscript
[kənskrípt]

n. conscription

v. 징집하다, 입대시키다 syn. draft, call up

4 He was ***conscripted*** to the navy despite his protests.

n. [kánskript] *BrE.* 징집병 syn. *AmE.* draftee ant. volunteer

flaunt
[flɔːnt]

v. 과시하다, 자랑하다, 뽐내다 syn. show off

5 She likes to ***flaunt*** her wealth at every opportunity.

voca+ If you've got it, flaunt it. 가지고 있으면 과시하라.

obliterate
[əblítərèit]

n. obliteration

v. 1. 완전히 파괴하다 syn. destroy
2. (기억 · 감정을) 지우다, 삭제하다 syn. erase
3. (가려서) 보이지 않게 하다

6 Hiroshima was ***obliterated*** by the atomic bomb in 1945.
7 Paul tried to ***obliterate*** her from his memory.
8 The mudslide had ***obliterated*** all signs of the village.

1 그녀는 법조계에서 성공하기 위해 많은 장벽을 넘어서야 했다. 2 돔 위에 독수리 상이 있다. 3 그녀는 그 소년이 넘어지는 것을 보자 움찔했다. 4 그는 저항했지만 결국 해군에 징집되었다. 5 그녀는 기회 있을 때마다 자신의 재력을 과시하기를 좋아한다. 6 히로시마는 1945년 원자폭탄에 의해 완전히 파괴되었다. 7 Paul은 그녀를 기억에서 지우려고 애썼다. 8 산사태는 모든 마을의 흔적을 지워 버렸다.

sedentary
[sédəntèri]

a. 앉아 있는 시간이 많은, 활동량이 적은

1 A ***sedentary*** lifestyle increases the risk of obesity and high blood pressure.

voca+ sedentary job[occupation] 사무직

beneficiary
[bènəfíʃièri]

n. 수익자, (보험금 · 상속재산 등의) 수혜자

2 Mr. Robinson's grandchildren are the ***beneficiaries*** of his insurance policy.

dearth
[dəːrθ]

n. 부족, 결핍 syn. scarcity, deficiency, shortage

3 There was a ***dearth of*** talented engineers in the country.

adulterate
[ədʌ́ltərèit]

n. adulteration 불순품, 저질품
a. adulterated

v. 다른 것을 섞어 질을 떨어뜨리다

4 It was said that the gold had been ***adulterated*** with a cheap compound.

IDIOMS

be all ears 열심히 귀를 기울이다 (to be very keen to hear)

5 I ***was all ears*** when she mentioned what I would receive.

not by a long shot 결코 ~않다 (not at all)

6 He had not told Rory everything, ***not by a long shot***.

1 좌식 생활 양식은 비만과 고혈압의 위험을 증가시킨다. 2 Robinson씨의 손자들이 보험금의 수혜자이다. 3 그 나라에는 재능있는 기술자들이 부족했다. 4 그 금에는 값싼 혼합물이 섞여 있었다고들 했다. 5 내가 받을 것에 대해 그녀가 언급하는 것을 귀 기울여 들었다. 6 그는 결코 Rory에게 모든 것을 말하지 않았다.

exercise

A Match the words in the left column to the sentences in the right column.

ⓐ **adulterate**: pollute or make impure

ⓑ **sedentary**: characterized by lack of physical activity

ⓒ **beneficiary**: one who receives funds or otherwise benefits from something

ⓓ **eminent**: highly regarded or important, standing above others

ⓔ **philanthropy**: the act of doing charitable things for the well-being of human-kind

1. He is a(n) ___________ member of the community.
2. I wouldn't like a(n) ___________ job. I prefer to be active.
3. If I were rich, I would become involved in ___________.
4. This beverage is ___________(e)d with sugar.
5. I'd like to buy life insurance and name my son as the ___________.

B Choose the word or phrase that best explains the underlined word.

1. If you have a lot of ***clout***, you can _______________ people.
   ⓐ influence ⓑ confuse ⓒ offend ⓓ deceive

2. A ***vendor*** is a person who _______________ merchandise.
   ⓐ eats ⓑ cooks ⓒ sells ⓓ makes

3. Something that is ***adjacent*** to the house is _______________ it.
   ⓐ behind ⓑ beside ⓒ in front of ⓓ in

4. When you ***repent*** of your sins, you _______________.
   ⓐ are punished for them ⓑ feel guilty
   ⓒ learn from your mistakes ⓓ deny them

5. If you are ***conscripted***, you _______________ the army.
   ⓐ voluntarily join ⓑ run away from
   ⓒ are discharged from ⓓ are forced to join

정답 및 해설 p.374

C Choose the option that is closest in meaning to the underlined word.

1. ***flaunt*** a new car
ⓐ purchase ⓑ crash ⓒ boast of ⓓ insure

2. a ***robust*** build
ⓐ strong ⓑ slim ⓒ short ⓓ frail

3. ***degenerate*** with age
ⓐ improve ⓑ weaken ⓒ ripen ⓓ shift

D Choose the option that is the opposite of the underlined word.

1. ***proliferate*** nuclear arms
ⓐ eliminate ⓑ develop ⓒ protest ⓓ test

2. times of ***strife***
ⓐ recession ⓑ change ⓒ harmony ⓓ success

3. an ***impartial*** mediator
ⓐ skilled ⓑ biased ⓒ famous ⓓ compassionate

E Choose the best word or phrase.

1. An ***obstinate*** person always does what he wants and ____________ to change his mind.
ⓐ agrees ⓑ hopes ⓒ likes ⓓ refuses

2. What should swimmers in the ocean ***beware*** of?
ⓐ sunscreen ⓑ sharks ⓒ their children ⓓ clouds

3. You ***wince*** when you ____________.
ⓐ eat something good ⓑ can't hear someone
ⓒ have a secret to tell ⓓ suddenly feel pain

4. Who would be off work on ***maternity*** leave?
ⓐ someone who was injured ⓑ someone who is on a business trip
ⓒ someone who is stressed out ⓓ someone who has a new baby

acquisitive
[əkwízətiv]

n. acquisitiveness 탐욕
acquisition 획득

a. 얻고자 하는, 욕심이 많은 syn. greedy

1 In an *acquisitive* world, people are judged by their wealth.
2 There have been many mergers and *acquisitions* in the telecommunications sector.

adore
[ədɔ́ːr]

n. adoration
a. adoring 숭배[흠모]하는
adorable 귀여운, 반할 만한

v. 1. 숭배하다, 존경하다 syn. worship, revere
2. 무척 좋아하다 syn. love

3 Let us *adore* God for all His work.
4 I'm sure you will *adore* this book.

bewilder
[biwíldər]

n. bewilderment
a. bewildering
bewildered

v. 당황하게 하다, 어리둥절하게 하다 syn. perplex, confuse, confound

5 Joan was *bewildered* by the critical articles in the press commenting on her new book.

prescient
[préʃənt]

n. prescience 선견지명

a. 선견지명이 있는, 앞을 내다본

6 It was foolish to ignore his *prescient* warning.

fabricate
[fǽbrikèit]

n. fabrication

v. 1. (이야기 · 정보 등을) 꾸며내다, 조작하다 syn. invent, make up
2. 만들다, 제작하다 syn. manufacture

7 The CEO was arrested and charged with *fabricating* accounting details.
8 The company *fabricates* office furniture.

1 욕망이 들끓는 세상에서는 부로 사람을 평가한다. 2 통신분야에서 기업의 인수합병이 많이 이루어져 왔다. 3 하나님이 하신 모든 일을 경배합시다. 4 네가 이 책을 무척 좋아할 거라고 확신해. 5 Joan은 그녀의 새 책에 대한 미디어의 혹평에 당황했다. 6 앞을 내다본 그의 경고를 무시한 것은 어리석은 일이었다. 7 그 CEO는 회계 수치를 조작한 혐의로 체포되어 기소되었다. 8 그 회사는 사무용 가구를 제작한다.

impel
[impél]

v. ~하도록 시키다[강요하다] syn. force, compel

1 Hunger *impelled* him *to* steal food.

voca+ impel sb to-v ~가 …하게 하다

pilgrimage
[pílgrimidʒ]

n. pilgrim 순례자

n. 1. 성지 순례, 순례 여행
2. (명소 · 고적 등을 찾는) 긴 여행

2 make[go on] a *pilgrimage* to Mecca
3 Elvis Presley's home has become a place of *pilgrimage*.

voca+ the Pilgrims 1620년에 Mayflower호를 타고 미국 Plymouth에 정착한 영국 청교도단

conspiracy
[kənspírəsi]

v. conspire
n. conspirator 공모자
a. conspiratorial

n. 음모, 공모 syn. intrigue, collusion

4 The directors were accused of *conspiracy* to defraud the company.

voca+ conspiracy against ~에 대한 음모
conspiracy of silence 침묵[비밀]을 지키자는 모의
conspiracy theory 음모설(사건 등의 배후에 음모가 있다는 믿음)

amiable
[éimiəbl]

n. amiability

a. 호감을 주는, 상냥한 syn. affable, genial

5 Her *amiable* character pleased everyone.

voca+ amiable character[mood/conversation] 정감 있는 성격[분위기/대화]

resolute
[rézəlùːt]

n. resolution
1. 결의, 결심
2. 해결책
3. 해상도

a. 결심이 굳은, 단호한 (doing something in a very determined way because of strong beliefs, aims, etc.) syn. decisive ant. irresolute

6 Be *resolute* in war, defiant in defeat, and magnanimous in victory.

voca+ New Year's resolution 새해 결심

1 배고픔은 그가 음식을 훔치게끔 만들었다. 2 메카로 성지순례를 떠나다 3 Elvis Presley의 집은 명승지가 되었다. 4 임원들은 회사 자금을 빼돌리려 공모한 혐의로 기소되었다. 5 그녀의 붙임성 있는 성격은 모든 사람들을 즐겁게 했다. 6 전쟁할 때는 단호하고, 패배했을 때는 굴하지 말며, 승리했을 때는 관대하라.

verify
[vérəfài]

n. verification
a. verifiable 입증할 수 있는

v. (진실임을) 입증하다, 확인하다 syn. confirm, prove

❶ He *verified* that the accused had been with him at the time of the robbery.

querulous
[kwérələs]

a. 불평이 많은, 화를 잘 내는

❷ His *querulous* voice annoyed his wife.

lavish
[lǽviʃ]

n. lavishness

a. 1. 사치스러운, 호화로운 syn. extravagant
2. 아낌없는, 후한 syn. generous

❸ He led a very *lavish* lifestyle.
❹ Robert was *lavish* in his praise for my performance.

v. 아낌없이 주다

voca+ lavish A on[upon] B B에게 A를 아낌없이 주다

disparity
[dispǽrəti]

n. 격차, 불균형, 불일치 ant. parity

❺ The *disparities* between the haves and the have-nots cause social unrest.

| Nuance | "차이/불일치" 관련 어휘 뉘앙스 차이

disparity 격차, 불균형	주로 불평등한 상태에 있는 대상들 간의 차이 ❻ a disparity between the rates of pay for men and women
difference 다름, 상이	세부 항목 · 사실 · 특성 · 속성상의 차이 ❼ a difference in color and size
dissimilarity 부동(不同)	유사한 대상 혹은 사람 간의 차이 ❽ a dissimilarity between the twins' personalities
divergence 차이	같은 것에서 갈라져 나와 달라진 것들 사이의 차이 ❾ a divergence between British and American English
discrepancy 불일치	같거나 일치해야 하는 것 사이에 나타내는 차이 ❿ a discrepancy between words and actions

❶ 그는 피고인이 강도 사건 발생 당시 자신과 함께 있었다는 것을 입증했다. ❷ 그의 투덜거리는 목소리는 그의 아내를 짜증나게 했다. ❸ 그는 매우 사치스러운 생활을 했다. ❹ Robert는 내 성과에 대한 칭찬을 아끼지 않았다. ❺ 가진 자와 못 가진 자 사이의 격차는 사회 불안을 낳는다. ❻ 남녀 간 급여의 불균형 ❼ 색깔과 크기 차이 ❽ 쌍둥이 간의 성격 차이 ❾ 영국 영어와 미국 영어의 차이 ❿ 말과 행동의 불일치

embody
[imbɑ́:di]

n. embodiment 체현, 화신

v. 1. (사상 · 감정 등을) 표현하다, 상징하다 syn. represent
2. 포함하다 syn. include, contain

1 Words *embody* our thoughts and express our feelings.
2 Our newest car *embodies* the latest technology.
3 He was portrayed in the movie as the *embodiment* of evil.

grievous
[grí:vəs]

v. grieve
n. grief

a. 비통한, 괴로운, (고통이) 심한

4 Marie's death was a *grievous* loss to all who knew her.

intermittent
[ìntərmítənt]

ad. intermittently

a. 때때로 중단되는, 간헐적인 syn. sporadic

5 There will be *intermittent* showers in L.A. today.
6 This web browser *intermittently* freezes for several seconds.

voca+ intermittent spring 간헐천

restrict
[ristríkt]

n. restriction
a. restricted

v. 1. (크기 · 양 등을) 제한하다, 한정하다
2. (활동 등을) 규제하다, 통제하다

7 The event organizers *restricted* the number of seats open to the public.
8 The government is trying to strengthen the efforts to *restrict* smoking in public places.

prone
[proun]

n. proneness

a. 1. (좋지 않은 쪽으로) ~하는 경향이 있는, ~하기 일쑤인 syn. liable, likely
2. 엎드린, 배를 깔고 누운 syn. prostrate ant. supine 등 대고 누운

9 He is *prone to* being lazy if he's not given anything to do.
10 I found her lying *prone* on the ground.

voca+ accident[injury / error]-prone 사고를 당하기[다치기 / 실수하기] 쉬운

1 언어는 우리의 사고를 구체화하며 우리의 감정을 표현한다. 2 우리의 최신 자동차는 최첨단 기술을 보유하고 있습니다. 3 그는 영화에서 악의 화신으로 그려졌다. 4 Marie의 죽음은 그녀를 알았던 모든 이들에게 심한 상실감을 주었다. 5 오늘 LA에는 때때로 소나기가 내리겠습니다. 6 이 웹브라우저는 중간중간 몇 초 동안 멈추곤 한다. 7 행사 기획자들은 일반인들에게 개방되는 좌석 수를 제한했다. 8 정부는 공공 장소에서 흡연을 규제하려는 노력을 강화하려 하고 있다. 9 그는 할 일이 주어지지 않으면 게으름을 피우는 경향이 있다. 10 나는 그녀가 땅에 엎드려 있는 것을 보았다.

rudimentary
[rù:dəméntəri]

n. rudiments 원리, 기초

a. 1. 초보적인, 기본의 syn. basic, fundamental ant. sophisticated
2. 미발달의 syn. undeveloped

1 Jim only has a *rudimentary* knowledge of computers.
2 Some fish have *rudimentary* legs.

voca+ rudimentary organ 흔적기관

surrogate
[sə́:rəgət]

a. 대리(인)의 syn. substitute

3 He acted like a *surrogate* father for some of his students.

voca+ surrogate mother 대리모

n. 대리인, 대체물

yolk
[jouk]

n. (달걀의) 노른자위 ant. white

4 Break the egg and separate the egg *yolk* from the white.

paltry
[pɔ́:ltri]

a. 1. (금액이) 얼마 안 되는 syn. meager
2. 하찮은, 보잘것없는 syn. insignificant, worthless

5 He received a *paltry* sum for his painting.
6 Don't waste time talking about *paltry* issues.

voca+ paltry sum 얼마 안 되는 금액

obsolescent
[àbsəlésənt]

n. obsolescence
a. obsolete 쓸모없게 된, 구식의

a. 쇠퇴해 가는, 구식이 되어가는 syn. waning

7 The Navy's warships are becoming *obsolescent*.

1 Jim은 컴퓨터에 대한 초보적인 지식만 갖고 있다. 2 어떤 물고기들은 완전히 발달되지 않은 다리를 갖고 있다. 3 그는 자신의 몇몇 제자들의 대부 노릇을 했다. 4 달걀을 깨서 노른자와 흰자를 분리해라. 5 그는 자신의 그림 값으로 얼마 안 되는 돈을 받았다. 6 시덥잖은 일에 대해 얘기하면서 시간을 낭비하지 마라. 7 해군 전함들은 구닥다리로 전락해가고 있다.

disruptive

[disrʌ́ptiv]

v. disrupt
n. disruption

a. 교란하는, 혼란[문제]을 일으키는

1 The child was expelled from school for *disruptive* behavior.

sludge

[slʌdʒ]

a. sludgy

n. 1. 진흙, 진창 syn. mud, slime
2. 침전물, 찌꺼기 syn. sediment

2 The motorbike struggled to pass through the *sludge*.
3 Sewage *sludge* is a good source of nutrients for the soil.

consign

[kənsáin]

n. consignment
1. 배송 2. 위탁

v. 1. 보내다, 발송하다
2. (눈에 띄지 않게) 치우다, (버리려고) 치워 두다
3. (나쁜 상황에) 처하게 만들다

4 The goods were *consigned to* your address.
5 He *consigned* his old shoes to the back of the closet.
6 The car accident *consigned* him *to* a wheelchair.

fluke

[fluːk]

a. fluky
(=flukey)

n. 요행, 뜻밖의 행운

7 It was just a *fluke* that I won the game.

IDIOMS

be out of the woods 위기[위험]에서 벗어나다 (to no longer be in danger or difficulty)

8 When the accused *was out of the woods*, he could go back to his normal life.

can't make heads or tails of something 이해[구별]할 수 없다 (to be completely unable to understand something)

9 People *can't make heads or tails of* her plan.

1 그 학생은 질서를 어지럽히는 행동을 해서 퇴학당했다. 2 오토바이는 진창길을 통과하려고 안간힘을 썼다. 3 하수 침전물은 토양에 양분을 공급하는 훌륭한 원천이다. 4 상품이 귀하의 주소로 배송되었습니다. 5 그는 낡은 신발을 벽장 깊숙이 치워뒀다. 6 차 사고로 그는 휠체어 신세를 지게 되었다. 7 내가 경기에서 승리한 것은 운이 좋았던 것뿐이다. 8 피고인은 혐의가 없다는 판결을 받고 나서 정상 생활로 돌아갈 수 있었다. 9 사람들은 그녀의 계획을 이해하지 못한다.

exercise

A Match the words in the left column to the sentences in the right column.

ⓐ **impel**: to urge or force someone to do something

ⓑ **lavish**: costing a lot of money, large in amount

ⓒ **conspiracy**: a secret plot, normally illegal, with a group of participants

ⓓ **paltry**: insufficient, not enough

ⓔ **sludge**: soft, wet dirt

1. He wasn't satisfied with his __________ salary.
2. The __________ to overthrow the government was unsuccessful.
3. They had a(n) __________ wedding; it was like a fairytale.
4. Wipe the __________ off your shoes before you come in.
5. I'll try to __________ him to tell the truth.

B Choose the word or phrase that best explains the underlined word.

1. If you are ***bewildered***, you are __________.
   ⓐ confident ⓑ confused ⓒ frightened ⓓ perceptive

2. If there is a ***disparity*** between two things, there is a __________.
   ⓐ difference ⓑ relationship ⓒ similarity ⓓ misunderstanding

3. If you win because of a ***fluke***, you are __________.
   ⓐ skilled ⓑ wealthy ⓒ lucky ⓓ competitive

4. If you are ***prone*** to a disease, you have an increased chance of __________.
   ⓐ being diagnosed with it ⓑ surviving it
   ⓒ being immune to it ⓓ dying from it

5. If you are ***querulous***, you __________ a lot of things.
   ⓐ achieve ⓑ are curious about
   ⓒ complain about ⓓ take pleasure in

정답 및 해설 p.375

C Choose the option that is closest in meaning to the underlined word.

1. be ***resolute*** from the start
   ⓐ uneasy ⓑ determined ⓒ flexible ⓓ disorganized

2. ***consign*** the electronic equipment
   ⓐ send ⓑ advertise ⓒ exchange ⓓ manufacture

3. ***disruptive*** behavior
   ⓐ idle ⓑ modest ⓒ troublesome ⓓ attractive

D Choose the option that is the opposite of the underlined word.

1. an ***amiable*** mood
   ⓐ hostile ⓑ courteous ⓒ straightforward ⓓ adorable

2. ***intermittent*** fighting
   ⓐ heavy ⓑ useless ⓒ steady ⓓ unexpected

3. ***rudimentary*** testing
   ⓐ strict ⓑ regular ⓒ compulsory ⓓ advanced

E Choose the best word or phrase.

1. Which of the following would someone ***fabricate***?
   ⓐ a poem ⓑ a concert ⓒ an excuse ⓓ a massage

2. Which of the following would you ***verify***?
   ⓐ findings ⓑ light bulbs ⓒ sports ⓓ criminals

3. Which of the following are ***obsolescent***?
   ⓐ computers ⓑ typewriters ⓒ telephones ⓓ refrigerators

4. A ***surrogate*** mother ________________.
   ⓐ gives up her child
   ⓑ educates a group of babies
   ⓒ adopts a baby from an agency
   ⓓ carries and delivers a baby for someone else

adversary
[ǽdvərsèri]
a. adversarial

n. 적, 상대 syn. opponent

1 Those two politicians are *adversaries* in the election.

blade
[bleid]

n. 1. (칼 · 도구 등의) 날
2. (노 · 프로펠러 등의) 평평한 부분
3. (식물 · 곡식 등의) 잎사귀, 가는 잎

2 razor *blade*
3 the *blades* of an airplane propeller
4 a *blade* of grass

contempt
[kəntémpt]
a. contemptible 경멸할 만한
contemptuous 경멸하는

n. 1. 경멸, 모욕, 멸시 syn. scorn, disdain
2. [법률] 모욕죄

5 The company showed utter *contempt* for its workers on strike.
6 She was jailed for *contempt* of court.

voca+ beneath contempt 경멸할 가치조차 없는

deprivation
[dèprivéiʃən]
v. deprive
a. deprived

n. 부족, 결핍, 궁핍 syn. lack, want, privation

7 Sleep *deprivation* is a very serious concern.

facet
[fǽsit]

n. 1. (사람 · 사물 · 문제 등의) 일면, 양상, 국면 syn. aspect, phase
2. (보석의) 단면

8 Her novel describes every *facet* of teenage life.
9 the *facets* of a diamond

voca+ multi-faceted 다면적인, 복합적인

1 저 두 정치인들이 선거의 경쟁자이다. 2 면도날 3 비행기 프로펠러의 날개 4 풀잎 5 그 회사는 파업 중인 직원들을 완전히 업신여겼다. 6 그녀는 법정 모독죄로 구속되었다. 7 수면 부족은 매우 심각한 문제이다. 8 그녀의 소설은 십대들 삶의 모든 양상을 묘사하고 있다. 9 다이아몬드의 단면들

disguise
[disgáiz]

a. disguised

v. 1. 변장하다, 위장하다
2. (사실 · 감정을) 숨기다, 감추다 syn. hide, conceal

1 To get into the party, I *disguised* myself as a band member.
2 I couldn't *disguise* my disappointment.

n. 변장, 가장, 위장

3 She wore glasses and a wig as a *disguise*.

voca+ in disguise 변장을 하고

imperative
[impérətiv]

a. 매우 중요한, 긴급한 syn. vital

4 It is *imperative* that you get to the office by 8 a.m. tomorrow.

n. 책무, 긴급한 과제

5 Reducing air pollution has become an *imperative*.

voca+ moral imperative 도덕적 책무[의무]

misanthrope
[mísənθròup]

n. misanthropy 염세, 인간 혐오
a. misanthropic

n. 사람을 싫어하는 사람, 염세주의자 (=misanthropist)

6 The *misanthrope* chose to live alone.

pneumonia
[nju:móunjə]

n. 폐렴

7 His cold turned into *pneumonia*.

voca+ acute[chronic] pneumonia 급성[만성] 폐렴

subdue
[səbdjú:]

a. subdued

v. 1. 진압하다, 정복하다 syn. defeat, conquer
2. (감정 등을) 억제하다 syn. suppress, control

8 Prison guards managed to *subdue* the rioting inmates.
9 Joanne had to *subdue* the urge to smoke a cigarette.

---

1 그 파티장에 들어가기 위해 나는 밴드 멤버로 위장했다. 2 나는 실망감을 감출 수 없었다. 3 그녀는 변장을 위해 안경과 가발을 썼다. 4 너는 반드시 내일 오전 8시까지 사무실로 와야 한다. 5 대기 오염을 줄이는 것은 당면 과제가 되었다. 6 그 염세주의자는 혼자 살기를 택했다. 7 그의 감기가 폐렴으로 발전되었다. 8 교도관들은 폭동을 일으킨 수감자들을 간신히 진압했다. 9 Joanne은 담배 피우고 싶은 욕구를 억제해야 했다.

vice
[vais]

a. vicious

n. 1. 악습, 악덕, 부도덕한 행위 ant. virtue
2. (성 · 마약 관련) 범죄

1 Playing computer games too much is my only *vice*.
2 The police unveiled a new plan to tackle *vice* in the city.
3 *vicious* circle

abate
[əbéit]

n. abatement

v. 약해지(게 하)다, 줄(이)다 syn. decrease, slacken (off)

4 The storm has started to *abate*.

ammunition
[æ̀mjuníʃən]

n. 1. 탄약, 총탄 syn. shell, bullet
2. (비난하는 데) 유용한 정보, 공격 수단

5 The rebels surrendered when they ran out of *ammunition*.
6 His behavior gave his boss all the *ammunition* she needed to fire him.

emancipate
[imǽnsipèit]

n. emancipation
a. emancipated

v. (정치적 · 사회적으로) 해방하다

7 The Civil War *emancipated* the slaves in the U.S.A.
8 the *Emancipation* Proclamation

| Nuance | "해방하다 / 풀어주다" 관련 어휘 뉘앙스 차이

emancipate 해방하다	기존에 없던 정치적 · 법적 권리를 갖게 해주다. 9 emancipate slaves
free 석방하다, 해방하다	구속이나 제한 등에서 풀어주다. 10 Jack was freed from prison yesterday.
liberate 해방하다	통제받고 있던 죄수 · 도시 · 국가 등을 자유롭게 하다. 11 Algeria was liberated from France in 1962.
release 풀어주다, 방면하다	일시적인 구속이나 속박 후 풀어주다. 12 The whales were released back into the wild.
discharge 퇴원시키다, 제대시키다	의무나 책임으로부터 면제시키다. 13 I was discharged from the Army in 1998.

1 컴퓨터 게임을 너무 많이 하는 것이 내 유일한 나쁜 습관이다. 2 경찰은 도시 내의 성 · 마약 범죄에 대처하기 위한 새로운 계획을 공개했다. 3 악순환 4 폭풍이 잦아들기 시작했다. 5 폭도들은 탄약이 다 떨어지자 항복했다. 6 그의 행동은 사장이 그를 해고하는 데 필요한 모든 구실을 제공했다. 7 남북 전쟁은 미국의 노예들을 해방시켰다. 8 (링컨 대통령의) 노예 해방 선언 9 노예들을 해방시키다 10 Jack은 어제 석방되었다. 11 알제리는 1962년에 프랑스로부터 독립했다. 12 고래들은 다시 야생으로 보내졌다. 13 나는 1998년에 제대했다.

colloquial
[kəlóukwiəl]

n. colloquialism 구어적 표현

a. 구어(口語)의, 회화의 syn. conversational, informal ant. literary

1 His *colloquial* style of speaking sounded familiar to me.

delude
[dilú:d]

n. delusion 망상
a. deluded 속고 있는
delusive 현혹시키는

v. 속이다, 현혹시키다 syn. deceive

2 She is just *deluding* herself if she thinks he's going to marry her.

voca+ delude sb into v-ing ~를 속여 …하게 하다

embroider
[imbrɔ́idər]

n. embroidery

v. 1. 수놓다, 자수하다
2. (이야기를) 과장하다, 윤색하다 syn. embellish, dramatize

3 She *embroidered* the cushion cover with flowers.
4 Alan *embroidered* his work history to get the job.

groove
[gru:v]

a. grooved

n. 홈, 패인 곳

5 You should slide your ID card along this *groove*.

voca+ be stuck in a groove 틀에 박힌 생활을 하다
in the groove 최상의 컨디션으로, 최고조로

interrogation
[intèrəgéiʃən]

v. interrogate
n. interrogator 심문[질문]자

n. 심문, 취조 syn. inquisition

6 The suspects were held by the police for *interrogation*.

1 그의 구어체 말투는 나에게 친숙하게 들렸다. 2 그가 그녀와 결혼할 거라고 생각한다면, 그건 그녀의 착각일 뿐이다. 3 그녀는 방석 덮개에 꽃무늬를 수놓았다. 4 Alan은 그 일자리를 얻으려고 자신의 경력을 부풀렸다. 5 신분증을 이 홈을 따라 통과시켜야 한다. 6 용의자들은 조사를 받기 위해 경찰에게 억류되었다.

offset
[ɔ́(:)fset]

v. 상쇄하다, 차감 계산하다 syn. counterbalance

1 The savings I made on flight bookings were ***offset*** by an increase in hotel prices.

proponent
[prəpóunənt]

n. 옹호자, 지지자 syn. advocate ant. opponent

2 The journalist is a leading ***proponent*** of women's rights.

ruffle
[rʌ́fl]

v. 1. 구기다, 헝클어뜨리다 syn. disarrange
2. 짜증나게 하다, 화나게 하다 syn. annoy

3 He ***ruffled*** his son's hair playfully.
4 Brian is easily ***ruffled*** when under pressure at work.

voca+ ruffle one's feathers 화나게 하다

n. 주름 장식 syn. frill

5 Her blouse has a ***ruffle*** of lace around the neck.

surveillance
[sərvéiləns]

n. 감시, 망보기 syn. observation

6 The police have kept the suspect *under **surveillance***.

voca+ under surveillance 감시 하에
surveillance camera 감시 카메라

contraband
[kɑ́ntrəbæ̀nd]

n. 수출입 금지 제품, 밀수품

7 The suspects were caught in possession of a large amount of ***contraband***.

voca+ smuggle[run] contraband 밀수입하다

a. 수출입 금지의, 불법의

8 ***contraband*** cigarettes

1 내가 비행편 예약에서 절약한 돈이 호텔 경비의 증가로 인해 상쇄되었다. 2 그 언론인은 대표적인 여권 옹호자이다. 3 그는 아들의 머리를 장난스럽게 헝클어뜨렸다. 4 Brian은 업무 압박을 받으면 짜증을 잘 낸다. 5 그녀의 블라우스는 목 주위에 레이스 주름 장식이 있다. 6 경찰은 그 용의자를 감시해 왔다. 7 용의자들은 대량의 밀수품을 소지하고 있다가 적발되었다. 8 수출입 금지 담배

ductile
[dʌ́ktail]

n. ductility

a. (금속이) 변형하기 쉬운, 연성의

1 Gold and silver are ***ductile*** metals.

foreclose
[fɔːrklóuz]

n. foreclosure

v. 1. (담보물의) 소유권을 빼앗다
2. (가능성을) 배제하다, 막다 syn. exclude

2 The bank ***foreclosed on*** his house.

3 His resignation ***foreclosed*** the possibility of the two companies merging.

oligarchy
[áligɑ̀ːrki]

n. 소수 독재정치(자), 과두정치 ant. polyarchy 다두정치

4 An ***oligarchy*** is a small group of people who control and run a particular country or organization.

demagogue
[déməgɑːg]

n. demagoguery 민중 선동 (=demagogy)
a. demagogic

n. 선동가 (=demagog)

5 McCarthy was a ***demagogue*** who used the fear of communism.

IDIOMS

beat[flog] a dead horse 헛수고하다, (끝난 일을) 다시 문제 삼다
(to waste your effort by trying to do something that is no longer possible)

6 Sending your manuscript to another publishing house is just ***beating a dead horse***.

catch someone red-handed 현행범으로 체포하다
(to catch someone in the act of doing something bad or illegal)

7 The FBI ***caught*** the mayor ***red-handed*** with the drugs.

1 금과 은은 연성 금속이다. **2** 은행은 그의 집을 압류했다. **3** 그의 사임으로 인해 두 회사가 합병할 가능성은 없어졌다. **4** 과두란 특정 국가나 조직을 장악하고 운영하는 소수의 집단을 뜻한다. **5** McCarthy는 공산주의에 대한 공포심을 이용한 선동가였다. **6** 네 원고를 또다른 출판사에 보내는 것은 헛수고일 뿐이다. **7** FBI는 마약을 소지하고 있던 그 시장을 현행범으로 체포했다.

day **12**

exercise

A Match the words in the left column to the sentences in the right column.

ⓐ **pneumonia**: a serious illness that affects the lungs and makes it difficult to breathe

ⓑ **vice**: an immoral practice or habit with serious consequences

ⓒ **colloquial**: (of language) informal

ⓓ **demagogue**: a leader who people follow because he or she speaks passionately about things that concern them

ⓔ **oligarchy**: a system of government in which the people are ruled by a few powerful people

1. I am trying to learn some more __________ expressions.
2. __________ can be quite serious, and can even cause death if not treated.
3. The militant group took over the leadership of the country and established a(n) __________.
4. Drinking too much is a dangerous __________.
5. The __________ had many followers.

B Choose the word or phrase that best explains the underlined word.

1. If you ***delude*** someone, you __________ them.
   ⓐ deceive ⓑ ignore ⓒ protect ⓓ attack

2. If something is ***contraband***, it is __________.
   ⓐ useless ⓑ musical ⓒ valuable ⓓ illegal

3. If something is ***imperative***, you __________ to do it.
   ⓐ have the option ⓑ are willing ⓒ are obliged ⓓ are unable

4. If you are under ***surveillance***, you are __________.
   ⓐ being watched ⓑ pretending to be someone else
   ⓒ avoiding the police ⓓ being considered for promotion

5. If you are a ***misanthrope***, you __________.
   ⓐ can't stay calm ⓑ have poor memory
   ⓒ are afraid of heights ⓓ prefer being alone

정답 및 해설 p.375

C Choose the option that is closest in meaning to the underlined word.

1. his old ***adversary***
ⓐ neighborhood ⓑ opponent ⓒ colleague ⓓ master

2. ***emancipated*** slaves
ⓐ mistreated ⓑ escaped ⓒ captured ⓓ liberated

3. ***abate*** symptoms
ⓐ reduce ⓑ worsen ⓒ ignore ⓓ describe

D Choose the option that is the opposite of the underlined word.

1. the ***proponent*** of a cause
ⓐ author ⓑ validity ⓒ critic ⓓ supporter

2. the ***contempt*** for rules
ⓐ respect ⓑ disbelief ⓒ violation ⓓ significance

3. ***ruffle*** your hair
ⓐ rinse ⓑ smooth ⓒ mess up ⓓ dry

E Choose the best word or phrase.

1. Which of the following is part of a ***disguise***?
ⓐ a wig ⓑ a wallet ⓒ a bowling ball ⓓ a newspaper

2. Which of the following mostly results from sleep ***deprivation***?
ⓐ stomachache ⓑ sore muscles
ⓒ impaired judgment ⓓ increased productivity

3. Which of the following would you ***embroider***?
ⓐ a wristwatch ⓑ a pillow ⓒ a chore ⓓ a picture frame

4. When an ***interrogation*** takes place, there are many ______________.
ⓐ patients cured ⓑ questions asked
ⓒ suspects jailed ⓓ items stolen

adverse
[ædvə́ːrs]

a. 해로운, 부정적인 syn. unfavorable

1 The drug may have some ***adverse*** effects on patients.

blunder
[blʌ́ndər]

n. 큰 실수, 터무니없는 실책

2 Youth is a ***blunder***; Manhood a struggle; Old age a regret.

v. 1. (부주의로 인해) 크게 실수하다
2. 머뭇거리며 움직이다, 어물어물하다

3 The best worker sometimes ***blunders***.
4 She ***blundered*** around in the darkness.

voca+ blunder into 실수로 ~에 처하다[부딪히다]

contender
[kənténdər]

v. contend

n. 경쟁자, 라이벌 syn. rival

5 Korea is a strong ***contender*** for the World Cup.

voca+ leading[strong/serious] contender 유력한 경쟁자

dismay
[disméi]

a. dismayed

n. 실망, 놀람, 당황

6 In ***dismay***, I couldn't say anything.

voca+ to one's dismay 실망스럽게도, 놀랍게도
be filled with dismay 놀라 당황하다, 대경실색하다

v. 당황케 하다, 실망시키다

vigorous
[vígərəs]

n. vigor

a. 1. 활발한, 격렬한, 힘찬 syn. strenuous
2. 강건한, 원기 왕성한 syn. energetic

7 After the operation, you should avoid ***vigorous*** exercise.
8 a ***vigorous*** young man

1 그 약은 환자에게 해로운 영향을 끼칠 수도 있다. 2 청춘은 실수요, 성년은 투쟁이요, 노년은 후회이다. 3 최고의 일꾼도 때로는 실수한다. 4 그녀는 어둠 속에서 더듬거리며 돌아다녔다. 5 한국은 월드컵에서 유력한 경쟁자이다. 6 나는 놀라서 아무 말도 할 수 없었다. 7 수술 뒤에는 격렬한 운동을 피해야 합니다. 8 원기 왕성한 젊은 남자

implication
[ìmpləkéiʃən]

v. imply 암시하다
implicate 연루시키다

n. 1. (예상되는) 결과, 영향 2. 함축, 암시 3. 연루, 관계

1 What are the *implications* of these proposals?
2 She accused my husband and, *by implication*, me too of dishonesty.
3 The president resigned after his *implication* in a corruption scandal.

voca+ by implication 암시적으로

mock
[mɑk]

v. (흉내내며) 놀리다, 조롱하다 syn. laugh at, make fun of

4 My sisters often *mock* me, saying that I am a princess.

a. 1. 가짜의 syn. sham 2. 모의의

5 *mock* modesty
6 a *mock* interview[examination]

pollen
[pɑ́lən]

n. 꽃가루

7 I'm allergic to *pollen*.

subordinate
[səbɔ́ːrdinət]

n. subordination

a. 1. (지위 등이) 하위[급]의
2. 덜 중요한, 부차적인 syn. secondary

8 All members of the team are *subordinate to* the captain.
9 In life, everything is *subordinate to* happiness.

n. 부하, 하급자 syn. inferior

10 the relationship between *subordinates* and superiors

v. [səbɔ́ːrdənèit] 덜 중요하게 취급하다, 홀대하다

11 His family has been *subordinated to* his career.

fallacy
[fǽləsi]

n. 잘못된 생각[신념], 오류 syn. misconception

12 It is a *fallacy* that only girls read romantic novels.

1 이 제안들로 인해 예상되는 결과는 무엇인가? 2 그녀는 내 남편을, 그리고 넌지시 나까지도 정직하지 못하다고 비난했다. 3 대통령은 부패 의혹에 연루된 후에 사임했다. 4 언니들은 나를 공주라며 자주 놀려댄다. 5 거짓 겸손 6 모의 인터뷰[시험] 7 나는 꽃가루 알러지가 있다. 8 팀원 모두는 주장 밑에 있다. 9 인생에서 행복보다 더 중요한 것은 없다. 10 하급자와 상급자 간의 관계 11 그는 가족보다 일을 더 중요하게 여겨왔다. 12 소녀들만 연애 소설을 읽는다는 것은 잘못된 생각이다.

amoral
[eimɔ́ːrəl]

n. amorality

a. 도덕 관념이 없는, 도덕을 완전 무시하는

1 The politician did foolish, ***amoral***, and cowardly things for votes.

commemorate
[kəmémərèit]

n. commemoration
a. commemorative

v. 기념하다, 축하하다 syn. memorialize

2 The museum opened to ***commemorate*** the 100th anniversary of the poet's birthday.

voca+ in commemoration of ~을 추모[기념]하여

demise
[dimáiz]

n. 1. 종말, 종지부, 사라짐
2. 사망, 서거

3 The ***demise*** of the business left 100 workers unemployed.
4 the senator's untimely ***demise***

demote
[dimóut]

n. demotion

v. (지위 · 계급 등을) 떨어뜨리다, 강등시키다 ant. promote

5 William was ***demoted*** after losing a big account at work.

| Nuance | "떨어뜨리다" 관련 어휘 뉘앙스 차이

demote 강등시키다	등급 · 지위 · 계급 등을 낮추다. 6 He was demoted from captain to lieutenant.
debase 떨어뜨리다	인품 · 품질 · 가치 등을 저하시키다. 7 debase the original purpose of Miss Universe
degrade 격하시키다	창피와 불명예를 느끼도록 함부로 대하다. 8 a movie that degrades the handicapped
demean 떨어뜨리다	사회적 평판이나 품위를 떨어뜨리다. 9 language that demeans women

1 그 정치인은 표를 얻기 위해 어리석고 도덕을 무시한 비겁한 짓들을 했다. 2 그 박물관은 그 시인의 탄생 100주년을 기념하여 개관했다. 3 기업의 도산으로 100명의 직원들이 일자리를 잃었다. 4 그 상원의원의 느닷없는 사망 5 William은 직장에서 큰 거래처를 놓친 뒤 강등되었다. 6 그는 대위에서 중위로 강등되었다. 7 미스 유니버스 대회의 본래 목적을 손상시키다 8 장애인을 비하하는 영화 9 여자를 비하하는 말

empirical
[impírikəl]

a. 경험적인, 실험에 근거를 둔 ant. theoretical

1 His conclusions are based on *empirical* evidence.

voca+ empiricism [철학] 경험론

guile
[gail]

a. guileful
guileless 정직한, 숨김없는

n. 교활, 간계, 술책 syn. cunning, deceit, craft

2 The coach used all his *guile* to win a victory for his team.

intestine
[intéstin]

a. intestinal

n. [신체] 장 syn. gut

3 Food passes from the stomach through the small *intestine* to the large *intestine*.

voca+ large[small] intestine 대장[소장]

ominous
[ɑ́:mənəs]

a. 불길한, 나쁜 징조의 syn. sinister, threatening, menacing

4 The dark sky looked *ominous*.

voca+ good[bad] omen 길조[흉조]

void
[vɔid]

n. 1. 빈 공간, 공석, 빈 상태 syn. vacancy, emptiness
2. 공허함, 허전함

5 Before the creation of the universe, space was regarded as a silent *void*.

6 Her son's death left a terrible *void*.

a. 1. 법적 효력이 없는
2. ~이 없는, 결여된 syn. devoid

7 The agreement will be considered *null and void*.

8 Her eyes were *void of* all expression.

voca+ null and void [법률] 무효인, 법적 효력이 없는

v. 무효로 하다, 취소하다 syn. nullify, invalidate

1 그의 결론은 경험적 증거에 근거하고 있다. 2 감독은 자기 팀의 승리를 위해 온갖 술책을 썼다. 3 음식은 위장에서 소장을 거쳐 대장으로 간다. 4 어두운 하늘은 불길해 보였다. 5 생성 이전의 우주는 고요하고 텅빈 공간으로 여겨졌다. 6 아들의 죽음은 그녀에게 끔찍한 공허감을 남겼다. 7 그 합의는 법적 효력이 없는 것으로 간주될 것이다. 8 그녀의 눈에는 표정이 전혀 없었다.

rupture
[rʌ́ptʃər]

n. 1. 파열
2. (관계의) 단절, 불화 syn. rift
3. [의학] 탈장 syn. hernia

1 the *rupture* of a blood vessel
2 a *rupture* in relations between two countries
3 A *rupture* can cause brain damage if not cured properly.

v. 1. 파열하다[시키다] 2. (관계를) 단절시키다

susceptible
[səséptəbl]

n. susceptibility

a. 1. (질병에) 걸리기 쉬운, (부상에) 취약한 syn. vulnerable, liable
2. 민감한, 영향을 받기 쉬운
3. ~의 여지가 있는, ~이 가능한

4 Children are more *susceptible to* disease.
5 A lot of new products are targeted at *susceptible* young children.
6 Her works are *susceptible* to many interpretations.

propriety
[prəpráiəti]

n. 예의바름, 타당(한 행동) ant. impropriety

7 They conducted themselves with *propriety*.

aberrant
[əbérənt]

a. 비정상적인 syn. abnormal, deviant

8 The actor's *aberrant* behavior was commented on by many people.

contrite
[kɑːntráit]

n. contrition

a. 죄를 깊이 뉘우치는, 참회하는 syn. repentant, remorseful

9 Ben gave a *contrite* admission of his guilt.

1 혈관 파열 2 두 나라 간의 불화 3 적절한 치료를 받지 않으면 탈장은 뇌손상을 야기할 수도 있다. 4 아이들은 병에 걸리기가 더 쉽다. 5 많은 신제품이 감수성이 예민한 어린 아이들을 주요 대상으로 삼고 있다. 6 그녀의 작품은 여러 가지 해석의 여지가 있다. 7 그들은 예의 바르게 잘 처신했다. 8 그 배우의 일탈 행동은 많은 사람들의 입방아에 올랐다. 9 Ben은 자신의 죄를 깊이 뉘우치며 인정했다.

forlorn
[fərlɔ́ːrn]

a. 1. 버려진, 외로운, 황량한 syn. desolate, forsaken
2. 가망 없는, 절망적인 syn. hopeless

1 The *forlorn* girl tried to catch a glimpse of her parents.
2 I knew that winning the race was a *forlorn* hope.

omniscient
[amníʃənt]
n. omniscience

a. 모르는 것이 없는, 박식한 syn. all-knowing

3 Students tend to expect teachers to be *omniscient*.

voca+ omniscient narrator [문학] 전지적 작가

sojourn
[sóudʒəːrn]

n. (일시적인) 머무름, 체류

4 a *sojourn* in France for a few months

v. (집이 아닌 곳에 일시적으로) 머물다, 체류하다

dichotomy
[daikátəmi]

n. 이분법, 양분 (a difference between two opposite things or ideas)

5 There is a *dichotomy* of policy *between* two factions in the government.

IDIOMS

castles in the air 백일몽, 비현실적인 소망 (plans or hopes that have little chance of happening)
6 She is building *castles in the air* about being a supermodel.

chicken out 그만두다, 무서워서 손을 떼다 (to decide not to do something because of fear)
7 He *chickened out* on sky diving.

1 그 버려진 소녀는 부모를 잠깐이라도 보려고 애썼다. 2 나는 경주에서 우승할 가망이 없다는 것을 알고 있었다. 3 학생들은 교사가 모든 것을 다 알 것이라고 기대하는 경향이 있다. 4 프랑스에서의 몇 개월간 단기 체류 5 정부 내 두 파벌 간에 정책이 양분되어 있다. 6 그녀는 수퍼모델이 되겠다는 허황된 꿈을 꾸고 있다. 7 그는 무서워서 스카이 다이빙에서 손을 뗐다.

exercise

A Match the words in the left column to the sentences in the right column.

ⓐ **fallacy**: incorrect idea or reasoning

ⓑ **rupture**: to burst or break open

ⓒ **forlorn**: appearing sad, as though abandoned

ⓓ **susceptible**: likely to be affected

ⓔ **void**: lacking or empty

1. Your conclusion is based on ________.
2. She's quite ________ to illness.
3. The water balloon ________(e)d when it hit the ground.
4. The office was ________ of activity on Saturday.
5. I felt sorry for the ________ girl.

B Choose the word or phrase that best explains the underlined word.

1. If you *dismay* someone, you ________ him or her.
   ⓐ disappoint ⓑ mislead ⓒ forsake ⓓ appreciate

2. *Empirical* findings are ________.
   ⓐ theoretical ⓑ unmistakable ⓒ suspicious ⓓ observable

3. If you behave with *guile*, you are ________.
   ⓐ helpful ⓑ unstable ⓒ sly ⓓ conventional

4. If you are on a *sojourn*, you are ________.
   ⓐ settling down for good ⓑ staying temporarily
   ⓒ wandering from place to place ⓓ planning to return

5. If you are *subordinate* to someone, you ________.
   ⓐ tell them what to do ⓑ train them in their job
   ⓒ do what they tell you ⓓ work together as equals

정답 및 해설 p.376

C Choose the option that is closest in meaning to the underlined word.

1. make a ***blunder***
   ⓐ decision ⓑ noise ⓒ mistake ⓓ change

2. a ***mock*** trial
   ⓐ unfair ⓑ fake ⓒ public ⓓ lengthy

3. a slow ***demise***
   ⓐ process ⓑ development ⓒ recovery ⓓ failure

D Choose the option that is the opposite of the underlined word.

1. ***adverse*** consequences
   ⓐ trivial ⓑ favorable ⓒ uncertain ⓓ foreseeable

2. a ***vigorous*** exercise
   ⓐ easy ⓑ brisk ⓒ regular ⓓ excessive

3. ***aberrant*** behavior
   ⓐ careless ⓑ normal ⓒ courageous ⓓ vulnerable

E Choose the best word or phrase.

1. What does a ***contender*** hope to be?
   ⓐ the winner ⓑ the cooperator ⓒ the competitor ⓓ the judge

2. Which of the following produces ***pollen***?
   ⓐ allergies ⓑ factories ⓒ farmers ⓓ flowers

3. You use your ***intestines*** to ________________.
   ⓐ breathe ⓑ reproduce ⓒ digest food ⓓ process information

4. You ***commemorate*** people by ________________.
   ⓐ writing them memos ⓑ having a ceremony in their honor
   ⓒ calling them names ⓓ telling lies about them to the newspaper

obsession
[əbséʃən]
a. obsessive

n. 강박관념, 집착

❶ Most students suffer from an ***obsession*** with exams.

voca+ be obsessive about/have an obsession with ~에 강박관념을 갖다

blur
[bləːr]
a. blurred (=blurry)

n. 1. (시각적으로) 흐림, 선명하지 않음 2. (기억 등이) 흐릿한 것

❷ Everything is a ***blur*** when I take my glasses off.
❸ The early years of my life are just a ***blur***.

v. 1. (시야 · 감각을) 흐리게 하다 2. (차이를) 불분명하게 하다

❹ He lent me his eyeglasses, but they ***blurred*** my vision.
❺ Many commercials ***blur*** the line between art and advertising.

contradictory
[kὰntrədíktəri]
v. contradict
n. contradiction

a. 모순된, 양립할 수 없는 syn. conflicting

❻ The witness has given two ***contradictory*** statements.

voca+ self-contradictory 자기 모순의, 자가당착의

fastidious
[fæstídiəs]
n. fastidiousness

a. 까다로운, 꼼꼼한 syn. meticulous

❼ My father is ***fastidious about*** planning everything.

implicit
[implísit]

a. 1. 암시하는, 함축적인 syn. implied ant. explicit
2. 내재하는, 암묵적으로 존재하는
3. 절대적인, 무조건적인, 맹목적인 syn. absolute, blind

❽ His comments contained an ***implicit*** threat.
❾ Credit is ***implicit in*** most contracts.
❿ They had ***implicit*** faith in his powers.

❶ 대부분의 학생들은 시험에 대해 강박관념을 가지고 있다. ❷ 나는 안경을 벗으면 다 흐릿하게 보인다. ❸ 내 유년기는 흐릿한 기억으로만 남아 있다. ❹ 그가 그의 안경을 빌려줬지만, 시야가 흐렸다. ❺ 많은 광고들이 예술과 선전의 경계선 상에 있다. ❻ 그 증인은 모순된 두 가지 진술을 했다. ❼ 아버지는 매사를 꼼꼼히 계획하신다. ❽ 그의 발언에는 은연 중 위협이 담겨 있었다. ❾ 대부분의 계약에서는 기본적으로 서로 간의 신용이 존재한다. ❿ 그들은 그의 권력에 절대적인 신뢰를 갖고 있었다.

irresolute
[irézəlùːt]

n. irresolution

a. 결단력 없는, 우유부단한 syn. indecisive ant. resolute

1 He was somewhat *irresolute* about everything.

modulate
[mádʒəlèit]

n. modulation

v. 1. (음색 · 음조 등을) 변화시키다
2. 조절하다, 조정하다
3. [음악] 조바꿈을 하다
4. [통신] 변조하다

2 She *modulated* her voice and spoke louder.
3 These treatments effectively *modulate* the curative process.
4 *modulate* from major to minor
5 *modulate* a radio signal

voca+ FM(frequency modulation) FM방송(주파수 변조)
AM(amplitude modulation) AM방송(진폭 변조)

restrain
[ristréin]

n. restraint
a. restrained 절제된, 차분한

v. 1. 제지하다, 제한하다 syn. restrict, limit
2. (감정 · 행동 등을) 억누르다, 자제하다 syn. control

6 The policy would help *restrain* gas price increases.
7 She was so angry that she could hardly *restrain* herself.

voca+ restrain sb from v-ing ~가 …하지 못하게 하다

subsequently
[sʌ́bsikwəntli]

a. subsequent

ad. 그 후에, 훗날에 syn. afterwards

8 The book was *subsequently* made into a musical.

virtuous
[və́ːrtʃuəs]

n. virtue

a. 덕이 높은, 고결한 syn. moral ant. wicked

9 He stresses his *virtuous* behavior and hides his vices.

voca+ virtuous[vicious] circle[cycle] 선순환[악순환]

1 그는 매사에 다소 우유부단했다. 2 그녀는 목소리를 바꾸고 목청을 높였다. 3 이 치료법들은 치유 과정을 효과적으로 조절한다. 4 장조에서 단조로 조바꿈을 하다 5 무선 신호를 변조하다 6 그 정책은 휘발유 가격 인상을 억제하는 데 도움이 될 것이다. 7 그녀는 너무 화가 나서 좀처럼 진정할 수가 없었다. 8 그 책은 나중에 뮤지컬로 만들어졌다. 9 그는 자신의 선한 행동은 강조하고 악행은 숨긴다.

amplify
[ǽmpləfài]

n. amplification
amplifier 증폭기, 앰프

v. 1. (소리를) 증폭시키다, (크기 · 효과 등을) 크게 하다 syn. magnify
2. 부연 설명하다

1 The government's policy *amplified* the anger of the poor.
2 The man refused to *amplify* his earlier remark.

potent
[póutənt]

n. potency

a. 1. 강력한, 효과가 센 syn. powerful
2. (남성이) 성적 능력이 있는 ant. impotent

3 Fear can be a *potent* weapon for controlling people.

demolish
[dimáliʃ]

n. demolition

v. 1. (건물 등을) 부수다, 파괴하다
2. (이론 · 사상 등을) 뒤집다, ~의 허구성을 증명하다
3. (스포츠 · 게임 등에서) 쉽게 이기다, 압승을 거두다

4 The typhoon *demolished* many houses.
5 The lawyer completely *demolished* her evidence.
6 L.A. *demolished* Texas 10-0.

voca+ demolition job [정치] 중상모략, [스포츠] 압승

belittle
[bilítl]

n. belittlement

v. 과소평가하다, 경시하다

7 Tony's father *belittled* his son's success in acting.

Nuance	"(가치를) 떨어뜨리다 / 경시하다" 관련 어휘 뉘앙스 차이
belittle 과소평가하다	노력이나 성과의 가치를 낮추어 보다. 8 belittle the effort
depreciate 저하시키다	상품이나 화폐의 가치나 가격 등을 낮추다. 9 depreciate the value
disparage 얕보다, 깔보다	가치를 인정하지 않거나 존경심 없이 비방하다. 10 disparage psychology as pseudoscience

1 정부 정책은 빈민들의 노여움을 증폭시켰다. 2 그 남자는 이전의 발언에 대해 부연 설명하기를 거부했다. 3 공포는 사람들을 통제하는 강력한 무기가 될 수 있다. 4 태풍은 많은 주택을 파괴했다. 5 변호사는 그녀가 제시한 증거가 완전히 거짓임을 입증했다. 6 LA가 텍사스를 10대 0으로 격파했다. 7 Tony의 아버지는 자신의 아들이 연기에서 거둔 성공을 무시했다. 8 노력을 과소평가하다 9 가치를 떨어뜨리다 10 심리학을 사이비 과학이라고 깎아내리다

sarcastic
[sɑːrkǽstik]

n. sarcasm

a. 빈정거리는, 비꼬는

1 Your *sarcastic* attitude shows that you don't take this class seriously.
2 I didn't notice the *sarcasm* in Mr. Jones' remarks.

commence
[kəméns]

n. commencement
1. 시작 2. *AmE* 졸업식

v. 시작하다[되다], 개시하다 syn. initiate, embark on

3 The course *commenced* on March 1 this year.
4 *commencement* day

gulp
[gʌlp]

v. 1. 꿀꺽 삼키다[마시다], 급히 먹다
2. 심호흡하다

5 The thirsty man *gulped down* the water.
6 He *gulped* for air after he held his breath for one minute.

voca+ gulp for air 숨을 가쁘게 들이마시다
gulp back (the tears) (울음을) 꾹 참다

n. 1. 꿀꺽꿀꺽 마심 2. 한 번에 마시는 양

voca+ in one gulp/at a gulp 한입에, 단숨에

intoxicated
[intɑ́ksikèitid]

n. intoxication
a. intoxicating

a. 1. 술 취한 syn. drunk ant. sober
2. 도취된, 흥분한

7 He was fined for driving while *intoxicated*.
8 The actor was *intoxicated* with her beauty.

onerous
[ɑ́nərəs]

n. onerousness

a. 부담스러운, 힘겨운 syn. burdensome

9 He quit his job because his workload was too *onerous*.

1 네 비꼬는 태도는 네가 이 수업을 진지하게 생각하지 않는다는 것을 보여준다. 2 나는 Jones씨의 말 속에 담긴 빈정거림을 눈치 채지 못했다. 3 강의는 올해 3월 1일에 시작되었다. 4 학위수여식 5 목마른 남자는 물을 벌컥벌컥 들이켰다. 6 그는 1분 동안 숨을 참은 후에 숨을 크게 들이 마셨다. 7 그는 음주 운전으로 벌금형을 받았다. 8 그 배우는 그녀의 아름다움에 도취되었다. 9 그는 업무량이 너무 과중해서 직장을 그만두었다.

prosecute
[prásəkjù:t]

n. prosecution
prosecutor 검사, 검찰관

v. 1. 기소하다, 고소[고발]하다
2. (전쟁 · 활동 등을) 계속하다, 속행하다

1 He was ***prosecuted for*** fraud.
2 We cannot ***prosecute*** this case without solid evidence.

ruthless
[rú:θlis]

n. ruthlessness

a. 비정한, 무정한, 잔인한 syn. merciless, pitiless

3 He was notorious for being a ***ruthless*** businessman.

sustainable
[səstéinəbl]

v. sustain
n. sustainability
a. sustained 지속된, 일관된

a. 1. (환경 파괴 없이) 계속 유지될 수 있는, 친환경적인
2. (같은 수준으로) 유지[지속]할 수 있는

4 ***Sustainable*** agriculture is becoming a standard.
5 The government promised ***sustainable*** economic growth.

voca+ sustainable development 지속 가능한[환경 친화적] 개발

impede
[impí:d]

n. impediment
방해, (신체적) 장애

v. 지연시키다, 방해하다 syn. hinder, hamper

6 His chances of winning were ***impeded*** by his injury.

conundrum
[kənʌ́ndrəm]

n. 1. 어려운 일, 문제
2. 수수께끼 syn. riddle, enigma

7 the ethical ***conundrum*** given by stem cell research
8 Oedipus solved the ***conundrum*** of the Sphinx.

feign
[fein]

a. feigned

v. ~인 체하다, ~을 가장하다

9 He ***feigned*** illness to get a day off school.

voca+ feign sleep[insanity / indifference] 자는[미친/무관심한] 척하다

1 그는 사기 혐의로 기소되었다. 2 우리는 확실한 증거 없이는 이 소송을 계속할 수 없다. 3 그는 비정한 사업가로 악명이 높았다. 4 친환경적인 농업은 (농업의) 표준이 되고 있다. 5 정부는 지속적인 경제 성장을 약속했다. 6 부상으로 인해 그가 이길 가능성이 줄었다. 7 줄기 세포 연구에 의해 제기된 윤리적 문제 8 오이디푸스는 스핑크스의 수수께끼를 풀었다. 9 그는 학교를 하루 빠지려고 꾀병을 부렸다.

stalemate
[stéilmèit]

n. 1. 교착 상태, 궁지 syn. deadlock, impasse
2. [체스] 쌍방의 수가 막힌 상태

1 The president and the Congress are at a ***stalemate***.

voca+ end in stalemate (협상 등이) 교착 상태로 끝나다
break the stalemate 난국을 타개하다

nerve
[nəːrv]

a. nervous
1. 초조한, 긴장한
2. 신경질적인

n. 1. 신경, 신경 조직
2. 용기, 담력 syn. guts, courage
3. (복수로) 신경과민, 신경 씀
4. 뻔뻔스러움, 무례함

2 peripheral ***nerves***
3 It took a lot of ***nerve*** for him to talk to her.
4 The war of ***nerves*** between the U.S. and Iran has been going on for some time.
5 He didn't even say sorry. What a ***nerve*** he has!

voca+ get on one's nerves ~을 짜증나게[신경 쓰게] 하다
have the nerve to-v 뻔뻔스럽게도 ~하다

v. 용기를 불어 넣다

6 She ***nerved*** herself to ask him out.

oscillate
[ásəlèit]

n. oscillation

v. 1. (두 점 사이를) 움직이다, 진동하다 syn. swing
2. (기분 · 의견 등이) 갈팡질팡하다

7 The needle on the dial ***oscillated*** between "full" and "empty."
8 His feeling ***oscillated*** between relief and frustration.

IDIOMS

a close call[shave] 위기일발, 구사일생 (a narrow escape from a dangerous or unpleasant situation)

9 We had ***a close call*** when our car almost crashed into a tree this morning.

cold comfort 위로가 되지 못하는 말, 달갑지 않은 일
(little or no comfort because the situation is so difficult or unpleasant)

10 The drop in inflation is ***cold comfort*** to those still in debt.

1 대통령과 의회는 교착 상태에 있다. 2 말초신경 3 그가 그녀에게 말을 건네는 데는 엄청난 용기가 필요했다. 4 미국과 이란 간의 신경전은 한동안 계속되고 있다. 5 그는 미안하다는 말도 하지 않았어. 정말 뻔뻔한 사람이야! 6 그녀는 용기를 내어 그에게 데이트 신청을 했다. 7 계기판의 바늘이 '충분'과 '부족' 사이를 왔다갔다 했다. 8 그의 감정은 안도감과 좌절감 사이에서 오락가락했다. 9 오늘 아침 우리 차가 나무에 부딪칠 뻔했을 때 정말 아슬아슬했다. 10 인플레이션의 감소는 여전히 부채가 있는 사람들에게는 별 위로가 되지 못한다.

exercise

A Match the words in the left column to the sentences in the right column.

ⓐ **sustainable**: using methods that do not harm the environment

ⓑ **impede**: to delay or stop the progress of something

ⓒ **ruthless**: without caring about other people's pain

ⓓ **demolish**: to bring down or destroy

ⓔ **irresolute**: undecided or unsure

1. The storm may __________ the construction project.
2. I am __________ about accepting the job. I need to think about it some more.
3. The apartment building will be __________ (e)d so that a shopping center can be built.
4. We need to stop wasting our natural resources and aim for __________ living.
5. The __________ dictator ordered the arrest of all citizens who disagreed with his policy.

B Choose the word or phrase that best explains the underlined word.

1. If you ***belittle*** someone, you make them feel __________.
   ⓐ proud ⓑ renowned ⓒ exhausted ⓓ unimportant

2. When something ***commences***, it __________.
   ⓐ begins ⓑ explodes ⓒ wears down ⓓ is canceled

3. When you are ***restrained***, you are being __________.
   ⓐ encouraged to speak ⓑ prevented from acting
   ⓒ beaten as a punishment ⓓ congratulated for success

4. If you are in a ***conundrum***, you have a __________.
   ⓐ reputation to keep ⓑ secret to keep
   ⓒ story to tell ⓓ problem to solve

5. When an argument ends in ***stalemate***, __________.
   ⓐ the problem is resolved ⓑ it ends without any conclusion
   ⓒ both sides get what they want ⓓ one side is convinced

정답 및 해설 p.376

C Choose the option that is closest in meaning to the underlined word.

1. ***feign*** an injury
ⓐ suffer ⓑ heal ⓒ fake ⓓ cause

2. an ***onerous*** task
ⓐ dangerous ⓑ difficult ⓒ enjoyable ⓓ additional

3. a ***virtuous*** leader
ⓐ popular ⓑ hard-working ⓒ victorious ⓓ honorable

D Choose the option that is the opposite of the underlined word.

1. a ***potent*** drug
ⓐ new ⓑ cheap ⓒ weak ⓓ illegal

2. ***blur*** the issue
ⓐ clarify ⓑ solve ⓒ discuss ⓓ bring up

3. ***contradictory*** advice
ⓐ well-intended ⓑ unwelcome ⓒ effective ⓓ consistent

E Choose the best word or phrase.

1. Which of the following probably ***oscillates***?
ⓐ a refrigerator ⓑ stereo speakers ⓒ a fan ⓓ a doormat

2. Which of the following would cause you to become ***intoxicated***?
ⓐ red wine ⓑ uncooked chicken
ⓒ fresh vegetables ⓓ decaffeinated coffee

3. When you ***prosecute*** a person, you try to show that they are __________.
ⓐ praiseworthy ⓑ mentally ill ⓒ competent ⓓ guilty

4. You should ***amplify*** your voice when __________.
ⓐ in a library ⓑ taking the subway
ⓒ telling a secret ⓓ giving a speech

aesthetic
[esθétik]

n. aesthete 예술 애호가
aestheticism
유미주의, 예술지상주의

a. 미(美)의, 미적 감각이 있는, 미학의 (=esthetic)

1 As an artist, she has a well-developed *aesthetic* sense.

n. (복수로) 미학

2 *Aesthetics* is the study of art and beauty.

cramped
[kræmpt]

cramp
v. 방해[제한]하다 n. 쥐, 경련

a. 1. 비좁은, 갑갑한 ant. spacious
2. (필체 등이) 읽기 힘든, 빽빽하게 쓰여진

3 Steven's apartment is nice but *cramped*.
4 His writing is very *cramped* and difficult to read.

diminution
[dìminú:ʃən]

v. diminish
a. diminutive 아주 작은

n. 감소, 축소 syn. reduction, decline

5 The man seemed to weaken following the *diminution* of his health.

dispense
[dispéns]

n. dispensation
dispenser 내용물을 일정하게 제공하는 기기[장치]
dispensary 약국, 조제실

v. 1. 분배하다, 제공하다 syn. distribute, give out
2. 조제하다

6 The machine *dispenses* a range of drinks and snacks.
7 A pharmacist is a person who is qualified to *dispense* drugs.

voca+ dispense with ~을 생략[제거]하다, ~없이 지내다
dispense justice 판결을 내리다, 형량을 정하다

feasible
[fí:zəbl]

n. feasibility

a. 실행[실현] 가능한, 그럴듯한 syn. practicable, viable, workable

8 Solar heating is technically and economically *feasible*.

voca+ feasibility study (실현 가능성을 조사하는) 타당성[예비] 조사

1 예술가로서 그녀는 뛰어난 미적 감각을 갖고 있다. 2 미학은 예술과 아름다움에 관한 학문이다. 3 Steven의 아파트는 좋긴 하지만 비좁다. 4 그의 글씨는 너무 빼곡해서 읽기 힘들다. 5 그 남자는 건강이 쇠약해진 뒤부터 약해지는 것 같았다. 6 그 기계는 다양한 음료와 과자를 제공한다. 7 약사는 약을 조제할 수 있는 자격이 있는 사람이다. 8 태양열 난방은 기술적으로나 경제적으로 실현 가능성이 있다.

impoverish
[impávəriʃ]

n. impoverishment
a. impoverished

v. 1. 가난하게 하다 ant. enrich
2. (질을) 저하시키다, 열악하게 만들다 syn. deteriorate, deplete

1 Government policy will ***impoverish*** the working classes.
2 Too much development has ***impoverished*** the land.

retain
[ritéin]

n. retention
1. 보유, 유지
2. 기억력
3. (분비물의) 이상 정체
a. retentive 기억력이 좋은

v. 1. 계속 유지하다, 보존하다 syn. preserve
2. 기억하다, 마음에 간직하다
3. (변호사 등을) 고용하다

3 I ***retained*** the business after my partner passed away.
4 Many students study to pass a test and don't ***retain*** the information.
5 She ***retained*** a lawyer to win her inheritance back.

voca+ retaining fee/retainer 변호사 수임료

subsidiary
[səbsídièri]

a. 보조의, 부수적인 syn. auxiliary, secondary

6 I'm taking sociology as a ***subsidiary*** subject.

n. 자회사 (a company that is owned or controlled by a larger company)
syn. affiliate

7 The company plans to establish ***subsidiaries*** in the U.K.

vivacity
[vivǽsəti]

a. vivacious

n. 생기, 쾌활함, 활발함 syn. liveliness

8 a character full of energy and ***vivacity***

voucher
[vautʃər]

v. vouch 보증하다, 확언하다

n. (현금 대용의) 상품권, 할인권

9 a ***voucher*** for a free salad

voca+ travel voucher 여행 상품권
gift voucher[certificate] 상품권

1 정부 정책은 노동자 계층을 궁핍하게 만들 것이다. 2 지나친 개발이 토양의 질을 떨어뜨렸다. 3 나는 동업자가 죽은 뒤에도 그 사업을 계속했다. 4 많은 학생들이 시험에 통과하기 위해 공부하고 나서는 공부한 것을 잊어버린다. 5 그녀는 유산을 돌려받기 위해 변호사를 고용했다. 6 나는 부수 과목으로 사회학을 수강하고 있다. 7 그 회사는 영국에 자회사를 설립할 계획이다. 8 에너지와 생기가 넘치는 성격 9 샐러드 무료 시식권

wart
[wɔːrt]

a. warty

n. 1. (피부의) 사마귀
2. 결점

1 He has a huge *wart* on his cheek.
2 She loves him, *warts and all*.

voca+ warts and all 결점까지 포함하여 모두, 있는 그대로

anomaly
[ənάməli]

a. anomalous

n. 이례적인 것, 예외, 변칙 syn. abnormality

3 She noticed some *anomalies in* the contract.

voca+ magnetic anomaly (지구 자장의) 자기(磁氣) 이상

complacent
[kəmpléisənt]

n. complacency

a. 자만하는, 안주하는, 흡족해 하는 syn. self-satisfied

4 You must not get *complacent* now that you have had some success.

assent
[əsént]

n. 동의, 승인

5 She nodded her *assent to* the proposal.

v. 동의하다, 찬성하다

| Nuance | "동의하다/찬성하다" 관련 어휘 뉘앙스 차이

assent 동의하다, 찬성하다	협의나 심의를 거쳐 공식적으로 동의하다. 6 assent to the suggestion
concur 일치하다	둘 이상의 의견이 일치하다. 7 concur with the evaluation
accede 응하다, 동의하다	반대했던 제안이나 요구에 승복하여 동조하다. 8 accede to demands
acquiesce 묵인하다, 따르다	그다지 원하지 않지만 마지못해 동의하다. 9 They acquiesced in the decision without arguing.
consent 승낙하다, 동의하다	자발적으로 동의하다. 10 Her parents consented to her marriage.

1 그는 뺨에 큰 사마귀가 있다. 2 그녀는 있는 그대로의 그를 사랑한다. 3 그녀는 계약서에서 몇 가지 이상한 점을 발견했다. 4 지금 조금 성공했다고 자만하면 안 된다. 5 그녀는 고개를 끄덕여 그 제안에 대한 동의를 나타냈다. 6 제안에 찬성하다 7 평가에 동의하다 8 요구에 응하다 9 그들은 별다른 논쟁 없이 그 결정을 묵인했다. 10 그녀의 부모는 그녀의 결혼을 승낙했다.

denote
[dinóut]

n. denotation
a. denotative

v. 나타내다, 의미하다 syn. indicate, represent

1 The line on the graph *denotes* the changes in prices.

enthrall
[inθrɔ́:l]

a. enthralling
enthralled

v. 매료시키다, 마음을 사로잡다 syn. fascinate, charm

2 The talented author wrote a book that *enthralled* mystery novel fans.

3 Watching the stars in the dark desert sky was an *enthralling* experience.

havoc
[hǽvək]

n. 대혼란, 대파괴

4 The gunman wreaked *havoc* in the crowd.

voca+ wreak[play/cause] havoc 혼란을 일으키다

intrigue
[intrí:g]

a. intriguing
intrigued

v. 1. 흥미[호기심]를 자아내다 syn. attract
2. 음모를 꾸미다

5 The history of India *intrigued* the student greatly.

6 They continued to *intrigue* against the government.

n. 음모 syn. conspiracy

7 She played no part in her party's political *intrigue*.

ornament
[ɔ́:rnəmənt]

a. ornamental

n. 장식, 장식물, 장신구 syn. decoration, accessory

8 Her living room is full of little china *ornaments*.

v. [ɔ́:rnəmènt] 장식하다 syn. decorate, adorn

1 그래프의 선은 가격의 변동을 의미한다. 2 그 재능 있는 작가는 추리소설 팬들을 매료시킨 책을 썼다. 3 어두운 사막 하늘에 떠 있는 별들을 바라보는 것은 매력적인 경험이었다. 4 총을 든 강도는 군중들 사이에 엄청난 혼란을 일으켰다. 5 인도의 역사는 그 학생에게 커다란 흥미를 불러 일으켰다. 6 그들은 계속 반정부 음모를 꾸몄다. 7 그녀는 자신이 속한 당의 정치적 음모에 가담하지 않았다. 8 그녀의 거실은 작은 사기 장식품들로 가득하다.

providence
[prάvədəns]

n. 1. 섭리, 신의 뜻
2. (P~) 신

1 The woman regarded his death as an act of *providence*.

voca+ divine providence 신의 섭리
tempt providence[fate] 하늘의 뜻을 거스르다, 무모한 짓을 하다

sacrament
[sǽkrəmənt]

a. sacramental

n. 1. (the ~) 성체, 성찬 (the bread and wine that are used at a religious ceremony)
2. (기독교의) 성례전, (가톨릭의) 성사 syn. Holy Communion

2 The priest gives the *sacrament* on Sundays.

voca+ receive the sacrament 성찬을 받다

swindle
[swíndl]

n. swindler 사기꾼

v. (돈을) 사기 쳐서 빼앗다, 사기치다 syn. cheat, defraud

3 He *swindled* the old woman *out of* her life's savings.

voca+ swindle A out of B 속여서 A로부터 B를 빼앗다

n. 사기

cornucopia
[kɔ̀ːrnjukóupiə]

n. 1. 풍요, 넉넉함 syn. abundance
2. [그리스 신화] 풍요의 뿔, 풍요의 상징

4 The jeweler displayed a *cornucopia* of every kind of gemstone imaginable.

voca+ a cornucopia of (다양한 종류의) 많은 ~

garrulous
[gǽrələs]

a. (쓸데없이) 수다스러운, 장황한 syn. talkative, chatty

5 We were fed up with his *garrulous* manner.

1 그 여자는 그의 죽음을 신의 뜻에 의한 것으로 여겼다. 2 목사는 일요일마다 성찬을 베푼다. 3 그는 그 노부인을 속여 평생 모은 돈을 가로챘다. 4 그 보석상은 상상할 수 있는 모든 종류의 보석을 전시해 놓았다. 5 우리는 그가 수다스럽게 떠들어대는 것에 넌더리가 났다.

osteoporosis
[ɑ̀ːstioupəróusis]

n. 골다공증 (a condition which causes the bones to weaken and be easily broken)

1 According to the WHO, one out of three women in India suffer from *osteoporosis*.

inflammatory
[inflǽmətɔ̀ːri]

v. inflame
n. inflammation 염증
a. inflammable
1. 가연성의 2. 쉽게 흥분하는

a. 1. 화나게 하는, 격앙시키는
2. [의학] 염증을 일으키는, 염증성의

2 He always uses *inflammatory* remarks.

voca+ anti-inflammatory 항염증의; 소염제

subjugate
[sʌ́bdʒugèit]

n. subjugation

v. 정복하다, 복종시키다 syn. subdue, conquer

3 In 1619, the Dutch *subjugated* the island of Java.

factitious
[fæktíʃəs]

a. 인위[인공]적인, 꾸며낸, 가상의 syn. sham

4 She told a *factitious* story about her role in the robbery.

voca+ factitious disorder [의학] 꾀병, 가장성 장애

IDIOMS

(come) rain or shine 무슨 일이 있어도 (whatever happens)

5 Don't worry. We'll be there – *come rain or shine*.

spill the beans 비밀을 누설하다 (to reveal a secret)

6 Someone *spilled the beans* about Joe's upcoming promotion.

1 WHO에 따르면 인도 여성 세 명 중 한 명이 골다공증에 걸려 있다고 한다. 2 그는 언제나 화를 돋우는 말을 한다. 3 1619년에 네덜란드인들이 Java섬을 점령했다. 4 그녀는 강도 사건에서 자신이 맡은 역할에 관해 거짓된 이야기를 꾸며냈다. 5 걱정 마. 우리는 무슨 일이 있어도 거기에 갈 거야. 6 누군가가 Joe가 곧 승진할 거라는 사실을 누설했다.

exercise

A Match the words in the left column to the sentences in the right column.

ⓐ **denote**: to mark, signify, or make known

ⓑ **dispense**: to provide or give out

ⓒ **cramped**: too small to be comfortable

ⓓ **garrulous**: overly talkative

ⓔ **inflammatory**: arousing negative emotions

1. The trip seemed longer because the backseat was so ___________.
2. He regretted making ___________ remarks.
3. We're going to install a machine to ___________ candy.
4. We'll use a red sticker to ___________ the sale price.
5. The ___________ youngster kept everyone's attention on him.

B Choose the word or phrase that best explains the underlined word.

1. If something is an ***anomaly***, it is _______________.
   ⓐ unusual ⓑ essential ⓒ heavy ⓓ unnamed
2. If someone has ***vivacity***, he or she is _______________.
   ⓐ original ⓑ annoying ⓒ lively ⓓ invisible
3. If you are ***enthralled*** with something, you are _______________.
   ⓐ detached ⓑ fascinated ⓒ indifferent ⓓ furious
4. If something is ***retained***, it is _______________.
   ⓐ delivered ⓑ kept ⓒ stolen ⓓ understood
5. When someone ***swindles*** you, you _______________.
   ⓐ enjoy yourself ⓑ lose money ⓒ go to jail ⓓ are impressed

C Choose the option that is closest in meaning to the underlined word.

1. ***impoverish*** the soil
ⓐ enrich ⓑ deplete ⓒ plow ⓓ flood

2. a ***subsidiary*** plan
ⓐ backup ⓑ practical ⓒ flexible ⓓ formal

3. cause ***havoc***
ⓐ disease ⓑ success ⓒ argument ⓓ destruction

D Choose the option that is the opposite of the underlined word.

1. a ***feasible*** solution
ⓐ radical ⓑ ambitious ⓒ impossible ⓓ long-term

2. ***subjugate*** people
ⓐ liberate ⓑ inspire ⓒ entertain ⓓ irritate

3. a ***factitious*** story
ⓐ short ⓑ absurd ⓒ comic ⓓ authentic

E Choose the best word or phrase.

1. Who would be most concerned with ***aesthetics***?
ⓐ a philosopher ⓑ a firefighter ⓒ a priest ⓓ a mathematician

2. Which of the following is affected by ***osteoporosis***?
ⓐ skin ⓑ lungs ⓒ stomach ⓓ bones

3. ***Ornaments*** are used for ________________.
ⓐ cleaning ⓑ gardening ⓒ decorating ⓓ heating

4. Where are you most likely to use a ***voucher***?
ⓐ a park ⓑ city hall ⓒ a church ⓓ a department store

abbreviate
[əbríːvièit]

n. abbreviation

v. 생략[축약]하다 syn. shorten, condense

1 The word "centimeter" *is* usually ***abbreviated to*** "cm."

voca+ be abbreviated to ~라고 축약되다

banish
[bǽniʃ]

n. banishment

v. 1. 추방하다 syn. expel, deport, exile
2. (근심 등을) 떨쳐버리다 syn. get rid of

2 The writer was ***banished*** to Siberia.
3 I was unable to ***banish*** my thoughts about him.

condemn
[kəndém]

n. condemnation
a. condemnatory
condemned
1. 사형선고를 받은
2. 철거될

v. 1. 비난하다 syn. denounce, criticize, censure
2. 유죄 판결을 내리다 syn. sentence, convict

4 The film was ***condemned*** for its sexism.
5 The spy was ***condemned*** to death.

deplore
[diplɔ́ːr]

n. deploration
a. deplorable 끔찍한

v. 비난하다, 규탄하다

6 We ***deplore*** the use of violence against children.

hospitable
[hɑ́spitəbl]

n. hospitality

a. 1. 대접이 좋은, 환대하는 ant. hostile
2. 개방적인 syn. receptive
3. (기후 · 환경이) 쾌적한, 생물이 살 수 있는

7 She is always ***hospitable*** to visitors.
8 He is ***hospitable*** to new ideas.
9 She moved to a more ***hospitable*** climate in Miami.

1 'Centimeter'라는 단어는 보통 'cm'으로 축약된다. 2 그 작가는 시베리아로 추방되었다. 3 나는 그에 대한 생각을 떨쳐버릴 수 없었다. 4 그 영화는 성차별주의로 인해 비난받았다. 5 그 스파이는 사형 선고를 받았다. 6 우리는 어린이에 대한 폭력을 규탄한다. 7 그녀는 언제나 방문객들을 잘 대접한다. 8 그는 새로운 생각에 개방적이다. 9 그녀는 기후가 더 쾌적한 마이애미로 이사 갔다.

omnipresent
[àmniprézənt]

n. omnipresence

a. 어디에나 있는 syn. ubiquitous

1 The *omnipresent* noise from traffic is annoying.

perilous
[pérələs]

n. peril

a. 위험한, 모험적인 syn. hazardous

2 You are walking into a *perilous* situation.

voca+ at one's peril 위험을 무릅쓰고

perseverance
[pə̀ːrsivíːrəns]

v. persevere

n. 인내, 불굴의 의지 syn. persistence, tenacity ant. surrender

3 The marathon winner attributed his success to *perseverance*.

dowry
[dáuəri]

n. (신부의) 지참금

4 Her parents gave away all their money as a *dowry* for their daughter's marriage.

spur
[spəːr]

n. 1. 자극, 격려 syn. impetus, incentive, impulse
2. 말의 박차

5 The report was a *spur* to the government to cut taxes.

voca+ win[earn] one's spurs 공을 세우다
on the spur of the moment 충동적으로, 갑작스럽게

v. 1. 자극[격려]하다 syn. incite, stimulate, prompt
2. 말에 박차를 가하다

6 Her goal *spurred* the team to victory.

1 어디에서나 들리는 차들의 소음은 짜증난다. 2 너는 위험한 상황에 들어서고 있어. 3 마라톤 우승자는 자신의 성공이 인내 덕분이라고 말했다. 4 그녀의 부모는 그들의 모든 돈을 딸의 결혼 지참금으로 내놓았다. 5 그 보고서는 정부가 세금을 감면하는 계기가 되었다. 6 그녀의 득점이 팀의 승리에 자극제가 되었다.

agitate
[ǽdʒitèit]

n. agitation
agitator 선동가
a. agitated 흥분한

v. 1. 동요시키다 syn. excite, disturb
2. 선동하다, 정치 운동을 하다
3. 휘젓다 syn. stir

1 He *agitated* me with his persistent questions.
2 The papers *agitated for* democracy.
3 *Agitate* the mixture to dissolve the powder.
4 The *agitated* crowd marched down the street.

avert
[əvə́:rt]

v. 1. 돌리다, 비키다, 외면하다 syn. turn away
2. (나쁜 일을) 피하다, 막다 syn. ward off, prevent

5 They *averted* their eyes from the accident.
6 I tried to *avert* running into him.

statutory
[stǽtʃutɔ̀:ri]

n. statute

a. 법정의, 법령의

7 The *statutory* fine for this offense is $250.

deplete
[diplí:t]

n. depletion
a. depleted

v. 고갈시키다

8 Freon *depletes* the ozone layer.
9 the *depletion* of fossil fuels

voca+ deplete A of B B에게서 A를 빼앗다[고갈시키다]

| Nuance | "고갈시키다" 관련 어휘 뉘앙스 차이

deplete 고갈시키다 | 천연 자원이나 자금 등을 감소시키다.
10 deplete the Earth's natural resources

drain 없애다, 고갈시키다 | 주로 재정적인 측면에서 고갈시키다.
11 drain a country of its resources

exhaust 소진시키다 | 체력을 바닥내거나 천연 자원 등을 다 써버리다.
12 Logging can exhaust the rain forest.

1 그는 집요한 질문으로 나를 괴롭혔다. 2 그 신문들은 민주주의 운동을 했다. 3 혼합물을 휘저어 가루를 녹여라. 4 흥분한 군중들이 거리를 행진해 내려왔다. 5 그들은 그 사고를 외면했다. 6 나는 그와 마주치지 않으려고 애썼다. 7 이 위법 행위에 대해 법으로 정해진 벌금은 250달러이다. 8 프레온은 오존층을 고갈시킨다. 9 화석 연료의 고갈 10 지구의 천연 자원을 고갈시키다 11 나라의 자원을 고갈시키다 12 벌목은 우림을 황폐하게 만들 수 있다.

covert
[kʌ́vərt]

a. 숨겨진, 비밀의, 은밀한 syn. clandestine, concealed ant. overt

1 He had no knowledge of *covert* operations.

n. (짐승의) 숨는 장소, 은신처

excavate
[ékskəvèit]

n. excavation
excavator 1. 굴착기
2. 발굴자

v. 1. (구멍 등을) 파다, 굴착하다
2. 발굴하다 syn. dig up

2 The turtle *excavates* a hole in the sand and lays its eggs in it.
3 Work is under way to *excavate* the ancient city.

reconcile
[rékənsàil]

n. reconciliation

v. 1. 화해시키다, 중재하다 syn. conciliate, resolve, settle
2. 조화시키다, 양립시키다 syn. harmonize

4 He has recently been *reconciled* with his father.
5 It is sometimes difficult to *reconcile* science with religion.

voca+ reconcile oneself to ~을 감수하다, 받아들이다

mar
[mɑːr]

v. 손상시키다, 훼손하다, 망치다 syn. ruin, blemish, spoil

6 The elections were *marred* by violence.

resilient
[rizíliənt]

n. resilience

a. 1. 곧 회복하는, 곧 기운을 차리는
2. 탄력 있는 syn. springy ant. stiff

7 He's *resilient* – he will get over the shock quickly.
8 Hair dye may leave hair less *resilient* than before.

1 그는 비밀 작전에 대해 전혀 알지 못했다. 2 바다거북은 모래밭에 구멍을 파고 그 속에 알을 낳는다. 3 고대 도시의 발굴 작업이 진행 중이다. 4 그는 최근에 아버지와 화해했다. 5 과학과 종교를 조화시키는 것은 때로는 어려운 일이다. 6 선거는 폭력 사태로 얼룩졌다. 7 그는 회복이 빠르다. 곧 충격에서 벗어날 것이다. 8 머리 염색약은 머리카락의 탄력을 이전보다 떨어뜨릴 수도 있다.

posterity
[pastérəti]

n. 자손, 후세 syn. descendants, offspring ant. ancestry

1 These works of art should be preserved for *posterity*.

resounding
[rizáundiŋ]

v. resound

a. 1. 철저한, 완전한
2. 울리는, 울려 퍼지는

2 The concert was a *resounding* success.
3 A *resounding* applause was given to the opera singer.

forbear
[fɔːrbέər]

n. forbearance
a. forbearing
참을성 있는, 관대한

v. 1. 참다
2. 삼가다, 그만두다 syn. refrain, cease

4 I could not *forbear* my laughter.
5 He *forbore* to talk about her failure.

n. (주로 복수로) 조상, 선조 (=forebear) syn. ancestor, forefather

6 I will come back to the land of my *forbears*.

utilitarian
[juːtìlətέəriən]

n. utilitarianism

a. 1. 실용적인, 실리적인 syn. practical, pragmatic
2. 공리주의의 (based on the belief that something is morally right if it helps the majority of people)

7 The furniture is plain and *utilitarian*.

culprit
[kʌ́lprit]

n. 1. 범인, 범죄자 syn. offender, criminal, malefactor
2. (문제의) 원인

8 Police managed to catch the *culprit*.
9 Plaque is the *culprit* of tooth decay.

---

1 이 예술 작품들은 후손들을 위해 보존되어야 한다. 2 공연은 대성공이었다. 3 그 오페라 가수는 울려퍼지는 박수갈채를 받았다. 4 나는 웃음을 참을 수 없었다. 5 그는 그녀의 실패에 대한 언급을 삼갔다. 6 나는 선조들의 땅으로 돌아올 것이다. 7 그 가구는 간소하며 실용적이다. 8 경찰은 간신히 범인을 잡았다. 9 치석은 충치의 원인이다.

exhort
[igzɔ́:rt]

n. exhortation

v. 간곡히 타이르다, 열심히 설득하다 syn. urge

1 The teacher kept *exhorting* us to work harder.

voca+ exhort sb to-v ~에게 …하도록 설득하다

loophole
[lú:phòul]

n. 허점, 맹점, 빠져나갈 구멍 syn. let-out, blind spot

2 Every law has a *loophole*.

relinquish
[rilíŋkwiʃ]

n. relinquishment

v. (소유권 · 권리 등을) 양도[포기]하다

3 No one wants to *relinquish* power once they have it.

extrapolate
[ikstrǽpəlèit]

n. extrapolation

v. 추론하다, (자료에 의거하여) 추측하다 syn. deduce, infer

4 Some people try to *extrapolate* a trend without supporting evidence.

voca+ extrapolate A from B B에서 A를 추론하다

IDIOMS

a ballpark figure[estimate] 어림수, 대충의 짐작 (approximate figure or quantity)

5 Can you give me *a ballpark figure* of how much it costs to rent a car?

tie the knot 결혼하다 (to marry)

6 The couple *tied the knot* yesterday after a 13-year romance.

1 선생님은 우리에게 더 열심히 공부하라고 계속 타이르셨다. **2** 모든 법에는 허점이 있다. **3** 일단 권력을 잡으면 아무도 그것을 넘겨주고 싶어하지 않는다. **4** 어떤 사람들은 뒷받침할 근거도 없이 경향성을 추론해 내려고 한다. **5** 차 한 대를 빌리는 데 대강 얼마나 드는지 알려줄 수 있어요? **6** 그 커플은 13년간의 연애 끝에 어제 결혼했다.

exercise

A Match the words in the left column to the sentences in the right column.

ⓐ **culprit**: a person who has committed a crime	1. The couple was saving for their daughter's ______________.
ⓑ **dowry**: a sum of money given to a groom by the bride's family	2. My mother is always very __________ when I bring friends home.
ⓒ **resilient**: able to recover easily	3. The environmental activist made a passionate speech to ____________ people to recycle their trash.
ⓓ **hospitable**: making guests feel at home	4. The ____________ got away with the stolen goods.
ⓔ **exhort**: to induce action by means of a strong appeal	5. Children are quite ____________ to injuries.

B Choose the word or phrase that best explains the underlined word.

1. If you ***condemn*** a person, you ___________________ him or her.
   ⓐ criticize ⓑ permit ⓒ advocate ⓓ release

2. If you conserve something for ***posterity***, you conserve it for your ___________________.
   ⓐ ancestors ⓑ antiquity ⓒ descendants ⓓ acquaintances

3. If you are ***banished*** from a country, you are ___________________.
   ⓐ taking a vacation ⓑ sent away ⓒ put in jail ⓓ invited

4. If something is ***statutory***, it is controlled by ___________________.
   ⓐ weather ⓑ hierarchy ⓒ genes ⓓ law

5. When you ***extrapolate***, you ___________________.
   ⓐ dissect an animal ⓑ make an inference
   ⓒ uncover something hidden ⓓ invent something useful

C Choose the option that is closest in meaning to the underlined word.

1. ***spur*** an argument
ⓐ compromise ⓑ incite ⓒ settle ⓓ win

2. ***relinquish*** all rights
ⓐ renounce ⓑ enhance ⓒ preserve ⓓ demand

3. His reputation was ***marred***.
ⓐ improved ⓑ exaggerated ⓒ denied ⓓ damaged

D Choose the option that is the opposite of the underlined word.

1. a ***covert*** operation
ⓐ secret ⓑ harmless ⓒ risky ⓓ well-known

2. ***deplete*** natural resources
ⓐ develop ⓑ conserve ⓒ exhaust ⓓ rely on

3. a ***perilous*** journey
ⓐ short ⓑ frightening ⓒ safe ⓓ boring

E Choose the best word or phrase.

1. Which of the following would be ***excavated***?
ⓐ a ghost ⓑ ancient ruins ⓒ a politician ⓓ a report

2. Where might one find a ***loophole***?
ⓐ in clothing ⓑ on a rope ⓒ in the ground ⓓ in a contract

3. Which of the following would most likely be ***deplored***?
ⓐ violence ⓑ a celebration ⓒ energy resources ⓓ a job advertisement

4. The couple wasn't able to ***reconcile*** their ________________.
ⓐ divorce ⓑ mortgage ⓒ differences ⓓ children

coherent
[kouhíərənt]

v. cohere
n. coherence

a. 명료한, 조리있는, 논리적인 ant. incoherent

1 Victoria gave a *coherent* account of the accident.

concede
[kənsíːd]

n. concession
1. 협상을 위한 양보
2. 사업권, 면허
3. *BrE.* 할인

v. 1. 마지못해 인정[시인]하다, (경기 · 토론 등에서) 패배를 인정하다
syn. admit, give in
2. (권리 등을) 마지못해 넘겨주다, 양보하다

2 The politician quickly *conceded* defeat.
3 The leader *conceded* power *to* his successor.
4 They'll give no *concessions to* the terrorists.
5 Kazakhstan has been selling oil *concessions to* many countries.

demographic
[dìːməgrǽfik]

n. demographics 인구 통계
demography 인구 (통계)학

a. 인구 통계의

6 *demographic* changes in Korea
7 No one has exact *demographics* on the area.

erode
[iróud]

n. erosion

v. 1. 침식하다[시키다] syn. wear[rub] away
2. 점차 저하시키다, 손상시키다 syn. wear down

8 The cliffs are being *eroded* by the ocean waves.
9 Repeated exam failure has *eroded* his confidence.
10 rapid *erosion* of the beach

heed
[hiːd]

a. heedless 부주의한

v. (충고 · 경고 등에) 주의를 기울이다 syn. pay attention to

11 They didn't *heed* our warnings to stay away from the water.

n. 주의

voca+ pay heed to/take heed of ~에 주의를 기울이다

1 Victoria는 사고 경위를 논리정연하게 설명했다. 2 그 정치가는 재빨리 패배를 인정했다. 3 그 지도자는 후임자에게 권력을 넘겨주었다. 4 그들은 테러리스트들에게 절대 양보하지 않을 것이다. 5 카자흐스탄은 여러 나라에 석유 사업권을 팔아 왔다. 6 한국의 인구 통계상 변화 7 아무도 그 지역의 정확한 인구 통계를 갖고 있지 않다. 8 절벽은 파도에 의해 침식되고 있다. 9 연이은 낙방은 그의 자신감을 점차 저하시켰다. 10 해안의 급속한 침식 11 그들은 물가에 가지 말라는 우리의 경고에 주의를 기울이지 않았다.

lapse
[læps]

a. lapsed 1. 신앙을 잃은
2. [법률] 실효한

n. 1. 잠깐의 실수, 착오
2. 시간의 경과[간격], 기간 syn. interval

1 He had a momentary *lapse* of memory.
2 The usual time *lapse* between sending and receiving a letter is three days.

v. 1. (권리 · 효력이) 만료되다, 끝나다 syn. expire
2. 잠깐 중단되다, 서서히 끊기다

3 Your membership has *lapsed*.
4 When the conversation *lapsed*, I went to the washroom.
5 He used to be a *lapsed* Christian.

voca+ lapse into ~한 상태에 빠지다

precursor
[prikə́:rsər]

n. 선구자, 전신(前身), 전조 syn. forerunner

6 Alchemy is the *precursor* of modern chemistry.

sovereign
[sávərən]

n. sovereignty 주권, 통치권

a. 1. (한 국가에서) 최고 권력을 지닌
2. 주권을 가진, 독립국의 syn. autonomous

7 It is said that the source of *sovereign* power is the people.
8 The US described North Korea as a *sovereign* state.
9 South Korea reasserted *sovereignty* over Tokdo Island.

n. 최고 권력자, 군주

poignant
[pɔ́injənt]

n. poignancy

a. 가슴에 사무치는, 애절한, 마음을 짠하게 만드는

10 The novel is a *poignant* story of a man who longs to go back to his hometown.

docile
[dásl]

n. docility

a. (사람 · 동물이) 온순한, 다루기 쉬운

11 We bought a young, *docile* dog.

1 그는 순간적으로 깜박 잊었다. 2 편지를 보내고 받는 데 걸리는 기간은 보통 3일이다. 3 귀하의 회원 기간이 만료되었습니다. 4 대화가 잠시 중단된 사이 나는 화장실로 갔다. 5 예전에 그는 신앙을 버린 기독교인이었다. 6 연금술은 현대 화학의 전신이다. 7 국가 최고 권력의 원천은 국민이라고들 한다. 8 미국은 북한을 주권 국가라고 규정했다. 9 대한민국은 독도에 대한 주권을 재확인했다. 10 그 소설은 고향으로 돌아가길 갈망하는 한 남자의 애절한 이야기이다. 11 우리는 어리고 온순한 개 한 마리를 샀다.

lucrative
[lú:krətiv]

a. 돈벌이가 되는, 큰 이익을 남기는 syn. highly profitable

1 The company is searching for a *lucrative* market.

tangible
[tǽndʒəbl]

n. tangibility

a. 1. 명백한, 확실한 ant. intangible
2. 만져볼 수 있는, 실체가 있는, 유형(有形)의

2 Without *tangible* evidence, they'll lose the case.

3 *Tangible* assets are property such as buildings and equipment.

tremble
[trémbl]

v. (추위 · 놀람 · 분노 등으로) 떨다[떨리다], 몸서리를 치다 syn. shake, shiver

4 His whole body *trembled with* fear.

expatriate
[ekspéitriət]

n. 국외 거주자, 추방된 사람

5 Many *expatriates* shop at this imported food store.

a. 국외로 이주한[추방된]

6 *expatriate* workers

v. [ekspéitrièit] 국외로 추방하다

7 The general *expatriated* the president.

| Nuance | "추방하다" 관련 어휘 뉘앙스 차이

expatriate 추방하다, 이주하다 | 무력 또는 법을 동원하여 국외로 추방하거나 스스로 국적을 버리고 외국으로 이주하다.
8 The new leader expatriated the royal family.

expel 내쫓다, 추방하다 | 범법 행위 또는 정치적 이유로 국내 거주 외국인을 추방하다.
9 Two foreign diplomats were expelled from South Africa.

exile 유배시키다 | 정치적인 이유로 강제로 다른 나라로 떠나보내다.
10 Napoleon was exiled to St. Helena in 1815.

extradite 송환하다 | 외국으로 도주한 범인을 본국으로 인도하다.
11 A member of the Mafia was extradited from the US to Italy.

banish 추방하다 | 죄로 인해 거주지에서 영구 추방하다.
12 The spy was found guilty of treason and banished from the country.

1 그 회사는 큰 수익을 거둘 수 있는 시장을 찾고 있다. 2 확실한 증거가 없으면 그들은 소송에서 질 것이다. 3 유형 자산은 건물이나 장비 같은 재산이다. 4 그의 온몸이 공포로 인해 떨렸다. 5 많은 외국인 거주자들이 이 수입 식품점에서 물건을 구입한다. 6 외국인 이주 노동자들 7 그 장군이 대통령을 국외로 추방했다. 8 새 지도자는 왕족을 추방했다. 9 두 명의 외교관이 남아프리카 공화국에서 추방되었다. 10 나폴레옹은 1815년에 St. Helena로 유배되었다. 11 마피아 단원이 미국에서 이탈리아로 송환되었다. 12 그 스파이는 반역죄 혐의가 드러나 본국에서 영구 추방되었다.

corrosion
[kəróuʒən]

v. corrode

a. corrosive
1. 부식성의 2. 해로운

n. (금속 등의) 부식, 점진적인 파괴

1 The surface of the aircraft is coated with paint to prevent *corrosion*.

2 a highly *corrosive* substance

indoctrinate
[indáktrinèit]

n. indoctrination

v. 교화하다, 세뇌시키다 syn. brainwash

3 They *indoctrinated* three new members into the cult.

4 political *indoctrination*

metaphysics
[mètəfíziks]

a. metaphysical

n. 형이상학 (a part of philosophy that deals with the nature of existence, and what is outside of the physical world)

5 *Metaphysics* tries to explain existence and truth.

6 *metaphysical* questions such as "Who am I?" and "Why do I live?"

superlative
[supə́ːrlətiv]

a. 최고의, 최상급의 syn. first-rate

7 the *superlative* special effects of the film

n. 1. 최고의 찬사[표현]
2. [문법] 최상급

8 The book has earned *superlatives* from critics and fans.

9 "Largest" is the *superlative* of "large."

affix
[əfíks]

v. 붙이다, 부착하다 syn. attach, stick

10 I had to *affix* several labels *to* the package.

n. [ǽfiks] [문법] 접사

11 *Affixes* are a group of letters added to the beginning(prefix) or end(suffix) of a word.

---

1 항공기의 표면은 부식을 방지하기 위해 페인트칠이 되어 있다. 2 부식성이 강한 물질 3 그들은 세 사람을 세뇌시켜 사이비 종교 단체에 가입시켰다. 4 정치적 교화 5 형이상학은 존재와 진리를 설명하고자 한다. 6 '나는 누구인가?'나 '나는 왜 사는가?'와 같은 형이상학적인 질문들 7 그 영화의 최상급 특수효과 8 그 책은 비평가와 애독자들로부터 최고의 찬사를 받았다. 9 'largest'는 'large'의 최상급이다. 10 나는 그 소포에 꼬리표를 몇 개 붙여야 했다. 11 접사는 단어의 앞(접두사)과 뒤(접미사)에 붙는 일련의 철자들이다.

squad
[skwɑd]

n. 1. (경찰의) 계, 전담반
2. (군대의) 분대 (소대(platoon)보다 작은 단위)
3. (특정 목적으로 뽑힌) 스포츠팀

1 drug[fraud/vice] *squad*
2 The bomb *squad* detected explosives in the parcel.
3 England's World Cup *squad*

unilateral
[jùːnilǽtərəl]

n. unilateralism
ad. unilaterally

a. 일방적인

4 What do you think of *unilateral* decisions to invade other countries?
5 North Korea *unilaterally* canceled the talks.

voca+ bilateral 양자간의, 쌍방의
multilateral 다자간의, 다원적인

carcinogenic
[kɑ̀ːrsənədʒénik]

n. carcinogen 발암물질

a. 암을 유발하는, 발암성의

6 Tobacco smoke includes at least 43 different *carcinogenic* substances.

erudite
[érədàit]

n. erudition

a. 박식한, 전문적 지식을 갖춘 syn. learned [lə́ːrnid]

7 He is *erudite* in philosophy.
8 a person of great *erudition*

lethargic
[ləθɑ́ːrdʒik]

n. lethargy 무기력증, 권태

a. 무기력한, 아무것도 하고 싶지 않은 syn. listless

9 The illness left him feeling *lethargic*.
10 The patient with chronic low blood pressure may complain of *lethargy*.

1 마약[사기/풍기 단속] 전담반 2 폭탄 제거반은 그 소포 안에서 폭발물을 찾아냈다. 3 잉글랜드 월드컵 대표팀 4 다른 나라를 침공하겠다는 일방적인 결정에 대해 어떻게 생각하는가? 5 북한은 일방적으로 회담을 취소했다. 6 담배 연기는 적어도 43종의 발암 물질을 포함하고 있다. 7 그는 철학에 조예가 깊다. 8 매우 박학다식한 사람 9 병 때문에 그는 무기력해졌다. 10 만성 저혈압 환자는 무기력증을 겪을 수도 있다.

flammable
[flǽməbl]

a. 가연성의, 불에 타기 쉬운 syn. inflammable, combustible
ant. nonflammable

1 Caution! Highly *flammable* chemicals!

protracted
[prətrǽktid]

a. (예정보다) 길어진, 오래 끄는 syn. prolonged

2 Frank bought the business after *protracted* negotiations with the previous owner.

redeem
[ridíːm]

n. redemption
1. 구원, 구제 2. 상환, 약속이행
a. redemptive

v. 1. (결점 · 잘못을) 만회하다
2. (상품권으로) 지불하다, (쿠폰을) 사용하다
3. (빚을) 상환하다, (저당물을) 되찾다
4. (악으로부터) 구원하다, 구제하다

3 He tried to *redeem* himself by being extra nice to me.
4 This coupon can be *redeemed* at any of our stores.
5 She has money to *redeem* her jewelry from the pawn shop.
6 The religious group tried to *redeem* the so-called sinners.
7 Christians believe in the *redemption* through Jesus Christ.
8 debt *redemption*

usurp
[juːzə́rp]

n. usurper 강탈자

v. (지위 · 권력을) 불법 행사하다, 빼앗다

9 They tried to *usurp* her inheritance.

IDIOMS

turn over a new leaf 새 사람이 되다, 개과천선하다 (to start behaving in a better way)

10 He claims he's *turning over a new leaf* this year.

the ball is in someone's court ~가 대응[결정]할 차례이다 (it is one's turn to take action or to reply)

11 I said all I could, now *the ball's in his court.*

1 경고! 가연성이 매우 높은 화학물질임! 2 Frank는 전 기업주와의 긴 협상 끝에 사업체를 매입했다. 3 그는 내게 필요 이상으로 잘해 주면서 자신의 잘못을 만회하려 했다. 4 이 쿠폰은 우리 상점의 어느 지점에서든 사용할 수 있습니다. 5 그녀는 전당포에 잡힌 자신의 보석을 되찾아올 돈을 갖고 있다. 6 그 종교 단체는 죄인이라 일컬어지던 사람들을 구원하려 애썼다. 7 기독교인들은 예수 그리스도를 통한 구원을 믿는다. 8 부채 상환 9 그들은 그녀의 상속 재산을 빼앗으려 했다. 10 그는 올해 새 사람이 되기로 했다고 주장한다. 11 내가 할 말은 다 했으니, 이제 그가 답변할 차례이다.

day 17 exercise

A Match the words in the left column to the sentences in the right column.

ⓐ **poignant**: causing a sharp feeling of sadness

ⓑ **squad**: an organized group with a specific purpose

ⓒ **usurp**: to take someone's power without having the right to do this

ⓓ **tremble**: to shake slightly

ⓔ **erudite**: having extensive knowledge

1. His younger brother tried to __________ the throne.
2. The movie brought back __________ memories of her miserable life.
3. His hands began to __________ when he asked her to marry him.
4. He is very __________ and well-informed.
5. The drug __________ arrested the two suspects.

B Choose the word or phrase that best explains the underlined word.

1. If you ***concede*** to someone's point of view, you __________ it.
   ⓐ doubt ⓑ change ⓒ criticize ⓓ admit

2. If you ***heed*** someone's advice, you __________ it.
   ⓐ ignore ⓑ listen to ⓒ seek ⓓ go against

3. If something is a ***precursor*** to an event, it happens __________ the event.
   ⓐ before ⓑ in the middle of ⓒ instead of ⓓ because of

4. If a region is ***sovereign***, it is __________.
   ⓐ at war ⓑ thriving ⓒ well-known ⓓ independent

5. Something that is ***carcinogenic*** causes __________.
   ⓐ acne ⓑ cancer ⓒ obesity ⓓ allergies

정답 및 해설 p.378

C Choose the option that is closest in meaning to the underlined word.

1. a memory ***lapse***
ⓐ aid ⓑ failure ⓒ token ⓓ flashback

2. ***affix*** a label
ⓐ attach ⓑ print ⓒ rename ⓓ design

3. ***indoctrinate*** people
ⓐ punish ⓑ injure ⓒ liberate ⓓ brainwash

D Choose the option that is the opposite of the underlined word.

1. a ***docile*** child
ⓐ intelligent ⓑ creative ⓒ industrious ⓓ disobedient

2. ***flammable*** clothing
ⓐ practical ⓑ fireproof ⓒ fashionable ⓓ expensive

3. feel ***lethargic***
ⓐ guilty ⓑ dizzy ⓒ energetic ⓓ strange

E Choose the best word or phrase.

1. Which of the following can be a ***tangible*** asset?
ⓐ equipment ⓑ patent ⓒ copyright ⓓ reputation

2. Which of the following is likely to ***erode*** over time?
ⓐ technology ⓑ literature ⓒ species ⓓ mountains

3. Which of the following results from ***corrosion***?
ⓐ sand ⓑ rust ⓒ glass ⓓ fire

4. If you have a ***lucrative*** job, you ________________.
ⓐ meet many people ⓑ work part-time
ⓒ earn a lot of money ⓓ do all the work at home

aggravating
[ǽgrəvèitiŋ]

v. aggravate
n. aggravation

a. 1. (상황 · 병 등을) 악화시키는 syn. exacerbating
2. 짜증나게 하는 syn. irritating

1 Military intervention is ***aggravating*** the existing tensions.
2 Her constant complaining is really ***aggravating***.

sanction
[sǽŋkʃən]

n. 1. (복수로) (상대 국가에 대한) 제재 syn. ban, restraint
2. 공식적 허가, 인가 syn. authorization

3 economic ***sanctions*** against Cuba
4 The diplomat made comments about the crisis without government ***sanction***.

voca+ impose[lift] sanctions 제재를 가하다[풀다]

v. 허가하다, 인가하다 syn. permit, approve

countenance
[káuntənəns]

n. 용모, 표정

5 His ***countenance*** went from happy to sad.

v. 허락[용인]하다, 지지하다 syn. approve

6 The principal couldn't ***countenance*** a bad attitude toward teaching.

derogatory
[dirágətɔ̀:ri]

a. 모욕적인, 경멸적인 syn. insulting

7 I'm angry at your ***derogatory*** remarks about my family.

fiscal
[fískəl]

a. 국고의, 재정의, 회계의 syn. financial

8 The government began a conservative ***fiscal*** policy.

voca+ fiscal[financial] year 회계연도
fiscal crisis 재정 위기

1 군사적 개입이 현재의 긴장 상태를 악화시키고 있다. 2 그녀의 끊임없는 불평은 정말 짜증난다. 3 쿠바에 대한 경제 제재 4 그 외교관은 정부의 재가 없이 위기 상황에 대해 언급했다. 5 그의 표정은 행복해 보였다가 슬프게 바뀌었다. 6 교장은 교육에 대한 불손한 태도를 용인할 수 없었다. 7 나는 우리 가족에 대한 너의 모욕적인 말에 무척 화가 난다. 8 정부는 보수적인 재정 정책을 펴기 시작했다.

incline
[inkláin]

n. inclination
a. inclined

v. 1. 마음이 내키다[내키게 하다], ~하고 싶은 생각이 들다[들게 하다]
2. 경사지다, 기울다[기울이다] syn. tilt

1 His straightforward manner *inclined* me *to* believe him.
2 The land *inclines* toward the shore.

voca+ incline to[towards] (태도 · 의견 등이) ~로 기울다
be inclined to(-v) ~하고 싶다, ~하는 경향이 있다

n. 경사 syn. slope

3 a steep[slight] *incline*

mutation
[mju:téiʃən]

v. mutate
n. mutant 변종

n. 돌연변이

4 It is said that radiation can cause *mutation*.

voca+ gene mutation 유전자 돌연변이

preliminary
[prilímənèri]

a. 예비의, 준비의 syn. preparatory

5 The project is still in its *preliminary* stages.

n. 1. (주로 복수로) 사전 준비, 서두
2. 예선

6 After a few *preliminaries*, she said the main ideas.
7 Korea got through the 2006 World Cup *preliminaries*.

voca+ without preliminaries 단도직입적으로

revenue
[révənjù:]

n. 세입, (정기적) 수입원 syn. income ant. expenditure

8 Taxes provide most of the government's *revenue*.

voca+ the Internal Revenue Service 미 국세청(IRS)

invert
[invə́:rt]

n. inversion 역, 전도
a. inverse 반대의, 역의
inverted 뒤집힌

v. (순서 · 위치 등을) 거꾸로 하다, 뒤집다 syn. reverse

9 The police officer *inverted* her bag and spilled the contents.

1 그의 솔직한 태도 때문에 나는 그에게 믿음이 갔다. 2 그 땅은 해안 쪽으로 경사가 져 있다. 3 가파른[완만한] 경사 4 방사능은 돌연변이를 일으킨다고 한다. 5 그 프로젝트는 아직 준비 단계이다. 6 약간의 서두 다음에 그녀는 요지를 말했다. 7 한국은 2006 월드컵 예선을 통과했다. 8 세금은 정부의 수입원 중 대부분을 차지한다. 9 경찰관이 그녀의 가방을 뒤집어 속에 든 것들을 쏟아놓았다.

wane
[wein]

v. 1. 약해지다, 감소하다 syn. fade, dwindle
2. (달이) 이울다, 이지러지다 ant. wax

1 My enthusiasm for the game had *waned* by the end.
2 Each month the moon waxes and *wanes*.

n. 쇠퇴, 약화

voca+ on the wane 쇠퇴하고 있는, (달이) 기울고 있는

antipathy
[æntípəθi]

a. antipathetic

n. 반감, 혐오 syn. aversion, distaste

3 She had an *antipathy* toward gossip magazines.

pundit
[pʌ́ndit]

n. 전문가, 권위자 syn. expert

4 She is a well-known sports *pundit* and is often asked to comment on events.

voca+ political[media/fashion] pundit 정치[미디어/패션] 전문가

indict
[indáit]

n. indictment
a. indictable 고발되어야 할

v. 기소하다, 고발하다

5 He was *indicted for* ID theft.

Nuance	"기소하다/고발하다" 관련 어휘 뉘앙스 차이
indict 기소하다, 공소를 제기하다	중죄에 대해 공식적으로 고소하여 법정에 세우다. 6 the indicted suspect
accuse 고소하다, 고발하다	사법적인 절차나 소환장 등으로 고발하다. 7 be accused of conspiracy to murder
charge 고발하다	검찰이 죄가 있는 것으로 판단하여 기소하다. 8 be charged with drug possession
impeach 탄핵하다	고위 공무원 혹은 정치가를 중대한 범죄 혐의로 고발하다. 9 impeach the president

1 게임에 대한 내 열정은 끝날 때 쯤엔 사그라 들어 있었다. 2 매달 달은 차고 기운다. 3 그녀는 가십을 다루는 잡지에 대해 혐오감을 갖고 있었다. 4 그녀는 유명한 스포츠 전문가로서 경기에 대해 평해 달라는 요청을 자주 받는다. 5 그는 명의 도용 혐의로 기소되었다. 6 기소된 용의자 7 살인 공모 혐의로 고발되다 8 마약소지죄로 고발되다 9 대통령을 탄핵하다

complicity
[kəmplísəti]

n. accomplice 공범
a. complicit

n. (범행 · 비행에의) 공모, 연루 syn. collusion

1 She is suspected of ***complicity*** in the crime.

divert
[divə́:rt]

n. diversion
a. diversionary 주의를 딴데로 돌리는

v. 1. (방향 · 흐름을) 바꾸다, 전환하다
2. (시간 · 돈 등을) 유용하다, 다른 목적으로 돌려 쓰다
3. 주의를 딴데로 돌리다 syn. distract
4. 즐겁게 해주다, 기분 전환시키다 syn. entertain, amuse

2 The dam will ***divert*** water from the area for the use of the city.
3 The company planned to ***divert*** more resources into research.
4 The political crisis has ***diverted*** media attention away from other issues.
5 He ***diverted*** us with his jokes.

hideous
[hídiəs]

a. 흉측한, 끔찍한, 소름끼치는 syn. repulsive, ugly

6 The horror film was about a ***hideous*** monster.

summon
[sʌ́mən]

v. 1. 소환하다, 호출하다
2. (회의 등을) 소집하다 syn. convene
3. (용기 · 힘을) 내다, 불러일으키다

7 He ***summoned*** the waiter for the bill.
8 The bank ***summoned*** a meeting of creditors.
9 I had to ***summon*** the courage to ask her to marry me.

obstruct
[əbstrʌ́kt]

n. obstruction
a. obstructive

v. 1. (길 · 통로 등을) 막다, 차단하다 syn. block
2. (진행 · 행동 등을) 방해하다 syn. hinder

10 A new office building ***obstructed*** the view from my window.
11 The campaigners are trying to ***obstruct*** the construction of a new power plant.

1 그녀는 그 범죄에 연루되었다는 혐의를 받고 있다. 2 그 댐은 도시가 쓸 물을 그 지역에서 끌어올 것이다. 3 회사는 더 많은 자금을 연구에 유용하기로 계획했다. 4 정치적 위기상황은 언론의 관심이 다른 사안들에 미치지 못하게 했다. 5 그는 농담으로 우리를 즐겁게 해 주었다. 6 그 공포 영화는 끔찍한 괴물에 대한 것이었다. 7 그는 계산서를 가져오라고 웨이터를 불렀다. 8 은행은 채권자 회의를 소집했다. 9 나는 그녀에게 청혼할 용기를 내야 했다. 10 새로 생긴 사무실 건물이 내 창가에서 보이던 전망을 가로막았다. 11 그 운동가들은 새 발전소 건설을 저지하려고 애쓰고 있다.

chastise
[tʃæstáiz]

n. chastisement

v. 1. 몹시 비난하다 syn. castigate, rebuke
2. 체벌하다

1 The minister *chastised* his church members for their greed.
2 Her father *chastised* her with a rod.

bulk
[bʌlk]

n. 1. (the ~) 대부분 syn. majority
2. 대량, 거대함 syn. mass
3. 부피, 크기 syn. volume, dimensions

3 The *bulk* of volunteers were young women.
4 The office buys paper in *bulk* to keep costs down.
5 Elephants and whales have huge *bulk*.

a. 대량의

voca+ bulk mail (우송료 할인) 대량 우편
bulk buying[orders] 대량 구매[주문]

v. 늘리다, 커지게 하다

voca+ bulk large 커지다, 중요해지다 bulk up (근육 등을) 부풀리다, 늘리다
bulk out (더하여) 커지게[만족스러워지게] 하다

tardy
[tá:rdi]

n. tardiness

a. 더딘, 늦은

6 He is always *tardy* in paying his bills.

agrarian
[əgrέəriən]

a. 농업의, 농지의

7 *agrarian* reform and land settlement services

voca+ agrarian economy 농업 기반 경제

debacle
[deibá:kl]

n. 완전한 실패, 와해, 붕괴 syn. fiasco

8 The current *debacle* could lead to the king's downfall.

1 목사는 교인들의 탐욕에 대해 거세게 비난했다. 2 그녀의 아버지는 그녀를 매로 때렸다. 3 자원 봉사자들 대부분이 젊은 여자들이었다. 4 사무실에서는 구매 비용을 낮추기 위해 종이를 대량으로 구매한다. 5 코끼리와 고래는 몸집이 거대하다. 6 그는 언제나 대금 결제를 늦게 한다. 7 농업 개혁과 농지 정착 서비스 8 현재의 엄청난 실패는 왕의 폐위로 이어질 수도 있다.

gullible
[gʌ́ləbl]

n. gullibility

a. 속이기 쉬운, 어리숙한 syn. naive, credulous

1 My sister is very ***gullible***; she believes everything I tell her.

parsimonious
[pὰːrsəmóuniəs]

n. parsimony

a. 인색한, 지나치게 아끼는 syn. stingy, tight-fisted

2 The woman was too ***parsimonious*** to eat properly.

voracious
[vəréiʃəs]

n. voracity

a. 1. 먹성 좋은, 대식하는
2. (취미 · 지식 등에) 열성적인, 골몰하는 syn. avid

3 Teenagers often have ***voracious*** appetites.
4 He's a ***voracious*** reader of historical novels.

taciturn
[tǽsətə̀ːrn]

n. taciturnity

a. 말수가 적은, 과묵한, 무뚝뚝한 ant. talkative

5 My grandfather was a ***taciturn*** man who spoke only when necessary.

IDIOMS

double-edged 양날의, 상반된 의미[용도]를 지닌 (having two completely different meanings[purposes])

6 Nuclear power can be a ***double-edged*** sword.

eat one's words 먼저 한 말을 취소하다, 실언을 인정하다 (to admit what you said was wrong)

7 You'll have to ***eat your words*** if you are wrong.

1 내 여동생은 정말 잘 속는다. 그녀는 내가 하는 말을 다 믿는다. 2 그 여자는 돈을 아끼느라 제대로 먹지도 않았다. 3 십대들은 왕성한 식욕을 갖고 있는 경우가 많다. 4 그는 역사 소설의 열렬한 애독자이다. 5 우리 할아버지는 필요할 때만 말씀하시는 과묵한 분이었다. 6 원자력은 양날의 검이 될 수 있다. 7 네가 틀렸다면 전에 한 말이 틀렸다는 것을 인정해야 할 거야.

exercise

A Match the words in the left column to the sentences in the right column.

ⓐ **incline**: to lean towards an opinion or an action

ⓑ **aggravating**: annoying or irritating

ⓒ **voracious**: consuming in large quantities

ⓓ **taciturn**: reserved, not talkative

ⓔ **sanction**: to give formal permission or approval

1. That music is __________! Turn it off!
2. I'm __________(e)d to agree with Mr. Smith.
3. He has a(n) __________ appetite.
4. The government will __________ the release of the prisoners.
5. The __________ woman made me uncomfortable.

B Choose the word or phrase that best explains the underlined word.

1. If you are ***indicted***, you __________.
   ⓐ are accused of a crime ⓑ will testify at a hearing
   ⓒ are convicted of a crime ⓓ will call the police

2. If you ***obstruct*** traffic, you __________ it.
   ⓐ direct ⓑ block ⓒ avoid ⓓ endure

3. If your application is ***tardy***, it is __________.
   ⓐ unreadable ⓑ overdue ⓒ well-written ⓓ perfect

4. When you ***divert*** someone's attention, you __________ him or her.
   ⓐ attract ⓑ distract ⓒ reject ⓓ entertain

5. When you ***summon*** someone, you want the person to __________.
   ⓐ return your call ⓑ follow your orders
   ⓒ move out of your way ⓓ come to you

정답 및 해설 p.378

C Choose the option that is closest in meaning to the underlined word.

1. buy in ***bulk***
ⓐ bargain prices ⓑ large quantities ⓒ second hand ⓓ good condition

2. a ***hideous*** witch
ⓐ capable ⓑ funny ⓒ genuine ⓓ ugly

3. an ***inverted*** triangle
ⓐ tiny ⓑ massive ⓒ symbolic ⓓ upside down

D Choose the option that is the opposite of the underlined word.

1. a ***preliminary*** hearing
ⓐ final ⓑ lengthy ⓒ public ⓓ mandatory

2. a ***derogatory*** remark
ⓐ suggestive ⓑ unheard ⓒ complimentary ⓓ regrettable

3. be filled with ***antipathy***
ⓐ rage ⓑ sincerity ⓒ humiliation ⓓ admiration

E Choose the best word or phrase.

1. For which of the following would you ***chastise*** a child?
ⓐ a good report card ⓑ a bad dream
ⓒ an upset stomach ⓓ cheating on a test

2. Which of the following is a source of government ***revenue***?
ⓐ taxes ⓑ elections ⓒ health care ⓓ politicians' salaries

3. ***Agrarian*** societies are involved in producing ________________.
ⓐ crops ⓑ machinery ⓒ media ⓓ processed fish

4. A ***gullible*** person tends to easily ________________ lies.
ⓐ dispute ⓑ invent ⓒ detect ⓓ believe

allay
[əléi]

v. (걱정 · 불안 등을) 가라앉히다, 누그러뜨리다 syn. relieve, ease

1 The CEO's statement was designed to *allay* shareholders' anxiety.

bureaucratic
[bjùərəkrǽtik]

n. bureaucracy 관료제
bureaucrat 관료

a. 관료적인, 관료주의의 (involving complicated official rules and processes)

2 The economy was being slowed down by *bureaucratic* inefficiency.

voca+ bureaucratic procedure 관료주의적 절차

counterattack
[káuntərətæ̀k]

n. 반격, 역습

3 The team's strategy was to score goals by employing rapid *counterattacks*.

v. 반격하다, 역습하다

eccentric
[ikséntrik]

n. eccentricity

a. 별난, 특이한 syn. odd, bizarre

4 He was known to be an *eccentric* man with unusual tastes.

n. 괴짜, 기인 syn. oddball, crank

5 His colleagues consider him an *eccentric*.

impulsive
[impʌ́lsiv]

n. impulse

a. 충동적인 syn. impetuous

6 *Impulsive* behavior often leads people into trouble.

voca+ impulsive buying[shopper] 충동 구매[구매자]

1 CEO의 발표는 주주들의 불안감을 가라앉히려는 의도에서 나온 것이었다. 2 관료주의적인 비효율성으로 인해 경기가 둔화되고 있었다. 3 그 팀의 전략은 빠른 역습으로 득점하는 것이었다. 4 그는 취향이 독특하고 별난 사람으로 알려져 있었다. 5 그의 동료들은 그를 괴짜라고 여긴다. 6 충동적인 행동은 자주 사람들을 곤란에 빠지게 한다.

flatter
[flǽtər]

n. flattery
flatterer 아첨꾼
a. flattered 우쭐해진
flattering (실제보다) 돋보이게 하는, 추켜세우는

v. 1. 아첨하다, 비위를 맞추다
2. 돋보이게 하다

1 He always ***flatters*** me. I don't believe him.
2 The color red ***flatters*** her.
3 Those jeans are so ***flattering***; they make your body look perfect.

voca+ flatter oneself 자만[자신]하다

indigent
[índidʒənt]

n. indigence

a. 궁핍한, 빈곤한 syn. impoverished

4 The government is providing aid to ***indigent*** citizens.

naughty
[nɔ́:ti]

n. naughtiness

a. 1. 장난이 심한, 버릇없는, 못된 syn. mischievous
2. 외설적인

5 The teacher disciplined all ***naughty*** children.
6 There was only one ***naughty*** scene in the entire movie.

prelude
[prélju:d]

n. 1. (사건 · 행동 등의) 전조, 서막
2. [음악] 서곡, 전주곡 syn. overture ant. postlude

7 The announcement was seen as a ***prelude to*** sweeping changes.
8 The orchestra played a ***prelude*** before the ballet began.

revoke
[rivóuk]

n. revocation

v. (공식적으로) 취소하다, 무효로 하다 syn. annul

9 His license was ***revoked*** for driving under the influence of alcohol.

day 11 day 12 day 13 day 14 day 15 day 16 day 17 day 18 day 19 day 20

1 그는 늘 내게 아첨을 한다. 나는 그를 믿지 않는다. 2 빨간색은 그녀를 돋보이게 한다. 3 그 청바지 정말 멋져 보이는데, 청바지 때문에 네 몸매가 완벽해 보여. 4 정부는 빈곤한 국민들에게 원조를 제공하고 있다. 5 교사는 버릇없는 아이들 모두에게 벌을 주었다. 6 그 영화에서 외설적인 장면은 딱 하나 있었다. 7 그 발표는 전면적인 변화를 알리는 서막으로 보였다. 8 발레가 시작되기 전에 관현악단이 서곡을 연주했다. 9 음주 운전으로 인해 그의 면허가 취소되었다.

superb
[su:pə́:rb]

a. 뛰어난, 훌륭한 syn. splendid, outstanding

1 The hotel is equipped with ***superb*** facilities.

appalling
[əpɔ́:liŋ]

v. appall 소름끼치게[질겁하게] 하다

a. 끔찍한, 몹시 나쁜 syn. awful, atrocious, dreadful

2 The refugees had to survive under ***appalling*** conditions.
3 He was ***appalled*** by the photographs of the war.

comprise
[kəmpráiz]

v. ~로 이루어지다, ~을 구성하다 syn. consist of, make up

4 Hindus ***comprise*** 82% of India's population.

voca+ be comprised of ~로 구성되다

premise
[prémis]

n. 1. 전제 (an idea that forms the basis for an argument)
2. (복수로) 건물, 토지 (the buildings and land that a shop, company, etc. uses)

5 The scientist's theory was founded on a questionable ***premise***.
6 The school is moving to new ***premises*** next month.

voca+ major[minor] premise (삼단논법의) 대[소]전제

v. 전제로 하다

| Nuance | "전제하다 / 추정하다" 관련 어휘 뉘앙스 차이

premise 전제하다	결과를 도출하기 위해 특정 사실이나 의견을 토대로 두다. 7 a policy that is premised on increasing profits
presume 추정하다	확신하지 못하나 사실일 것이라 추정하다. 8 He is presumed innocent until we have evidence of guilt.
assume 가정하다, 간주하다	근거 없이 단순 가정하다. 9 Let's assume what she says is true.
presuppose 전제로 하다	필요조건으로 사전에 가정하다. 10 Solutions presuppose problems.

1 그 호텔은 훌륭한 시설을 갖추고 있다. 2 피난민들은 끔찍한 생활 환경에서 살아남아야 했다. 3 그는 전쟁 사진을 보고 소름이 끼쳤다. 4 인도 인구의 82%가 힌두교도이다. 5 그 과학자의 이론은 의문의 여지가 있는 전제에 토대를 두고 있었다. 6 그 학교는 다음 달에 새 건물로 이사갈 예정이다. 7 이윤 증가를 전제로 한 정책 8 죄를 입증할 증거를 확보하기 전까지 그는 무죄로 간주된다. 9 그녀가 하는 말이 사실이라고 가정하자. 10 문제가 있어야 해결책이 존재한다.

destitute
[déstitù:t]

n. destitution

a. 극빈의, 빈털터리의 syn. penniless, indigent

1 The tsunami resulted in thousands being left *destitute*.

voca+ be destitute of ~이 결여되다

erroneous
[iróuniəs]

ad. erroneously

a. 잘못된, 틀린 syn. inaccurate, fallacious

2 Some people skip breakfast in the *erroneous* belief that they will lose weight.

3 an *erroneously* listed phone number

hierarchy
[háiərὰ:rki]

a. hierarchical

n. 1. 계층[계급] 제도, 서열 syn. pecking order
2. 권력층, 지배층

4 We still have social and economical *hierarchy* in modern society.

5 Candidates are chosen by the party *hierarchy*.

6 the *hierarchical* structure of medieval society

invoke
[invóuk]

n. invocation

v. 1. (법에) 호소하다, (법을) 발동하다
2. 떠오르게 하다, 연상시키다 syn. evoke
3. (신에게) 도움을 청하다, 기원하다 syn. pray
4. 혼령을 불러내다

7 He *invoked* an international law that protects refugees.

8 His photographs *invoke* feelings of the early 20th century.

9 He *invoked* God to help her to escape her difficulties.

10 The shamans were doing rituals to *invoke* evil.

panacea
[pæ̀nəsí:ə]

n. 만병통치약 syn. cure-all

11 They consider science a *panacea for* future problems.

---

1 지진해일은 수천 명의 사람들을 빈털터리로 만들었다. 2 어떤 사람들은 살이 빠질 것이라는 잘못된 믿음 때문에 아침식사를 거른다. 3 잘못 등록된 전화번호 4 현대 사회에는 여전히 사회적, 경제적 계층이 존재한다. 5 후보들은 당의 지도층에 의해 선출된다. 6 중세 사회의 계급 구조 7 그는 난민을 보호하는 국제법에 호소했다. 8 그의 사진은 20세기 초반의 정서를 떠올리게 한다. 9 그는 그녀가 고난에서 벗어나게 도와달라고 신에게 빌었다. 10 무당들은 악령을 불러내는 의식을 하고 있었다. 11 그들은 과학이 미래의 문제를 모두 해결해줄 것이라 믿는다.

quota
[kwóutə]

n. 할당(량), 몫 syn. share, allotment

❶ A *quota* has been placed on all imports from China.

voca+ meet[make/achieve] a quota 할당량을 채우다
Screen Quota System 스크린쿼터제도(자국영화 의무상영제)

scanty
[skǽnti]

n. scantiness
ad. scantily

a. 1. 부족한, 불충분한
2. (옷이) 작은, 노출이 많은

❷ There is only *scanty* evidence of her involvement.
❸ *Scanty* clothing has become commonplace among young women these days.

voca+ scantily clad[dressed] 노출이 많은 옷차림의

tarnish
[tɑ́:rniʃ]

a. tarnished

v. 1. (평판 · 이미지 등을) 손상시키다, 실추시키다 syn. sully, taint
2. (금속 등이) 변색되다[시키다], 녹슬다[녹슬게 하다] syn. discolor

❹ The photos *tarnished* the celebrity's reputation.
❺ Silver *tarnishes* when it is exposed to air.
❻ He claimed he would improve the company's *tarnished* image.

n. 변색

ambience
[ǽmbiəns]

a. ambient

n. 분위기, 환경 (=ambiance) syn. atmosphere

❼ The hotel offers a pleasant *ambience* and excellent service.

debauchery
[dibɔ́:tʃəri]

n. debauchee 난봉꾼
a. debauched

n. 방탕, 난봉 (behavior that is considered to be immoral because it involves a lot of alcohol, illegal drugs, or sex) syn. dissipation

❽ He was sent to prison, convicted of *debauchery* and sexual immorality.

❶ 모든 중국산 수입품에 할당량이 지정되었다. ❷ 그녀가 연루되었다는 증거는 매우 부족하다. ❸ 요즘 젊은 여자들 사이에 노출이 심한 옷이 흔해졌다. ❹ 그 사진들은 그 유명 인사의 명성을 손상시켰다. ❺ 은은 공기 중에 노출되면 변색된다. ❻ 그는 회사의 실추된 이미지를 개선하겠다고 힘주어 말했다. ❼ 그 호텔은 쾌적한 분위기와 훌륭한 서비스를 제공한다. ❽ 그는 방탕과 성적 방종으로 유죄 판결을 받아 수감되었다.

heterodox
[hétərədɑ̀:ks]

a. 이교의, 이단의, 이설의 ant. orthodox

1 The ***heterodox*** opinions of yesterday's thinkers are seen as fairly normal nowadays.

patrimony
[pǽtrəmòuni]

n. 상속[세습] 재산, 유산 syn. inheritance

2 He wasted his ***patrimony*** on drinking and gambling.

pivotal
[pívətl]

pivot
n. 1. [기계] 회전축 2. 중심, 중추
v. 한 점을 중심으로 돌다

a. 중추적인, 중요한 syn. crucial

3 The Bank of England has a ***pivotal*** role in the London money market.

4 The abduction is the ***pivot*** on which the movie turns.

garner
[gɑ́:rnər]

v. (노력 끝에) 모으다, 획득하다 syn. acquire, gather

5 He has ***garnered*** enough votes to remain as head councilor.

IDIOMS

drink like a fish 술을 많이 마시다 (to drink too much alcohol)

6 Luke ***drinks like a fish***, completely unable to control himself.

eat (someone) alive ~을 혹독하게 비난하다 (to criticize someone very angrily)

7 If she finds out, she'll ***eat you alive***!

1 과거 사상가들의 이단적인 의견은 요즘에는 아주 당연한 것으로 여겨진다. 2 그는 물려받은 재산을 음주와 도박에 탕진했다. 3 영국 은행은 런던 화폐 시장에서 중요한 역할을 한다. 4 그 영화는 유괴 사건을 중심으로 돌아갔다. 5 그는 시의원 대표직을 유지하는 데 충분한 표를 얻었다. 6 Luke는 자신을 전혀 통제할 수 없을 정도로 술을 마셔댄다. 7 그녀가 알게 되면 널 심하게 비난할 거야!

day **19**

exercise

A Match the words in the left column to the sentences in the right column.

ⓐ **comprise**: to be made up of

ⓑ **destitute**: lacking necessities, extremely poor

ⓒ **hierarchy**: a power structure with upper levels having more power and importance

ⓓ **quota**: a minimum requirement or an upper limit as to how much of an activity is necessary or permitted

ⓔ **tarnish**: to make worse or less admirable

1. He was saddened by the ___________ conditions of the school.
2. His lies will ___________ my reputation.
3. The fisherman reached his ___________ for the season.
4. I am at the bottom of the ___________, but I hope to move up.
5. Milkshakes ___________ milk and ice cream.

B Choose the word or phrase that best explains the underlined word.

1. If something is ***erroneous***, it is ______________.
   ⓐ steady ⓑ incorrect ⓒ offensive ⓓ acceptable

2. If circumstances are ***appalling***, they are ______________.
   ⓐ favorable ⓑ stable ⓒ impressive ⓓ terrible

3. If you ***flatter*** someone, you ______________ him or her.
   ⓐ compliment ⓑ chastise ⓒ advise ⓓ abuse

4. If your meal is ***superb***, it is ______________.
   ⓐ simple ⓑ quick ⓒ outstanding ⓓ abundant

5. When you give a ***prelude*** to something, you ______________ it.
   ⓐ introduce ⓑ interrupt ⓒ analyze ⓓ summarize

C Choose the option that is closest in meaning to the underlined word.

1. an ***eccentric*** man
   ⓐ conservative ⓑ noisy ⓒ unusual ⓓ intelligent

2. a starting ***premise***
   ⓐ basis ⓑ topic ⓒ question ⓓ remark

3. ***revoke*** privileges
   ⓐ give back ⓑ pass up ⓒ come by ⓓ take away

D Choose the option that is the opposite of the underlined word.

1. ***indigent*** children
   ⓐ spoiled ⓑ needy ⓒ wealthy ⓓ lonely

2. an ***impulsive*** purchase
   ⓐ expensive ⓑ online ⓒ planned ⓓ wasteful

3. ***allay*** concerns
   ⓐ worsen ⓑ share ⓒ reduce ⓓ ignore

E Choose the best word or phrase.

1. Which of the following would be likely to have the nicest ***ambience***?
   ⓐ a factory ⓑ a playground ⓒ a highway ⓓ a restaurant

2. A woman who engages in ***debauchery*** might ________________.
   ⓐ starve herself ⓑ work out
   ⓒ drink too much ⓓ go to sleep regularly

3. Most people consider ________________ to be highly ***bureaucratic***.
   ⓐ churches ⓑ local gyms
   ⓒ government offices ⓓ convenience stores

4. When children are ***naughty***, we might ________________.
   ⓐ give them candy ⓑ give them chores to do
   ⓒ punish them ⓓ let them take a rest

allocate
[ǽləkèit]
n. allocation

v. 할당하다, 배분하다 syn. allot

❶ More funding needs to be *allocated to* healthcare.

voca+ allocate A B A에게 B를 할당[배분]하다

counterfeit
[káuntərfit]

a. 모조의, 위조의 syn. fake ant. genuine

❷ The *counterfeit* diamond necklace looked like the real thing.

v. 위조하다, 모조품을 만들다

❸ The man admitted *counterfeiting* the $100 bills.

ecstasy
[ékstəsi]
a. ecstatic

n. 1. 황홀함, 희열, 무아지경 syn. rapture
2. (E~) 환각제

❹ This rich chocolate cake is pure *ecstasy*!

voca+ go into ecstasies over[about] ~에 황홀해지다, 매우 흥분하다

flourish
[flə́:riʃ]
a. flourishing

v. 1. 번영[번성]하다 syn. thrive
2. (동 · 식물이) 잘 자라다
3. 알아채도록 흔들어대다, 손에 쥐고 흔들다

❺ Small businesses are *flourishing*.
❻ Many plants *flourish* in warm, humid climates.
❼ They wept with joy, *flourishing* their nation's flag.

n. 1. (눈에 띄기 위한) 과장된 몸짓 2. 인상적인 부분[행위]

❽ He ended the dance with a *flourish*.

improvident
[imprɑ́vidənt]

a. 절약하지 않는, 헤픈 syn. extravagant, prodigal ant. provident

❾ She is kind and beautiful, but hopelessly *improvident*.

❶ 보건 분야에 더 많은 자금이 할당되어야 한다. ❷ 가짜 다이아몬드 목걸이는 마치 진품처럼 보였다. ❸ 그 남자는 100달러짜리 지폐를 위조했다는 것을 인정했다. ❹ 이 진한 초콜릿 케이크는 황홀함 그 자체야! ❺ 중소기업들이 번창하고 있다. ❻ 많은 식물들이 따뜻하고 습윤한 기후에서 잘 자란다. ❼ 그들은 국기를 흔들며 기쁨의 눈물을 흘렸다. ❽ 그는 화려한 동작으로 춤을 마무리했다. ❾ 그녀는 친절하고 아름답지만 구제불능으로 씀씀이가 헤프다.

indispensable
[ìndispénsəbl]

a. 필수적인, 불가결의 syn. essential ant. dispensable

1 He said that democracy is *indispensable* to peace.

negligence
[néglidʒəns]

a. negligent 태만한
negligible 무시할 수 있는, 사소한

n. 1. 태만, 부주의, 소홀함 syn. neglect
2. [법률] 과실

2 Their *negligence* resulted in a forest fire.
3 The doctor was sued for medical *negligence*.

voca+ sue A for criminal[professional / medical] negligence
형사상[업무상 / 의료상] 과실로 A를 고소하다

death through negligence / (involuntary) manslaughter
과실치사

rigorous
[rígərəs]

n. rigor

a. 1. 철저한, 면밀한 syn. thorough
2. 혹독한, 엄격한 syn. severe, strict

4 The company has *rigorous* quality control measures for its products.
5 *rigorous* military training

amenity
[əménəti]

n. (주로 복수로) 편의 시설물 syn. facility

6 The hotel has many *amenities*, including a heated swimming pool.

weave
[wi:v]

v. 1. (직물 등을) 짜다, 뜨다
2. (이야기 등을) 만들어내다, (여러 요소를) 짜맞추다
3. 누비고 다니다

7 a hand-*woven* scarf
8 She *wove* facts and fiction together in her stories.
9 His car was *weaving* in and out of traffic.

n. 짜는 법, 짠 것

voca+ weave-wove[wouv]-woven[wóuvən] 1, 2번 뜻일 때 동사 변화
weave-weaved-weaved 3번 뜻일 때 동사 변화

1 그는 민주주의가 평화를 위해 필수적이라고 말했다. 2 그들의 부주의로 인해 산불이 났다. 3 그 의사는 의료상 과실로 고소당했다. 4 그 회사는 자사 제품에 대한 철저한 품질 관리 척도를 갖고 있다. 5 혹독한 군사 훈련 6 그 호텔에는 온수 수영장을 비롯한 많은 편의 시설이 있다. 7 손으로 짠 목도리 8 그녀는 자신이 쓰는 이야기에 사실과 허구를 섞었다. 9 그의 차가 차량들 사이를 이리저리 빠져나가고 있었다.

conciliatory
[kənsíliətɔ̀ːri]

v. conciliate
n. conciliation

a. 회유하는, 달래는 syn. pacifying, appeasing

1 The mayor made some *conciliatory* remarks to the angry public.

2 The school district made some changes to *conciliate* the teachers.

detrimental
[dètriméntl]

n. detriment

a. 해로운, 피해를 입히는 syn. damaging, injurious

3 Lead produces *detrimental* effects on the nervous system.

euthanasia
[jùːθənéiʒə]

n. 안락사 (the act of ending the life of an individual suffering from an incurable or painful condition) syn. mercy killing

4 Governments hesitate to make *euthanasia* legal.

rebuke
[ribjúːk]

v. 꾸짖다, 비난하다

5 I was *rebuked* by my boss for my error.

n. 비난, 문책

| Nuance | "비난하다/꾸짖다" 관련 어휘 뉘앙스 차이

rebuke 책망하다	옳지 않다는 것을 알고 저지른 일에 대하여 호되게 비난하다. 6 be rebuked for making an offensive remark
scold 꾸짖다	주로 부모나 교사가 아이들을 꾸짖다. 7 scold the child for being late
reprimand 질책하다	잘못에 대해 공식적으로 질책하다. 8 The boy was reprimanded for fighting at school.
reproach 나무라다	상대방의 행동에 대해 실망하여 비난하다. 9 She began to reproach herself for her cowardice.

1 시장은 화난 시민들을 달래기 위한 발언을 했다. 2 그 학군에서는 교사들을 회유하기 위해 몇 가지 변화를 시도했다. 3 납은 신경계에 해로운 영향을 미친다. 4 정부에서는 안락사를 합법화하는 것을 망설이고 있다. 5 나는 실수를 해서 상사에게 문책을 받았다. 6 무례한 말을 한 것에 대해 비난받다 7 지각한 것에 대해 아이를 꾸짖다 8 그 소년은 학교에서 싸운 것 때문에 질책을 받았다. 9 그녀는 자신의 비겁함에 대해 자책하기 시작했다.

evanescent
[èvənésənt]

n. evanescence

a. 곧 사라지는, 오래 못 가는 syn. transient, ephemeral

1 Memory is *evanescent*, changing with the passage of time.

hoist
[hɔist]

v. (줄 등을 이용하여) 끌어올리다 syn. lift

2 The cargo was *hoisted* aboard by crane.

voca+ hoist a flag[sail] 국기를 게양하다[돛을 올리다]

n. 올리는 기계, 화물용 승강기

irrigation
[ìrəgéiʃən]

v. irrigate

n. 관개 (supplying water to land through pipes so that crops will grow)

3 We can reduce water use with improved *irrigation*.

paranoid
[pǽrənɔ̀id]

n. paranoia 피해망상증, 편집증

a. 피해망상의, 편집증적인 (=paranoiac)

4 She is *paranoid* that the project will fail.

n. 편집증 환자 (=paranoiac)

5 *Paranoids* are hard to treat because they don't even trust their doctors.

rash
[ræʃ]

n. rashness

a. 경솔한, 성급한 syn. impulsive, reckless

6 Think twice before making *rash* decisions.

n. 1. 발진, 두드러기
2. (불쾌한 사건 등의) 다발, 빈발 syn. spate

7 I *break out in a rash* if I eat chicken.

8 a *rash* of car thefts

voca+ come[break] out in a rash 발진이 생기다
heat rash 땀띠

1 기억이란 금새 사라지며, 시간의 흐름에 따라 변하기도 한다. 2 화물은 기중기에 의해 배[비행기]에 올려졌다. 3 우리는 개선된 관개로 물의 소비량을 줄일 수 있다. 4 그녀는 그 프로젝트가 실패할 거라는 피해망상에 사로잡혀 있다. 5 편집증 환자는 주치의조차 믿지 않기 때문에 치료하기가 어렵다. 6 결정을 성급하게 내리기 전에 두 번 생각해라. 7 나는 닭고기를 먹으면 두드러기가 생긴다. 8 차량 절도 사건의 다발적 발생

scribble
[skríbl]

n. scribbler 시시한 글쟁이

v. 휘갈겨 쓰다, 낙서하다 syn. scrawl

1 My young cousin just *scribbled* all over my new notebook.

n. 휘갈겨 쓴 글씨, 낙서

2 a *scribbler* of sentimental verse

temperance
[témpərəns]

a. temperate
1. 절제하는 2. 온대 기후의

n. 1. 금주, 술을 끊음
2. 절제, 자제 syn. moderation

3 a *temperance* group[society]
4 *Temperance* in behavior is important.
5 He is *temperate* in his eating and drinking habits.

suspend
[səspénd]

n. suspension
1. 정지, 유보
2. 정직, 정학
3. [기계] 완충장치
suspense 불안감, 서스펜스

v. 1. 일시 정지하다, 유예시키다, 보류하다
2. 정직[정학]시키다
3. 매달다

6 The baseball game was *suspended* because of the rain.
7 He was *suspended from* school for smoking.
8 A lamp was *suspended* from the ceiling.
9 There's been a *suspension* of the court's decision.

voca+ suspended sentence 집행 유예

decadent
[dékədənt]

n. decadence

a. 쾌락적인, 퇴폐적인

10 a *decadent* life of excessive consumption and no sense of responsibility

hypochondriac
[hàipəkάndriæ̀k]

n. 심기증 환자 (someone who always worries about their health and thinks that they may be ill, even when they are not)

11 She's a *hypochondriac*; she goes to the doctor's office every week with some imaginary illness.

---

1 어린 사촌 동생이 내 새 공책에 온통 낙서를 해 놓았다. 2 감상적인 시를 쓰는 별 볼 일 없는 작가 3 금주 단체[모임] 4 행동을 절제하는 것은 중요하다. 5 그는 절제된 식습관과 음주 습관을 가지고 있다. 6 비 때문에 야구 경기가 잠시 중단되었다. 7 그는 흡연을 해서 정학당했다. 8 전등 하나가 천장에 매달려 있었다. 9 법원 판결이 유예되었다. 10 과소비와 무책임으로 점철된 퇴폐적인 삶 11 그녀는 심기증 환자로 자신이 병에 걸렸다고 상상해서 매주 병원에 간다.

pediatrician
[pìːdiətríʃən]

n. pediatrics 소아과

n. 소아과 의사

1 He was a gentle ***pediatrician*** who cared for thousands of children.

wanton
[wɑ́ːntən]

n. wantonness

a. 1. 이유없이 해를 끼치는, 악의적인 syn. unprovoked
2. (여성이) 음란한, 행실이 좋지 않은

2 the ***wanton*** killing of innocent civilians
3 She was blamed for ***wanton*** behavior.

debilitate
[dibílətèit]

n. debility
a. debilitating

v. 쇠약하게 하다, (기능 등을) 약화시키다 syn. weaken, sap

4 The hurricane ***debilitated*** the tourism industry.
5 a ***debilitating*** disease

collusion
[kəlúːʒən]

v. collude
a. collusive

n. 공모, 결탁 (the secret cooperation to do something dishonest or illegal)

6 Oil companies have been charged with price ***collusion***.

IDIOMS

fill someone's shoes ~이 하던 일을 맡다, ~을 대신하다 (to do the job that someone used to do)

7 It's going to be tough to find someone to ***fill Mark's shoes***.

(way) off the mark 부정확한 (not correct)

8 Our estimate of our vacation expenses was ***(way) off the mark***.

1 그는 수천 명의 아이들을 보살핀 자상한 소아과 의사였다. 2 무고한 시민 살해 3 그녀는 문란한 행실로 비난받았다. 4 허리케인으로 인해 관광산업이 쇠퇴했다. 5 몸을 쇠약하게 하는 병 6 석유 회사들이 가격 담합 혐의로 고발당했다. 7 Mark의 일을 대신할 사람을 구하기는 힘들 것이다. 8 우리의 휴가 비용 추산은 정확하지 않았다.

day 20 exercise

A Match the words in the left column to the sentences in the right column.

ⓐ **suspend**: to temporarily withhold privileges

ⓑ **detrimental**: having a severely negative impact

ⓒ **pediatrician**: a doctor who specializes in babies and young children

ⓓ **negligence**: the quality of being careless

ⓔ **debilitate**: to make something weak and less effective

1. My son is very sick. I have to make an appointment with the ___________.
2. A stroke can ___________ language ability.
3. The man's ___________ cost him his life.
4. The woman can't drive because her license is ___________(e)d.
5. Smoking is ___________ to your health.

B Choose the word or phrase that best explains the underlined word.

1. If money is ***counterfeit***, it is ___________.
   ⓐ stolen ⓑ taxed ⓒ fake ⓓ saved

2. If something is ***indispensable***, it is ___________.
   ⓐ delicious ⓑ wasteful ⓒ problematic ⓓ necessary

3. If you are a ***hypochondriac***, you always think you are ___________.
   ⓐ overweight ⓑ diseased ⓒ unattractive ⓓ victimized

4. When you ***allocate*** funds, you ___________ them.
   ⓐ divide ⓑ invest ⓒ spend ⓓ count

5. When you ***hoist*** something, you ___________ it.
   ⓐ bury ⓑ lift ⓒ throw ⓓ unload

정답 및 해설 p.379

C Choose the option that is closest in meaning to the underlined word.

1. ***flourish*** in a damp environment
ⓐ thrive ⓑ change ⓒ seed ⓓ adapt

2. ***rebuke*** an employee
ⓐ promote ⓑ fire ⓒ scold ⓓ question

3. have all of the ***amenities***
ⓐ conveniences ⓑ possibilities ⓒ problems ⓓ staff

D Choose the option that is the opposite of the underlined word.

1. a ***rash*** decision
ⓐ important ⓑ quick ⓒ careful ⓓ risky

2. be in ***ecstasy***
ⓐ misery ⓑ debt ⓒ confusion ⓓ deep thought

3. ***rigorous*** training
ⓐ special ⓑ athletic ⓒ easy ⓓ tiresome

E Choose the best word or phrase.

1. Which of the following would you ***weave***?
ⓐ a necklace ⓑ a river ⓒ a basket ⓓ a statue

2. ***Irrigation*** is the practice of supplying land with ______________.
ⓐ electricity ⓑ water ⓒ insecticide ⓓ fertilizer

3. Which of the following would you ***scribble***?
ⓐ a job application ⓓ a research paper
ⓒ a telephone message ⓑ an email to a client

4. Which of the following would be described as ***evanescent***?
ⓐ a perfect mood ⓑ a work day
ⓒ a construction project ⓓ a chronic illness

endow
[indáu]

n. endowment

v. 1. (학교 · 병원 등에) 기부하다
2. (재능 · 특징 등을) 부여하다 syn. invest

1 He *endowed* money to the hospital for a new wing.
2 All people *are endowed with* certain inalienable rights.

voca+ be endowed with ~을 타고나다

autocracy
[ɔːtákrəsi]

n. autocrat 독재자
a. autocratic

n. 독재 정치[국가], 독재 권력 syn. dictatorship, despotism

3 The country was an *autocracy* for 50 years.

coincidence
[kouínsidəns]

v. coincide
a. coincidental 우연한
coincident
1. 동시에 발생하는
2. 일치하는, 꼭 맞는

n. 1. 우연의 일치, 동시 발생 syn. chance
2. (의견 · 이해 등의) 일치 syn. accord

4 What a *coincidence*! We were just talking about you.
5 A *coincidence* of interests between the two rivals led to cooperation.

voca+ by coincidence[accident] 우연히

dedicate
[dédikèit]

n. dedication
a. dedicated
1. 헌신적인, 몰두하는
2. 전용의, 특정 목적의

v. 1. (시간 · 노력을) 바치다, 헌신하다 syn. devote
2. (저작물을) 헌정하다

6 Maria *dedicated her life to* helping others.
7 He *dedicated* his first book to his mother.
8 a *dedicated* sports channel

voca+ dedicate oneself[one's life] to ~에 헌신[전념]하다

punctuate
[pʌ́ŋktʃuèit]

n. punctuation 구두점

v. 1. 구두점을 찍다
2. 방해하다, (말을) 가로막다 syn. interrupt

9 None of his essays was *punctuated* correctly.
10 Her speech was *punctuated* by questions from the audience.

1 그는 병원에 새 부속 건물을 지을 돈을 기부했다. 2 모든 사람들은 몇 가지의 불가침 권리를 가지고 태어난다. 3 그 나라는 50년간 독재국가였다. 4 기막힌 우연의 일치네! 우리는 방금 네 얘기를 하고 있었어. 5 두 라이벌의 이해 관계가 맞아 떨어져 서로 협력하게 되었다. 6 Maria는 남을 돕는 데 평생을 바쳤다. 7 그는 자신의 첫번째 책을 어머니에게 바쳤다. 8 스포츠 전용 채널 9 그의 에세이들 중 구두점이 정확히 사용된 것은 하나도 없었다. 10 그녀의 연설은 청중들의 질문 때문에 방해를 받았다.

intact
[intǽkt]

a. 온전한, 손상되지 않은 syn. undamaged

1 The castle remained *intact* even after the long war.

outrage
[áutrèidʒ]

a. outrageous

n. 1. 경악, 격분, 분개 syn. indignation
2. 경악스러운 일, 참사 syn. atrocity

2 There was public *outrage* over the president's dishonesty.
3 a memorial service for those who died in the bomb *outrage*

v. 경악케 하다

apparatus
[æ̀pərǽtəs]

n. 1. (한 벌의) 기구, 장치 syn. equipment, kit
2. (정치 활동 등의) 조직
3. [신체] 기관

4 an oxygen breathing *apparatus*
5 The state *apparatus* has long been without real power.
6 the digestive *apparatus*

recede
[risíːd]

v. 1. (소리 · 형체가) 멀어지다 syn. fade
2. (기억 · 감각이) 희미해지다, 약해지다

7 The sun *receded into* the horizon.
8 The pain in his head had *receded* a little.

sheer
[ʃiər]

a. 1. 완전한, 순전한 syn. pure, utter
2. 매우 가파른, 깎아지른 듯한 syn. steep
3. (직물이) 얇은, 속이 비치는

9 The look of *sheer* terror on his face was unforgettable.
10 a *sheer* cliff
11 I saw him hiding behind the *sheer* curtains.

v. 갑자기 방향을 바꾸다

12 The bike *sheered off* to the right.

voca+ sheer off[away] 방향을 바꾸다, 떨어져 나가다

1 그 성은 오랜 전쟁 후에도 온전히 남아 있었다. 2 대통령의 부정 행위에 국민들은 분개했다. 3 폭탄 참사로 인한 사망자들을 위한 추도식 4 산소 호흡 장치 5 정부 조직은 오랫동안 실권이 없었다. 6 소화 기관 7 태양이 지평선 너머로 사라져갔다. 8 그의 두통이 조금 가셨다. 9 엄청난 공포에 휩싸인 그의 표정이 잊혀지지 않았다. 10 깎아지른 듯한 절벽 11 나는 그가 얇은 커튼 뒤에 숨어 있는 것을 보았다. 12 자전거는 갑자기 오른쪽으로 방향을 틀었다.

threshold
[θréʃhòuld]

n. 1. 입구, 문지방 syn. doorway
2. 발단, (반응 등의) 시작점

1 They stepped across the *threshold* and into their new home.
2 She has a high pain *threshold*.

voca+ on the threshold of ~을 막 시작하려 하는

pious
[páiəs]

n. piety

a. 1. 신앙심이 깊은, 독실한 syn. religious, devout ant. profane
2. 위선적인, 독실한 체하는

3 Abdul is a *pious* Muslim.
4 I'm annoyed with *pious* speeches by politicians.

assuage
[əswéidʒ]

v. (고통 · 불쾌한 감정 등을) 완화하다, 덜어 주다 syn. relieve, alleviate

5 Nothing could *assuage* her guilt.

unremitting
[ʌ̀nrimítiŋ]

a. 끊임없는, 끈질긴

6 The *unremitting* noise of his neighbors angered him.

| Nuance | "계속되는" 관련 어휘 뉘앙스 차이

unremitting 끊임없는	ㅣ나쁜 일이 오랫동안 개선되지 않고 계속되는 7 unremitting pain[poverty]
continual 잇따른, 빈번한	ㅣ주로 불쾌한 일이 되풀이되는 8 continual problems[interruptions]
continuous 그칠 줄 모르는	ㅣ어떤 상황이 중단되지 않고 물 흐르듯 계속되는 9 continuous flow[speech]
incessant 끊임없는, 쉴 새 없는	ㅣ소음과 같은 불쾌한 것이 오랫동안 끊임없이 일어나는 10 incessant noise[chatter]

1 그들은 입구를 지나 새 집으로 걸어 들어갔다. 2 그녀는 고통을 매우 잘 견딘다. 3 Abdul은 독실한 이슬람교도이다. 4 나는 정치인들의 위선적인 말에 짜증이 난다. 5 무엇도 그녀의 죄책감을 덜어주지 못했다. 6 이웃집에서 나는 끊임없는 소음이 그를 화나게 했다. 7 계속되는 통증[빈곤] 8 되풀이되는 문제[방해] 9 계속되는 흐름[연설] 10 끊임없는 소음[수다]

conspicuous
[kənspíkjuəs]

a. 1. 눈에 잘 띄는, 두드러지는 ant. inconspicuous
2. 대단한, 엄청난

1 He signaled in a *conspicuous* manner.
2 a *conspicuous* success[failure]

voca+ conspicuous consumption 과시적 소비
conspicuous by one's[its] absence (있어야 할 곳에) 없어서 눈에 띄는

dilate
[dailéit]

n. dilation

v. (신체 부위) 확대되다[시키다] ant. contract

3 When there is less light, the pupils in our eyes *dilate*.

voca+ dilate on[upon] ~에 대해 자세히 말하다[쓰다]

relish
[réliʃ]

v. 1. 즐기다, 음미하다 syn. savor
2. (계획 · 생각으로) 들뜨다, 즐거워하다

4 Jim always *relishes* debates.
5 Tara is *relishing* the idea of visiting Tokyo.

n. 1. 즐거움, 만끽 syn. zest
2. (핫도그 · 햄버거 등의) 소스

6 She sat back and sipped her coffee *with relish*.
7 a hamburger with cheese and *relish*

malnutrition
[mæ̀lnjuːtríʃən]

n. 영양실조

8 refugees suffering from *malnutrition*

extricate
[ékstrəkèit]

v. (곤란한 상황에서) 구해내다, 빠져나오다

9 Police *extricated* the survivors from the car accident.

1 그는 눈에 잘 띄게 신호를 보냈다. 2 대성공[대실패] 3 빛의 양이 적어지면 눈의 동공이 확대된다. 4 Jim은 항상 토론을 즐긴다. 5 Tara는 도쿄에 갈 생각에 들떠 있다. 6 그녀는 의자에 깊숙이 기대 앉아서 커피를 조금씩 음미하며 마셨다. 7 치즈와 소스가 들어 있는 햄버거 8 영양실조로 고통받고 있는 난민들 9 경찰이 교통사고 현장에서 생존자들을 구해냈다.

bequeath
[bikwíːð]

v. (재산 · 지식 등을) 물려주다, 남기다 syn. leave

1 His father *bequeathed* a fortune *to* him.

transitory
[trǽnzitɔ̀ːri]

n. transition 전환, 변화, 이동

a. 일시적인, 잠시 동안의 syn. temporary, transient, fleeting

2 Peace between the two nations was only *transitory*.
3 a country now in *transition*

smear
[smiər]

a. smeary

v. 1. 마구 칠하다, 바르다 syn. daub
2. (먼지 · 기름 등으로) 더럽히다
3. (거짓말로) 명예를 훼손하다, 비방하다 syn. slander

4 The child *smeared* paint on the wall.
5 The suntan lotion *smeared* my sunglasses.
6 She sued the magazine after it had *smeared* her private life.

n. 1. 얼룩, 더러움
2. 중상모략, 근거 없는 비방

voca+ smear campaign 인신공격, 흑색 비방전

emanate
[émənèit]

n. emanation

v. (감정 · 특질 · 냄새 등을) 내뿜다, 발산하다

7 She *emanates* glamor and wealth.

insidious
[insídiəs]

a. (병 등이) 서서히 진행되는, 모르는 사이에 해를 입히는

8 The *insidious* disease had finally taken his life.

1 그의 아버지는 그에게 큰 재산을 물려주었다. 2 두 나라 간의 평화는 일시적인 것일 뿐이었다. 3 전환기에 있는 국가 4 그 아이는 벽에다 페인트를 마구 칠했다. 5 선탠 로션이 내 선글라스를 더럽혔다. 6 그녀는 자신의 사생활에 대한 거짓 보도를 한 잡지를 고소했다. 7 그녀는 매력과 재력을 뽐낸다. 8 서서히 진행되던 그 병은 마침내 그의 목숨을 앗아갔다.

belligerent
[bəlídʒərənt]

n. belligerence

a. 1. 공격적인, 적대적인, 호전적인 syn. hostile, aggressive
2. 전쟁 중인 syn. warring

1 Barbara is a *belligerent* young woman.
2 The *belligerent* countries are intent on continuing their dispute.

n. 전쟁 중인 국가, 교전국

absolution
[æ̀bsəlú:ʃən]

n. (기독교의) 면죄, 사죄

3 Pope John Paul II granted him *absolution*.

profligate
[prɑ́fligət]

n. profligacy

a. 낭비하는, 방종한 syn. wasteful, prodigal

4 He is infamous for his *profligate* lifestyle.

n. 방탕한 자, 난봉꾼

prodigious
[prədídʒəs]

a. 엄청난, 막대한, 대단한 syn. enormous, colossal

5 Tim has a *prodigious* capacity for learning.

IDIOMS

pay lip service to 입에 발린 말을 하다, 실천 없이 말만 하다
(to say that you support something, but do nothing to prove it)

6 The mayor is *paying lip service to* the issue.

not mince (one's) words 단도직입적으로 말하다, 솔직히 말하다
(to say what you mean directly, even if it might offend people)

7 She *doesn't mince her words*, and this upsets her co-workers.

1 Barbara는 공격적인 젊은 여성이다. 2 전쟁 중인 그 나라들은 이 싸움을 계속할 작정이다. 3 교황 요한 바오로 2세는 그의 죄를 사했다. 4 그는 방탕한 생활로 악명이 높다. 5 Tim은 매우 뛰어난 학습 능력을 갖고 있다. 6 시장은 그 사안에 대해 입에 발린 말을 하고 있다. 7 그녀는 단도직입적으로 말을 해서 동료들을 기분 나쁘게 한다.

exercise

A Match the words in the left column to the sentences in the right column.

ⓐ **smear**: to spread a sticky or greasy substance on something

ⓑ **malnutrition**: poor health due to lack of nutrients

ⓒ **belligerent**: hostile or aggressive

ⓓ **apparatus**: a device that serves a function

ⓔ **unremitting**: persistent

1. After I __________ sunscreen on your back, I'll go wash my hands.
2. This handy __________ helps you peel potatoes in seconds.
3. She was __________ in her efforts to persuade her co-workers.
4. __________ is a serious problem in many developing countries.
5. The man became __________ when he was confronted by the police.

B Choose the word or phrase that best explains the underlined word.

1. If something is ***punctuated*** by something, it is ______________ by it.
   ⓐ improved ⓑ educated ⓒ interrupted ⓓ deceived

2. If a curtain is ***sheer***, it is ______________.
   ⓐ handsewn ⓑ see-through ⓒ high-quality ⓓ shiny

3. If you are ***endowed*** with something, you ______________.
   ⓐ are surprised by it ⓑ feel upset about it
   ⓒ have a favorable quality ⓓ have to pay it back

4. If you look ***conspicuous***, you ______________.
   ⓐ are puzzled ⓑ seem tired ⓒ are embarrassed ⓓ stand out

5. If an event is a ***coincidence***, it ______________.
   ⓐ happens by chance ⓑ interferes with another event
   ⓒ has not taken place ⓓ occurs ahead of schedule

정답 및 해설 p.380

C Choose the option that is closest in meaning to the underlined word.

1. ***dedicate*** yourself to your work
ⓐ devote ⓑ behave ⓒ discourage ⓓ volunteer

2. ***assuage*** pain
ⓐ inflict ⓑ suffer ⓒ stand ⓓ soothe

3. ***transitory*** benefits
ⓐ contradictory ⓑ short-term ⓒ mutual ⓓ commercial

D Choose the option that is the opposite of the underlined word.

1. ***relish*** the performance
ⓐ cancel ⓑ applaud ⓒ dislike ⓓ attend

2. ***profligate*** spending
ⓐ overall ⓑ additional ⓒ reasonable ⓓ wasteful

3. an ***intact*** structure
ⓐ impressive ⓑ broken ⓒ complex ⓓ decorative

E Choose the best word or phrase.

1. Which of the following might ***recede*** with age?
ⓐ hairline ⓑ skin ⓒ teeth ⓓ wrinkle

2. Where is the ***threshold*** of your house?
ⓐ the yard ⓑ the basement ⓒ the entrance ⓓ the chimney

3. Which of the following ***dilates***?
ⓐ pupils ⓑ fingernails ⓒ tongues ⓓ earlobes

4. You might seek ***absolution*** if ________________.
ⓐ you don't know the answer ⓑ you are in danger
ⓒ your business is failing ⓓ you have sinned

appendix
[əpéndiks]

v. append 부록으로 싣다

n. 1. (책의) 부록 (복수형 appendices)
2. 맹장 (복수형 appendixes)

1 an *appendix* at the end of the book
2 He was in hospital for two weeks with *appendix* problems.
3 The author *appended* five pages on historical background.

autopsy
[ɔ́:tɑpsi]

n. 부검, 검시 syn. post-mortem (examination)

4 The *autopsy* showed that she had died of heart failure.

voca+ perform[carry out] an autopsy 부검하다

bizarre
[bizɑ́:r]

a. 이상한, 기묘한, 설명하기 어려운 syn. weird, strange

5 John was embarrassed with her *bizarre* behavior.

arsenal
[ɑ́:rsənəl]

n. 1. 비축된 무기, 군수 물자 2. 무기고, 군수품 창고

6 China's nuclear *arsenal*

voca+ arsenal of 많은 ~, ~의 총체

graze
[greiz]

v. 1. 풀을 뜯어먹다[뜯게 하다]
2. 긁히다, 찰과상을 입다
3. 살짝 스치다, 가볍게 닿다 syn. brush
4. (식사 대신) 이것저것 가볍게 먹다

7 The sheep were *grazing* quietly.
8 He fell to the ground, *grazing* his face.
9 The bullet *grazed* the police officer's hand.
10 I'm not hungry because I've been *grazing* all day.

n. 찰과상, (살짝) 긁힌 상처

11 Her arms were covered with cuts and *grazes* after the fall.

1 (책의) 권말 부록 2 그는 맹장염으로 2주 동안 병원에 입원해 있었다. 3 저자는 역사적 배경에 관한 5페이지 분량의 부록을 실었다. 4 부검 결과 그녀는 심장마비로 죽었다는 것이 밝혀졌다. 5 John은 그녀의 기묘한 행동에 당황했다. 6 중국이 비축한 핵무기 7 양들이 조용히 풀을 뜯고 있었다. 8 그는 땅에 넘어져서 얼굴을 긁혔다. 9 총알이 경찰관의 손을 스쳤다. 10 나는 하루 종일 이것저것 먹었더니 배고프지 않다. 11 넘어지는 바람에 그녀의 팔은 크고 작은 상처투성이가 되었다.

integrate
[íntəgrèit]

n. integration
a. integrated

v. 1. (효율성을 높이기 위해) 통합하다, 결합하다
2. (사회 · 조직 등의) 일원이 되다[되게 하다], ~에 융화되다[되게 하다]

1 Teachers *integrate* games *with* education.
2 We need a person who can *integrate with* a team.

voca+ integrate A with[into] B A와 B를 통합하다

ludicrous
[lú:dikrəs]

n. ludicrousness

a. 터무니없는, 말도 안 되는 syn. absurd, ridiculous

3 It was a *ludicrous* idea to rob such a well-guarded bank.

austere
[ɔ:stíər]

n. austerity

a. 1. 수수한, 꾸미지 않은 syn. plain
2. 엄격한, 진지한 syn. strict, serious
3. 금욕적인, 절제된 syn. ascetic
4. 긴축 재정의

4 Her apartment was small and *austere*.
5 My father was an *austere*, silent man.
6 the Buddhist monks' *austere* way of life
7 *austere* economic policy

collaboration
[kəlæ̀bəréiʃən]

v. collaborate
n. collaborator
a. collaborative

n. 1. 협동, 공동 작업[연구], 합작품 syn. teamwork
2. (적국에 대한) 협조, 부역

8 The opera is a *collaboration* between two of the best composers in the world.
9 The soldier was charged with *collaboration* with the enemy.

voca+ in collaboration with ~와 협동하여

shimmer
[ʃímər]

a. shimmering

v. 은은하게 빛나다, 가물거리다

10 Her eyes were *shimmering* in the moonlight.
11 A *shimmering* light that signaled land came into view.

1 교사들은 교육과 게임을 결합한다. 2 우리는 팀에 융화될 수 있는 사람이 필요하다. 3 그처럼 경비가 철저한 은행을 턴다는 것은 말도 안 되는 생각이었다. 4 그녀의 아파트는 작고 간소했다. 5 아버지는 엄격하고 말수가 없는 분이었다. 6 스님들의 금욕적인 생활 방식 7 긴축 재정 정책 8 그 오페라는 세계 최고의 작곡가 두 명의 합작품이다. 9 그 병사는 적과 내통한 혐의로 기소되었다. 10 그녀의 눈이 달빛을 받아 은은히 빛나고 있었다. 11 육지가 있음을 나타내는 가물거리는 불빛이 보이기 시작했다.

thrive
[θraiv]

a. thriving

v. (사업 등이) 번창하다, (동 · 식물이) 잘 자라다 syn. flourish

1 His business *thrived* despite a recession.

voca+ thrive on (힘든 일을) 견뎌내다, 즐기다

abstinence
[ǽbstənəns]

v. abstain
a. abstinent

n. 금욕, 절제 (=abstention) ant. indulgence

2 *Abstinence* is one of the ways to avoid AIDS.
3 He promised to *abstain from* alcohol.

voca+ abstinence from food[sex] 음식[성생활] 절제

indolence
[índələns]

a. indolent

n. 게으름, 나태 syn. idleness, laziness

4 *Indolence* is the sleep of the mind.

insolent
[ínsələnt]

n. insolence

a. 무례한, 불손한, 버릇없는

5 She was punished for her *insolent* behavior toward her teacher.

| Nuance | "무례한" 관련 어휘 뉘앙스 차이

insolent 무례한, 불손한	마땅히 공경해야 할 사람에게 버릇없이 행동하는 6 You insolent child!
impertinent 건방진, 버릇없는	연장자에게 주제넘는 말이나 질문을 하는 7 She asked me impertinent questions after just meeting me.
impolite 무례한, 실례되는	무심코 무례한 말이나 행동을 하는 8 It may be impolite to ask someone's age.
ill-mannered 버릇없는	사회생활에 적합하지 않은 행동을 하는 9 Her children are incredibly ill-mannered.

1 경기 침체에도 불구하고 그의 사업은 번창했다. 2 금욕은 에이즈를 예방하는 방법들 중 하나이다. 3 그는 술을 끊겠다고 약속했다. 4 나태는 정신의 수면 상태이다. 5 그녀는 교사에 대한 버릇없는 행동 때문에 벌을 받았다. 6 이 버릇없는 녀석! 7 그녀는 나를 만난 지 얼마 되지도 않았는데 주제넘은 질문을 했다. 8 다른 사람의 나이를 묻는 것은 실례가 될 수 있다. 9 그녀의 아이들은 심하게 버릇이 없다.

constrain
[kənstréin]

n. constraint
a. constrained

v. 1. 제한하다, 규제하다 syn. restrict, limit
2. (억지로) ~하게 하다 syn. force

1 The report shows taxes in Brazil *constrain* IT market growth.
2 I *felt constrained to* do what he said.

voca+ constrain A from v-ing A가 ~하지 못하게 하다
be[feel] constrained to-v (억지로) ~하도록 강요당하다

dispassionate
[dispǽʃənit]

a. 냉정한, 중립적인, 공정한 syn. impartial, detached

3 Take a *dispassionate* view of the situation.

exuberant
[igzúːbərənt]

n. exuberance

a. 1. 활기찬, 생기 넘치는
2. 화려한, 다채로운

4 Billy has an *exuberant* personality.
5 *exuberant* paintings by Italian artists

incessant
[insésənt]

a. (짜증스럽게) 계속되는, 끊임없는 syn. perpetual

6 His girlfriend's *incessant* whining irritated him.

mandate
[mǽndeit]

a. mandatory
법으로 규정된, 의무적인

n. 1. (유권자에게 위임받은) 권한, 정책 수행권
2. (공적인) 명령, 지시

7 The president was given a *mandate* to introduce educational reform.
8 a *mandate* to release political prisoners

v. 1. ~에게 위임하다[권한을 주다]
2. 지시하다, (법으로) 규정하다

9 The council is *mandated* to change traffic laws.
10 constitutionally *mandated* civil rights
11 Wearing helmets is *mandatory* for motorcyclists.

1 그 보고서는 브라질의 세금이 IT 시장의 성장을 제한하고 있음을 보여준다. 2 나는 그의 말대로 해야 한다고 느꼈다. 3 상황을 냉철하게 봐라. 4 Billy는 성격이 활달하다. 5 이탈리아 화가들이 그린 현란한 색감의 그림들 6 여자친구의 끊임없는 푸념이 그를 짜증나게 했다. 7 대통령은 교육개혁안을 도입할 권한을 부여받았다. 8 정치범들을 석방하라는 지시 9 지방자치단체는 교통 법규를 개정할 권한을 위임받았다. 10 헌법으로 규정된 시민권 11 모터사이클 운전자들은 헬멧을 착용하도록 법으로 규정되어 있다.

placate

[pléikeit]

a. placatory

v. 달래다, 회유하다, 진정시키다 syn. appease, pacify

1 The promises did little to *placate* the angry demonstrators.

reminisce

[rèmənís]

n. reminiscence

a. reminiscent (~을) 생각나게 하는

v. 추억을 떠올리다, 추억에 잠기다

2 The woman was *reminiscing* about her life before marriage.

3 a scene *reminiscent of* the classic Hollywood film

voca+ reminiscent of ~을 생각나게 하는

solicit

[səlísit]

n. solicitation

solicitor

1. 탄원자
2. *AmE.* 방문 판매원
3. *BrE.* 법무관

v. 1. 간청하다, 탄원하다

2. (방문하여) 구매를 종용하다, 강매하다 (to try to sell something by visiting people and persuading them to buy it)

3. (매춘부가) 호객 행위를 하다

4 She is *soliciting* donations for orphans.

5 *Soliciting* in this building is not allowed.

6 If prostitutes *solicit* openly, they will be prosecuted.

translucent

[trænslú:sənt]

n. translucence

a. 반투명의, 살짝 비치는

7 The glass in the bathroom window is *translucent*.

enact

[inǽkt]

n. enactment

v. 1. (법률 · 규칙 등을) 제정하다

2. 상연하다, 연기(演技)하다

8 legislation *enacted* by the National Assembly

9 The play was *enacted* using sign language.

1 그 약속은 분노한 시위대를 진정시키는 데 거의 도움이 되지 않았다. 2 그 여자는 결혼하기 전의 삶을 추억하고 있었다. 3 헐리우드 고전 영화를 생각나게 하는 장면 4 그녀는 고아들을 위한 기부를 요청하고 있다. 5 이 건물은 잡상인 출입이 금지되어 있습니다. 6 매춘부가 드러내 놓고 호객 행위를 하면 처벌의 대상이 된다. 7 욕실 창문의 유리는 반투명이다. 8 국회에 의해 제정된 법률 9 그 연극은 수화로 공연되었다.

insipid
[insípid]

n. insipidness
(=insipidity)

a. 1. 맛이 안 나는, 밍밍한 syn. flavorless
2. 무미건조한, 재미없는 syn. dull

1 The *insipid* coffee was cheap anyway.
2 He's such an *insipid* man.

profane
[prəféin]

n. profanity 욕설, 신성 모독

a. 1. 신성 모독의, 불경스러운
2. 세속적인 syn. secular ant. sacred

3 She disliked the use of *profane* language in the band's songs.
4 stories of *profane* love

v. 모독하다

congruent
[káŋgruənt]

n. congruence

a. 1. 적합한, 잘 들어맞는 syn. suitable, appropriate
2. [수학] 합동의

5 The movie may not be *congruent with* Korean values.
6 *Congruent* triangles have the same size and shape.

exacerbate
[igzǽsərbèit]

n. exacerbation

v. 악화시키다 syn. worsen, aggravate

7 Cleave's interference *exacerbated* the situation.

IDIOMS

put words into someone's mouth ~가 하려는 말을 멋대로 넘겨짚다
(to suggest that someone has said something when they really meant something else)

8 Stop *putting words into my mouth* – I never said I disliked him.

be[go] on the wagon 술을 끊다 (to give up drinking)

9 Do you want a beer, or *are* you still *on the wagon*?

1 그 밍밍한 커피는 어쨌건 싸긴 했다. 2 그는 정말 재미없고 지루한 사람이다. 3 그녀는 그 밴드의 노래에 나오는 불경스러운 말들을 싫어했다. 4 세속적인 사랑 이야기 5 그 영화는 한국적인 가치관에 맞지 않을지도 모른다. 6 합동 삼각형들은 크기와 모양이 같다. 7 Cleave의 간섭이 상황을 악화시켰다. 8 멋대로 넘겨짚지 마. 나는 그 남자가 싫다고 한 적 없어. 9 맥주 하나 마실래? 아니면 아직도 술을 끊은 상태니?

exercise

A Match the words in the left column to the sentences in the right column.

ⓐ **integrate**: to join or become part of

ⓑ **exacerbate**: to make worse

ⓒ **translucent**: not transparent, but clear enough to allow light to pass through

ⓓ **indolence**: laziness

ⓔ **abstinence**: the practice of avoiding something you enjoy

1. Smoking will only __________ your illness.
2. She was fired for her __________.
3. The only way to recover from alcoholism is __________.
4. It is difficult to __________ into a culture when you don't speak the language.
5. If you put a(n) __________ purple film over the lamp, the whole room will seem purple.

B Choose the word or phrase that best explains the underlined word.

1. When you are ***dispassionate*** about something, you are __________.
   ⓐ upset ⓑ unbiased ⓒ unaware ⓓ curious

2. When you ***reminisce***, you __________ something.
   ⓐ recall ⓑ celebrate ⓒ describe ⓓ change

3. If a boy is ***insolent***, he is being __________.
   ⓐ helpful ⓑ messy ⓒ rude ⓓ imaginative

4. If something is ***incessant***, it __________.
   ⓐ needs help
   ⓑ is hard to motivate
   ⓒ is incorrect
   ⓓ never stops

5. If you are part of a ***collaboration***, you are __________.
   ⓐ breaking the law
   ⓑ cooperating with others
   ⓒ volunteering your time
   ⓓ competing for a promotion

정답 및 해설 p.380

C Choose the word that is closest in meaning to the underlined word.

1. an ***insipid*** novel
ⓐ popular ⓑ dull ⓒ inspiring ⓓ unpublished

2. a ***ludicrous*** plan
ⓐ ambitious ⓑ original ⓒ ridiculous ⓓ attainable

3. an ***austere*** teacher
ⓐ strict ⓑ energetic ⓒ inventive ⓓ knowledgeable

D Choose the word that is the opposite of the underlined word.

1. an ***exuberant*** fan
ⓐ crazed ⓑ loyal ⓒ disappointed ⓓ unenthusiastic

2. ***placate*** your friend
ⓐ entertain ⓑ flatter ⓒ support ⓓ provoke

3. ***congruent*** ideas
ⓐ incompatible ⓑ innovative ⓒ uninteresting ⓓ unbelievable

E Choose the best word or phrase.

1. What would you find in an ***arsenal***?
ⓐ treasures ⓑ weapons ⓒ information ⓓ criminals

2. Which of the following animals prefers to ***graze***?
ⓐ cattle ⓑ tigers ⓒ hamsters ⓓ fish

3. Which of the following would be most likely to ***shimmer***?
ⓐ clouds ⓑ donkeys ⓒ dirt ⓓ stars

4. Doctors perform an ***autopsy*** when ______________.
ⓐ a tumor needs to be removed
ⓑ a patient suffers from a stroke
ⓒ the cause of death is unknown
ⓓ a person is having a heart attack

appliance
[əpláiəns]

n. 가정용 기구, 가전제품

1 Major *appliances* include stoves, refrigerators, washing machines, and dishwashers.

voca+ household[kitchen] appliance 가전[주방]제품

avenge
[əvéndʒ]

n. avenger 복수하는 사람

v. ~에 대해 복수하다, 앙갚음을 하다

2 He was determined to *avenge* his father's death.

voca+ avenge oneself on ~에게 복수하다

commitment
[kəmítmənt]

v. commit

a. committed 열의를 다하는, 강하게 믿는

n. 1. 약속, 공약
2. 헌신, 열성, 충성 syn. dedication
3. 의무, 책임

3 the company's *commitment* to customer service

4 She is known for her *commitment* to the peace movement.

5 I have a lot of financial *commitments*.

6 He is a *committed* Socialist.

voca+ make[meet] a commitment 약속을 하다[이행하다]

deem
[di:m]

v. ~라고 여기다, 간주하다 syn. consider

7 The project was *deemed* a great success.

enhance
[inhǽns]

n. enhancement
enhancer 강화제

v. 향상시키다, 개선하다 syn. improve, boost

8 The company is trying to *enhance* its image.

voca+ flavor enhancer 화학 조미료
performance enhancing drug 경기력 향상 (불법)약물

1 주요 가전제품에는 스토브, 냉장고, 세탁기, 식기세척기가 있다. 2 그는 아버지의 죽음에 대해 복수를 하겠다고 굳게 다짐했다. 3 회사의 대(對)고객 약속 4 그녀는 열성적인 평화 운동으로 유명하다. 5 나는 돈을 써야 할 곳이 많다. 6 그는 열성적인 사회주의자이다. 7 그 프로젝트는 대성공으로 여겨졌다. 8 그 회사는 이미지를 개선하려고 노력하고 있다.

grim
[grim]

n. grimness

a. 1. 암울한, 걱정스러운 syn. depressing
2. (표정 · 태도가) 심각한, 험악한
3. (장소 · 외관이) 보기 흉한, 불쾌한

1 He suffered a severe injury and his chances for living are *grim.*
2 I have never seen Clive with such a *grim* face.
3 The old factory looks rather *grim*.

voca+ hang[hold] on for grim death (두려움에) 꽉 잡다
Grim Reaper 죽음의 신, 사신(死神)

intricate
[íntrikət]

n. intricacy

a. 복잡한, 세밀한

4 the *intricate* patterns of the wallpaper

scrupulous
[skrúːpjuləs]

n. scrupulousness

a. 1. 양심적인, 도덕적인 ant. unscrupulous
2. 꼼꼼한, 철저한 syn. meticulous

5 Not all doctors are as *scrupulous* as Mike is.
6 Her new job requires *scrupulous* attention to detail.

radiate
[réidièit]

n. radiation
a. radiant 빛나는, 환한

v. 1. (감정 · 성향 등) 내보이다, 드러나다
2. (빛 · 열 등) 방출하다[되다], 발산하다[시키다] syn. emit, give off
3. (중심점에서) 사방으로 퍼지다, 뻗어나가다

7 She *radiates* warmth and kindness.
8 The sun *radiates* light and heat.
9 The pain originated in my shoulder and *radiated* down my back.

sibling
[síbliŋ]

n. 형제자매

10 Vinnie is an only son; he wishes he had a *sibling*.

voca+ sibling rivalry 형제자매 간의 경쟁 의식

1 그는 심각한 부상을 입어서 살 가망이 별로 없다. 2 나는 Clive가 그렇게 심각한 표정을 짓는 것을 본 적이 없다. 3 그 낡은 공장은 다소 흉해 보인다. 4 벽지의 정교한 무늬 5 모든 의사들이 Mike처럼 양심적이지는 않다. 6 그녀의 새 일은 세부사항에 대한 꼼꼼한 주의를 필요로 한다. 7 그녀는 따뜻하고 친절한 분위기를 풍긴다. 8 태양은 빛과 열을 내뿜는다. 9 통증이 어깨에서 시작하여 등을 타고 내려가며 퍼졌다. 10 Vinnie는 외아들이라 형제나 남매가 있었으면 하고 바란다.

thrust
[θrʌst]

v. 1. 들이밀다, 쑤셔 넣다
2. 달려들다, 공격하다
3. 떠맡기다, 강요하다

1 He *thrust* me roughly toward the wall.
2 The robber *thrust at* Dylan with a knife.
3 His boss *thrust* more pressure *upon* him.

n. 1. 취지, 요점 2. 돌격, 추진(력)

4 What is the *thrust* of his speech?

acrid
[ǽkrid]

a. 1. (냄새 · 맛이) 매운, 쓴 syn. pungent
2. 신랄한, 혹독한 syn. harsh

5 the *acrid* smoke of burning rubber
6 His *acrid* remark surprised his friend.

autonomous
[ɔːtɑ́nəməs]
n. autonomy

a. 자치적인, 자율적인

7 Sicily is an *autonomous* region of Italy.

decrepit
[dikrépit]
n. decrepitude

a. 낡아빠진, 노쇠한, 쇠약해진

8 Most of the houses in this village are old and *decrepit*.

| Nuance | "약한" 관련 어휘 뉘앙스 차이

decrepit 노쇠한, 낡은	늙어서 기력이 없거나 오래 사용하여 낡아빠진 9 a decrepit old man
feeble 연약한	어려서 연약하거나 병에 걸려 약해진 10 The baby's heartbeat was feeble.
fragile 부서지기 쉬운	약해서 다치거나 부서지기 쉬운 11 fragile bones
frail 허약한	나이가 들거나 병에 걸려 야위고 약해진 12 a frail 100-year-old lady

1 그는 나를 벽 쪽으로 거칠게 밀었다. 2 강도는 칼을 들고 Dylan에게 달려들었다. 3 사장은 그에게 더 많은 압력을 가했다. 4 그 사람 말의 요점이 뭐야? 5 고무 태우는 매캐한 연기 6 그의 신랄한 발언이 친구를 놀라게 했다. 7 Sicily는 이탈리아의 자치 지역이다. 8 이 마을의 집들 대부분이 오래되고 낡아빠졌다. 9 노쇠한 남자 10 그 아기의 심장 박동은 약했다. 11 부러지기 쉬운 뼈 12 100세의 쇠약한 노부인

contour
[kɑ́ntuər]

a. contoured
1. 형태에 맞게 만들어진
2. 굴곡이 진

n. 1. 윤곽, 외곽
2. 지도의 등고선 (=contour line)
(a line on a map showing points that are of equal heights above sea level)

1 The painting showed the *contours* of the landscape.
2 a *contour* map
3 a *contoured* handgrip

disperse
[dispə́:rs]

n. dispersal
(=dispersion)

v. 흩어지다[흩어지게 하다], 해산하다[시키다] syn. scatter

4 The government sent orders to *disperse* the crowds that had assembled outside Parliament.

equanimity
[é:kwənímәti]

n. 평정(심), 침착함

5 He took the shocking news with remarkable *equanimity*.

remit
[rimít]

n. remittance 송금(액)
remission
1. (병의) 완화
2. (부채) 탕감, 면제
3. 감형

v. 1. 송금하다, 돈을 보내다 syn. forward
2. (빚 · 형벌을) 면제하다, 경감하다
3. (결정을) 위임하다, 맡기다

6 He *remitted* all of his savings to his home country.
7 *remit* a fine
8 The case was *remitted to* the Supreme Court on appeal.
9 The bank has a *remittance* fee of $10 for sending money abroad.

incisive
[insáisiv]

n. incisiveness

a. (말 · 생각 등이) 예리한, 날카로운 syn. penetrating, acute, keen

10 He was impressed with her *incisive* understanding of the matter.

1 그 그림은 풍경의 윤곽을 보여주었다. 2 등고선 지도 3 체형에 맞는 손잡이 4 정부는 의회 밖에 모인 군중들을 해산시키라는 명령을 내렸다. 5 그는 놀라울 정도로 침착하게 그 충격적인 소식을 받아들였다. 6 그는 저축한 돈 전부를 고국으로 보냈다. 7 벌금을 면제하다 8 그 사건은 대법원 항소심으로 넘어갔다. 9 그 은행의 해외 송금 수수료는 10달러이다. 10 그는 그 문제에 대한 그녀의 날카로운 이해력에 깊은 인상을 받았다.

placid
[plǽsid]

n. placidity (=placidness)

a. 차분한, 잔잔한 syn. tranquil, calm

1 It is easy to babysit her because she is a *placid* baby who rarely cries.

exult
[igzʌ́lt]

n. exultation
a. exultant

v. (성취 등에) 매우 기뻐하다, 기뻐서 날뛰다 syn. rejoice

2 The inventor *exulted in* his realization that he had created something totally unique.

3 The *exultant* crowd poured into the streets as their team won the football championship.

solvent
[sɑ́lvənt]

n. solvency

a. 지불 능력이 있는 ant. insolvent

4 The company became financially *solvent* by the end of the year.

n. 용매, 용제 (a substance that can dissolve another substance)

5 industrial *solvents* for removing oil

treachery
[trétʃəri]

a. treacherous
1. 위험한, 불안정한
2. 배반하는

n. 배반, 배신 syn. betrayal, disloyalty

6 The spy is known for his cruelty and *treachery*.

7 Snow and ice are making driving conditions *treacherous*.

blasphemy
[blǽsfəmi]

v. blaspheme
a. blasphemous

n. 신성 모독, 불경(스러운 언동)

8 His remarks were taken as *blasphemy* by religious leaders.

1 그녀는 잘 울지 않는 순한 아기여서 돌보기 쉽다. 2 그 발명가는 자신이 완전히 새로운 것을 만들어냈다는 것을 깨닫고는 매우 기뻐했다. 3 환희에 찬 군중들은 자신들의 팀이 축구 결승에서 우승하자 거리로 쏟아져 나왔다. 4 그 회사는 그 해 말에 재정적으로 회생했다. 5 기름을 제거하는 산업용 용제 6 그 스파이는 잔인하고 배신을 잘 하기로 유명하다. 7 눈과 얼음 때문에 운전하기가 매우 위험하다. 8 그의 발언은 종교 지도자들에게 신성 모독으로 여겨졌다.

amicable
[ǽmikəbl]

a. 우호적인, 원만한 ant. hostile

1 Eventually they reached an *amicable* agreement.

curtail
[kəːrtéil]

n. curtailment

v. 제한하다, 축소하다

2 The minister has defended the government's rights to *curtail* individual freedom.

profuse
[prəfjúːs]

n. profusion

a. 많은 양의, 풍부한

3 He went into shock because of the *profuse* bleeding.

voca+ a profusion of 많은, 풍부한
in profusion 풍부하게, 굉장히 많이
profuse apology 장황한 변명

prudish
[prúːdiʃ]

n. prudery
(=prudishness)
prude 성에 과민한 사람

a. 성에 대해 과민한, 지나치게 엄격한 syn. strait-laced

4 Koreans are known to be *prudish* in their manner.

IDIOMS

save face 체면을 지키다, 창피를 면하다 (to avoid being embarrassed or losing people's respect)

5 She *saved face* by pretending that someone else had caused the accident.

pay through the nose 너무 많은 돈을 지불하다, 바가지 쓰다 (to pay much more for something than it is really worth)

6 He had to *pay through the nose* to get his car repaired.

1 결국 그들은 원만한 합의에 이르렀다. 2 그 장관은 개인의 자유를 제한하는 정부의 권리를 옹호해 왔다. 3 그는 과다 출혈로 쇼크 상태에 빠졌다. 4 한국인들은 성(性)에 대해 지나치게 엄격하다고 알려져 있다. 5 그녀는 다른 누군가가 그 사고를 일으킨 체해서 창피를 면했다. 6 그는 차를 수리하는 데 엄청나게 많은 돈을 써야 했다.

exercise

A Match the words in the left column to the sentences in the right column.

ⓐ **autonomous**: independent, not under the control of an outside force

ⓑ **incisive**: sharp or clever

ⓒ **radiate**: to give off or to be sent out

ⓓ **decrepit**: old and worn out

ⓔ **disperse**: to distribute or spread

1. Heat ___________(e)d from the pipe.
2. The region will become ___________ if they win the election.
3. The wind will ___________ the seeds of the flower.
4. The ___________ house is not fit to live in.
5. The man made some ___________ comments at the conference.

B Choose the word or phrase that best explains the underlined word.

1. If you ***enhance*** something, you make it ______________.
   ⓐ better ⓑ shorter ⓒ brighter ⓓ harder

2. When an activity is ***curtailed***, it is ______________.
   ⓐ restricted ⓑ overlooked ⓒ encouraged ⓓ legalized

3. When you commit ***treachery***, you ______________ someone.
   ⓐ murder ⓑ cure ⓒ abduct ⓓ betray

4. Someone who engages in ***blasphemy*** ______________ his or her God.
   ⓐ prays to ⓑ quotes ⓒ believes in ⓓ insults

5. If you ***avenge*** yourself on a man, you ______________.
   ⓐ return a favor to him ⓑ scold him for a wrongdoing
   ⓒ punish him for harming you ⓓ give him information

정답 및 해설 p. 381

C Choose the option that is closest in meaning to the underlined word.

1. an ***intricate*** design
ⓐ detailed ⓑ original ⓒ terrible ⓓ realistic

2. a ***placid*** stream
ⓐ flowing ⓑ polluted ⓒ winding ⓓ calm

3. show ***equanimity***
ⓐ courtesy ⓑ contempt ⓒ stability ⓓ pity

D Choose the option that is the opposite of the underlined word.

1. an ***amicable*** conversation
ⓐ dull ⓑ polite ⓒ hostile ⓓ humorous

2. ***exult*** in the news
ⓐ hide ⓑ grieve ⓒ doubt ⓓ exaggerate

3. ***grim*** prospects
ⓐ hopeful ⓑ frightening ⓒ limited ⓓ fair

E Choose the best word or phrase.

1. Which of the following is the best example of an ***appliance***?
ⓐ a flowerpot ⓑ a toaster ⓒ a sofa ⓓ a rug

2. Who would be your ***sibling***?
ⓐ your uncle ⓑ your father ⓒ your sister ⓓ your daughter

3. Which of the following would smell ***acrid***?
ⓐ a flower ⓑ smoke ⓒ a bakery ⓓ cosmetics

4. When you have a ***commitment***, you should ________________.
ⓐ make it a priority ⓑ handle a complaint
ⓒ never compromise ⓓ never ask questions

cavity
[kǽvəti]

n. 1. 충치 2. [의학] 강(인체 내의 구멍이나 빈 공간)

1 I've had two ***cavities*** filled.

voca+ oral[chest/abdominal] cavity 구강[흉강/복강]

aversion
[əvə́ːrʒən]

n. 몹시 싫어함, 혐오 syn. hatred, antipathy

2 She has an ***aversion to*** public speaking.

rally
[rǽli]

n. 1. 대규모 집회, 시위
2. (주가 등의) 반등, 회복세 syn. recovery
3. 장거리 자동차 경주
4. (테니스 등에서) 랠리, 연속적으로 공을 쳐 넘기기

3 hold an anti-war ***rally***
4 a ***rally*** in shares on the Korean stock market
5 Congratulations on your victory in the Safari ***Rally***.

v. 1. (~을 지지하러) 모이다[모으다], 뭉치다
2. 회복하다 syn. recover

6 They ***rallied*** to win the game.
7 After a long illness, my father ***rallied*** his strength.

voca+ rally around 함께 ~를 돕다

grudge
[grʌdʒ]

a. grudging 마지못해 하는
ad. grudgingly 마지못해

n. 앙심, 원한

8 The criminal had a ***grudge*** against the world.

voca+ bear[hold] a grudge against ~에게 원한을 품다

v. ~을 하기 싫다, 마지못해 ~하다, 투덜거리다

9 I ***grudge*** having to pay so much tax.
10 He ***grudgingly*** admitted he made a mistake.

1 나는 충치 두 개를 때웠다. 2 그녀는 연설이나 발표하는 것을 몹시 싫어한다. 3 반전 집회를 열다 4 한국 주식 시장의 주가 반등 5 사파리 랠리 우승을 축하합니다. 6 그들은 경기에서 이기기 위해 뭉쳤다. 7 긴 투병 끝에 아버지는 기력을 회복했다. 8 그 범죄자는 세상에 앙심을 품고 있었다. 9 나는 그렇게 많은 세금을 물기 싫다. 10 그는 마지못해 자신이 실수했다고 인정했다.

tentative
[téntətiv]

n. tentativeness

a. 1. 임시의, 확정되지 않은 syn. temporary, provisional
2. 망설이는, 자신 없는 syn. hesitant

1 The two parties came to a *tentative* agreement.
2 a *tentative* attitude

chronological
[krɑ̀nəlɑ́dʒikəl]

n. chronology 발생 순서, 연대기

a. 연대순의, 발생 순서대로 배열된

3 The list is arranged *in chronological order*.
4 The book includes a *chronology* of her life and works.

voca+ in chronological order 연대 순으로, 발생 순서대로

pensive
[pénsiv]

a. 수심에 잠긴, 생각에 잠긴

5 He became *pensive*, hardly talking to anyone.

defer
[difə́ːr]

n. deferment (=deferral)

v. (일정을) 연기하다 syn. postpone, put back

6 He *deferred* his decision on taking the job.

voca+ defer to ~를 받아들이다, ~에 따르다

enigma
[inígmə]

a. enigmatic

n. 수수께끼(같은 인물), 신비로운 존재 syn. mystery, riddle

7 The whereabouts of the terrorist leader is still an *enigma*.

slaughter
[slɔ́ːtər]

n. 1. (가축의) 도살 2. 대학살 syn. massacre

8 pigs taken for *slaughter*
9 the *slaughter* of innocent civilians

v. 1. 도살하다 syn. butcher 2. 학살하다
3. (경기 등에서) 완패시키다

10 They *slaughtered* us in the game!

1 두 정당은 임시 합의를 보았다. 2 자신 없는 태도 3 그 목록은 연대 순으로 정리되어 있다. 4 그 책에는 그녀의 생애와 작품을 소개한 연표가 들어 있다. 5 그는 수심에 잠겨 거의 아무하고도 말하지 않았다. 6 그는 그 일의 수락 여부 결정을 미루었다. 7 그 테러리스트 지도자의 행방은 여전히 수수께끼이다. 8 도살용으로 데려간 돼지들 9 죄없는 민간인들의 대학살 10 그들이 그 경기에서 우리에게 압승을 거뒀어!

obese

[oubíːs]

n. obesity

a. 비만인, 과체중의

1 *Obese* people have a higher risk of heart disease.

2 A high calorie diet can lead to *obesity*.

admonish

[ədmániʃ]

n. admonition (=admonishment)

v. 호되게 꾸짖다, 훈계하다 syn. reprove, rebuke

3 He was *admonished for* bullying his classmates.

4 Parental *admonitions*, like "Eat your vegetables," vary by culture.

banal

[bənǽl]

n. banality

a. 진부한, 독창성이 없고 시시한 syn. trite, stale

5 Her commonplace writing style made her essay seem *banal*.

congenital

[kəndʒénitl]

a. 선천적인, 타고난 ant. acquired 후천성의

6 *Congenital* heart defects are commonly found in newborns.

voca+ congenital deformity[abnormality] 선천적 기형

| Nuance | "타고난/내재된" 관련 어휘 뉘앙스 차이

congenital 선천적인

| 질병 · 기형 등을 태어날 때부터 지니고 있는

7 congenital disease

innate 타고난, 내재적인

| 특질 · 능력 등을 천부적으로 타고난

8 children's innate ability to learn language

inherent 고유의, 본래의

| 고유의 성격을 이루는 부분이라 따로 떼어낼 수 없는

9 Violence is inherent in human nature.

intrinsic 본질적인

| 어떤 것을 구성하는 데 본질적이고 필수적인

10 Understanding customers is intrinsic to a successful business.

1 비만인 사람들은 심장병에 걸릴 위험이 더 높다. 2 고칼로리 식단은 비만을 일으킬 수 있다. 3 그는 반 친구들을 괴롭히다가 혼났다. 4 "채소를 많이 먹어라."와 같은 부모님의 훈계는 문화마다 다르다. 5 그녀의 평범한 문체는 그녀의 수필을 시시해 보이게 했다. 6 선천적 심장 결함은 신생아에게서 흔히 발견된다. 7 선천성 질환 8 아이들의 타고난 언어 학습 능력 9 폭력은 인간의 본성이다. 10 고객을 이해하는 것은 사업 성공에 필수적인 것이다.

contrive
[kəntráiv]

n. contrivance
a. contrived 작위적인

v. 1. (좋지 않은 일을) 꾀하다, 계획하다, 획책하다
2. (어려운 상황에서) 용케 해내다, 성공시키다
3. 발명하다, (묘책을) 고안해내다 syn. devise

1 We *contrived* a plan to sneak into the theater.
2 Somehow I *contrived* to get tickets for the concert.
3 Richter *contrived* a scale to measure the force of an earthquake.

disseminate
[disémineit]

n. dissemination

v. (정보 등을) 널리 알리다, 유포하다 syn. spread

4 The human rights group tried to *disseminate* information about torture.

fern
[fəːrn]

a. ferny

n. [식물] (고사리 · 이끼 등의) 양치식물 (a type of plant with leaves shaped like feathers, but no flowers)

5 *Ferns* like rich, moist, well-draining soil.

increment
[íŋkrəmənt]

a. incremental 점차 증가하는

n. 1. (급여의) 정기적 인상
2. (수 · 양적) 증대, 증가

6 You will receive annual *increments* every March.
7 the *increment* in productivity
8 Conservatives want *incremental* political reforms rather than radical ones.

matriarchy
[méitriàːrki]

n. matriarch 여자 가장
a. matriarchal [mèitriáːrkl]

n. 모계[모권] 사회 ant. patriarchy 부계 사회

9 *Matriarchy* is a society that is controlled by women.

1 우리는 극장에 몰래 들어갈 계획을 꾸몄다. 2 나는 어렵게 공연 티켓을 구했다. 3 리히터는 지진의 강도를 측정하는 척도를 고안했다. 4 그 인권 단체는 고문의 실태를 널리 알리려고 노력했다. 5 양치류는 비옥하고 습하면서도 배수가 잘 되는 흙을 좋아한다. 6 당신은 매년 3월에 정기 임금 인상을 받을 것이다. 7 생산성 증대 8 보수주의자들은 급진적인 것보다는 점진적인 정치 개혁을 원한다. 9 모계 사회는 여성에 의해 지배되는 사회이다.

plaster
[plǽstər]

n. 1. 회반죽 (a substance covering walls and ceilings to give a smooth surface)
2. *BrE.* 반창고 (*AmE.* Band-Aid)

1 The ***plaster*** on the walls was damaged.

v. 1. 표면을 완전히 뒤덮다 2. (벽 · 천장 등에) 회반죽을 칠하다

2 The wall was ***plastered with*** posters of presidential candidates.

voca+ be plastered all over the papers (어떤 소식이) 주요 기사거리가 되다

renounce
[rináuns]

n. renunciation

v. 1. (지위 · 권리 등에 대해) 공식적으로 포기 선언을 하다
2. (믿음 · 신념 등에 대해) 공식적으로 부인 선언을 하다

3 He ***renounced*** his US citizenship.
4 The priest was famous for his ***renunciation*** of current values.

sparse
[spaːrs]

n. sparseness

a. 적은, 드문드문 있는

5 rural areas with ***sparse*** population

deviate
[díːvièit]

n. deviation

v. (일상적인 것에서) 벗어나다, 이탈하다

6 He had to ***deviate from*** his normal route due to a traffic jam.

a. [díːviət] (일반적인 것에서) 벗어난, 비정상적인 (=deviant)

7 Any ***deviation*** from official policy may be fatal to the prime minister.

voca+ deviation from route 항로 이탈 standard deviation [수학] 표준편차

epidemic
[èpidémik]

n. 1. 유행병, 전염병 2. (전염병 · 범죄 등의) 유행, 급증

8 Hand washing is a good way to prevent a flu ***epidemic***.
9 Iraq is suffering an ***epidemic*** of street crime.

a. 1. 유행병의 2. (사상 · 풍속 등이) 유행하고 있는

1 벽의 회칠이 훼손되었다. 2 그 벽은 대통령 후보자 포스터들로 완전히 뒤덮였다. 3 그는 미국 시민권을 공식적으로 포기했다. 4 그 신부는 현대적 가치관을 거부한 것으로 유명했다. 5 인구가 희박한 시골 지역 6 그는 교통 체증 때문에 평소 이용하던 길을 벗어나야 했다. 7 공식적인 정책에서 이탈하는 것은 수상에게 치명적일 수 있다. 8 손을 씻는 것은 유행성 독감을 예방하는 좋은 방법이다. 9 이라크는 급증하는 노상범죄로 곤란을 겪고 있다.

epidermis
[èpidə́ːrmis]

n. 표피, 상피 (the outer layer of the skin)

1 UV radiation can cause damage to the *epidermis* of the skin.

brandish
[brǽndiʃ]

v. (무기 · 흉기를) 휘두르다 syn. wield

2 The man was arrested after ***brandishing*** a gun in a public building.

intravenous
[ìntrəvíːnəs]

a. 정맥 내의 (=IV)

3 While in the coma, he received *intravenous* feeding.

voca+ vein 정맥
artery 동맥
intravenous injection 정맥 주사

prolific
[prəlífik]

a. 1. 많이 만들어 내는, 다작[다산]의
2. 수많은, 풍부한

4 He is a ***prolific*** actor, having starred in over 100 films.

5 a TV celebrity with a ***prolific*** following of female fans

IDIOMS

see red 매우 화나다, 격노하다 (to become very angry)

6 The thought of her betraying him made him ***see red***.

pull someone's leg ~에게 농담하다, 장난치다 (to tell someone something that is not true, as a joke)

7 Are you really quitting your job or are you ***pulling my leg***?

1 자외선은 피부 표피를 손상시킬 수 있다. 2 그 남자는 공공 건물에서 총을 휘두르다 체포되었다. 3 그는 혼수상태에 빠져 있는 동안 정맥을 통해 영양 공급을 받았다. 4 그는 많은 작품을 하는 배우로 100여 편의 영화에서 주연을 맡았다. 5 수많은 여성 팬들을 거느리고 있는 TV 스타 6 그녀가 자신을 배신했다는 생각이 들자 그는 무척 화가 났다. 7 너는 진짜로 직장을 그만둘 거니, 아니면 농담하는 거니?

day **24** exercise

A Match the words in the left column to the sentences in the right column.

ⓐ **congenital**: present since birth

ⓑ **epidermis**: the outer layer of the skin

ⓒ **contrive**: to make or invent something in a clever way

ⓓ **renounce**: to give something up officially

ⓔ **prolific**: able to produce an abundance of works

1. Tattoos are permanent because the needle goes right through the ________.
2. They ________(e)d a way to get their bicycles back from the thief.
3. He ________(e)d his American citizenship to join the Korean army.
4. She is a(n) ________ writer. She's written over thirty novels.
5. Many children suffer from ________ heart disease.

B Choose the word or phrase that best explains the underlined word.

1. If something is an ***enigma***, it is ________.
   ⓐ enlightening ⓑ frightening ⓒ boring ⓓ puzzling

2. If you bear a ***grudge*** against a man, you feel ________ toward him.
   ⓐ anger ⓑ loyalty ⓒ responsibility ⓓ compassion

3. If someone catches an ***epidemic*** disease, he has a(n) ________ disease.
   ⓐ heart ⓑ serious ⓒ infectious ⓓ chronic

4. If you have an ***aversion*** to something, you ________.
   ⓐ are good at it ⓑ hate it
   ⓒ are attracted to it ⓓ don't understand it

5. If a story is ***chronological***, events ________.
   ⓐ seem disorganized ⓑ are exaggerated
   ⓒ are not true ⓓ appear in order of time

C Choose the option that is closest in meaning to the underlined word.

1. ***defer*** decisions
ⓐ make ⓑ delay ⓒ reach ⓓ follow

2. hold a ***rally***
ⓐ exhibition ⓑ debate ⓒ contest ⓓ gathering

3. an ***obese*** child
ⓐ overweight ⓑ playful ⓒ smart ⓓ studious

D Choose the option that is the opposite of the underlined word.

1. a ***tentative*** plan
ⓐ definite ⓑ realistic ⓒ practical ⓓ ambitious

2. ***admonish*** a child
ⓐ teach ⓑ abuse ⓒ praise ⓓ care for

3. a ***banal*** book
ⓐ second-hand ⓑ unique ⓒ immoral ⓓ famous

E Choose the best word or phrase.

1. Who would you see if you had a ***cavity***?
ⓐ a surgeon ⓑ a dentist ⓒ a lawyer ⓓ a carpenter

2. Who ***slaughters*** animals for sale?
ⓐ a cook ⓑ a butcher ⓒ a vet ⓓ a farmer

3. Which of the following would you ***disseminate***?
ⓐ information ⓑ willpower ⓒ a wound ⓓ an argument

4. Who holds power in a ***matriarchy***?
ⓐ royalty ⓑ the church ⓒ women ⓓ the wealthy

apprehend
[æ̀prihénd]

n. apprehension
1. 불안, 염려 2. 체포 3. 이해

a. apprehensive
우려[염려]하는

v. 1. 체포하다
2. 이해하다, 파악하다

1 The thieves were ***apprehended*** by the security guards.
2 Sally didn't ***apprehend*** that she was in danger.

ratio
[réiʃou]

n. 비율 (a relationship between two things expressed by numbers)

3 The ***ratio*** of men to women at the company is 3:2.

entity
[éntəti]

n. (독립된) 개체, 단위

4 The club operates as a separate ***entity*** from the department.

grumble
[grʌ́mbəl]

v. 1. 투덜거리다, 불평하다 syn. moan
2. 낮게 울리다, 우르릉거리다 syn. rumble

5 He's always ***grumbling*** about something.
6 Everything darkened and the thunder ***grumbled*** in the distance.

n. 불평

7 My main ***grumble*** is concerning the stupidity of the rules.

loom
[lu:m]

v. 1. (거대한 형체가) 불쑥 나타나다, 어렴풋이 드러나다
2. (곤란한 일이) 임박하다, 곧 발생할 듯하다

8 Dark clouds ***loomed*** in the sky.
9 War between the two nations is ***looming on the horizon***.

voca+ loom large 불가피해[중요하게] 보이다

n. 직조기, 베틀

10 She weaves pretty cloth on her ***loom***.

1 도둑들은 경비들에게 붙잡혔다. 2 Sally는 자신이 위험에 처해 있다는 것을 몰랐다. 3 그 회사의 남녀 비율은 3:2이다. 4 동호회는 부서에서 독립된 별개의 단위로 운영된다. 5 그는 늘 무언가에 대해 불평한다. 6 주위가 어두워지더니 멀리서 천둥소리가 우르릉거렸다. 7 내 주된 불만은 그 어처구니 없는 규칙에 관한 것이다. 8 하늘에서 먹구름이 불쑥 나타났다. 9 두 국가 간에 금방이라도 전쟁이 터질 것으로 보인다. 10 그녀는 베틀로 예쁜 천을 짠다.

overwhelm
[òuvərhwélm]

a. overwhelming
저항할 수 없는, 엄청난, 압도적인

v. 1. 압도하다, 놀라게[당황하게] 하다
2. 압도적으로 이기다, 물리치다 syn. overpower

1 The treasures in the museum ***overwhelm*** visitors.
2 Brazil's soccer players ***overwhelmed*** their Mexican opponents.
3 He had an ***overwhelming*** urge to kiss her.

voca+ be overwhelmed by[with] ~에 압도되다

deficient
[difíʃənt]

n. deficiency

a. 1. 결핍된, 부족한 syn. lacking
2. 미흡한, 부실한

4 The research showed that the children were ***deficient in*** vitamin A.
5 the country's ***deficient*** welfare services
6 Pregnant women often suffer from iron ***deficiency***.

woo
[wu:]

v. 1. (지지 · 구매 등을) 호소하다, 얻기 위해 설득하다
2. 구애[구혼]하다 syn. court

7 He is trying to ***woo*** the voters with promises of reform.
8 He ***wooed*** her for months and then married her.

sneer
[sniər]

a. sneering

v. 비웃다, 코웃음치다 syn. scorn, disdain

9 He ***sneered at*** people who liked pop music.

n. 냉소, 비웃음

10 She looked at my old cell phone with a ***sneer***.

judicious
[dʒu:díʃəs]

a. 분별력 있는, 신중한 syn. prudent ant. injudicious

11 Steve made a ***judicious*** decision not to join the group.

1 박물관에 소장된 보물들은 관람객들을 놀라게 한다. 2 브라질 축구 선수들이 멕시코 선수들을 압도적으로 물리쳤다. 3 그는 그녀에게 키스하고 싶은 충동을 참기 힘들었다. 4 조사 결과 그 아이들은 비타민 A 결핍인 것으로 나타났다. 5 그 나라의 부실한 복지 체제 6 임산부들은 철분 결핍으로 고생하는 일이 잦다. 7 그는 개혁 약속으로 유권자들의 지지를 얻으려 애쓰고 있다. 8 그는 그녀에게 몇 달 동안 구애하여 결혼했다. 9 그는 대중음악을 좋아하는 사람들을 비웃었다. 10 그녀는 내 구식 휴대전화를 비웃으며 바라보았다. 11 Steve는 그 단체에 가입하지 않기로 신중한 결정을 내렸다.

barter
[bɑ́ːrtər]

v. 물물교환하다

1 He *bartered* his CDs *for* her comic books.

voca+ barter A for B A와 B를 물물교환하다

n. 물물교환제, 교환품

2 Do you think the *barter* was fair?

convene
[kənvíːn]

n. convenor
1. *BrE.* 노조간부
2. 회의 소집인

v. 소집하다, 불러 모으다 (to arrange a group of people for a meeting)

3 The president *convened* the ministers to discuss the matter.

incur
[inkə́ːr]

v. (나쁜 결과 · 손실을) 초래[자초]하다

4 He had *incurred* the anger of his colleagues by stealing their clients.

deprecate
[déprikèit]

n. deprecation
a. deprecating

v. (강하게) 비판하다, 비난하다

5 The man *deprecated* the government for its misuse of public funds.

6 Despite his self-*deprecation*, he does have a talent for literature.

| Nuance | "비난하다" 관련 어휘 뉘앙스 차이

deprecate 비판하다
| 강한 어조로 어떤 행동을 비난하거나 반대하다.
7 deprecate the effects of TV on children

condemn 비난하다
| 도덕적으로 옳지 않다고 여겨 강한 어조로 비난하다.
8 Politicians universally condemn this act of terrorism.

denounce 규탄하다
| 어떤 대상에 대한 비판이나 반대를 공식적으로 표명하다.
9 His behavior was denounced as immoral.

deplore 개탄하다
| 특정한 행동이나 사건의 비윤리성을 공식적으로 강하게 비난하다.
10 deplore the use of violence against innocent people

1 그는 자신의 CD들을 그녀의 만화책과 맞바꾸었다. 2 그 물물교환이 공평했다고 생각하나요? 3 대통령은 그 문제를 논의하기 위해 장관 회의를 소집했다. 4 그는 동료들의 고객을 가로채 그들을 화나게 만들었다. 5 그 남자는 정부의 공금 유용을 강한 어조로 비판했다. 6 그의 자아비판에도 불구하고 그는 정말 문학에 재능이 있다. 7 아이들에게 미치는 TV의 영향에 대해 강하게 비판하다 8 정치인들은 모두 이런 테러 행위를 규탄한다. 9 그의 행동은 비윤리적이라고 비난받았다. 10 무고한 사람에 대한 폭력 사용을 비난하다

tranquil
[trǽŋkwil]

v. tranquilize
n. tranquility
tranquilizer 진정제

a. 잔잔한, 조용한, 평화로운 syn. still, serene

1 Hugh led a *tranquil* life in the countryside.
2 He takes *tranquilizers* to control his mood swings.

feud
[fjuːd]

n. 장기간의 불화, 다툼

3 a long-running *feud between* the two families

v. 오랫동안 다투다, 반목하다

rebuff
[ribʌ́f]

v. 거절하다, 거부하다 syn. reject

4 She *rebuffed* his attempts to talk with her.

n. 퉁명스러운 반응, 거절 syn. rejection, snub

5 His suggestion to his boss was met with a flat *rebuff*.

dissuade
[diswéid]

n. dissuasion

v. ~않도록 설득하다, 단념시키다 ant. persuade

6 Phil tried to *dissuade* her *from* leaving school.
7 *Dissuasion* can be used to tackle the problem of nations acquiring nuclear weapons.

voca+ dissuade A from v-ing A를 설득하여 ~하지 않게 하다

maverick
[mǽvərik]

n. 독창적으로 행동[생각]하는 사람, 이단아 (an unusual person who has different ideas and ways of behaving from other people)

8 He was seen as a *maverick* in the scientific community.

a. 이단아의, 독특한

9 a *maverick* artist[writer]

1 Hugh는 시골에서 평온한 삶을 살았다. 2 그는 심한 감정 기복을 다스리기 위해 진정제를 복용한다. 3 두 집안 간의 오래된 불화 4 그녀는 자신과 대화하려는 그의 시도를 거부했다. 5 그가 사장에게 한 제안은 단칼에 거절당했다. 6 Phil은 그녀가 학교를 그만두지 않도록 설득하려고 애썼다. 7 국가들이 핵무기를 보유하려는 문제는 설득과 만류를 통해 해결할 수 있다. 8 그는 과학계의 이단아로 보였다. 9 독특한 예술가[작가]

plausible
[plɔ́ːzəbl]

n. plausibility

a. 그럴듯한 (reasonable and likely to be true)　ant. implausible

1 His reasons to quit his job sounded *plausible* to me.
2 The *plausibility* of his defense is being questioned by lawyers.

splinter
[splíntər]

n. (유리 · 나무 · 금속 등의) 부서진 조각, 파편

3 *splinters* of glass

v. 쪼개다[쪼개지다], (조직 등이) 분열되다　syn. shatter

4 Communities have *splintered* as technology has progressed.

voca+ splinter group[party] (정당 등의) 분파

tumult
[túːmʌlt]

a. tumultuous

n. 소란, 소동, (정신적) 혼란　syn. turmoil, commotion

5 The whole city was *in tumult* during the festival.
6 People burst into *tumultuous* applause as he came out on stage.

brittle
[brítl]

a. 1. 부서지기[부러지기] 쉬운, 불안정한　syn. fragile
2. 냉담한, 차가운

7 Bones can become *brittle* as we get older.
8 She gave a *brittle* laugh and turned away.

voca+ brittle bone disease / osteoporosis 골다공증

pernicious
[pəːrníʃəs]

a. 유해한, 해로운

9 A rise in the frequency of *pernicious* viruses concerns medical experts.

voca+ pernicious anemia 악성 빈혈

1 그가 직장을 그만둔 이유는 내가 보기에는 그럴 만했다. 2 그의 방어가 정당했는가에 대해 변호사들이 의문을 제기하고 있다. 3 깨진 유리 조각 4 기술이 발전함에 따라 공동체들이 분열되었다. 5 축제기간 동안 도시 전체가 소란스러웠다. 6 그가 무대로 나오자 우레와 같은 박수가 터져나왔다. 7 나이가 들어감에 따라 뼈가 쉽게 부러질 수 있다. 8 그녀는 차갑게 웃고는 돌아섰다. 9 악성 바이러스의 발생 빈도가 증가하여 의료 전문가들이 우려하고 있다.

idiosyncrasy
[ìdiəsíŋkrəsi]

a. idiosyncratic

n. 고유의 특징, 특이한 성질[습관] (a strange or unusual way of behaving, or a feature that someone or something has) syn. eccentricity

1 Always wearing sunglasses, even indoors, is one of his *idiosyncrasies*.

carnage
[kɑ́ːrnidʒ]

n. 대학살, 살육 syn. massacre, bloodbath, slaughter

2 The civil war in Sudan has resulted in terrible *carnage*.

apocalypse
[əpɑ́kəlips]

a. apocalyptic

n. 1. 세상의 종말
2. 대재난, 대참사
3. (the A~) [성서] 요한계시록

3 A single nuclear war could lead to the *apocalypse*.

4 The movie showed an *apocalyptic* representation of life after a nuclear war.

perennial
[pəréniəl]

a. 1. 고질적인, 장기간 반복되는
2. [식물] 다년생의, 2년 이상을 사는

5 High unemployment rates are a *perennial* problem in Korea.

6 *perennial*[annual/biennial] plants

n. 다년생 식물

IDIOMS

sleep on it (중요한 문제를) 숙고하다, 더 고민하다
(to think about something more clearly before making a decision)

7 There's no rush. *Sleep on it* and tell me what you think tomorrow.

smoke and mirrors 눈속임, 진실을 은폐하는 수단
(something intended to prevent people from clearly seeing or understanding something)

8 This new policy appears to be more *smoke and mirrors*.

1 실내에서도 늘 선글라스를 쓰는 것이 그의 괴벽 중 하나이다. 2 수단의 내전은 끔찍한 살육을 불러왔다. 3 단 한 번의 핵전쟁이 세상의 종말을 부를 수도 있다. 4 그 영화는 핵전쟁 이후의 삶을 종말론적 표현으로 보여 주었다. 5 높은 실업률은 한국의 고질적인 문제이다. 6 다년생[1년생/2년생] 식물 7 급할 거 없어. 잘 생각해 보고 내일 네 생각을 말해 줘. 8 이 새 정책은 더 교묘한 눈속임인 것 같다.

day 25 exercise

A Match the words in the left column to the sentences in the right column.

ⓐ **grumble**: to complain
ⓑ **idiosyncrasy**: a unique characteristic
ⓒ **tumult**: a confusing and noisy situation
ⓓ **overwhelm**: to cause someone to have a strong emotion
ⓔ **deprecate**: to criticize, to show disapproval

1. I was ___________(e)d with his sudden kiss.
2. He was known for his strange ___________.
3. She ___________(e)d all day about missing her favorite TV show.
4. The teacher unfairly ___________(e)d the student's efforts.
5. The novel describes the ___________ of the war years.

B Choose the word or phrase that best explains the underlined word.

1. If you ***sneer*** at someone, you show ___________.
ⓐ respect ⓑ forgiveness ⓒ contempt ⓓ disappointment

2. If people are in a ***feud***, they are ___________.
ⓐ planning ⓑ fighting ⓒ rehearsing ⓓ researching

3. If a man is a ***maverick***, he has ___________ ideas.
ⓐ considerate ⓑ unique ⓒ immoral ⓓ acceptable

4. If something is ***pernicious***, it is ___________.
ⓐ harmful ⓑ tedious ⓒ dead ⓓ creative

5. If the directors ***convene***, they ___________.
ⓐ hold a meeting ⓑ take a break
ⓒ reach an agreement ⓓ retire from public life

정답 및 해설 p. 382

C Choose the option that is closest in meaning to the underlined word.

1. ***barter*** goods
ⓐ sell ⓑ produce ⓒ trade ⓓ design

2. ***brittle*** bones
ⓐ weak ⓑ broken ⓒ tiny ⓓ aching

3. a ***plausible*** excuse
ⓐ ridiculous ⓑ pitiful ⓒ impulsive ⓓ reasonable

D Choose the option that is the opposite of the underlined word.

1. ***apprehend*** a suspect
ⓐ release ⓑ defend ⓒ chase ⓓ identify

2. ***dissuade*** a person
ⓐ insult ⓑ confuse ⓒ encourage ⓓ confine

3. ***deficient*** funds
ⓐ stolen ⓑ adequate ⓒ borrowed ⓓ public

E Choose the best word or phrase.

1. Who would you likely try to ***woo***?
ⓐ someone you don't know ⓑ someone you desire
ⓒ someone who feels sad ⓓ someone who needs help

2. Where would you likely find ***carnage***?
ⓐ at the supermarket ⓑ on a battlefield
ⓒ at the library ⓓ on a ship

3. Which of the following would you ***rebuff***?
ⓐ an offer ⓑ an issue ⓒ a car ⓓ a garden

4. You might get a ***splinter*** if you handle ____________.
ⓐ rubber ⓑ mud ⓒ wool ⓓ wood

abduct
[æbdʌ́kt]
n. abduction
abductor 유괴범

v. 유괴하다 syn. kidnap

1 The girl was ***abducted*** by kidnappers, but later let go.

ballot
[bǽlət]

n. 1. 투표 syn. vote 2. 투표용지 (=ballot paper)

2 The president is elected by universal, equal, direct, and secret ***ballot*** by the people.
3 invalid ***ballot***

voca+ cast ballots 투표하다 absentee ballot 부재자 투표(용지)

v. 1. (~에 대해) 투표를 하도록 요구하다 2. 투표하다

4 Committee members were ***balloted*** on the proposal.

voca+ ballot for[against] ~에 찬성[반대] 투표를 하다

deport
[dipɔ́ːrt]
n. deportation
deportee 추방된 자

v. (국외로) 추방하다 syn. banish, exile

5 Two employees of the North Korean Embassy in Moscow were ***deported*** from Russia.

voca+ deport oneself 처신하다, 행동하다

dreary
[dríəri]
n. dreariness

a. 1. 황량한, 음산한 syn. bleak, dismal
2. 지루한, 따분한 syn. dull ant. cheerful

6 She looked out over a ***dreary*** landscape of gray buildings.
7 It was a ***dreary*** life studying all the time.

genesis
[dʒénəsis]

n. 1. 발생, 기원 syn. origin 2. (G~) [성서] 창세기

8 Tracing the ***genesis*** of a family is the theme of the novel *Roots*.

1 그 소녀는 유괴범들에게 납치됐지만 후에 풀려났다. 2 대통령은 국민에 의한 보통, 평등, 직접, 비밀 선거를 통해 선출된다. 3 무효표 4 위원들은 그 제안에 대해 투표하도록 요구받았다. 5 모스크바에 있는 북한 대사관 직원 두 명이 러시아에서 추방되었다. 6 그녀는 회색 건물들이 늘어선 황량한 풍경을 바라보았다. 7 늘 공부만 하는 따분한 생활이었다. 8 한 가족의 뿌리를 추적하는 것이 소설 'Roots'의 주제이다.

hostile
[hɔ́stail]

n. hostility

a. 1. 적대적인, 비우호적인 ant. amicable
2. (환경 등이) 부적합한, 척박한
3. 적(敵)의 ant. friendly

1 I'm not *hostile to* illegal immigrants.
2 The grains failed to grow in the *hostile* climate of extreme cold.
3 *hostile* territory

stake
[steik]

n. 1. 말뚝, 막대기 syn. pole, stick
2. 내기에 건 돈, 배당액, 지분 syn. bet

4 He planted a *stake* in the garden.
5 high *stakes*

voca+ at stake 위험에 처한, ~이 걸려 있는

liable
[láiəbl]

n. liability

a. 1. 책임을 져야 할, ~할 의무가 있는 syn. responsible
2. ~하기 쉬운, 자칫하면 ~하는 syn. apt, prone

6 You are *liable for* any damages.
7 We're all *liable to* become irritated when tired.

periodic
[pìəriɑ́dik]

n. periodical 정기간행물

a. 주기적인, 정기적인

8 A head injury can cause *periodic* dizziness and headaches.

recur
[rikə́ːr]

n. recurrence
a. recurrent
(=recurring)

v. 1. 재발하다, 되풀이되다 syn. reappear
2. (생각 · 기억이) 되살아나다
3. 의지하다, 호소하다 syn. resort

9 I don't know why the same dream keeps *recurring*.
10 The memory of her appearance often *recurs* to me.
11 *recur to* violence[arms]

1 나는 불법 이민자들에게 적대감을 갖고 있지 않다. 2 혹한의 척박한 기후에서 곡식들은 자라지 못했다. 3 적군 점령지 4 그는 정원에 말뚝을 박았다. 5 큰 배당금 6 당신은 모든 파손에 대해 배상해야 합니다. 7 우리 모두는 지치면 짜증을 내기 쉽다. 8 머리 부위의 부상은 주기적인 어지러움과 두통을 일으킬 수 있다. 9 왜 계속 같은 꿈을 되풀이해서 꾸는지 모르겠다. 10 그녀 모습에 대한 기억이 자주 떠오른다. 11 폭력[무기]에 의존하다

agnostic
[ægnástik]

n. agnosticism 불가지론

n. 불가지론자 (someone who is not sure if God exists), 회의론자

1 He believes in evolution and is an *agnostic* when it comes to religion.

a. 불가지론의

carcass
[ká:rkəs]

n. 1. (짐승의) 시체, 몸통
2. (건물 · 차 등의) 잔해

2 The lion's *carcass* lay rotting in the sun.

3 After the accident, the *carcasses* of burnt-out vehicles were cleared.

credentials
[kridénʃəlz]

n. (항상 복수로) 1. 자격, 능력 syn. certificate, license
2. 신임장

4 His *credentials* proved he could do the job.

5 The new French Ambassador to the U.S. presented his *credentials* to President George Bush.

abdicate
[ǽbdikèit]

n. abdication

v. (지위 · 권리 등을) 포기하다, 버리다

6 A republic was declared after the king *abdicated*.

| Nuance | "포기하다 / 단념하다" 관련 어휘 뉘앙스 차이

abdicate 포기하다	권력 또는 지위를 포기하거나 책임을 저버리다. 7 abdicate the throne
renounce 포기하다	권리 · 지위 · 직함 등을 공식적이며 자발적으로 포기하다. 8 renounce a title[right]
resign 사임하다	직위 등을 임기 만료 전에 공식적으로 그만두다. 9 resign as president
relinquish 양도하다	의지와 상관없이 포기하는 것으로, 미련 · 유감 등의 뜻이 내포된다. 10 relinquish control of a company

1 그는 진화론을 믿으며 종교에 있어서는 불가지론자이다. 2 사자의 시체가 햇볕 아래에서 썩고 있었다. 3 사고 후 불에 탄 차량의 잔해가 치워졌다. 4 그의 자격증은 그가 그 일을 할 수 있음을 입증했다. 5 새로 임명된 주미 프랑스 대사는 George Bush 대통령에게 신임장을 제출했다. 6 왕이 물러난 뒤 공화정이 선포되었다. 7 퇴위하다 8 직함[권리]을 포기하다 9 회장직을 사임하다 10 회사 경영권을 내주다

forfeit
[fɔ́ːrfit]

v. 몰수당하다, 박탈당하다

1 He had to *forfeit* his medal after being disqualified.

n. 벌금, 몰수(된 것) syn. fine, penalty

2 Throwing objects on the playing field will result in a *forfeit*.

a. 몰수된, 상실한

preposterous
[pripɑ́stərəs]

a. 터무니없는, 매우 불합리한 syn. absurd, outrageous

3 The movie's plot was *preposterous*.

municipal
[mjuːnísəpl]

n. municipality 지방자치체

a. 시의, 지방자치의 syn. local, civic

4 The *municipal* council has decided to destroy all illegal structures in the city.

precipitate
[prisípətèit]

n. precipitation
a. precipitative

v. 1. 촉진시키다, 재촉하다 syn. hasten, accelerate
2. 침전시키다, 침전되다
3. 응결하여 비[눈/우박]이 되다

5 World War I was *precipitated* by a political assassination.
6 Cooling the beaker helps *precipitate* the compound.
7 Water vapor condenses to form clouds and *precipitates* as rain or snow.

a. 성급한, 경솔한

8 a *precipitate* action

retaliate
[ritǽlièit]

n. retaliation
a. retaliatory

v. 보복하다, 앙갚음하다 syn. avenge, revenge

9 That soccer player usually *retaliates* if fouled.

1 그는 실격된 뒤에 메달을 몰수당해야 했다. 2 경기장에 물건을 던지면 벌금을 물게 될 것이다. 3 그 영화의 줄거리는 엉터리였다. 4 시의회는 그 도시의 모든 불법 건축물들을 철거하기로 결정했다. 5 1차 세계대전은 한 정치 요인의 암살에 의해 촉발되었다. 6 비커를 식히면 그 화합물을 빨리 침전시킬 수 있다. 7 수증기가 응축되어 구름을 형성하고 비나 눈으로 응결된다. 8 성급한 행동 9 그 축구선수는 누군가가 자신에게 반칙을 하면 대개 보복을 한다.

staunch
[stɑːntʃ]

n. staunchness

a. 1. 지조 있는, 충실한, 완고한 syn. faithful, steadfast
2. 견고한, 튼튼한

1 He was a *staunch* opponent of fascism.
2 a *staunch* bridge

v. (출혈 등을) 멈추게 하다 (=stanch)

3 He *staunched* the flow of blood with a cloth.

strut
[strʌt]

v. 활보하다, 거들먹거리며 걷다

4 The horse *strutted* with great majesty.

n. 1. 점잔빼는 걸음걸이, 활보
2. 받침대, 버팀목

5 The *struts* held up the old structure.

venerate
[vénərèit]

n. veneration

v. 존경하다, 공경하다 syn. admire, esteem ant. scorn

6 In many cultures, spirits are *venerated* and feared.

circumvent
[sə̀ːrkəmvént]

n. circumvention

v. 1. 회피하다, 빠져나갈 길을 찾다 syn. evade, avoid
2. 우회하다, 돌아가다 syn. bypass

7 The corrupt politicians tried to find ways to *circumvent* the law.
8 We headed south to *circumvent* construction.

exonerate
[igzɑ́nərèit]

n. exoneration

v. ~의 결백을 입증하다, ~의 무죄를 밝히다 syn. acquit

9 She was *exonerated* of any guilt.

1 그는 파시즘에 완강하게 반대했던 사람이다. 2 견고한 다리 3 그는 헝겊으로 흘러나오는 피를 막았다. 4 그 말은 대단한 위용을 뽐내며 걸었다. 5 버팀목들이 그 낡은 구조물을 지탱했다. 6 여러 문화권에서 혼령은 경외의 대상이다. 7 부패한 정치인들은 법망을 빠져나갈 방법을 찾으려 했다. 8 우리는 공사장을 우회하려고 남쪽으로 향했다. 9 그녀의 모든 혐의에 대해 결백이 입증되었다.

maladroit
[mæ̀lədrɔ́it]

n. maladroitness

a. 서툰, 요령 없는, 어색한 syn. clumsy

1 His *maladroit* handling of the car almost caused a serious traffic accident.

recant
[rikǽnt]

n. recantation

v. (신앙 · 주장 등을) 공식적으로 부인하다, 철회하다 syn. retract

2 Galileo was forced to *recant* his belief in the Copernican theory.

euphoria
[juːfɔ́ːriə]

a. euphoric

n. 1. 행복(감), 도취 syn. ecstasy
2. [의학] 병적 쾌감, 다행증(多幸症)

3 The winning team was still in a state of *euphoria* the following day.

extoll
[ikstóul]

v. 격찬하다, 매우 칭찬하다 ant. condemn

4 Her book *extolling* the benefits of exercise sold millions of copies.

IDIOMS

behind bars 수감된 (in prison)

5 She has been *behind bars* for a decade.

a drop in the bucket[ocean] 아주 적은 양, 구우일모 (a very small amount)

6 He is so rich that a million dollars is *a drop in the bucket[ocean]* for him.

1 그가 서툴게 차를 운전해서 하마터면 심각한 교통사고가 날 뻔했다. 2 갈릴레오는 코페르니쿠스 이론에 대한 믿음을 버리라고 강요받았다. 3 그 우승팀은 다음 날까지도 기쁨에 도취되어 있었다. 4 운동의 장점을 극찬하고 있는 그녀의 책은 수백만부가 팔렸다. 5 그녀는 10년째 수감되어 있다. 6 그는 아주 큰 부자여서 1백만 달러도 그에게는 새발의 피다.

exercise

A Match the words in the left column to the sentences in the right column.

ⓐ **ballot**: a piece of paper used for voting

ⓑ **deport**: to force someone to leave a country

ⓒ **staunch**: strong or firm, with regards to beliefs

ⓓ **exonerate**: to free from accusation or blame

ⓔ **carcass**: a dead body

1. I am a(n) __________ believer in human rights.
2. I cast my __________ this afternoon.
3. The hungry animals ripped the __________ apart.
4. The witness will __________ the defendant of all charges.
5. He was __________(e)d from the country for illegal activities.

B Choose the word or phrase that best explains the underlined word.

1. When something ***recurs***, it ______________ again.
ⓐ happens ⓑ disappears ⓒ tries ⓓ changes

2. When you ***strut***, you ______________ with confidence.
ⓐ decide ⓑ perform ⓒ insist ⓓ walk

3. When you ***circumvent*** something, you ______________ it.
ⓐ destroy ⓑ invent ⓒ avoid ⓓ discover

4. When an idea is ***preposterous***, it is ______________.
ⓐ basic ⓑ absurd ⓒ creative ⓓ destructive

5. When the queen ***abdicated*** the throne, she ______________.
ⓐ fought the king for it ⓑ gave it up
ⓒ occupied the position ⓓ claimed it for her own

C Choose the option that is closest in meaning to the underlined word.

1. the ***genesis*** of humankind
ⓐ origin ⓑ religion ⓒ development ⓓ intelligence

2. a child that was ***abducted*** from the park
ⓐ returned ⓑ injured ⓒ rescued ⓓ kidnapped

3. play cards for high ***stakes***
ⓐ chances ⓑ percentages ⓒ bets ⓓ cost

D Choose the option that is the opposite of the underlined word.

1. a ***maladroit*** movement
ⓐ clumsy ⓑ graceful ⓒ rapid ⓓ helpful

2. a feeling of ***euphoria***
ⓐ pride ⓑ delight ⓒ sympathy ⓓ misery

3. a ***dreary*** day
ⓐ cheerful ⓑ depressing ⓒ chilly ⓓ peaceful

E Choose the best word or phrase.

1. Which of the following things could not be ***forfeited***?
ⓐ a crime ⓑ property ⓒ a bank account ⓓ a computer

2. Which of the following entities does the ***municipal*** government preside over?
ⓐ a nation ⓑ a group of nations ⓒ a state ⓓ a city

3. Which of the following would a ***hostile*** person most likely do?
ⓐ support a campaign ⓑ argue with others
ⓒ treat others with respect ⓓ hide where no one will find them

4. Your Honor, my client would like to ***recant*** his ________________.
ⓐ crime ⓑ marriage ⓒ testimony ⓓ license

arbitrary
[ɑ́ːrbətrèri]
n. arbitrariness

a. 자의[임의]적인, 독단적인 syn. random

1 He should not have made such an *arbitrary* decision.

compulsory
[kəmpʌ́lsəri]
n. compulsion

a. 강제적인, 의무의, 필수의 syn. mandatory, obligatory

2 Students should undertake nine years of *compulsory* education in Korea.

deliberate
[dilíbərət]
n. deliberation
ad. deliberately

a. 1. 의도적인, 계획된 syn. intentional, planned ant. accidental
2. 신중한 syn. measured

3 It was a *deliberate* misrepresentation of facts.
4 He walks in a slow, *deliberate* way.

v. [dilíbərèit] 신중히 생각하다, 숙고하다

5 The jury *deliberated* for hours before reaching the verdict.
6 I *deliberately* chose this apartment for its natural light.

equator
[ikwéitər]
a. equatorial

n. 적도

7 Ecuador lies on the *equator*.
8 *Equatorial* climates are very hot and wet.

haunt
[hɔːnt]
a. haunted
haunting 잊혀지지 않는

v. 1. (집 · 장소 등에) 귀신이 자주 출몰하다
2. (불쾌한 것이) 지속적으로 괴롭히다

9 They say ghosts *haunt* this house.
10 He was *haunted* by nightmares of the accident.

n. (특정인이) 자주 다니는 곳, 아지트 syn. hangout

11 The club is a favorite *haunt* of jazz fans.

1 그는 그런 자의적인 결정을 내리지 말았어야 했다. 2 한국 학생들은 9년간의 의무교육을 받아야 한다. 3 그것은 고의적인 사실 왜곡이었다. 4 그는 천천히 조심스럽게 걷는다. 5 배심원단은 평결을 내기 전 몇 시간 동안 숙고했다. 6 나는 자연광 때문에 일부러 이 아파트를 선택했다. 7 에콰도르는 적도상에 있다. 8 적도 지방의 기후는 매우 덥고 습하다. 9 이 집은 귀신이 나온다고들 한다. 10 그는 사고의 악몽에 계속 시달렸다. 11 그 클럽은 재즈 음악 팬들이 즐겨 찾는 곳이다.

lament
[ləmént]

n. lamentation
a. lamentable 통탄할, 한심한

v. ~에 애도[유감]를 표하다 syn. mourn, bewail

1 The nation *lamented* the death of their president.

n. 애도 · 비탄의 시[노래 · 글]

2 She read a *lament* at his funeral.

paralyze
[pǽrəlàiz]

n. paralysis 마비, 중풍
a. paralytic

v. 마비시키다, 무력하게 만들다

3 Botox injections *paralyze* the muscles in the face.
4 One of the most frequent causes of *paralysis* is stroke.

crude
[kru:d]

n. crudeness (=crudity)

a. 1. 대강의, 어림짐작의
2. 조잡한, 투박한
3. 무례한, (성적으로) 노골적인 syn. vulgar
4. 천연의, 가공하지 않은 syn. raw ant. refined

5 We made a *crude* estimate of how much cement we needed.
6 The ancient culture used *crude* tools for digging.
7 His *crude* jokes offended me.
8 *crude* rubber

n. 원유 (=crude oil)

soothe
[su:ð]

a. soothing

v. (고통 · 불안 등을) 달래다, 진정시키다 syn. calm, pacify

9 We tried to *soothe* the crying child.
10 Aromatherapy is usually coupled with a *soothing* massage.

voca+ soothe away (고통 · 불쾌감 등을) 없애다

treason
[trí:zən]

a. treasonable (=treasonous)

n. 반역(죄), 이적 행위

11 They were charged with committing *treason* against the government.
12 The jury found their activities to be *treasonable*.

1 온 국민이 대통령의 죽음을 애도했다. 2 그녀는 그의 장례식에서 추도사를 읽었다. 3 보톡스 주사는 안면 근육을 마비시킨다. 4 중풍의 가장 흔한 원인 중 하나는 뇌졸중이다. 5 우리는 필요한 시멘트 양을 대강 계산해 보았다. 6 고대 문화권에서는 땅을 파는 데 조잡한 도구를 사용했다. 7 그의 외설스러운 농담이 나를 화나게 했다. 8 천연 고무 9 우리는 우는 아이를 달래려 애썼다. 10 향기 요법은 보통 몸을 풀어주는 마사지와 병행해서 한다. 11 그들은 정부에 대해 반역 행위를 한 혐의로 기소되었다. 12 배심원 일동은 그들의 행위가 반역이라는 평결을 냈다.

affinity
[əfínəti]

n. 1. 친밀함, 공감
2. 유사점, 밀접한 관계 syn. likeness

1 She had an *affinity* and affection *for* Korea.
2 There is an *affinity between* Spanish and Portuguese.

beset
[bisét]

v. 곤란하게 만들다, 위험에 빠뜨리다

3 The country has been *beset* by civil war and anarchy.

corroborate
[kərɑ́bərèit]

n. corroboration
a. corroborative

v. (주장 · 이론 등을) 뒷받침하다, 입증하다

4 The theory was *corroborated* by many experiments.
5 *corroborative* evidence

arbitrate
[ɑ́ːrbitrèit]

n. arbitration
arbitrator 중재자, 조정자

v. 중재하다, 조정하다

6 The union will *arbitrate* on behalf of the workers.
7 Both sides finally agreed to go to *arbitration*.

| Nuance | "개입하다" 관련 어휘 뉘앙스 차이

arbitrate 조정하다	요청을 받아 공식적으로 나서서 분쟁을 해결하다. 8 WTO agreed to arbitrate a dispute between the US and Japan.
intercede 중재하다, 조정하다	자신이 가진 영향력을 이용하여 선처를 호소하거나 분쟁 해결을 위해 중재하다. 9 The priest interceded on behalf of the criminal.
interfere 간섭하다	상대방이 원치 않거나 쓸데없는 개입 · 간섭을 하다. 10 Please stop interfering and let me make my own decisions.
mediate 중재하다	분쟁 당사자 간에 합의점을 찾도록 돕다. 11 mediate the peace talks

1 그녀는 한국에 친밀감과 애정을 갖고 있었다. 2 스페인어와 포르투갈어는 밀접한 관계가 있다. 3 그 나라는 내전과 무정부 상태로 인해 위험에 빠져 있다. 4 그 이론은 많은 실험으로 입증되었다. 5 확실한 증거 6 노동조합이 노동자들을 대신하여 중재에 나설 것이다. 7 마침내 양측은 중재에 들어가기로 합의했다. 8 WTO는 미국과 일본 간의 분쟁을 조정하는 데 동의했다. 9 목사는 범죄자를 대신하여 중재에 나섰다. 10 제발 간섭하지 말고 저 혼자 결정하게 놔두세요. 11 평화 협상을 중재하다

lucid
[lú:sid]

n. lucidity

a. 분명한, 명쾌한, 이해하기 쉬운

1 This is such a *lucid* explanation that anyone can understand it.

indignant
[indígnənt]

n. indignation

a. 분개한, 분노한 syn. resentful

2 Frank was *indignant at* the service he received at the store.
3 His voice rose *in indignation*.

meddle
[médl]

n. meddler 참견하는 사람
a. meddlesome 참견하기 좋아하는
meddling

v. 간섭하다, 참견하다, 끼어들다 syn. interfere

4 You have no right to *meddle in* my affairs.
5 We have very *meddlesome* neighbors who won't give us a moment of peace.

plight
[plait]

n. 곤경, 어려운 상황[처지] syn. predicament

6 The *plight* of the homeless is often forgotten.

reproach
[ripróutʃ]

a. reproachful

n. 1. 비난, 비판(의 말)
2. 치욕, 망신, 수치 syn. discredit

7 The boss had a few words of *reproach* for Bob's mistake.
8 His behavior brought *reproach* upon himself.

voca+ above[beyond] reproach 흠 잡을 데 없는

v. 비난하다, 나무라다 syn. condemn

9 She *reproached* him for spending too much money on the car.

voca+ reproach oneself 자신을 책망하다

1 이것은 누구나 이해할 수 있는 아주 명쾌한 설명이다. 2 Frank는 그 가게에서 받은 서비스에 화가 났다. 3 그는 화가 나서 목소리가 커졌다. 4 너는 내 일에 끼어들 권한이 없어. 5 우리 이웃 사람들은 참견하기를 무척 좋아해서 조용히 지낼 틈을 주지 않는다. 6 노숙자들의 비참한 상황은 곧잘 잊혀진다. 7 사장은 Bob의 실수를 비난하는 말을 몇 마디 했다. 8 그는 자신의 행동으로 인해 망신을 당했다. 9 그녀는 그가 자동차에 너무 많은 돈을 쓴다고 나무랐다.

sprawl
[sprɔːl]

a. sprawled 사지를 쭉 편
sprawling 마구 팽창하는

v. 1. (팔다리를) 쭉 펴고 눕다, 아무렇게나 뻗다
2. (도시 · 건물 등이) 보기 흉하게 팽창하다, 난립하다

1 I *sprawled* out on the huge hotel bed.
2 The town *sprawled* along the riverside.

n. 1. 무계획적인 도시 팽창(스프롤 현상), 건물이 난립한 지역
2. 사지를 쭉 편 모습

3 Urban *sprawl* has changed the city dramatically.

ramification
[ræ̀mifikéiʃən]

n. (주로 복수로) 부수적[부가적] 결과 syn. implication

4 You must consider all the *ramifications* of the decision.

undaunted
[ʌ̀ndɔ́ːntid]

a. (어려움에도) 굴하지 않고 계속하는, 기죽지 않는 syn. undeterred

5 She's *undaunted* by the rain that threatens to cancel her camping trip.

tout
[taut]

v. 1. (알리기 위해) 극구 칭찬하다, 선전하다
2. 호객 행위를 하다, 손님을 끌다
3. *BrE.* 암표를 팔다 syn. *AmE.* scalp

6 She is being *touted as* the next mayor of Seoul.
7 Street vendors were *touting* for business by the subway station.
8 £20 seats for the show were being *touted* for £100.

voca+ be touted as ~로 부각되다, ~로서 부상하다

n. *BrE.* 암표 장수 syn. *AmE.* scalper

erratic
[irǽtik]

ad. erratically

a. 불규칙한, 종잡을 수 없는, 변덕스러운 syn. unpredictable

9 His pulse was becoming *erratic*.
10 Stocks increased *erratically* this morning.

1 나는 널찍한 호텔 침대에 사지를 쭉 펴고 누웠다. 2 도시 지역이 강변을 따라 난립해 있었다. 3 무질서한 도시 주변 확장으로 인해 그 도시가 엄청나게 변화되었다. 4 너는 그 결정의 모든 파급 효과를 고려해야 한다. 5 그녀는 비로 인해 캠핑 계획이 취소될 수도 있지만 아랑곳하지 않는다. 6 그녀는 차기 서울 시장감으로 떠오르고 있다. 7 노점 상인들이 지하철 역 옆에서 손님들을 끌고 있었다. 8 그 공연의 20파운드짜리 좌석이 웃돈을 붙여 100파운드에 팔리고 있었다. 9 그의 맥박이 불규칙해지고 있었다. 10 오늘 오전 주가가 종잡을 수 없을 정도로 올랐다.

lassitude
[lǽsitù:d]

n. 피로, 무기력 syn. weariness

1 Symptoms of the disease include general *lassitude*.

proscribe
[prouskráib]
n. proscription

v. (공식적으로) 금지하다 syn. forbid, prohibit

2 Some religions *proscribe* birth control.

tenacious
[tənéiʃəs]
n. tenacity

a. 완강한, 집념이 강한, 고집스러운 syn. determined, adamant

3 Jack is one of the most competitive and *tenacious* people I know.

4 She has enough *tenacity* to win the award.

rectify
[réktifài]
n. rectification

v. 바로잡다, 정정하다 syn. correct, set right

5 The school will take the necessary steps to *rectify* the problem.

IDIOMS

the last[final] straw (파국으로 몰고 가는) 마지막 사건[동기]
(the last in a series of bad events that makes it impossible to accept the situation anymore)

6 His insulting my mother was *the last straw*.

take something with a grain of salt 반신반의하다, 곧이곧대로 믿지 않다
(not to completely believe what you hear)

7 Don't believe her. *Take* what she says *with a grain of salt*.

1 그 병의 증상들 중 하나는 만성 피로이다. 2 몇몇 종교는 산아제한을 금지한다. 3 Jack은 내가 알고 있는 경쟁심과 집념이 가장 강한 사람 중 하나이다. 4 그녀는 그 상을 받을 만한 강한 집념을 갖고 있다. 5 학교 당국은 그 문제를 바로잡기 위해 필요한 조치를 취할 것이다. 6 그가 우리 어머니를 모욕하자 나는 더 이상 참을 수 없었다. 7 그녀를 믿지 마. 그녀가 하는 말은 액면 그대로 들으면 안 돼.

day **27** exercise

A Match the words in the left column to the sentences in the right column.

ⓐ **soothe**: to make somebody or something feel better

ⓑ **plight**: a bad and unfortunate situation

ⓒ **reproach**: to express disapproval

ⓓ **ramification**: an additional result of an action, plan or statement

ⓔ **tenacious**: stubbornly determined, unyielding

1. Your mother will __________ you if she finds out what you have done.
2. I hope you will consider the __________ (e)s of your decision before you act.
3. This __________ young woman would not give up.
4. This cream will __________ your sunburn.
5. We gave some money to the poor to help with their __________.

B Choose the word or phrase that best explains the underlined word.

1. If a decision is ***arbitrary***, it's probably __________.
   ⓐ difficult ⓑ controversial ⓒ random ⓓ unconfirmed

2. If you are ***paralyzed***, you can't __________.
   ⓐ move ⓑ vote ⓒ criticize ⓓ breathe

3. If you have an ***affinity*** for something, you __________ it.
   ⓐ notice ⓑ like ⓒ ignore ⓓ don't understand

4. If you are ***undaunted*** by something, you are __________.
   ⓐ not interested ⓑ distressed ⓒ afraid ⓓ not discouraged

5. If a course is ***compulsory***, you __________ it.
   ⓐ don't need to do ⓑ have completed ⓒ have to take ⓓ want extra help with

정답 및 해설 p. 383

C Choose the option that is closest in meaning to the underlined word.

1. ***meddle*** in a matter
   ⓐ interfere ⓑ discover ⓒ participate ⓓ worry

2. ***rectify*** a situation
   ⓐ create ⓑ describe ⓒ correct ⓓ guide

3. ***crude*** oil
   ⓐ healthy ⓑ unrefined ⓒ soiled ⓓ stored

D Choose the option that is the opposite of the underlined word.

1. a ***deliberate*** action
   ⓐ dangerous ⓑ accidental ⓒ significant ⓓ intentional

2. ***corroborate*** the theory
   ⓐ confirm ⓑ contradict ⓒ develop ⓓ support

3. ***erratic*** behavior
   ⓐ predictable ⓑ illegal ⓒ abnormal ⓓ considerate

E Choose the best word or phrase.

1. Which of the following countries lies on the ***equator***?
   ⓐ Canada ⓑ Ecuador ⓒ South Korea ⓓ Australia

2. Which of the following might ***haunt*** a house?
   ⓐ new tenants ⓑ firefighters ⓒ mice ⓓ ghosts

3. Which of the following would you ***lament***?
   ⓐ a death ⓑ a triumph ⓒ a marriage ⓓ a detour

4. An ***indignant*** person thinks something is ______________.
   ⓐ unfair ⓑ ugly ⓒ brilliant ⓓ possible

affluent
[ǽfluənt]

n. affluence

a. 부유한, 풍족한 syn. wealthy, prosperous

1 The department store has ***affluent*** customers.

brisk
[brisk]

n. briskness

a. 1. (동작 등이) 활발한, 재빠른 syn. vigorous
2. (사업이) 호황인
3. (날씨가) 상쾌한, 쌀쌀한

2 I go for a ***brisk*** walk every morning to stay fit.
3 The restaurant was doing a ***brisk*** business.
4 a ***brisk*** fall morning

correlation
[kɔ̀:rəléiʃən]

v. correlate
a. correlative

n. 상관관계, 인과관계

5 a ***correlation*** between smoking and lung cancer

voca+ close[strong/high] correlation 밀접한 상관관계

ditch
[ditʃ]

n. 도랑, 개천

6 I crashed into the ***ditch*** at the end of the road.

voca+ last-ditch attempt[effort] 마지막 시도, 안간힘

v. 1. (물건 · 관계 등을) 버리다, 끝내다
2. *AmE.* 학교를 빠지다 syn. skip
3. (비행기를) 바다에 빠뜨리다, 불시 착수하다

7 Not a few dogs are ***ditched*** when they get sick.
8 Why did you ***ditch*** the computer class?
9 The pilot had to ***ditch*** his aircraft.

predominant
[pridɑ́:mənənt]

v. predominate
n. predominance

a. 지배적인, 주된, 두드러진 syn. dominant, paramount

10 Red is the ***predominant*** color in most of his paintings.

1 그 백화점에는 부유한 고객들이 있다. 2 나는 건강을 유지하기 위해 매일 아침 빠른 걸음으로 산책을 한다. 3 그 식당은 호황을 누리고 있었다. 4 맑고 쌀쌀한 가을날 아침 5 흡연과 폐암의 상관관계 6 나는 길 끝에 있던 도랑에 빠졌다. 7 적지 않은 개들이 병들면 버려진다. 8 왜 컴퓨터 수업을 빼먹었니? 9 그 비행기 조종사는 비행기를 바다에 불시착시켜야 했다. 10 그의 그림들 대부분에서 붉은 색이 가장 두드러진다.

incite
[insáit]

n. incitement

v. 선동하다, 부추기다 syn. provoke, stir up

1 He *incited* the crowd *to* go wild.

voca+ incite sb to-v ~를 …하도록 선동하다

mumble
[mʌ́mbl]

v. 중얼거리다 syn. mutter

2 Tim *mumbled* something in response to my criticism.

voca+ mumble to oneself 혼잣말로 중얼거리다

figurative
[fígjərətiv]

a. 1. 비유적인, 상징적인 ant. literal
2. [미술] 조형의, 형상 묘사의 ant. abstract

3 a *figurative* expression
4 *figurative* paintings depicting everyday life

voca+ in a figurative sense 비유적인 의미에서
figurative arts 조형 미술

retrospective
[rètrəspéktiv]

n. retrospect

a. 1. 회고의
2. *BrE.* [법률] 소급하는 (effective from a particular date in the past)
syn. retroactive

5 write a *retrospective* book
6 Some people pointed out the unfairness of this *retrospective* law.

n. 회고전 (an exhibition of an artist's work from their whole career)

7 a *retrospective* of Picasso

somber
[sɑ́mbər]

n. somberness

a. 1. 침울한, 우울한 syn. grave, solemn
2. (색 등이) 어두운, 칙칙한

8 All the players were in a *somber* mood after they lost the game.
9 She always wears *somber* clothes to work.

1 그는 군중들이 소요를 일으키도록 부추겼다. 2 Tim은 내 비난에 대한 대꾸로 무엇인가를 중얼거렸다. 3 비유적 표현 4 일상 생활을 묘사하는 구상화 5 회고록을 쓰다 6 몇몇 사람들이 이 소급법의 부당함을 지적했다. 7 Picasso 회고전 8 경기에서 진 후 모든 선수들은 침울한 기분이 되었다. 9 그녀는 언제나 칙칙한 색깔의 옷을 입고 출근한다.

vulnerable
[vʌ́lnərəbl]

n. vulnerability

a. 1. 약한, 상처 입기 쉬운 syn. susceptible ant. invulnerable
2. 공격[비난] 받기 쉬운

1 Janet is very *vulnerable* since the breakup with her boyfriend.
2 Baby lions are *vulnerable to* predators.

voca+ be vulnerable to ~에 취약하다, ~에 상처 받기 쉽다

pacify
[pǽsifài]

n. pacifier
1. *AmE.* 고무 젖꼭지
2. 달래는 것[사람]

v. 1. 달래다, 진정시키다 syn. appease
2. (전쟁 · 분쟁 등을 끝내고) 평화를 회복시키다

3 He *pacified* his girlfriend by hugging her.
4 The army temporarily *pacified* the troubled area.

derivative
[dirívətiv]

v. derive
n. derivation

n. 파생된 것, 파생어

5 "Happiness" is a *derivative* of "happy."

a. 모방한, 독창적이지 못한, 판에 박은 듯한

6 Simon was responsible for the *derivative* design.

exterminate
[ikstə́ːrminèit]

n. extermination
exterminator
(해충 등의)구제업자

v. 몰살시키다, 박멸하다, 완전히 없애다

7 All rats were *exterminated* to prevent the plague from spreading.

| Nuance | "없애다/근절하다" 관련 어휘 뉘앙스 차이

exterminate 완전히 없애다 | 특정한 생물 종류나 특정 장소의 동물 등을 대량으로 박멸하다.
8 exterminate cockroaches

eliminate 제거하다 | 불필요하거나 원치 않는 것을 완전히 없애다.
9 eliminate all opposition

eradicate 근절하다 | 질병, 사회 문제 등의 발생 원인을 완전히 제거하다.
10 eradicate crime in our community

root out 뿌리뽑다 | 나쁜 것, 불법인 것을 찾아내어 없애다.
11 root out corruption

1 Janet은 남자친구와 헤어진 이후로 마음이 매우 약해졌다. 2 사자 새끼들은 육식동물의 공격을 받기 쉽다. 3 그는 여자친구를 안아주면서 달래주었다. 4 군대가 분쟁 지역의 평화를 일시적으로 회복시켰다. 5 'happiness'는 'happy'의 파생어이다. 6 Simon이 그 모방한 디자인에 대해 책임이 있었다. 7 역병이 퍼지는 것을 막기 위해 모든 쥐들이 박멸되었다. 8 바퀴벌레를 박멸하다 9 모든 반대파를 제거하다 10 우리 사회의 범죄를 근절하다 11 부정부패를 뿌리뽑다

compliant
[kəmpláiənt]

v. comply
n. compliance

a. (요구 · 규칙 등을) 잘 따르는, 고분고분한 syn. obedient ant. defiant

1 She became more *compliant* in her behavior as she got older.

equilibrium
[ìːkwilíbriəm]

n. 1. 평형, 균형 syn. balance
2. (마음의) 평정

2 Economic *equilibrium* refers to a balance of supply and demand.
3 He tried to maintain his *equilibrium* throughout the debate.

voca+ equilibrium price 균형가격
in equilibrium 평형 상태의, 균형을 이룬

heterogeneous
[hètəroudʒíːniəs]

n. heterogeneity

a. 이종의, 이질적인 (consisting of parts or members that are very different from each other) ant. homogeneous

4 the *heterogeneous* population of the United States

introspective
[ìntrəspéktiv]

n. introspection

a. 내성적인, 자기 반성[성찰]의 syn. introverted

5 Susie is very *introspective*. She understands her weaknesses as well as her strengths.

antecedent
[æ̀ntəsíːdənt]

n. 1. 선례, 전례, 전력
2. (항상 복수로) 조상 syn. ancestors
3. [문법] 선행사 (a word or phrase to which the following word refers back)

6 The crisis in Mexico is without historical *antecedent*.
7 Her *antecedents* came from England.
8 In the sentence "I threw the ball to him and he caught it," "ball" is the *antecedent* of "it."

a. 선행의, 앞서는

1 그녀는 나이가 들면서 행동이 전보다 고분고분해졌다. 2 경제적 균형은 수요와 공급의 균형을 가리킨다. 3 그는 논쟁 내내 평정심을 유지하려고 노력했다. 4 미국의 이질적인 인구 집단 5 Susie는 자신에 대해 매우 냉철하다. 그녀는 자신의 장점뿐만 아니라 단점도 알고 있다. 6 멕시코의 위기는 역사적으로 유례가 없는 것이다. 7 그녀의 조상은 영국 출신이었다. 8 'I threw the ball to him and he caught it.'에서 'ball'은 'it'의 선행사이다.

illuminate
[ilúːmənèit]

n. illumination 빛
a. illuminating
1. 비추는 2. 해명하는, 계몽적인

v. 1. 조명하다, 밝게 비추다 syn. light up, brighten
2. 명백히 하다 syn. clear up, clarify

1 The parade was *illuminated* with Chinese lanterns.
2 This part of the book *illuminates* the author's intention.

prudent
[prúːdənt]

n. prudence

a. 신중한, 현명한 syn. cautious ant. imprudent

3 It may be *prudent* to avoid an investment in a small company like that.

saliva
[səláivə]

v. salivate [sǽləvèit]
군침을 흘리다
a. salivary

n. 침, 타액 syn. spit, spittle

4 DNA can be taken from hair, sweat, or *saliva*.
5 The smell of the delicious bread made the children *salivate*.

voca+ salivary glands 침샘

tamper
[tǽmpər]

v. 함부로 손대다[변경하다], (망가뜨리기 위해) 건드리다[조작하다]

6 I could see that my personal belongings had been *tampered with*.

voca+ tamper-proof (포장 · 용기 등이) 개봉 방지 처리된, 제품 보호 기능이 된
tamper-evident[resistant] (포장 · 용기 등이) 개봉 확인 기능이 되는

culpable
[kʌ́lpəbl]

n. culpability

a. 과실 있는, 비난할 만한, 범죄로 여겨지는 syn. blameworthy

7 If someone becomes fat, is junk food *culpable*?

voca+ culpable negligence 태만죄
culpable homicide 과실치사(우발적 살인)

1 행렬은 초롱불로 밝게 비추어져 있었다. 2 책의 이 부분이 저자의 의도를 분명히 보여주고 있다. 3 그런 작은 회사에는 투자를 피하는 것이 현명할지도 모른다. 4 DNA는 모발, 땀, 또는 침에서 추출할 수 있다. 5 맛있는 빵 냄새에 아이들은 군침을 흘렸다. 6 나는 누군가가 내 개인 물품에 손댔다는 것을 알 수 있었다. 7 어떤 사람이 뚱뚱해지면, 그것은 인스턴트 식품의 잘못인가?

gregarious
[grigέəriəs]

n. gregariousness

a. 1. 어울리기 좋아하는, 사교적인 syn. sociable ant. solitary
2. 군집성의, 떼지어 사는

1 She was very ***gregarious*** before she became ill.
2 Snow geese are ***gregarious*** birds.

palpitate
[pǽlpətèit]

n. palpitations (가슴이) 두근거림

v. (빠르고 불규칙적으로) 심장이 뛰다, 두근거리다 syn. pound, flutter

3 As the MC opened the envelope containing the winner's name, Peter's heart began to ***palpitate***.

virtuoso
[və̀ːrtʃuóusou]

n. virtuosity 탁월한 기량

n. (주로 음악 분야의) 거장, 대가, 명인 syn. master, maestro

4 Famous as an actress, Jones was also a ***virtuoso*** on the harp.

a. 거장의, 대가의

5 a ***virtuoso*** performance

assortment
[əsɔ́ːrtmənt]

a. assorted 다양한 종류의

n. 각양각색의 물건[사람], 모듬 syn. mixture

6 The refugees received emergency supplies containing an ***assortment*** of medicine, clothes, and food.
7 This item is sold in ***assorted*** sizes and colors.

IDIOMS

dog-eat-dog 냉혹하게 사리사욕을 추구하는, 치열하게 다투는 (fiercely competitive)
8 It's ***dog-eat-dog*** in show business.

cut something to the bone 최대한 줄이다 (to reduce something as much as possible)
9 After losing his job, he had to ***cut*** expenses ***to the bone***.

1 그녀는 병에 걸리기 전에 매우 사교적이었다. 2 흰기러기는 무리를 이루어 사는 새이다. 3 사회자가 우승자의 이름이 들어 있는 봉투를 개봉할 때 Peter의 가슴은 두근거리기 시작했다. 4 배우로서 유명한 Jones는 하프의 명인이기도 했다. 5 거장의 공연 6 피난민들은 약품, 옷, 음식이 함께 담긴 긴급 구호품을 받았다. 7 이 물건은 다양한 크기와 색깔로 판매되고 있다. 8 연예계는 약육강식의 세계이다. 9 그는 실직한 뒤에 지출을 최소한으로 줄여야 했다.

day **28** exercise

A Match the words in the left column to the sentences in the right column.

ⓐ **correlation**: a connection or relationship between two things

ⓑ **compliant**: ready to follow orders or do things to please others

ⓒ **tamper**: to touch or change something in order to damage it

ⓓ **assortment**: a mixture of different types of things

ⓔ **gregarious**: sociable, or tending to seek company

1. The ___________ fellow enjoyed parties and preferred not to be alone.
2. There is a(n) ___________ of delicious desserts on the table. Take your pick.
3. Research shows that there is a(n) ___________ between education and income.
4. Don't ___________ with the car, you'll only make it worse. I'll take it to a mechanic.
5. The young man was ___________ with his parents' wishes that he study medicine.

B Choose the word or phrase that best explains the underlined word.

1. If things are in ***equilibrium***, they are ________________.
   ⓐ available ⓑ active ⓒ balanced ⓓ absent

2. When you ***mumble***, you don't speak ________________.
   ⓐ politely ⓑ frankly ⓒ clearly ⓓ seriously

3. If you are ***vulnerable***, you can be easily ________________.
   ⓐ respected ⓑ hurt ⓒ pleased ⓓ promoted

4. When you are ***retrospective***, you think about your ________________.
   ⓐ past ⓑ success ⓒ death ⓓ appearance

5. When you are ***culpable***, you are ________________.
   ⓐ exhausted ⓑ defensive ⓒ skilled ⓓ blameworthy

정답 및 해설 p.383

C Choose the option that is closest in meaning to the underlined word.

1. a ***brisk*** movement
ⓐ energetic ⓑ gradual ⓒ enjoyable ⓓ slow

2. an ***affluent*** businessperson
ⓐ cruel ⓑ greedy ⓒ wealthy ⓓ wise

3. ***incite*** a riot
ⓐ suppress ⓑ encourage ⓒ survive ⓓ relate

D Choose the option that is the opposite of the underlined word.

1. a ***predominant*** feature
ⓐ necessary ⓑ minor ⓒ noticeable ⓓ main

2. a ***somber*** mood
ⓐ sad ⓑ frightful ⓒ grave ⓓ cheerful

3. a ***virtuoso*** of the arts
ⓐ specialist ⓑ collector ⓒ amateur ⓓ critic

E Choose the best word or phrase.

1. Which of the following would be most likely to ***palpitate***?
ⓐ a brain ⓑ a nose ⓒ a heart ⓓ a stomach

2. You try to ***pacify*** someone when he or she is ________________.
ⓐ tired ⓑ upset ⓒ missing ⓓ sick

3. Which of the following would you ***exterminate***?
ⓐ homework ⓑ cockroaches ⓒ advice ⓓ school

4. A ***prudent*** person is one who makes ________________ decisions.
ⓐ quick ⓑ selfish ⓒ secret ⓓ careful

benign
[bináin]

a. 1. 친절한, 인자한, 상냥한
2. [의학] 양성의, 암이 아닌 ant. malignant

1 I remember my grandfather as a ***benign*** old gentleman.
2 It wasn't cancer, only a ***benign*** tumor.

errant
[érənt]

a. (행동 등이) 그릇된, 부정한, 탈선한

3 The woman was suspicious that her husband was engaging in ***errant*** behavior.

expire
[ikspáiər]

n. expiration (=expiry)

v. 1. 만료되다, 끝나다 syn. terminate, run out
2. 죽다 syn. perish

4 My driver's license ***expires*** in June.
5 Ophelia ***expires*** in Act IV of *Hamlet*.
6 ***expiration*** date

introverted
[íntrəvə̀ːrtid]

n. introversion 내성적인 성격
introvert 내성적인 사람

a. 내성적인 ant. extroverted, outgoing

7 He seems ***introverted*** at times, but he actually is an outgoing person.

marital
[mǽrətl]

a. 결혼 (생활)의, 부부의 syn. matrimonial, conjugal

8 He is not married, so his ***marital*** status is single.

voca+ marital status: married / single / divorced 결혼 여부: 기혼 / 미혼 / 이혼

---

1 나는 우리 할아버지를 인자한 노신사로 기억하고 있다. 2 그것은 암이 아니라 양성 종양일 뿐이었다. 3 그 여자는 남편이 바람을 피우고 있다고 의심했다. 4 내 운전 면허는 6월에 만료된다. 5 Ophelia는 연극 'Hamlet'의 4막에서 죽는다. 6 만료일(유통 기한) 7 그는 때때로 내성적인 사람처럼 보이지만 실제로는 활달한 사람이다. 8 그는 결혼하지 않았으므로 그의 결혼 상황은 미혼이다.

pesticide
[péstisàid]

n. 살충제 syn. insecticide

1 vegetables grown without the use of *pesticides*

remorse
[rimɔ́ːrs]

a. remorseful
remorseless 냉혹한, 무정한

n. 후회, 양심의 가책 syn. regret, repentance

2 Mike was filled with *remorse* after the car crash.
3 The *remorseless* killer has been jailed for life.

reprehensible
[rèprihénsəbl]

a. 비난받을 만한, 괘씸한 syn. blameworthy, deplorable

4 Your aggression toward her is *reprehensible*.

stir
[stəːr]

a. stirring 자극하는, 감동시키는

v. 1. 휘젓다, 뒤섞다
2. 흔들다, 움직이다, 살랑거리게 하다
3. 자극하다, 감정을 일으키다 syn. stimulate

5 He *stirred* milk *into* his coffee.
6 The strong wind *stirred* the trees around us.
7 Her words *stirred* him *into* action.

voca+ stir up (분란 등을) 불러일으키다

n. 1. 뒤섞음, 휘젓기
2. 혼란, 소동, 흥분

voca+ cause[create] a stir 흥분[소동]을 일으키다

submissive
[səbmísiv]

v. submit
n. submission

a. 복종[순종]하는, 자기 주장을 하지 않는 syn. obedient ant. assertive

8 Many bosses want their workers to be *submissive*.

1 농약을 쓰지 않고 재배된 채소 2 Mike는 차 사고 이후 양심의 가책에 시달렸다. 3 그 비정한 살인자는 무기징역을 살고 있다. 4 그녀에 대한 너의 공격적인 태도는 비난받아 마땅하다. 5 그는 커피에 우유를 넣고 섞었다. 6 강한 바람이 우리 주위의 나무들을 흔들었다. 7 그녀의 말이 그의 행동을 이끌어냈다. 8 많은 고용주들은 직원들이 순종하기를 바란다.

vacillate
[vǽsileit]

n. vacillation

v. 갈팡질팡하다, 망설이다 syn. waver

1 He *vacillated between* going to college *and* getting a job.

claustrophobia
[klɔ̀ːstrəfóubiə]

a. claustrophobic

n. 밀실 공포증 (fear of being in enclosed spaces)

2 Tom experiences *claustrophobia* in elevators.

voca+ phobia 혐오증
acrophobia / fear of heights 고소 공포증

cogent
[kóudʒənt]

n. cogency

a. (논증 · 추론 등이) 설득력 있는, 명확한 syn. convincing

3 Her defense to the judge wasn't *cogent*.

succumb
[səkʌ́m]

v. 1. (유혹 등에) 굴복하다, 압도되다
2. (병 · 부상 등으로) 죽다, 고통을 겪다

4 I often *succumb to* her sweet talk.
5 Lewis *succumbed to* cancer in 1985.

voca+ succumb to ~에 굴복하다, (병으로) 죽다

| Nuance | "굴복하다 / 항복하다" 관련 어휘 뉘앙스 차이

succumb 굴복하다, 압도되다	자신보다 우세한 것에 압도당하여 굴복하다. 6 succumb to the throne
defer 따르다, 인정하다	권위 · 지식 등의 우월함을 인정하여 그 사람의 의견이나 결정을 따르다. 7 defer to the wisdom of a teacher
surrender 항복하다	전쟁 등에서 공식적으로 항복하다. 8 Japan surrendered to America right after the atomic bombing.
submit 복종하다, 굴복하다	저항을 시도하나 대안이 없어서 굴복하다. 9 submit to new rules

1 그는 대학에 갈지 취직을 할지 망설였다. 2 Tom은 엘리베이터 안에서 밀실 공포증을 느낀다. 3 판사에게 한 그녀의 변호는 설득력이 없었다. 4 나는 그녀의 감언이설에 곧잘 넘어간다. 5 Lewis는 1985년에 암으로 죽었다. 6 왕권에 굴복하다 7 선생님의 지혜를 따르다 8 일본은 원자 폭탄 투하 직후 미국에게 항복했다. 9 새 법칙을 따르다

inscription
[inskrípʃən]

v. inscribe
a. inscriptive

n. 새겨진 글자, 비문

1 The *inscriptions* on the stones were written in ancient Egyptian.
2 The names of the previous kings were *inscribed* on the monument.

oblivious
[əblíviəs]

n. oblivion 1. 망각 2. 의식 없음
obliviousness 염두에 두지 않음

a. 깨닫지 못하는, 안중에 없는 syn. unaware, unmindful

3 Jane seemed *oblivious to* the seriousness of her situation.
4 The singer who once enjoyed great popularity has gradually faded into *oblivion*.

prodigal
[prádigəl]

n. prodigality

a. 낭비하는, 방탕하게 쓰는 syn. extravagant, wasteful

5 *Prodigal* habits die hard.

voca+ prodigal son [성서] 회개한[돌아온] 탕아

n. 방탕아 (someone who leaves their family, but who is sorry later and returns)

progeny
[prádʒəni]

n. 1. 자식, 자손, 후계자 syn. descendants, offspring
2. 결과, 소산

6 He was proud of the achievements of his *progeny*.
7 The series are the *progeny* of his earlier writings.

deference
[défərəns]

a. deferential

n. 존경, 경의, 존중 syn. respect, honor

8 She decided not to marry him *in deference to* her father.

voca+ in[out of] deference to ~을 존중하여

1 그 돌들에 새겨진 글들은 고대 이집트어로 쓰여졌다. 2 역대 왕들의 이름이 기념비에 새겨졌다. 3 Jane은 자신이 처한 상황의 심각성을 깨닫지 못한 것 같았다. 4 한때 대단한 인기를 누렸던 그 가수는 점차 잊혀졌다. 5 낭비벽은 좀처럼 고치기 힘들다. 6 그는 자기 자식들의 업적을 자랑스러워했다. 7 그 시리즈는 그의 초기 저작의 산물이다. 8 그녀는 아버지의 의견을 존중해서 그와 결혼하지 않기로 결심했다.

reverence
[révərəns]

v. revere
a. reverent
(=reverential)

n. 경외, 숭배, 대단한 존경 syn. awe, admiration

1 Religious people have *reverence to* their god.
2 The football player was *revered* as a national hero.

voca+ Your Reverence 신부님[목사님]

sullen
[sʌ́lən]

n. sullenness

a. 1. 부루퉁한, 시무룩한 syn. sulky
2. (날씨가) 잔뜩 흐린, 맑지 않은

3 The boy's appearance was *sullen*.
4 The man looked up at the *sullen* sky.

wayward
[wéiwərd]

a. 말을 안 듣는, 제멋대로인, 통제불능의 syn. unruly ant. obedient

5 He tried everything to change his son's *wayward* behavior.

diatribe
[dáiətràib]

n. 통렬한 비난(의 말 · 글), 혹평

6 The NGO presented a *diatribe against* the government.

voca+ launch into a diatribe against ~에 대해 비난을 퍼붓다

exude
[igzú:d]

v. 1. (자신감 · 매력 · 분위기 등을) 발산하다
2. (냄새 · 액체 등이 지속적으로) 스며[배어] 나오다 syn. ooze

7 She *exuded* confidence.
8 Compared to many flowers, roses *exude* a strong fragrance.

voca+ exude from ~로부터 스며나오다[풍겨나오다]

1 신앙심이 깊은 사람들은 자신들의 신에 대해 경외심을 갖고 있다. 2 그 축구선수는 국가적 영웅으로 존경받았다. 3 그 소년의 표정은 시무룩했다. 4 그 남자는 잔뜩 찌푸린 하늘을 쳐다보았다. 5 그는 아들의 통제불가능한 행실을 고치기 위해 온갖 시도를 했다. 6 그 비정부 기구는 정부에 대해 통렬한 비난을 했다. 7 그녀에게서 자신감이 풍겨져 나왔다. 8 많은 꽃들과 비교했을 때, 장미는 향기가 강한 편이다.

mitigate
[mítigèit]

n. mitigation
a. mitigating

v. 완화하다, 경감하다, 덜어주다 syn. alleviate, relieve

1 Soil erosion is ***mitigated*** by the planting of trees.
2 His several years of voluntary service was regarded as *mitigating circumstances.*

voca+ mitigating circumstances[factors] [법률] (형기의) 경감 사유, 정상참작되는 사실

repugnant
[ripʌ́gnənt]

n. repugnance

a. 비위에 거슬리는, 불쾌한, 혐오스러운 syn. disgusting, repellent

3 Animal experiments are ***repugnant** to* many people.

acumen
[əkjúːmən]

n. 통찰력, 안목, 수완 syn. insight

4 He is blessed with great business ***acumen***.

voca+ business[financial / political] acumen 사업[경제 / 정치] 수완

fervor
[fə́ːrvər]

a. fervid

n. 열정, 열렬함 syn. enthusiasm

5 She has pursued her art career *with **fervor*** and dedication.
6 millions of ***fervid*** soccer fans

IDIOMS

a pain in the neck 골칫거리, 눈엣가시, 성가신 일 (someone or something that is very annoying)
7 It's *a pain in the neck* having to clean this stain.

bite the bullet 이를 악물고 참다, 과감히 맞서다 (to start dealing with an unpleasant or dangerous situation)
8 She wanted to give up, but had to *bite the bullet* to survive severe competition.

1 토양 침식은 나무를 심음으로써 완화된다. 2 그의 수년간의 봉사 활동이 정상참작되었다. 3 동물 실험은 많은 사람들에게 혐오감을 준다. 4 그는 뛰어난 사업 수완을 타고났다. 5 그녀는 열정과 헌신을 다해 자신의 예술 세계를 추구해왔다. 6 수백만의 열렬한 축구팬들 7 이 얼룩을 닦아내야 하는 것은 성가신 일이다. 8 그녀는 포기하고 싶었지만 혹독한 경쟁에서 살아남기 위해 이를 악물어야만 했다.

day 21 day 22 day 23 day 24 day 25 day 26 day 27 day 28 day 29 day 30

exercise

A Match the words in the left column to the sentences in the right column.

ⓐ **sullen**: silently angry or gloomy

ⓑ **reverence**: respect or high esteem

ⓒ **errant**: behaving badly or not following the rules

ⓓ **repugnant**: disgusting or offensive

ⓔ **acumen**: the ability to think quickly and make good judgments

1. Regard your parents with ___________.
2. The ___________ children were punished.
3. His business ___________ is what made him successful.
4. A(n) ___________ smell came from the fridge.
5. The girl was ___________ when she didn't get what she wanted.

B Choose the word or phrase that best explains the underlined word.

1. I show ***remorse*** when I feel ______________.
   ⓐ proud ⓑ guilty ⓒ bored ⓓ interested

2. ***Pesticides*** are used to ______________.
   ⓐ fertilize crops ⓑ kill insects
   ⓒ scare away predators ⓓ enhance the flavor of food

3. If you are ***introverted***, you are probably ______________.
   ⓐ talkative ⓑ tidy ⓒ shy ⓓ outgoing

4. If you ***succumb*** to demands, you ______________ them.
   ⓐ suggest ⓑ ask for
   ⓒ give in to ⓓ stand firm against

5. If you are ***oblivious*** of something, you are ______________ it.
   ⓐ unaware of ⓑ a supporter of
   ⓒ in denial of ⓓ related to

정답 및 해설 p. 384

C Choose the option that is closest in meaning to the underlined word.

1. a ***benign*** tumor
   ⓐ harmless ⓑ terminal ⓒ spreading ⓓ large

2. religious ***fervor***
   ⓐ faith ⓑ ceremony ⓒ enthusiasm ⓓ discrimination

3. ***exude*** confidence
   ⓐ lack ⓑ encourage ⓒ fake ⓓ show

D Choose the option that is the opposite of the underlined word.

1. a ***submissive*** partner
   ⓐ compliant ⓑ passive ⓒ domineering ⓓ former

2. a ***cogent*** argument
   ⓐ weak ⓑ organized ⓒ main ⓓ similar

3. ***mitigate*** a threat
   ⓐ imply ⓑ lessen ⓒ intensify ⓓ surrender

E Choose the best word or phrase.

1. Which of the following will ***expire***?
   ⓐ a funeral ⓑ snake skin boots ⓒ a credit card ⓓ a bicycle

2. Which of the following would have an ***inscription*** on it?
   ⓐ an address ⓑ a gravestone ⓒ a candidate ⓓ a computer

3. The couple made their ***marital*** ________________.
   ⓐ furniture ⓑ handbook ⓒ budgets ⓓ vows

4. If you had ***claustrophobia***, where would you feel uncomfortable?
   ⓐ outdoors ⓑ in a mall ⓒ on stage ⓓ in an elevator

arithmetic
[əríθmətìk]

n. 산수, 산술, 계산

1 mental *arithmetic*

a. 셈의, 산수의 (=arithmetical)

2 Students were given *arithmetic* problems to solve.

concur
[kənkə́ːr]

n. concurrence
a. concurrent 동시에 일어나는

v. 1. 동의하다
2. 동시에 발생하다 syn. coincide

3 "Absolutely!" *concurred* Jonathan.
4 Stephanie's Caribbean cruise *concurs with* hurricane season.
5 pollution *concurrent* with civilization

denomination
[dinɑ̀minéiʃən]

v. denominate 특정 화폐 단위를 붙이다
a. denominational 종파의

n. 1. [종교] 종파, 교파
2. (화폐 등의) 단위, 액면 (금액)

6 There are thousands of Christian *denominations* throughout the world.
7 coins of various *denominations*

depict
[dipíkt]

n. depiction

v. (그림 · 언어 등으로) 묘사하다

8 The novel *depicts* Korean society in the 1950s.

voca+ depict A as B A를 B로 묘사하다

9 the film's vivid *depiction* of a crime

evoke
[ivóuk]

n. evocation
a. evocative

v. (감정 · 기억 등을) 불러일으키다, 되살려내다 syn. bring back

10 The song *evoked* memories of my wedding day.
11 a picture *evocative of* the sea

1 암산 2 학생들에게 풀어야 할 산수 문제가 주어졌다. 3 "당연하지!"하고 Jonathan이 동의했다. 4 Stephanie의 카리브해 유람선 여행은 허리케인이 오는 시기와 겹친다. 5 문명과 동시에 발생하는 공해 6 전세계에는 수천 개의 기독교 종파가 있다. 7 다양한 단위의 동전들 8 그 소설은 1950년대의 한국 사회를 묘사하고 있다. 9 그 영화의 생생한 범죄 묘사 10 그 노래는 내 결혼식 날의 기억을 불러일으켰다. 11 바다를 생각나게 하는 그림

hindrance
[híndrəns]

v. hinder

n. 방해(하는 것), 장애물 syn. interference

1 He was more of a *hindrance* than a help.
2 An injury was *hindering* him *from* playing his best.

lethal
[líːθəl]

a. 치명적인, 죽음을 초래하는 syn. fatal, deadly

3 The amount of medicine she was about to take was *lethal*.

voca+ lethal dose 치사량 lethal weapon 치명적 무기[흉기]

penetrate
[pénətrèit]

n. penetration
a. penetrating
1. 꿰뚫는, 침투하는
2. 예리한, 현명한

v. 1. 뚫다, 뚫고 들어가다 syn. get through
2. (사상 · 문화 · 상품 등이) 침투하다, 스며들다
3. 이해하다, 규명하다, 간파하다

4 The knife had *penetrated* his skin.
5 Islam has *penetrated* deep into northern Africa.
6 Some say that science will *penetrate* the mysteries of life.
7 a *penetrating* question

spontaneous
[spɑntéiniəs]

n. spontaneity

a. 자연히 발생하는, 미리 계획하지 않은, 자발적인

8 The audience gave the speaker a *spontaneous* applause.
9 *Spontaneity* is important to me because I don't like routine.

relevance
[réləvəns]

a. relevant

n. 연관성, 타당성, 적합성 ant. irrelevance

10 I don't see the *relevance* of your question.
11 That comment is not *relevant to* this discussion.

voca+ relevant to ~와 연관성이 있는

1 그는 도움이 되기보다는 오히려 방해가 되었다. 2 그는 부상으로 인해 기량을 최고로 발휘하지 못했다. 3 그녀가 복용하려 했던 약의 분량은 치사량이었다. 4 칼이 그의 피부를 뚫고 들어갔다. 5 이슬람교는 북아프리카 내륙 깊숙이 파고들었다. 6 몇몇 사람들은 과학이 생명의 신비를 규명해 낼 거라고 말한다. 7 예리한 질문 8 청중들은 시키지 않았는데도 그 연사에게 진심에서 우러나오는 박수갈채를 보냈다. 9 나는 틀에 박힌 것을 좋아하지 않기 때문에 내게는 자발성이 중요하다. 10 네 질문은 연관성이 없어 보인다. 11 그 발언은 이 토론과 관련이 없다.

bluster
[blʌ́stər]

a. blustering (바람이) 세차게 부는 (=blustery)

v. 1. 고함치다, 괜히 화난 듯이 소리치다
2. 바람이 세게 불다

1 "I don't care," he *blustered*.
2 The wind was *blustering* across the lake.

n. 허세, 고함

3 She was tired of hearing his *bluster*.

courier
[kúriər]

n. 배달원, (급송) 택배원

4 I sent her a birthday present by *courier*.

dormant
[dɔ́ːrmənt]

n. dormancy

a. 잠복 중인, 휴지기의 ant. active

5 Mount Haleakala is the world's largest *dormant* volcano.

voca+ lie[remain] dormant 활동하지 않다, 잠재해 있다

obnoxious
[əbnάkʃəs]

n. obnoxiousness

a. 불쾌한, 무례한

6 We're not going to invite him to the party because we think he's *obnoxious*.

| Nuance | "불쾌한" 관련 어휘 뉘앙스 차이

obnoxious 역겨운, 몹시 불쾌한 | 일부러 무례하게 굴거나 극도로 불쾌한 감정을 유발하는
7 The teens' behavior was obnoxious.

repugnant 비위에 거슬리는 | 강한 혐오감이나 역겨움을 불러일으키는
8 Cannibalism seems repugnant in the modern world.

abhorrent 용납할 수 없는 | 비윤리적으로 여겨져서 절대 받아들일 수 없는
9 It is abhorrent to slaughter animals in a cruel way.

1 "난 상관 안해."라고 그는 괜히 큰소리를 쳤다. 2 호수 너머에서 바람이 거세게 불어왔다. 3 그녀는 그가 허세부리는 것을 듣기가 지겨웠다. 4 나는 그녀에게 택배로 생일 선물을 보냈다. 5 Haleakala산은 전세계에서 가장 큰 휴화산이다. 6 우리는 그가 몹시 불쾌한 사람이라고 생각하기 때문에 파티에 초대하지 않을 것이다. 7 그 십대들의 행동은 불쾌했다. 8 현대 사회에서 식인 풍습은 혐오감을 불러일으킨다. 9 동물을 잔인한 방법으로 도살하는 것은 절대 용납할 수 없다.

fluctuate
[flʌ́ktʃuèit]

n. fluctuation

v. (가격 등이) 변동하다, 오르내리다 syn. vary

1 Oil prices are *fluctuating* between $65 and $70 a barrel.
2 *fluctuation* in the exchange rate

indulge
[indʌ́ldʒ]

n. indulgence
a. indulgent
멋대로 하게 하는, 관대한

v. 1. (나쁜 것에) 탐닉하다, 빠지다
2. (욕망을) 충족시키다, (아이를) 제멋대로 하게 두다

3 It doesn't help to *indulge in* gossip.
4 *Indulging* your children will spoil them.

voca+ indulge yourself 마음껏 즐기다[먹다]
indulge in (좋지 않은 일에) 연루되다

morbid
[mɔ́ːrbid]

n. morbidity 1. 병적 상태 2. 사망률

a. 1. (죽음 등의) 음울한 것에 관심이 많은, 병적으로 몰입하는
2. 병적인, 병에 기인한

5 She read about the murder with *morbid* interest.
6 a *morbid* gene
7 This drug will contribute to the decrease in malaria *morbidity*.

pompous
[pάmpəs]

n. pomposity
(=pompousness)

a. 잘난 척하는, 거드름 피우는 syn. pretentious

8 I found their remarks *pompous* and annoying.

residue
[rézidjùː]

a. residual

n. 잔류물, 나머지, 찌꺼기

9 pesticide *residue* on agricultural produce
10 *residual* income

1 배럴당 석유 가격이 65달러에서 70달러 사이를 오르내리고 있다. 2 환율 변동 3 남의 뒷얘기에 열중하는 것은 좋을 것이 없다. 4 자녀가 하고 싶어하는 대로 다 들어주면 버릇이 나빠질 것이다. 5 그녀는 병적인 관심을 보이며 그 살인 사건에 관한 글을 읽었다. 6 질병과 관련된 유전자 7 이 약은 말라리아 환자들의 사망률 감소에 기여할 것이다. 8 내가 보기에 그들의 발언은 거만하고 짜증스러웠다. 9 농산물에 남아 있는 농약 잔류물 10 세금을 제한 실수입

static
[stǽtik]

a. 정체된, 움직임[변화] 없는 ant. dynamic

1 The birth rate in the country remains *static*.

n. 1. (전파 수신기의) 잡음
2. 정전기 (=static electricity)

2 There was so much *static* on the radio.

uproar
[ʌ́prɔ̀ːr]

a. uproarious 떠들썩한

n. 소란, 항의, 거센 비난

3 The newspaper article caused an *uproar*.
4 She threw an *uproarious* New Year's Eve party.

voca+ in (an) uproar 소란한

eclectic
[ekléktik]

n. eclecticism 절충주의

a. 취사선택한, 정선된, 절충된 (selecting the best items from a variety of sources)

5 I have an *eclectic* mix of furniture in my apartment.

exculpate
[ékskʌlpèit]

n. exculpation
a. exculpatory

v. ~의 무죄를 입증[선고]하다 syn. acquit

6 Paul will surely be *exculpated* when the truth is known.
7 *Exculpatory* evidence clears a person of guilt.

libel
[láibəl]

a. libelous

n. (글을 통한) 비방, 모함, 허위 사실 유포

8 The actor sued the newspaper for *libel*.

v. 글을 써서 비방[모함]하다

1 그 나라의 출산율은 변화가 없다. 2 라디오에서 잡음이 아주 많이 들렸다. 3 그 신문 기사는 거센 비난을 받았다. 4 그녀는 떠들썩한 송년 파티를 열었다. 5 내 아파트에는 필요에 따라 장만한 여러 가지 가구들이 있다. 6 진실이 밝혀지면 Paul은 반드시 무죄가 입증될 것이다. 7 무죄를 입증하는 증거는 피고인의 혐의를 벗겨 준다. 8 그 배우는 그 신문사를 명예훼손 혐의로 고소했다.

reincarnation
[rìːinkɑːrnéiʃən]

v. reincarnate

n. 윤회, 환생(한 사람 · 동물)

1 Buddhists believe in *reincarnation*.
2 I want to be *reincarnated* as a bird.

eerie
[íəri]

n. eeriness
ad. eerily

a. 괴이한, 섬뜩한, 오싹한

3 I had an *eerie* feeling that somebody was following me.
4 Her voice is *eerily* similar to my dead friend's.

disparage
[dispǽridʒ]

n. disparagement
a. disparaging

v. (업적 등을) 깔보다, 깎아내리다 syn. belittle

5 I have no intention of *disparaging* your achievements.
6 My sister was the target of his *disparagement*.

castigate
[kǽstigèit]

n. castigation

v. 신랄하게 비판하다, 꾸짖다, 벌하다 syn. chastise

7 I *castigated* myself *for* being so careless.

IDIOMS

be green with envy 부러워하다, 질투하다 (to be jealous of someone)

8 Julie is going to Europe and I'*m green with envy*.

be up to one's neck in something ~에 매여 있다, ~로 바쁘다 (to be completely involved in or busy with something)

9 She'*s up to her neck in* this project.

1 불교도들은 윤회를 믿는다. 2 나는 한 마리 새로 환생하고 싶다. 3 나는 누군가가 나를 미행하고 있다는 오싹한 느낌이 들었다. 4 그녀의 목소리는 죽은 내 친구의 목소리와 섬뜩할 정도로 비슷하다. 5 나는 네 업적을 깎아내릴 의도가 전혀 없다. 6 내 여동생은 그의 멸시의 대상이었다. 7 나는 너무도 부주의했던 내 자신을 탓했다. 8 Julie가 유럽에 간다니 정말 부럽다. 9 그녀는 이 프로젝트로 인해 정신없이 바쁘다.

day 30 exercise

A Match the words in the left column to the sentences in the right column.

ⓐ **penetrate**: to go into or through something

ⓑ **libel**: the act of spreading lies about someone in print

ⓒ **residue**: a substance left behind

ⓓ **exculpate**: to clear someone of guilt

ⓔ **relevance**: suitability or applicability

1. The newspaper editor was found guilty of ____________ when his claims were shown to be false.
2. There was bath oil ____________ left on the tub.
3. The witness's testimony has no ____________ to the case and should be disregarded.
4. The meteor ____________(e)d the earth's atmosphere.
5. The witness ____________(e)d the defendant.

B Choose the word or phrase that best explains the underlined word.

1. If you ***concur*** with a colleague, you ________________ with him or her.
   ⓐ compete ⓑ agree ⓒ argue ⓓ socialize

2. If something ***fluctuates***, it ________________.
   ⓐ grows ⓑ varies ⓒ flees ⓓ disappears

3. If a man is ***pompous***, he is ________________.
   ⓐ attractive ⓑ comic ⓒ dull ⓓ arrogant

4. If you ***depict*** something, you ________________ it.
   ⓐ carry ⓑ inspect ⓒ discover ⓓ describe

5. ***Morbid*** poems are ________________.
   ⓐ uplifting ⓑ puzzling ⓒ depressing ⓓ romantic

C Choose the option that is closest in meaning to the underlined word.

1. ***lethal*** poison
   ⓐ helpful ⓑ painful ⓒ fatal ⓓ unnecessary

2. work as a ***courier***
   ⓐ delivery person ⓑ designer ⓒ hairdresser ⓓ teacher

3. ***castigate*** a person
   ⓐ promote ⓑ criticize ⓒ introduce ⓓ congratulate

D Choose the option that is the opposite of the underlined word.

1. ***evoke*** sympathy
   ⓐ prevent ⓑ undergo ⓒ demand ⓓ cause

2. a ***spontaneous*** party
   ⓐ farewell ⓑ informal ⓒ planned ⓓ crowded

3. ***disparage*** an employee
   ⓐ require ⓑ flatter ⓒ blame ⓓ hire

E Choose the best word or phrase.

1. Which of the following is involved in ***arithmetic***?
   ⓐ meditation ⓑ division ⓒ athletics ⓓ virtues

2. Which of the following has ***denominations***?
   ⓐ sports ⓑ schools ⓒ businesses ⓓ religions

3. Most people try to ____________ ***obnoxious*** people.
   ⓐ avoid ⓑ understand ⓒ encourage ⓓ imitate

4. Who would be most likely to ***bluster***?
   ⓐ an honest person ⓑ an arrogant person
   ⓒ a shy person ⓓ a gorgeous person

Part Ⅱ

주제별 어휘

| 권장 학습법 |

◉ 마인드 맵(mind-map)의 흐름에 따라 주제별 어휘를 눈으로 훑어 내려가자.

◉ 맵에서 살펴 본 단어들을 voca check를 통해 확인하자.

◉ More Words에서 주제별 어휘를 추가적으로 알아보자.

◉ voca⁺를 통해 표제어와 관련된 다양한 표현들을 심도있게 학습하자.

◉ 하루에 학습한 어휘들을 연습문제(exercise)에서 복습하자.

◉ MP3 파일을 들으면서 암기하자.

day **31**

Environment & Development 환경과 개발

Environment & Development 환경과 개발

- **pollution** 오염
  - pollutants 오염원
  - fossil fuel 화석 연료
  - exhaust(fumes) 배기가스
  - sulfurous acid gas 아황산가스
  - toxic substances 유독 물질
  - particulates 미세먼지
  - yellow dust 황사(먼지)
  - nuclear waste 방사성 폐기물
  - NIMBY(Not In My Back Yard) 혐오시설 반대운동
  - PIMFY(Please In My Front Yard) 개발시설 유치운동
- **reckless development** 난개발
  - landfill 쓰레기 매립지
    - disposable 일회용품(의)
    - synthetic detergent 합성 세제
    - garbage disposal 음식물 쓰레기 분쇄기
    - sewage 하수 (오물)
    - sewer 하수도
  - incineration 소각
  - reclamation 간척
  - devastating 황폐화시키는
  - deforestation 산림 파괴
  - desertification 사막화
  - endangered species 멸종 위기에 처한 종
  - extinct species 멸종된 종
- **global warming** 지구온난화
  - carbon dioxide 이산화탄소
  - greenhouse effect 온실효과
  - depletion of the ozone layer 오존층 파괴
- **alternative energy** 대체에너지
  - fuel cell 연료 전지
  - hydrogen vehicle 수소 자동차
  - renewable energy 재생 에너지
  - nuclear fusion energy 핵융합 에너지
  - solar power plant 태양열 발전소
  - hydroelectric power plant 수력 발전소
  - tidal power plant 조력 발전소
  - geothermal power plant 지열 발전소
  - wind power plant 풍력 발전소
- **sustainable development** 지속가능한 발전
  - environmental policy 환경 정책
  - environment(ally)-friendly 환경친화적인
  - biodegradable 자연분해성의
  - natural restoration 자연 정화
  - environmental impact assessment 환경영향평가
  - PAYT(pay-as-you-throw) program 종량제
  - environment improvement charge 환경개선 분담금

Voca Check

정답 p.385

Complete the English translation by referring to the page on the left.

❶ ___________ causes serious problems, such as erosion and loss of habitats for animals.
산림 파괴는 침식이나 동물의 서식지 손실과 같은 심각한 문제를 야기한다.

❷ We are far too dependent on ___________s as an energy source.
우리는 에너지 자원으로서 화석 연료에 지나치게 의존한다.

❸ The presidential candidate promised to improve the government's ___________.
그 대통령 후보는 정부의 환경 정책을 개선하겠다고 약속했다.

❹ ___________ is a relatively clean, but dangerous energy source.
핵융합 에너지는 비교적 환경을 덜 오염시키지만 위험한 에너지 자원이다.

❺ ___________s use the movement of the ocean as an energy source.
조력 발전소는 해양의 운동력을 에너지 자원으로 이용한다.

❻ I buy only ___________ cleaning products.
나는 환경친화적인 세제만을 구입한다.

❼ It is more important than ever to wear sunscreen because of the ___________.
오존층 파괴 때문에 자외선 차단제를 바르는 것이 어느 때보다 중요하다.

❽ Developing a ___________ would benefit the environment.
수소 자동차를 개발하는 것은 환경에 도움이 될 것이다.

More Words

odor 악취
effluent 폐수
red tide 적조
potable 마실 수 있는, 식수의
photochemical smog 광화학 스모그
radioactive leak(age) 방사능 누출
preservative 방부제
combustible waste 가연성 쓰레기
eco-labelling 환경 마크 제도
Global Environment Facility 지구 환경 보호 기금
biodiversity 생물 다양성
poach 밀렵하다

pollutant
[pəlúːtənt]

n. **오염원, 오염 물질** syn. contaminant

1 New regulations will help reduce toxic air *pollutants*.

voca+ • release chemical[industrial] pollutants 화학[산업] 오염물을 배출하다

sewage
[súːidʒ]

n. **하수, 오수, 하수 오물**

2 The factory secretly dumped raw *sewage* into the river.

voca+ • sewer 하수구, 하수도 • raw sewage 정제하지 않은 오물
• treat sewage 하수를 처리하다
• sewage treatment[disposal] plant 하수 처리장

incineration
[insìnəréiʃən]

n. **소각**

3 In Germany, opposition to waste *incineration* is widespread.

voca+ • incinerate (버리기 위해) 태우다
• incineration plant 소각장 • incinerator 소각로

greenhouse effect

n. **온실효과** (the gradual warming of the air surrounding the earth as a result of heat being trapped by pollution)

4 Burning fossil fuels has been contributing to the *greenhouse effect*.

voca+ • refrigerant (프레온 등과 같은) 냉매제
• greenhouse gas (이산화탄소 등과 같이) 온실효과를 일으키는 가스
• carbon dioxide 이산화탄소(CO_2)
• the ozone layer 오존층

hydrogen vehicle

n. **수소 자동차** (=hydrogen-fueled car)

5 The study says *hydrogen vehicles* won't be available soon.

voca+ • hydrogen internal combustion engine 수소 내연 기관

1 새 법규는 독성이 있는 공기 오염 물질을 줄이는 데 도움이 될 것이다. 2 그 공장은 처리되지 않은 하수 오물을 강에 몰래 버렸다. 3 독일에서는 쓰레기 소각에 대한 반대 여론이 널리 퍼져 있다. 4 화석 연료의 연소가 온실효과를 가중시켜 왔다. 5 그 연구에 따르면 수소 자동차가 빠른 시일 내에 실용화되지는 않을 것이라고 한다.

alternative energy

n. 대체 에너지

1 The energy crisis is fueling an investment boom in *alternative energy*.

voca+
- alternative fuel 대체 연료
- clean energy 청정 에너지
- conventional energy 재래식 에너지
- nuclear[thermal] power plant 원자력[화력] 발전소

exhaust
[igzɔ́:st]

n. 1. 배기가스 (=exhaust fumes)
2. 배기관 (=exhaust pipe)

2 Car *exhaust* is the main reason for the city's pollution.

voca+
- incomplete combustion 불완전 연소
- carbon monoxide 일산화탄소(CO)
- soot 그을음

reclamation
[rèkləméiʃən]

n. 개간, 간척

3 The government allocated money for the land *reclamation* project.

voca+
- reclaimed land 간척지
- tide embankment 방조제
- tideland reclamation project 간석지 개간 사업

disposable
[dispóuzəbl]

a. 일회용의, 쓰고 버리는 syn. throwaway

4 I forgot to buy *disposable* contact lenses for the trip.

voca+
- disposable razor[diaper/syringe] 1회용 면도기[기저귀/주사기]

n. (주로 복수로) 일회용품

5 Tons of plastic *disposables* are dumped into landfills every day.

biodegradable
[bàioudigréidəbl]

a. 생물 분해성의, 자연 분해되는

6 The packaging is made of *biodegradable* plastic.

voca+
- biodegradable[non-biodegradable] garbage 썩는[썩지 않는] 쓰레기

1 에너지 위기가 대체 에너지에 대한 투자 열풍을 촉진하고 있다. 2 자동차 배기가스는 도시 공해의 주요 원인이다. 3 정부는 토지 간척 사업에 예산을 할당했다. 4 나는 여행에 가져갈 일회용 콘택트 렌즈를 깜박 잊고 사지 않았다. 5 매일 수톤의 플라스틱 일회용품이 매립지에 버려진다. 6 그 포장재는 자연 분해성 비닐로 만들어졌다.

desertification
[dizə̀ːrtəfikéiʃən]

n. 사막화

1 The yellow dust storms in Korea are the result of rapid *desertification* in China.

voca+ • UNCCD(United Nations Convention to Combat Desertification) 사막화 방지 협약
• dust bowl (모래 폭풍이 부는) 황진 지대

devastating
[dévəstèitiŋ]

a. 황폐화시키는, 파괴적인

2 Global warming will have *devastating* effects on coral reefs.

reckless development

n. 난개발 (a development process that disregards the environment)

3 *Reckless development* has destroyed many forests.

voca+ • development[environment]-oriented 개발[환경] 지향적인

sustainable development

n. 지속가능한 개발, 환경 친화적 개발 (a process of developing a place or a business while considering its environmental impact on the future)

4 World leaders pledged to pursue *sustainable development*.

voca+ • SDI(Sustainable Development Indicator) 지속가능한 개발 지표

landfill
[lǽndfil]

n. 쓰레기 매립지, 매립식 쓰레기 처리

5 The problem with *landfills* is that they can leak toxic substances.

voca+ • sanitary landfill 위생 매립 (쓰레기 매립으로 인해 환경오염이 발생하지 않도록 환경오염 방지대책 수립과 환경오염 방지시설을 설치한 뒤에 쓰레기를 매립하는 방식을 말한다. 보통 매립지를 선정하고 바닥에 가스관과 침출수를 처리할 수 있는 집수관을 설치한 다음 폐기물을 버리고 15~30cm 두께로 흙을 덮는다.)

1 한국의 황사는 중국의 급속한 사막화의 결과이다. **2** 지구 온난화는 산호초에 파괴적인 영향을 끼칠 것이다. **3** 난개발로 인해 많은 산림이 파괴되었다. **4** 전 세계 지도자들이 환경 친화적 개발을 추구하겠다고 공식적으로 약속했다. **5** 쓰레기 매립지의 문제점은 그곳에서 독성 물질이 유출될 수 있다는 것이다.

exercise

정답 및 해설 p.385

A Match the words in the left column to the sentences in the right column.

ⓐ **disposable**: meant to be thrown out after use

ⓑ **biodegradable**: capable of being decomposed naturally

ⓒ **landfill**: a garbage disposal method or a place in which garbage is buried

ⓓ **sustainable development**: the practice of developing at a rate that does not deplete the earth's resources

ⓔ **desertification**: a process that changes fertile land into desert

1. As ________ sites fill up, it is difficult to find new places to put our waste.
2. ________ diapers replaced cloth ones in the 1970s.
3. The increase in yellow dust in recent years is the result of ________.
4. We must pursue ________ so that future generations will be able to live comfortably.
5. Many fast food chains have switched from Styrofoam to ________ packaging.

B Choose the option that best completes the sentence.

1. The fish were dying because of the ______________ in the water.
   ⓐ species ⓑ tides ⓒ pollutants ⓓ exhaust fumes

2. Raw ______________ is being dumped into the river.
   ⓐ carbon dioxide ⓑ fossil fuel ⓒ particulates ⓓ sewage

3. Fumes from ______________ are a health risk.
   ⓐ incineration ⓑ nuclear waste ⓒ wind power ⓓ reclaimed land

4. We must develop ______________ sources to prepare for the expected energy crisis.
   ⓐ fossil fuels ⓑ alternative energy
   ⓒ biodegradable ⓓ devastating

5. ______________ is causing temperatures to rise.
   ⓐ Natural restoration ⓑ Reclamation
   ⓒ The greenhouse effect ⓓ Synthetic detergent

day 32

Biology & Life Sciences 생물학과 생명과학

Biology 생물학

- **classification of living things** 생물의 분류
  - kingdom 계
    - division (식물)문
    - phylum (동물)문
      - class 강
        - order 목
        - family 과
        - genus 속
        - species 종
        - mammal 포유류
          - primate 영장류
          - bird 조류
          - reptile 파충류
          - amphibian 양서류
          - rodent 설치류
          - crustacean 갑각류
- **metabolism** 신진대사
  - ingestion 섭취
  - digestion 소화
  - absorption 흡수
  - excretion 배설
  - secretion 분비
    - hormone 호르몬
    - enzyme 효소
  - respiration 호흡
  - photosynthesis 광합성
    - osmosis 삼투 (현상)
    - transpiration 증산
- **ecosystem** 생태계
  - producer 생산자
  - consumer 소비자
    - decomposer 분해자
    - predator 포식자
    - carnivore 육식동물
    - herbivore 초식동물
    - omnivore 잡식동물
  - food chain 먹이사슬
    - survival of the fittest 적자생존

Life Sciences 생명과학

- **bioengineering** 생명공학
  - stem cell 줄기세포
  - somatic cell 체세포
  - cultivate/incubate 배양하다
  - interbreed 이종교배시키다
    - crossbreeding 잡종교배
    - inbreeding 근친교배
  - IVF(in vitro fertilization) 시험관 수정
  - human embryo cloning 인간 배아복제
  - mutation 돌연변이
  - variant 변종
- **genetic engineering** 유전공학
  - gene 유전자
    - dominant 우성의
      - eugenics 우생학
    - recessive 열성의
  - chromosome 염색체
  - genome 유전자 지도, 게놈
  - gene manipulation 유전자 조작
  - GM(genetically modified) food 유전자 조작 식품

Voca Check

정답 p.385

Complete the English translation by referring to the page on the left.

❶ ___________s are born in the water and move onto the land.
양서류는 물에서 태어나 육지로 옮겨간다.

❷ Plants convert carbon dioxide into oxygen through a process called ___________.
식물은 광합성이라는 과정을 통해 이산화탄소를 산소로 변환시킨다.

❸ Darwin's theory of evolution is based on the "___________" principle.
다윈의 진화론은 '적자생존'의 법칙에 근거하고 있다.

❹ Humans eat both meat and vegetables. We are ___________s.
인간은 육류와 야채를 모두 먹는다. 우리는 잡식동물이다.

❺ Scientists hope that through ___________ research they will learn to grow organs to replace damaged ones.
과학자들은 줄기세포 연구를 통해 손상 기관을 대체할 기관을 배양하는 방법을 알고 싶어한다.

❻ Lizards, turtles and alligators are all ___________s.
도마뱀, 거북, 악어는 모두 파충류이다.

❼ ___________s are animals that are born from their mother's body and feed on their mother's milk during infancy.
포유동물은 어미의 몸에서 태어나며 유아기 동안 어미 젖을 먹는 동물들이다.

❽ Human beings have no predators. We are at the top of the ___________.
인간에게는 (잡아먹힐) 포식자가 없다. 우리는 먹이 사슬의 맨 꼭대기에 있다.

More Words

scientific term 학명
bioethics 생명윤리
biometrics 생체인식
asexual reproduction 무성생식
bisexuality 자웅동체
unisexuality 자웅이체
sporic plant 포자식물
chlorophyl(l) 엽록소
flora and fauna (특정 지역의) 동 · 식물군
parasite 기생동물, 기생충
warm-blooded[cold-blooded] animal 온혈[냉혈] 동물
seed leaf 떡잎

dominant
[dɑ́:minənt]

a. 우성의 ant. recessive

1 A *dominant* gene is one that is expressed or shows up, instead of another.

voca+ • dominant character[gene] 우성 형질[유전자]

species
[spí:ʃi:z]

n. (생물 분류상의) 종 (복수형 species)

2 The giant panda is an endangered *species*.

voca+ • The Origin of Species 종의 기원(Charles Darwin의 저서)

primate
[práimeit]

n. 영장류 (a member of the most developed group of mammals, including humans, monkeys, and apes)

3 There are many similarities between humans and other *primates*.

secretion
[sikrí:ʃən]

n. 분비(물)

4 He has a problem with his insulin *secretion*.

voca+ • secretory gland 분비선
• thyroid gland 갑상선
• endocrine[internal] secretion 내분비

respiration
[rèspiréiʃən]

n. 호흡

5 Doctors have instruments to measure heart beat and *respiration*.

voca+ • respiratory system 호흡계
• give[do] artificial respiration 인공 호흡을 하다
• CPR(cardio-pulmonary resuscitation) 심폐소생술

digestion
[daidʒéstʃən]

n. 소화(력)

6 Using ginger in a tea will aid your *digestion*.

voca+ • aid[disturb] digestion 소화를 돕다[방해하다]
• have good[poor] digestion 소화력이 좋다[나쁘다]

1 우성 유전자는 여타 유전자 대신 드러나는 유전자이다. 2 자이언트 판다는 멸종 위기에 처해 있는 종이다. 3 인간과 다른 영장류 사이에는 많은 유사점이 있다. 4 그는 인슐린 분비에 문제가 있다. 5 의사들은 심장 박동과 호흡을 측정할 기구를 가지고 있다. 6 차에 생강을 넣어 마시면 소화에 도움이 될 것이다.

transpiration
[trӕnspiréiʃən]

n. **증산 작용** (the process in which water passes from the surface of a plant's leaves into the air)

1 The air around plants can be cooled by the ***transpiration*** process.

consumer
[kənsúːmər]

n. **(먹이사슬의) 소비자**

2 Primary ***consumers*** are herbivores; they only eat plants.

voca+ • primary[secondary/tertiary] consumer 1차[2차/3차] 소비자

interbreed
[ìntərbríːd]

v. **이종교배 시키다** (to produce young animals from parents of different groups)
syn. hybridize

3 If you ***interbreed*** a donkey with a horse, you will get a mule.

voca+ • cross/hybrid/half-breed 잡종
• inbreeding 근친[동종] 교배(순수한 계통을 만들기 위한 같은 계통 간의 교배)

variant
[vériənt]

n. **변종** syn. strain, variety a. **변종의**

4 The H5N1 is a ***variant*** of bird flu seen in Asia.

IVF

n. **시험관 수정, 체외수정** (in vitro fertilization: a technique in which egg cells are fertilized outside the woman's body)

5 The couple is trying ***in vitro fertilization*** in order to have a baby.

voca+ • external[internal] fertilization 체외[체내]수정
• artificial insemination 인공수정
• test tube baby 시험관 아기
• surrogate mother 대리모

1 식물 주변의 공기는 증산 작용에 의해 냉각될 수 있다. 2 (먹이사슬의) 1차 소비자는 식물만 먹는 초식 동물이다. 3 당나귀와 말을 교배시키면 노새가 나온다. 4 H5N1은 아시아에서 발견되는 조류 인플루엔자의 변종이다. 5 그 부부는 아기를 갖기 위해 시험관 수정을 시도하고 있다.

cloning
[klóuniŋ]

n. 생물 복제

1 *Cloning* has many ethical considerations.

voca+
- clone 복제된 생물; 생물을 복제하다
- Dolly the sheep 복제양 돌리
- human cloning 인간 복제

gene
[dʒiːn]

n. 유전자

2 If *gene* mutations are not repaired, they can result in cancer.

voca+
- double helix 이중나선구조
- heredity 유전(적 형질)
- genetic code 유전자 정보[암호]
- genetic sequence 유전자 서열

eugenics
[juːdʒéniks]

n. 우생학 (the study of methods to improve the human race by selecting parents who will produce the strongest children) ant. dysgenics 열생학, 비우생학

3 In the 19th century, Francis Galton created a new science called *eugenics*.

GM food

n. 유전자 변형 식품 (genetically modified food)
syn. frankenfood (=frankenstein food)

4 The government insisted on risk assessment studies before it imported *GM food*.

voca+
- GMO (genetically modified organism) 유전자 변형 생물
- genetically-engineered[altered] 유전자 조작의

chromosome
[króuməsòum]

n. 염색체

5 A *chromosome* is a long piece of DNA containing many genes.

voca+
- sex chromosome 성염색체
- autosome 상[보통]염색체

1 생물 복제에는 윤리적으로 고려해야 할 점들이 많다. **2** 유전자 변형이 정상으로 돌아오지 않으면 암이 발생할 수 있다. **3** 19세기에 Francis Galton이 우생학이라는 새로운 과학을 만들어냈다. **4** 정부는 유전자 변형 식품을 수입하기 전에 위험도 평가 조사를 실시해야 한다고 주장했다. **5** 염색체는 많은 유전자를 갖고 있는 긴 DNA 조각이다.

exercise

정답 및 해설 p.385

A Match the words in the left column to the sentences in the right column.

ⓐ **species**: a group of animals or plants that share certain characteristics which distinguish them from others

ⓑ **respiratory**: relating to the process of breathing air in and out

ⓒ **gene**: a unit of DNA by which heritable traits are passed on to offspring

ⓓ **in vitro fertilization**: the act of fertilizing a woman's egg in a laboratory and then replacing it in her womb

ⓔ **interbreed**: to mate with an animal of a different species

1. Scientists think that there might be a(n) ________ that is related to obesity.
2. ________ has helped many couples to have a baby.
3. There are many different ________ of butterflies in the Amazon rain forest.
4. Asthma is a(n) ________ disease that makes it difficult to breathe.
5. Lions and tigers can ________ to create ligers.

B Choose the option that best completes the sentence.

1. Brown eyes are ________________ while blue eyes are recessive.
   ⓐ dominant ⓑ cloned ⓒ variant ⓓ manipulated

2. Monkeys, apes, and humans are all ________________.
   ⓐ producers ⓑ predators ⓒ primates ⓓ rodents

3. ________________ is the process our bodies undergo to break down the foods we eat.
   ⓐ Respiration ⓑ Mutation ⓒ Transpiration ⓓ Digestion

4. The sex of a baby is determined by two sex ________________. Two Xs mean a girl and an X and a Y mean a boy.
   ⓐ enzymes ⓑ chromosomes ⓒ species ⓓ hormones

5. Some people feel that ________________ is wrong because we should not duplicate living organisms.
   ⓐ cloning ⓑ GM food ⓒ photosynthesis ⓓ transpiration

IT & Internet 정보기술과 인터넷

IT(Information Technology) 정보기술

Information Society 정보화 사회

- telecommuting 재택근무
- ubiquitous 유비쿼터스, 어디에나 있는
- e-government 전자정부
- knowledge-based society 지식기반 사회

Information Revolution 정보 혁명

- bandwidth 통신기기 전송량
- frequency 주파수
- terminal 단말기
- information superhighway 초고속 정보 통신망
- optical cable 광케이블
- communications satellite 통신 위성
- GPS(global positioning system) 위성 위치 확인 시스템
- DMB(digital multimedia broadcasting) 디지털 멀티미디어 방송
- mobile[cell] phone 휴대전화
- state-of-the-art 최첨단의

Internet 인터넷

OS(operating system) 운영체제

- CPU(central processing unit) 중앙 처리 장치
- RAM(random access memory) 임의 추출 기억장치
- peripheral 주변기기
- compatible 호환성이 있는, 함께 사용 가능한
- configure 설정하다

Internet surfing 인터넷 활용

- log on to the Internet 인터넷에 접속하다
- browser 인터넷 열람 프로그램
- search engine 검색 엔진
- blog(web log) 블로그
- bulletin board 온라인 게시판
- P2P(peer to peer) file sharing 일대일 파일 공유
- ISP(internet service provider) 인터넷 서비스 제공자
- wireless Internet access 무선인터넷 접속
- LAN(local area network) 근거리 통신망
- broadband Internet 광대역 인터넷 (통신망)
- Internet penetration (rate) 인터넷 보급률

problems in cyperspace 사이버 공간상의 문제점

- invasion of privacy 사생활 침해
- spam (mail) 스팸 메일
- anonymity 익명성
- Internet addiction 인터넷 중독
- cybercrime 사이버 범죄
- copyright infringement 저작권 침해
- intellectual property 지적 재산
- digital divide 정보 격차
- netiquette 네티켓
- cyberporn 사이버 음란물
- censorship in cyberspace 인터넷 검열

Voca Check

정답 p.385

Complete the English translation by referring to the page on the left.

❶ The Internet is so much faster since I switched to a __________ connection.
광대역 인터넷 통신망으로 바꾼 이후 인터넷 속도가 훨씬 더 빨라졌다.

❷ __________ is fantastic. I don't have to drive in traffic and I can work in my pajamas.
재택근무는 환상적이다. 나는 차를 몰고 나갈 필요 없이 잠옷 차림으로 일을 할 수 있다.

❸ I'm still using Windows 98 because some of the software I use is not __________ with Windows XP.
나는 여전히 윈도우 98을 쓰고 있는데 그 이유는 내가 사용하는 몇몇 소프트웨어가 윈도우 XP와 호환되지 않기 때문이다.

❹ I'm going to switch to this new __________ because it offers a lower rate.
나는 새로운 인터넷 서비스 제공업체로 전환할 생각이다. 왜냐하면 거기가 더 저렴한 요금을 제공하기 때문이다.

❺ I used to write in a journal, but now I have a __________ where I can share my thoughts with others.
전에는 일기를 썼지만, 지금은 내 생각을 다른 사람들과 공유할 수 있는 블로그가 있다.

❻ I prefer Google to Yahoo as my __________.
나는 검색 엔진으로 야후보다 구글을 선호한다.

❼ You should practice proper __________ in online chats so as not to upset or offend anyone.
온라인 채팅을 할 때는 다른 사람을 화나게 하거나 불쾌하게 하지 않도록 올바른 네티켓을 지켜야 한다.

❽ Some feel that Internet users have too much __________ and should provide personal details.
몇몇 사람들은 인터넷 사용자들이 과도한 익명성을 가지고 있기 때문에 개인 정보를 제공해야 한다고 느낀다.

More Words

instant messenger 메신저
Internet portal site 인터넷 포털 사이트
run[manage] a website 웹사이트를 운영하다
web master[mistress] 웹사이트 관리자
(the) number of visitors 방문자 수
fee-based[free] site 유료[무료] 사이트
software developer 프로그램 개발자
internet café/cybercafé PC방

ISDN (integrated services digital network) 종합 정보 통신망
e-commerce 전자 상거래
data transmission speed 데이터 전송 속도
real-time 실시간의
webcast 인터넷을 통한 방송
authentication 인증
base station 기지국

ubiquitous
[ju:bíkwətəs]

a. 어디에나 존재하는, 편재하는 syn. omnipresent

❶ *Ubiquitous* technology enables people to connect to a network at any time and at any place.

state-of-the-art

a. 최신의, 최첨단 기술을 사용한 syn. cutting-edge

❷ This is a *state-of-the-art* cell phone with an MP3 player, a camera and GPS.

voca+ • early adopter 얼리 어답터, 최신 상품[기술] 사용자[구매자]

Internet penetration (rate)

n. 인터넷 보급률

❸ Korea boasts the world's highest *Internet penetration rate*.

voca+ • penetration of PCs PC 보급률

OS

n. 운영체제 (operating system: a system in a computer that helps all the programs work)

❹ Linux is a free and reliable computer *operating system*.

voca+ • 대표적인 OS로 MicroSoft사의 Windows와 그에 대항하여 OS의 무료화를 선언한 Linux가 있다.

compatible
[kəmpǽtəbl]

a. 호환 가능한, 호환성이 있는 (able to be used together, especially computer equipment from different companies)

❺ The new software is IBM *compatible*.

voca+ • compatibility 호환성
• plug-compatible 플러그가 공용인
• specifications (컴퓨터) 사양

DMB

n. 디지털 멀티미디어 방송 (digital multimedia broadcasting)

❻ With this *DMB*, I can get 7 radio stations and 13 TV channels on my cell phone.

❶ 유비쿼터스 기술은 사람들이 언제 어디서나 네트워크에 접속할 수 있게 해 준다. ❷ 이것은 MP3 플레이어, 카메라, GPS가 내장된 최첨단 휴대폰이다. ❸ 한국은 세계 최고의 인터넷 보급률을 자랑하고 있다. ❹ 리눅스는 무료이고 믿을 만한 컴퓨터 운영체제이다. ❺ 새로 나온 소프트웨어는 IBM과 호환 가능하다. ❻ DMB를 통해 나는 휴대전화로 라디오방송 7개와 TV 채널 13개를 수신할 수 있다.

peripheral
[pərífərəl]

n. 주변기기, 주변장치 (=peripheral device)

1 Printers and scanners are examples of ***peripherals***.

voca+
- USB(universal serial bus) PC와 주변기기를 접속하기 위해 만든 규격
- memory stick 메모리 스틱
- tablet 타블렛, 펜 형태의 마우스
- webcam 웹캠, 컴퓨터와 연결해서 사용하는 카메라

(web) browser

n. 웹 브라우저, 인터넷 검색[열람] 프로그램

2 Internet Explorer and Netscape are two major ***browsers*** used to access the Web.

voca+
- WWW(World Wide Web) 월드와이드웹
- URL(uniform resource locator) (인터넷에서) 서버 주소를 나타내는 방법
- interface (홈페이지 등의) 사용자 환경
- hyperlink 문서 이동, 하이퍼링크
- domain name 도메인 이름
- default 기본값, 시작 페이지
- favorite/bookmark 즐겨찾기

bulletin board

n. 온라인 게시판

3 Read the school's electronic ***bulletin board*** to find out what's going on.

voca+
- post/put up 글을 게시하다
- (the) number of hits[queries] 조회수
- BBS(bulletin board system) 전자 게시판 시스템
- SysOp(system operator) 게시판 운영자
- FAQs(frequently asked questions) 자주 묻는 질문들

P2P file sharing

n. 일대일 파일 공유 (peer-to-peer file sharing)

4 Napster was founded in 1999 as a ***peer-to-peer*** music ***file sharing*** service by 18-year-old Shawn Fanning.

voca+
- FTP(file transfer protocol) 파일 전송 규약(인터넷을 통해 한 컴퓨터에서 다른 컴퓨터로 파일을 전송하는 규약체계 혹은 프로그램)

1 프린터와 스캐너는 주변기기의 예이다. **2** Internet Explorer와 Netscape는 웹에 접속하는 데 이용되는 두 가지 주요 브라우저이다. **3** 무슨 일이 일어나고 있는지 알려면 교내 온라인 게시판의 글들을 읽어라. **4** Napster라고 하는 일대일 음악 파일 공유 서비스는 1999년에 Shawn Fanning이라는 18세 청년에 의해 만들어졌다.

LAN

n. (빌딩 · 사무실 내의) 근거리 통신망 (local area network)

1 A *LAN* is a network that connects computers that are close to each other, usually in the same building.

voca+
- broadband 광대역(의)
- data traffic 전송량
- WAN(wide area network) 광역 통신망
- VDSL(very high data rate digital subscriber line) 초고속 디지털 가입자 회선

cybercrime

[sáibərkràim]

n. 사이버 범죄

2 *Cybercrime* is one of the fastest-growing criminal activities.

voca+
- cyberterrorism 사이버 테러
- hacker 해커
- cyberbullying 사이버 왕따
- flaming 인터넷상의 언어 폭력
- phishing 인터넷 금융 사기
- firewall 방화벽 (정보 통신망의 불법 접근을 차단하는 보안 시스템)

digital divide

n. 정보 격차 (the gap existing between people with greater access and those with lesser access to technological resources and training)

3 Government and industry should take steps to reduce the *digital divide*.

voca+
- computer-illiterate 컴맹의

copyright infringement

n. 저작권 침해

4 *Copyright infringement* also involves illegal downloading of music to MP3 players.

voca+
- piracy / counterfeiting 무단 복제
- pirated version 해적판
- fair use 공정 이용 (저작권을 침해하지 않는 기간과 범위 내 사용)
- shareware 쉐어웨어 (일정 기간 동안 사용 및 복사가 가능한 샘플 소프트웨어)
- freeware 프리웨어 (누구나 무료로 사용할 수 있는 공개 소프트웨어)

1 LAN은 보통 같은 건물 안에 있는 서로 가까이 있는 컴퓨터들을 연결하는 네트워크이다. **2** 사이버 범죄는 가장 빠른 속도로 증가하고 있는 범죄 형태 중 하나이다. **3** 정부와 기업들은 정보 격차를 줄이기 위한 조치를 취해야 한다. **4** MP3 플레이어에 음악을 불법 다운로드하는 것도 저작권 침해에 포함된다.

exercise

정답 및 해설 p. 385

A Match the words in the left column to the sentences in the right column.

ⓐ **peripheral**: equipment that can be connected to and used with a computer

ⓑ **ubiquitous**: present everywhere

ⓒ **web browser**: a program that allows users to access the Internet

ⓓ **digital divide**: the socio-economic gap in relation to access to computers and the Internet

ⓔ **copyright infringement**: unauthorized and illegal copying of a work

1. I used to use Netscape, but now I use Explorer as my ________.
2. The Korean music industry has suffered from ________ because of free online music.
3. ________ computing will make computers an essential part of every aspect of our lives.
4. I bought a computer, and now I just need to get a few ________(e)s, like a webcam and a printer.
5. Victims of the ________ are people with limited access or no access to the Internet.

B Choose the option that best completes the sentence.

1. I use Windows XP. What ________________ do you use?
   ⓐ web log ⓑ search engine ⓒ operating system ⓓ browser

2. Most airports have a wireless ________________ so that you can access the Internet from your laptop.
   ⓐ URL ⓑ RAM ⓒ CPU ⓓ LAN

3. The new software is not ________________ with my operating system. So I can't install it.
   ⓐ ubiquitous ⓑ compatible ⓒ anonymous ⓓ wireless

4. Increasing PC and Internet ________________ can help close the digital divide.
   ⓐ penetration ⓑ cyberporn ⓒ spam mail ⓓ anonymity

5. If you use your credit card on a site that isn't secure, you might become a victim of ________________.
   ⓐ telecommuting ⓑ cybercrime ⓒ censorship ⓓ digital divide

day 34 International Relations 국제관계

International Relations 국제관계

Ministry of Foreign Affairs and Trade 외교통상부

- embargo 통상금지
- trade friction 무역마찰
- doctrine 외교 정책[원칙]
- signatory 조인국
- ratification 비준
- protocol 의정서, 국제규약
- bilateral[multilateral] agreement 상호[다자간] 협정
- treaty 조약
- international organization 국제기구
- international law 국제법
- FTA(free trade agreement) 자유무역 협정

- behind-the-scenes negotiations 물밑 협상
- diplomatic dispute 외교 분쟁
- territorial dispute 영유권 분쟁
- summit talks 정상회담
- diplomatic talks 외교협상
- delegate (재외) 대표, 사절
- ambassador 대사
- diplomat 외교관

- fisheries agreement 어업협정
- EEZ(exclusive economic zone) 배타적 경제수역

North Korea 대북관계

- nuclear inspections 핵사찰
- armistice 휴전
- arms race 군비 경쟁
- disarmament 군비 축소
- JSA(joint security area) 공동경비구역
- light water reactor project 경수로 사업
- food aid 식량원조
- DMZ(demilitarized zone) 비무장지대
- the 38th parallel 38선
- six-party talks 6자 회담

international politics 국제정치

- super powers 열강들(강대국)
- national interest 국익
- Pax Americana 팍스 아메리카나(미국중심주의)
- post-cold war 탈냉전
- multilateralism 다자주의
- strained relations 긴장 관계
- economic sanctions 경제 제재
- exile 국외 추방하다
- refugee 난민, 망명자
- (military) coup 쿠데타, 군부에 의한 정권 찬탈

Voca Check

정답 p.386

Complete the English translation by referring to the page on the left.

❶ An __________ can be used as an economic alternative to warfare.
통상금지는 전쟁의 경제적 대안으로 이용될 수 있다.

❷ Many African countries have suffered from civil wars and __________s.
아프리카의 많은 나라들이 내전과 쿠데타로 인해 고통 받고 있다.

❸ He was granted __________ status because of the civil war taking place in his home country.
그는 고국에 내전이 일어났기 때문에 난민으로 받아들여졌다.

❹ The Korean War never officially ended, but an __________ has been in effect since 1953.
한국 전쟁은 공식적으로 종전된 것이 아니라 1953년 이래 계속 휴전 상태에 있다.

❺ The Korean __________ met with representatives of companies which are responsible for major investments in Korea.
한국 대사는 한국에서 주요 투자를 맡고 있는 회사의 대표들과 만남을 가졌다.

More Words

UN (United Nations) 국제 연합

UN Security Council 유엔 안전보장 이사회

WHO (World Health Organization) 국제 보건 기구

IMF (International Monetary Fund) 국제 통화 기금

WTO (World Trade Organization) 국제 무역 기구

Amnesty International 국제 사면 위원회

UNESCO (United Nations Educational, Scientific, and Cultural Organization) 유엔 교육 과학 문화 기구

UNICEF (United Nations International Children's Emergency Fund) 유엔 아동 기금

IAEA (International Atomic Energy Agency) 국제 원자력 기구

APEC (Asia-Pacific Economic Cooperation) 아시아 태평양 경제협력체

OECD (Organization for Economic Cooperation and Development) 경제 협력 개발 기구

OPEC (Organization of Petroleum Exporting Countries) 석유 수출국 기구

ISO (International Standardization Organization) 국제 표준화기구

delegate
[déligit]

n. (재외) 대표, 사절, 파견위원

1 *Delegates* from 7 countries met to discuss the issue of foreign aid.

voca+ • delegation 대표단
• representative (입법 관련) 재내 대표, 국회의원

v. [déligeit] ~을 대표로 파견하다 syn. dispatch

2 The chairperson *delegated* him to attend the conference.

diplomat
[dípləmæ̀t]

n. 외교관 (someone who officially represents their government in a foreign country)

3 The government has warned *diplomats* in East Timor to leave immediately.

voca+ • recall[summon] a diplomat 외교관을 본국으로 소환하다
• ambassador 대사(최고위 외교관) • embassy 외교사절단; 대사관
• consul 영사(외국에서 자국민을 보호하고 통상과 문화 교류 업무를 하는 공무원)
• minister 공사 • secretary 서기관
• diplomatic envoy 외교사절
• inviolability 불가침권
• extraterritoriality 치외법권

treaty
[trí:ti]

n. 조약 (a written agreement between countries)

4 Some documents related to the South Korea-Japan *treaty* in 1965 were disclosed.

voca+ • sign[violate] a treaty 조약에 조인하다[조약을 위반하다]
• NPT/NNPT(Nuclear Non-Proliferation Treaty) 핵 확산 방지 조약

ratification
[ræ̀təfikéiʃən]

n. 비준, 승인 (making something valid by formally signing and confirming it)

5 They voted against *ratification* of the treaty.

voca+ • instruments of ratification (조약의) 비준서

1 7개 국가에서 온 파견위원들이 대외 원조와 관련된 안건에 대해 논의하기 위해 만났다. 2 의장은 그를 대표로 보내 회의에 참석하도록 했다. 3 정부는 동티모르 주재 외교관들에게 즉시 출국하라고 촉구했다. 4 1965년의 한일 조약 관련 문서 몇 건이 공개되었다. 5 그들은 투표 끝에 조약의 비준에 반대하기로 했다.

protocol
[próutəkɑ̀l]

n. **의정서, 국제규약** (an international agreement between two or more countries)

❶ The Kyoto ***Protocol*** is very important for protecting the environment.

FTA

n. **자유무역협정** (Free Trade Agreement)

❷ An ***FTA*** is an agreement between two or more countries which lifts certain government regulations on trade between them.

arms race

n. **군비(확장)경쟁** syn. armament race

❸ An ***arms race*** between the superpowers may threaten world peace.

voca+
- set off[curb] the arms race 군비경쟁을 촉발[억제]하다
- military alliance 군사동맹
- arms control 군비제한
- under arms 무장한, 전투 태세를 갖춘

talks
[tɔ:ks]

n. (항상 복수로) **회담**

❹ The Middle East peace ***talks*** were postponed.

voca+
- talks break down[collapse/fall apart] 회담이 결렬되다
- working-level talks 실무회담
- summit meeting[talks] 정상회담

doctrine
[dɑ́:ktrin]

n. **(보통 D~) 공식적 외교정책**

❺ "Preemption, rather than reaction" summarizes the Bush ***Doctrine***.

voca+
- military doctrine 군사 정책
- brinkmanship 벼랑 끝 외교 정책, 극단적 외교 정책 (=brinksmanship)
- the Monroe Doctrine 먼로 독트린, 미국의 고립주의 ("European powers should no longer interfere with the affairs of sovereign nations located in the Americas.")

---

❶ 교토 의정서는 환경 보호에 있어서 매우 중요하다. ❷ 자유무역협정은 두 개 이상의 나라 사이에서 무역에 관한 특정한 정부 규제를 폐지하는 국가간 협정이다. ❸ 강대국들 간의 군비 경쟁이 세계 평화를 위협할 수도 있다. ❹ 중동 평화 회담이 연기되었다. ❺ '대응보다 선제공격'이라는 말이 Bush 정부의 외교 정책을 요약해 준다.

economic sanctions

n. 경제 제재 syn. economic blockade 경제 봉쇄

1 They will strengthen pressure on North Korea through military and *economic sanctions*.

voca+
- embargo 수출입금지[통상금지] 조치
- diplomatic[military] sanctions 외교[군사] 제재
- apply[impose] economic sanctions on ~에 대한 경제 제재를 발효하다
- lift[remove] economic sanctions 경제 제재를 해제하다

multilateralism

[mʌ̀ltilǽtərəlìzəm]

n. 다국 간의 상호자유무역주의, 다자주의 (trade or diplomatic negotiations among several countries)

2 *Multilateralism* is an effective approach to resolving international disputes.

voca+
- unilateralism 일방주의
- bilateralism 상호주의

coup

[kuː]

n. 쿠데타, 군부에 의한 정권 찬탈 syn. military coup, coup d'état

3 The attempted *coup* was uncovered and the leader was arrested immediately.

Pax Americana

n. 팍스 아메리카나, 미국이 주도하는 세계 평화

4 *Pax Americana* denotes the peace that is supposed to be established in the world by the U.S.

voca+
- Pax Romana 로마제국에 의한 평화

signatory

[sígnətɔ̀ːri]

n. 조인국, (조약) 가맹국

5 About 160 countries are *signatories to* the Bern Convention.

1 그들은 군사 및 경제 제재를 통해 북한에 대한 압박을 강화할 것이다. **2** 다자주의는 국제 분쟁을 해결하는 효과적인 접근법이다. **3** 쿠데타 시도는 발각되었고, 주동자는 즉시 체포되었다. **4** 팍스 아메리카나는 미국에 의해 정착되었다고들 말하는 세계 평화를 일컫는다. **5** 약 160여 개국이 베른 협약의 조인국이다.

exercise

정답 및 해설 p.386

A Match the words in the left column to the sentences in the right column.

ⓐ **protocol**: an international agreement between two or more countries

ⓑ **talks**: formal discussions between governments, organizations, etc.

ⓒ **coup**: an attempt by the military to take control of the government

ⓓ **multilateralism**: trade or diplomatic negotiations among several countries

ⓔ **Free Trade Agreement**: an agreement between two or more countries to limit restrictions on imports and exports

1. Since the ________ in June, political and social tensions in the country have soared.
2. South Korea, China, Japan, Russia, the U.S. and North Korea will hold ________ regarding nuclear arms.
3. ________(e)s remove taxes and quotas between trading countries.
4. The Kyoto ________ was meant to reduce CO_2 emissions.
5. The UN and NATO are examples of organizations involved in ________.

B Choose the option that best completes the sentence.

1. The two countries finally agreed upon and signed a(n) ______________ in 2003.
ⓐ embargo ⓑ coup ⓒ treaty ⓓ sanction

2. I lived in several countries as a child because my father was a(n) ______________.
ⓐ diplomat ⓑ activist ⓒ monarch ⓓ politician

3. The agreement requires ______________ by 45 countries before it takes effect.
ⓐ cooperation ⓑ ratification ⓒ disarmament ⓓ abolition

4. North Korea urges the U.S. to lift ______________.
ⓐ territorial disputes ⓑ summit talks
ⓒ Pax Americana ⓓ economic sanctions

5. The cold war between the United States and the Soviet Union involved a nuclear ______________.
ⓐ trade ⓑ radiation ⓒ energy ⓓ arms race

day 35 Government & Politics 정부와 정치

- **Government** 정부
  - **separation of powers** 삼권분립
    - **legislature** 입법부
      - abolish (법률을) 폐지하다
      - enact a law 법률을 제정하다
      - submit a bill 법안을 제출하다
      - impeach the president 대통령을 탄핵하다
      - hold a hearing 청문회를 열다
      - lawmaker/member of Congress 국회의원
        - immunity 면책특권
      - National Assembly (한국)국회
    - **executive** 행정부
      - veto 거부권을 행사하다
      - chief executive 행정수반
      - minister 장관
        - prime minister 국무총리, 수상
        - secretary 미국 장관
      - cabinet 내각
      - bureaucracy 관료 정치[제도]
        - civil[public] servant 공무원
    - **judiciary** 사법부
      - rule of law 법치주의
      - constitutional amendment 헌법 개정
      - the Supreme Court 대법원
- **Politics** 정치
  - **election** 선거
    - by-election 보궐선거
    - election campaign 선거 운동, 선거 유세
    - nominate 후보로 추천[공천]하다
    - candidate 후보
    - referendum 국민투표
      - suffrage 참정권
    - cast a vote[ballot] 투표하다
    - voter turnout 투표율
    - exit poll 출구 조사
    - vote counting 개표
    - president-elect 대통령 당선자
    - inauguration 취임(식)
  - **political party** 정당
    - ruling party 여당
    - opposition party 야당
    - spokesperson 대변인
    - minority government 여소야대 (정부)
  - **political inclination** 정치 성향
    - conservative 보수적인/보수주의자
    - moderate 온건한/중도주의자
    - liberal 진보적인/진보주의자
    - radical 급진적인, 과격한/급진론자
    - extremist 극단주의자(의)

Voca Check

정답 p.386

Complete the English translation by referring to the page on the left.

❶ Many countries have ___________ed the death penalty, but it is still practiced in some.
많은 나라들이 사형제를 폐지했지만, 몇몇 국가에서는 여전히 실시되고 있다.

❷ Having won the election, the ___________ is celebrating with supporters.
선거에서 승리하고 나서 대통령 당선자는 지지자들과 함께 자축하고 있다.

❸ The president made a touching speech after being sworn in at her ___________ ceremony.
대통령은 취임식에서 선서를 한 후 감동적인 연설을 했다.

❹ The issue will be decided by public opinion. There will be a ___________ at the end of the month.
그 문제는 여론에 따라 결정될 것이다. 이달 말 국민투표가 있을 것이다.

❺ The low ___________ reflects political apathy among the people.
낮은 투표율은 국민들의 정치적 무관심을 반영하는 것이다.

❻ President George Bush and ___________ Tony Blair met to discuss the issue.
George Bush 대통령과 Tony Blair 총리는 그 사안을 논의하기 위해 만났다.

❼ The human rights activists cheered when ___________ upheld the ruling of the lower court.
인권 운동가들은 대법원이 하급 법원의 판결을 확정했을 때 환호했다.

❽ The ___________ is responsible for making laws.
입법부는 법을 제정하는 책임을 맡고 있다.

More Words

checks and balances 견제와 균형
Parliament (영국)국회
Congress (미국)국회
presidential system 대통령제
electoral college (미국 대통령/부통령) 선거인단
parliamentary cabinet system 의원 내각제
(the) Republican Party 미국 공화당
(the) Democratic Party 미국 민주당
run[stand] as an independent 무소속으로 출마하다
incumbent 현직의, 현직 의원
political[voter] apathy 정치[선거]에 대한 무관심
regionalism / regional animosity 지역주의, 지역 감정
the national[party] convention 전당 대회
pardon / amnesty 사면
special presidential pardon[amnesty] 대통령 특사
political prisoner 정치범

enact
[inǽkt]

v. 법률을 제정하다

❶ Although the law was *enacted*, it hasn't been enforced.

voca+ • enact a provision[regulation] 조항[규칙]을 제정하다

lawmaker
[lɔ́:mèikər]

n. 국회의원 syn. member of Congress[Parliament], assemblyperson

❷ He submitted his resignation as a *lawmaker*.

voca+ • former and incumbent lawmakers 전 · 현직 국회의원들
• independent Parliament member 무소속 의원
• senator 미 상원의원 • representative 미 하원의원

cabinet
[kǽbinət]

n. 내각

❸ The prime minister nominates the members of *cabinet*.

voca+ • cabinet reshuffle[shakeup] 개각(改閣)

veto
[ví:tou]

v. 거부권을 행사하다 n. 거부권

❹ The president *vetoed* the legislative bill.

voca+ • exercise[use] one's veto 거부권을 행사하다
• override a veto (거부된 법안을) 재가결하다

constitutional amendment

n. 헌법 개정

❺ He announced that the *constitutional amendment* did not pass.

voca+ • propose[initiate] a constitutional amendment 개헌을 발의[제의]하다

hearing
[híriŋ]

n. 청문회

❻ The ruling party promised to hold a public *hearing*.

voca+ • hold a hearing 청문회를 열다
• parliamentary[confirmation] hearing 국회[인사]청문회

❶ 그 법은 제정되기는 했지만 시행되지는 않고 있다. ❷ 그는 (국회)의원직 사퇴를 표명했다. ❸ 수상이 내각 각료들을 임명한다. ❹ 대통령은 입법안에 대해 거부권을 행사했다. ❺ 그는 헌법 개정안이 통과되지 않았다고 발표했다. ❻ 여당은 공청회를 열겠다고 약속했다.

candidate
[kǽndidèit]

n. 후보

1 Don't you feel this *candidate* is qualified?

voca+
- candidacy 입후보
- put up a candidate 후보자를 추천하다
- strong[leading] candidate 유력한 후보

suffrage
[sʌ́fridʒ]

n. 참정권

2 She spoke fiercely for women's *suffrage*.

voca+
- universal suffrage 보통선거권
- voting age 투표[선거권 취득] 연령
- Chartism 차티스트 운동(19세기 중반 선거권 획득을 위해 전개된 영국의 노동자 운동)

cast a vote

v. 투표하다

3 Less than 60% of the population had *cast their votes*.

voca+
- cast a vote for[against] 찬성표[반대표]를 던지다
- absentee vote[ballot] 부재자 투표
- put sth to the vote ~을 표결에 부치다

ruling party

n. 여당 syn. the party in power ant. opposition party

4 The unions will campaign against the *ruling party*'s candidates in the general elections.

voca+
- keep the ruling party in check 여당을 견제하다
- the ins and the outs 여당과 야당

by-election

n. 보궐선거 (a special election to replace a politician who has left Parliament or died)

5 Who won the last *by-election*?

voca+
- general election 총선거
- presidential election 대통령 선거

1 이 후보가 적격이라고 생각하지 않니? **2** 그녀는 여성의 참정권을 강력히 요구했다. **3** 전체 주민 중 투표한 사람은 60%도 안 되었다. **4** 노조들은 총선에서 여당 후보들에 대한 반대 운동을 벌일 것이다. **5** 지난번 보궐선거에서 누가 당선됐니?

election campaign

n. 선거 운동 syn. electioneering, canvassing

1 *Election campaigns* usually cost a great deal of money.

voca+
- election fraud 선거 비리
- campaign promise[pledge] 선거 공약
- negative[smear] campaign 인신공격 위주의 선거 운동

exit poll

n. 출구 조사

2 The *exit polls* revealed that more women voted than men.

voca+
- conduct exit polls 출구 조사를 실시하다
- margin of error 오차 (범위)

conservative

[kənsə́ːrvətiv]

a. 보수적인 n. 보수주의자

3 The Supreme Court Justice has very *conservative* views.

voca+
- moderate conservatives 온건 보수파
- hard-line conservatives 강경 보수파
- neo-conservatives 신 보수파

liberal

[líbərəl]

a. 진보적인, 자유주의적인 syn. progressive
n. 진보주의자, 자유주의자

4 She calls herself a *liberal* democrat, but she voted republican last year.

voca+
- liberal democracy 자유 민주주의
- political liberalism 정치적 자유주의

radical

[rǽdikəl]

a. 급진적인, 과격한 n. 급진론자

5 The candidate is too *radical* to get elected.

voca+
- radical left[right]-wing politician 과격한 좌파[우파] 정치인
- radical reforms 과감한 개혁

1 선거 운동에는 보통 엄청난 돈이 든다. **2** 출구 조사 결과 남성보다 여성이 더 많이 투표한 것으로 나타났다. **3** 그 연방 대법관은 매우 보수적인 시각을 견지하고 있다. **4** 그녀는 자신을 진보적인 민주당 지지자라고 하지만 지난 해 공화당에 투표했다. **5** 그 후보는 너무 급진적이어서 당선되기 어렵다.

exercise

정답 및 해설 p.386

A Match the words in the left column to the sentences in the right column.

ⓐ **exit poll**: a survey of voters immediately after they have voted

ⓑ **by-election**: a special election held in order to fill a vacancy

ⓒ **ruling party**: the political party holding the most power in government

ⓓ **lawmaker**: a member of the legislature; one who makes the laws

ⓔ **election campaign**: an attempt aimed at persuading voters to vote a certain way

1. The ________(e)s are debating the proposal.
2. If ________(e)s are any indication, the current president will serve another term.
3. Her ________ involved a lot of speeches and debates that were very successful.
4. The ________ has been in control for a long time.
5. A(n) ________ was held to replace the senator after he resigned.

B Choose the option that best completes the sentence.

1. Susan B. Anthony fought for women's ____________ so that women's voices would be heard.
   ⓐ inauguration ⓑ by-election ⓒ immunity ⓓ suffrage

2. I think it's important to take part in the political process of our country by ____________ on election day.
   ⓐ enacting a law ⓑ casting a vote
   ⓒ submitting a bill ⓓ impeaching the president

3. The president could prevent the bill from passing if he were to ____________ it.
   ⓐ balance ⓑ nominate ⓒ veto ⓓ propose

4. This ____________ promises to make a lot of changes if you vote for him.
   ⓐ secretary ⓑ candidate ⓒ spokesperson ⓓ president-elect

5. My father is traditional and dislikes change. He has very ____________ views.
   ⓐ conservative ⓑ liberal ⓒ radical ⓓ moderate

Law & Crime 법과 범죄

Law & Crime 법과 범죄

investigation 수사, 조사
- detective 형사
- suspect 용의자
  - witness 목격자
- warrant 영장
- wanted 지명 수배된
- arrest 체포[구속]하다
- be held in custody 구금되다
- be released on bail 보석으로 풀려나다
- autopsy/postmortem examination 검시
- forensic evidence 법의학적 증거
- C.S.I. (crime scene investigation) 범죄현장조사반

court of law 법정
- judge 판사
- prosecutor 검사
- public defender 국선 변호인
- defendant/the accused 피고
- plaintiff/accuser 원고
- jury 배심원단
- the judiciary 사법부

Constitution 헌법
- criminal law 형법
- civil law 민법
- ordinance 법령, 조례
- enforcement decree 시행령

breach 위반
- misdemeanor/minor offense 경범죄
- felony 중죄
- assault 폭행
- burglary 주거 침입
- sexual harassment 성희롱/성추행
- arson 방화
- kidnap 유괴하다/납치하다
  - hostage 인질
  - ransom 몸값
- homicide 살인죄
- assassinate 암살하다
- bribery 뇌물 수수죄
- embezzle 횡령하다
- fraud 사기
- plagiarism 표절
- smuggle 밀수하다

trial procedure 재판 절차
- sue 고소하다/소송을 걸다
  - case 사건
  - lawsuit 소송
- prosecute (검찰이) 기소하다
- plead (not) guilty (피고가) 유죄를 인정하(지 않)다
- plea bargain(ing) 유죄답변 교섭
- verdict (배심원이 재판장에게 전하는) 평결
  - acquit 무죄 판결을 내리다
  - convict 유죄 판결을 내리다
    - ex-con(vict) 전과자
    - sentence 형을 선고하다
    - be on probation 집행유예[보호관찰] 상태에 있다
    - correctional facility 교도소
    - death penalty 사형 선고

Voca Check

정답 p.387

Complete the English translation by referring to the page on the left.

❶ The ____________ has a strong case against the defendant.
검사는 피고를 사법처리할 충분한 논거를 가지고 있다.

❷ The ____________ says she can identify the murderer.
목격자는 살인범을 알아볼 수 있다고 말한다.

❸ The ____________ claims he is innocent, but the police believe they have the right person.
용의자는 자신이 결백하다고 주장하지만 경찰은 그가 범인이라고 생각한다.

❹ The ____________ is still used in some states of the US as punishment for murder.
사형은 미국의 몇몇 주에서 여전히 살인죄에 대한 형벌로 사용되고 있다.

❺ The family of the accused jumped for joy when a ____________ of "not guilty" was returned.
피고의 가족들은 무죄 평결을 받았을 때 뛸 듯이 기뻐했다.

❻ The plot to ____________ the president was intercepted by security.
대통령을 암살하려던 계획은 경호원에 의해 저지되었다.

❼ The man was found guilty based on ____________.
그 사람은 법의학적 증거를 근거로 유죄임이 밝혀졌다.

❽ It is the job of the courts to uphold the ____________ in order to protect citizens' rights.
국민의 권리를 보호하기 위해서 헌법을 수호하는 것이 법정의·의무이다.

More Words

advocate/attorney 변호사
the bench 판사직, 판사석
the bar 변호사 단체
written law/statute 성문법
customary law 관습법
case[common] law 판례법
accomplice 공범
parole 가석방
interrogation 취조
summons 소환장, 출두 명령
subpoena 증인 소환장
blackmail 공갈 협박
tax evasion 탈세
forgery 문서 위조
confiscate 압수하다
capital punishment 사형, 극형

smuggle
[smʌ́gəl]

v. 밀수하다

1 They were punished for *smuggling* drugs.

voca+ • smuggler 밀수업자
• drug trafficking 마약 밀거래
• mule 마약 운반책
• confiscate smuggled goods 밀수품을 압수하다

jury
[dʒúəri]

n. 배심원단 (a group of people who listen to the details of a case in court and decide whether someone is guilty or not)

2 The *jury* gave its verdict after three hours' deliberation.

voca+ • juror/juryman 배심원 • serve[sit] on a jury 배심원이 되다

detective
[ditéktiv]

n. 형사, 탐정 syn. investigator

3 The *detective* was investigating an armed robbery that occurred yesterday.

voca+ • private detective[investigator/eye] 사설 탐정
• detective agency 사설 탐정소

warrant
[wɔ́(:)rənt]

n. 영장 (a legal document that is signed by a judge, allowing the police to take a particular action)

4 A *warrant* has been issued for the arrest of the suspect.

voca+ • search[arrest/death] warrant 수색[구속/사형집행] 영장
• issue a warrant of attachment 압류 영장을 발부하다

custody
[kʌ́stədi]

n. 구류, 감금 (the state of being kept in prison, especially while waiting to go to court for trial)

5 Suspects can be held in police *custody* up to 48 hours.

voca+ • protective custody 보호구금
• take (sb) into custody (~를) 구금하다

1 그들은 마약 밀수 혐의로 처벌받았다. **2** 배심원단은 3시간의 심의 끝에 평결을 내렸다. **3** 그 형사는 어제 발생한 무장 강도 사건을 수사하고 있었다. **4** 용의자의 체포 영장이 발부되었다. **5** 용의자는 최대 48시간까지 경찰에 의해 구류될 수 있다.

plea bargain(ing)

n. **유죄 답변 교섭, 사전형량 조정제도, 플리바겐** (an agreement in which you say you are guilty in order to avoid a more serious punishment)

1 The suspect had a ***plea bargain*** with the prosecutor.

sexual harassment

n. **성추행, 성희롱**

2 This company has a zero-tolerance policy for ***sexual harassment***.

voca+
- sex crimes 성범죄
- sex offender 성범죄자
- rape 강간
- sexual abuse[assault] 성적 학대[폭행]

fraud

[frɑːd]

n. **사기 (행위), 사기꾼, 사칭하는 자**

3 He has been convicted of ***fraud*** twice.

voca+
- tax[insurance/credit card] fraud 조세[보험/신용카드] 사기
- electoral fraud 선거 부정
- forgery (공문서 · 지폐 등) 위조

plagiarism

[pléidʒərìzəm]

n. **표절**

4 This university has strict rules against ***plagiarism***.

voca+
- plagiarize 표절하다
- plagiarist 표절자, 도용인
- copyright 저작권
- copyleft 카피레프트(비상업적 용도로 무료 사용)
- fair use 저작권 침해가 되지 않는 범위 내의 이용

verdict

[və́ːrdikt]

n. **(배심원의) 평결**

5 The jury reached a unanimous ***verdict*** of not guilty.

voca+
- render[deliver] a (final) verdict (최종) 평결을 내리다
- unanimous[split] decision 만장일치의[의견이 분산된] 평결
- majority verdict 과반수 평결

---

1 용의자는 검사와 사전형량 조정에 합의했다. **2** 이 회사는 성희롱을 절대 용납하지 않는 정책을 취하고 있다. **3** 그는 두 차례 사기 혐의로 유죄 판결을 받았다. **4** 이 대학은 표절에 대한 엄격한 규정을 갖고 있다. **5** 배심원단은 만장일치로 무죄 평결을 내놓았다.

homicide
[há:məsàid]

n. 살인 (행위) syn. murder

■1 Another *homicide* occurred as police were still searching for clues.

voca+
- attempted murder 살인 미수
- serial killer 연쇄 살인범
- justifiable homicide 정당방위에 의한 살인
- manslaughter/culpable homicide 과실치사, 우발적 살인
- femicide 여성을 대상으로 한 살인

sue
[su:]

v. 고소하다, 소송을 제기하다

■2 We intend to *sue* the insurance company *for* damages.

voca+
- judicial procedure 소송절차
- civil[criminal] suit 민사[형사] 소송
- paternity suit 친자 확인 소송
- malpractice suit 의료사고 소송
- sue for libel[defamation/slander] 명예훼손으로 고소하다
- sue for divorce[custody] 이혼[자녀 양육권] 소송을 제기하다
- drop[discontinue] a lawsuit 소송을 취하하다

convict
[kənvíkt]

v. 유죄 판결을 내리다 ant. acquit

■3 The former police officer was *convicted of* bribery.

voca+
- conviction 유죄 판결
- acquittal 무죄 판결

n. [ká:nvikt] 죄수, 기결수

probation
[proubéiʃən]

n. 집행유예, 보호관찰 (a period of time during which a criminal has to obey the law and be supervised by a probation officer, instead of being sent to prison)

■4 Jack was fined and given 9 months' *probation*.

voca+
- probation officer 보호관찰관
- put[place] sb on[under] probation ~를 집행유예[보호관찰] 상태에 두다

■1 경찰이 여전히 단서를 찾고 있을 때 또다른 살인 사건이 발생했다. ■2 우리는 그 보험 회사에 손해배상 청구 소송을 제기하려 한다. ■3 그 전직 경찰관은 뇌물 수수 혐의로 유죄 판결을 받았다. ■4 Jack은 벌금형 및 집행유예 9개월에 처해졌다.

exercise

정답 및 해설 p.387

A Match the words in the left column to the sentences in the right column.

ⓐ **detective**: a person who investigates crimes

ⓑ **fraud**: the crime of deceiving people to obtain money

ⓒ **plagiarism**: intentionally copying the ideas or work of someone else

ⓓ **sexual harassment**: sexual behavior done to someone who does not want it

ⓔ **plea bargain**: an agreement in which an accused person pleads guilty to a less serious charge in order to get a less severe punishment

1. He was charged with ________ because of the way he treated his female staff.
2. Evidence of ________ has been found in the professor's latest paper.
3. The ________ found many important clues at the victim's apartment.
4. Her lawyer advised her to accept the ________ because the jury would probably convict her.
5. After cheating people out of their life savings, he was finally charged with ________.

B Choose the option that best completes the sentence.

1. He tried to ________________ drugs into the country, but his car was searched at the border.
   ⓐ acquire ⓑ prescribe ⓒ smuggle ⓓ ban

2. After deliberating for only four hours, the ________________ found her guilty.
   ⓐ witness ⓑ jury ⓒ fraud ⓓ victim

3. The judge issued a(n) ________________ for his arrest.
   ⓐ plea ⓑ investigation ⓒ officer ⓓ warrant

4. The suspect was held in ________________ until the trial.
   ⓐ custody ⓑ guilty ⓒ evidence ⓓ violation

5. Because he was on ________________, he couldn't leave the state.
   ⓐ bribery ⓑ sentence ⓒ probation ⓓ hostage

Economy 경제

Economy 경제

national economy 국가경제

- expansionary measures 적극[팽창]재정 정책
- austerity measures 긴축재정 정책
- deregulation 규제 철폐, 완화
- regulation 규제
- privatize 민영화하다
- nationalize 국유화하다
- developed[advanced] country 선진국
- developing country 개발도상국
- growth rate 성장률
- GDP(gross domestic product) 국내총생산
- GNP(gross national product) 국민총생산

trade 무역

- depreciation 평가절하
- appreciation 평가절상
- international competitiveness 국제 경쟁력
- competitive edge 경쟁우위
- dumping 덤핑
- impose tariffs 관세를 부과하다
- (trade) protectionism 보호 무역주의
  - subsidy 정부 보조금
- trade dispute[friction] 무역 마찰
  - retaliation 보복
  - retaliatory duties 보복 관
- multilateral trade 다자간 무역
- international trade 국제 무역
- trade surplus[deficit] 무역 흑자[적자]
- export/import 수출하다/수입하다

ups & downs 경기 활황과 불황

- business downturn 경기 하락
- recession 경기 후퇴
- stagnation 경기 침체
- depression 불경기
- sluggish 경기가 부진한
- panic (경제) 공황

- business upturn 경기 상승
- prosperous 번창[번성]하는
- brisk/buoyant/exuberant 활황의
- economic boom 경기 활황
  - bubble economy 거품경제
  - speculate 투기하다
  - real estate 부동산
  - income disparity 소득 불균형

price 물가

- stable 안정된
- fluctuate 변동하다
- soar/skyrocket 치솟다
- plummet 폭락하다
- deflation 물가 하락
- inflation rate 물가 상승률
- price index 물가 지수
- price collusion 가격 담합
- consumption 소비
- expenditure 지출, 경비

Voca Check

정답 p.387

Complete the English translation by referring to the page on the left.

❶ The company was successful because it had a ___________.
그 회사는 경쟁우위를 점했기 때문에 성공할 수 있었다.

❷ Share prices ___________ed to an all-time low.
주가가 사상 최저 수준으로 폭락했다.

❸ The government may do away with universal health care and ___________ the sector.
정부는 공공 의료를 폐지하고 그 분야를 민영화할지도 모른다.

❹ As a result of the high ___________, people's purchasing power has decreased.
높은 물가 상승률로 인해 사람들의 구매력이 감소하고 있다.

❺ The graduating class can expect to find good jobs as a result of the ___________.
졸업반 학생들은 경기 활황 덕분에 좋은 일자리 구하는 것을 기대할 수 있다.

❻ The ___________ between men and women needs to be addressed.
남성과 여성 사이의 소득 격차는 해소되어야 한다.

❼ Commuters may have trouble making ends meet as the price of gas is expected to ___________.
기름 값이 폭등할 것으로 예상됨에 따라 통근자들은 수지 균형을 맞추기 어려워질지도 모른다.

❽ I got involved in ___________ when I bought my first house fifteen years ago.
나는 15년 전에 처음으로 집을 샀을 때 부동산에 관여하게 되었다.

More Words

goods and services 재화와 용역
supply and demand 수요와 공급
capitalism 자본주의
socialism 사회주의
communism 공산주의
vicious cycle [circle] 악순환
virtuous cycle [circle] 선순환
foreign exchange reserves 외환 보유고
neoliberalism 신자유주의
niche market 틈새 시장
infrastructure 산업 기반 (시설)
VAT (value added tax) 부가가치세
CPI (consumer price index) 소비자 물가지수
monopoly 독과점

subsidy
[sʌ́bsədi]

n. **(정부의) 보조금** (money that is paid by the government to make prices lower, reduce the cost of producing goods, etc.)

1 *Subsidies* can help farmers when their crops fail.

voca+
- subsidize 보조금을 지급하다
- phase out subsidies 보조금을 단계적으로 폐지하다
- reduce[cut] subsidies 보조금을 삭감[폐지]하다

nationalize
[nǽʃənəlàiz]

v. **국영화하다** ant. privatize

2 All U.S. railways were *nationalized* during WWI and then returned to their private owners after the war.

voca+
- state-run[private] company[enterprise] 국영[민영] 기업

GDP

n. **국내총생산** (gross domestic product: the total value of all goods and services produced in a country, in one year, except for income received from abroad)

3 If the *GDP* continues to shrink, the country will enter a recession.

voca+
- GNP(gross national product) 국민총생산 (국내외를 막론하고 그 나라 국적을 가진 국민에 의해 생산되는 재화 및 서비스를 시장가격으로 평가한 총액)

depreciation
[diprìːʃiéiʃən]

n. **평가절하** (a reduction in the value or price of something) syn. devaluation

4 Lately, the *depreciation* of the dollar has lowered exports to North America.

voca+
- denomination 디노미네이션 (화폐의 실질 가치 변동 없이 호칭만 변경하여 단위를 절하하는 것)

appreciation
[əprìːʃiéiʃən]

n. **평가절상** (a rise in value, especially of land or possessions)

5 The U.S. dollar's *appreciation* will cause U.S. exports to decrease and imports to increase.

voca+
- revalue 재평가하다 (주로 평가절상하다)
- strong[weak] dollar 달러화 강세[약세]

1 작황이 안 좋을 때는 정부 보조금이 농민들에게 도움이 된다. **2** 1차 세계대전 중 미국의 모든 철도가 국유화되었다가 전쟁이 끝난 뒤 개인 소유자들에게 반환되었다. **3** GDP가 계속 줄어들면 그 나라는 경기 침체에 들어설 것이다. **4** 최근 달러화의 평가절하로 인해 북미 수출이 둔화되었다. **5** 미 달러화의 평가절상은 미국의 수출이 감소하고 수입이 증가하는 현상을 초래할 것이다.

dumping
[dʌ́mpiŋ]

n. 덤핑 (selling unwanted goods very cheaply, usually in other countries)

1 Several pharmaceutical companies were accused of *dumping* out-of-date medicines.

voca+
- anti-dumping tariffs[duty] 반덤핑 관세
- file an anti-dumping complaint 반덤핑 제소를 하다

multilateral trade

n. 다자간[다각] 무역

2 *Multilateral trade* talks collapsed.

voca+
- FTA(Free Trade Agreement) 자유무역협정
- WTO(World Trade Organization) 세계무역기구
- NTB(non-tariff barriers) 비관세장벽

stagnation
[stægnéiʃən]

n. 경기 침체

3 Despite a period of economic *stagnation*, luxury brands are still doing well.

voca+
- inflation 인플레이션 (화폐가치 하락으로 물가가 지속적으로 상승하는 현상)
- stagflation 스테그플레이션 (경제 불황과 물가 상승이 겹쳐진 상황)
- boost[revitalize] the economy 경기를 부양[회복]하다
- economic stimulus package 경기 부양책

plummet
[plʌ́mit]

v. 폭락하다 syn. plunge

4 The company's stocks *plummeted* when the CEO retired.

panic
[pǽnik]

n. 경제 공황 (sudden economic downturn) syn. crisis

5 In 1997, the financial *panic* broke out in Thailand, and it soon spread across Asia.

voca+
- stock market panic 주식 공황
- the Great Depression (1930년대) 미국의 경제 대공황
- the New Deal 뉴딜정책 (미국 루스벨트 대통령이 공황 타개를 위해 펼쳤던 정책)

1 몇몇 제약 회사들이 구식 약품을 덤핑 처리한다는 비난을 받았다. 2 다자간 무역 회담이 결렬되었다. 3 경기 침체기임에도 불구하고 사치품들은 여전히 잘 팔리고 있다. 4 그 회사의 주식은 CEO가 은퇴하자 폭락했다. 5 1997년에 태국에서 경제 공황이 발생하여 곧 아시아 전역으로 퍼졌다.

fluctuate
[flʌ́ktʃuèit]

v. (가격 등이) 변동하다, 계속 변화하다

1 Oil prices *fluctuate* based on supply and demand conditions.

voca+ • sharp[wide] fluctuation 큰 폭의 변동

prosperous
[prάspərəs]

a. 호황의, 번창[번성]하는 syn. flourishing, thriving

2 Their business is a *prosperous* one, fortunately.

voca+ • economic prosperity[boom] 경제 호황, 호경기
• business cycle 경기 변동
• boom and bust cycle 경기 부침 주기

speculate
[spékjəlèit]

v. 투기하다

3 He *speculated in* stocks and lost a fortune.

voca+ • speculate in[on] ~에 투기하다
• speculator 투기꾼
• bonanza / windfall 횡재
• REIT (real estate investment trust) 부동산 투자 신탁, 리츠

income disparity

n. 소득 불균형 syn. income gap

4 An immense *income disparity* exists between those living in large cities and those living in rural areas.

voca+ • the rich-get-richer and the poor-get-poorer 부익부 빈익빈
• polarization[redistribution] of wealth 부의 양극화[재분배]

austerity measures

n. 긴축재정 정책 syn. belt-tightening measures
ant. expansionary measures

5 The government has considered *austerity measures* in order to prevent a financial crisis.

voca+ • tax revenues[expenditures] 세입[세출]
• compile[execute] a budget 예산을 편성[집행]하다
• Ministry of Finance and Economy 재정경제부

1 석유 가격은 수요와 공급 조건에 따라서 변동한다. 2 그들의 사업은 다행히도 번창하고 있다. 3 그는 주식 투기를 해서 많은 돈을 잃었다. 4 대도시 주민들과 시골 주민들 사이에는 커다란 소득 불균형이 존재한다. 5 정부는 금융 위기를 막기 위해 긴축재정 정책을 고려하고 있다.

exercise

정답 및 해설 p.387

A Match the words in the left column to the sentences in the right column.

ⓐ **nationalize**: to change a private company into a government-run one

ⓑ **appreciation**: an increase in value

ⓒ **dumping**: the act of exporting unwanted goods at a lower price than they are sold on the domestic market

ⓓ **multilateral trade**: trade between three or more countries

ⓔ **speculate**: to take the risk for the purpose of earning a big profit

1. Iran's Parliament voted to ________ the oil industry.
2. Developed countries must end ________ of agricultural products on developing countries.
3. I prefer safe investments, but my husband likes to ________.
4. The couple made a lot of money when they sold their house because of the ________ in real estate.
5. The five nations were engaging in ________.

B Choose the option that best completes the sentence.

1. The government decided to provide the textile industry with a(n) ________________.
   ⓐ inflation ⓑ monopoly ⓒ subsidy ⓓ price index

2. The ________________ is a measure of the value of all goods produced within a country's borders.
   ⓐ GDP ⓑ GNP ⓒ CPI ⓓ NTB

3. From a US manufacturer's perspective, ________________ of the dollar leads to decreased imports because fewer foreign products can be purchased with the same amount of money.
   ⓐ appreciation ⓑ regulation ⓒ retaliation ⓓ depreciation

4. There was a period of ________________ in the 1970s, when economic growth rate was less than 2%.
   ⓐ business upturn ⓑ speculation ⓒ stagnation ⓓ recovery

5. As the price of gas ________________, fewer people drove to work.
   ⓐ fluctuated ⓑ declined ⓒ stabilized ⓓ soared

Company 회사

Company 회사

enterprise 기업

- entrepreneur 기업가
- corporation 법인기업 — Inc.(incorporated) 주식회사
- conglomerate 대기업, 재벌 — affiliate 계열사 — subsidiary 자회사
- state-owned enterprise 공기업 (=public corporation)
- multinational (corporation) 다국적기업
- venture 벤처기업 — start-up 신생기업
- franchise 체인점, 연쇄점
- consortium 기업연합
- M&A(mergers & acquisitions) 인수합병
- hostile[friendly] takeover 적대적[우호적] 인수

organization 조직

- department 부서
- rank and file(r) 평사원
- supervisor 총책임자, 상관
- board members 임원진
- board of directors 중역[간부]회의
- CEO(chief executive officer) 최고경영자
- top management 최고경영진
- (labor) union 노동조합
- (on) strike 파업 (중인)
- boycott 보이콧, 불매운동

business management 경영

- financial statement 재무제표
- account book/ledger 회계 장부
- accountant 회계사 — CPA(certified public accountant) 공인회계사
- surplus 흑자
- deficit 적자
- mismanagement 부실경영
- fraudulent accounting 분식회계 — slush fund 비자금
- insolvency/bankruptcy 파산, 부도
- liquidation 부채청산, 회사정리
- strategic partnership 전략적 제휴
- subcontract 하청을 주다

personnel 인사

- recruit 채용하다 — applicant 지원자 — résumé 이력서 — reference 추천서
- designate 임명하다
- performance evaluation 업무수행 평가
- promote 승진시키다
- demote 좌천시키다
- lay-off 정리해고 — downsizing 조직축소
- discharge/fire 해고하다
- resign 사임하다
- retire 퇴직하다
- retirement pay 퇴직금
- pension 연금
- employee[fringe] benefits 복리후생

Voca Check

정답 p.388

Complete the English translation by referring to the page on the left.

❶ Most fast food outlets operate as ___________s.
대부분의 패스트푸드점은 체인점으로 운영된다.

❷ Most of the employees are satisfied with the company because of their ___________.
대부분의 직원들은 복리후생 때문에 회사에 만족하고 있다.

❸ He will get a raise if he does well on his ___________.
업무수행 평가에서 높은 점수를 얻는다면 그는 봉급 인상을 받을 것이다.

❹ A lot of employees will lose their jobs as a result of ___________.
조직 축소로 인해 많은 직원들이 일자리를 잃을 것이다.

❺ ___________ seemed to be the only option as the company was running up huge debts.
회사가 엄청난 부채에 허덕이고 있었기 때문에, 부도만이 유일한 선택으로 보였다.

❻ Now that the business has failed, it has gone into ___________.
그 업체는 도산했고 부채청산에 들어갔다.

❼ The employees were relieved when the company announced there would be no ___________s.
회사측에서 정리해고가 없을 것이라고 발표하자 직원들은 안심했다.

❽ Instead of competing, the companies formed a ___________ and shared resources.
경쟁하는 대신 그 회사들은 기업연합을 결성하여 자원을 공유했다.

More Words

temporary position 임시직
permanent position 정규직
placement agency 직업 소개소
scout 스카우트하다
workload 업무량
paycheck 급여
maternity[sick] leave 출산 휴가[병가]
headquarters/head office 본사 (건물)
go into the black[red] 흑자[적자]를 내다
lucrative 돈벌이가 되는
assets and liabilities 자산 및 부채
restructuring 구조조정
curtail 삭감하다
cutback 삭감
monopoly 독점하다

corporation
[kɔ̀ːrpəréiʃən]

n. 회사, 법인기업

1 How long have you worked for this *corporation*?

voca+
- Inc.(incorporated) 주식회사(의)
- corporation aggregate 사단법인
- corporate transparency[ethics] 기업 투명성[윤리]

conglomerate
[kənglɑ́ːmərət]

n. (여러 계열사를 가지고 있는) 대기업, 재벌, 그룹 (a huge business group that consists of several different companies)

2 Korea has many family-owned *conglomerates* like Samsung, LG and Hyundai.

voca+
- headquarters/head office 본사
- branch 지점
- affiliate 계열사
- subsidiary 자회사

department
[dipɑ́ːrtmənt]

n. (회사의) 부서

3 She is the manager of the public relations *department*.

voca+
- personnel[accounting/customer service/R&D] department
  인사[회계/고객지원/연구개발] 부서

supervisor
[súːpərvàizər]

n. 총책임자, 상관, 상사

4 She is now a *supervisor* of 50 staff members.

voca+
- co-worker/colleague/fellow worker 직장 동료
- subordinate 부하직원

retire
[ritáir]

v. (노령 등으로) 퇴직하다

5 She *retired* at age 60 and wrote a book.

voca+
- retiree 퇴직자
- age limit 정년
- pension/annuity 연금
- retirement pay[payment/money] 퇴직금
- voluntary retirement[resignation] 명예퇴직

1 너는 이 회사에서 일한 지 얼마나 됐니? 2 한국에는 삼성, LG, 현대와 같이 한 집안이 소유한 재벌 회사들이 많이 있다. 3 그녀는 홍보부 부장이다. 4 그녀는 직원 50명을 거느린 총책임자이다. 5 그녀는 60세 때 정년퇴임하여 책 한 권을 썼다.

(labor) union

n. 노동조합

1 The *labor union* voted to go on strike.

voca+
- wage negotiation 임금 협상
- wage hike[freeze] 임금 인상[동결]
- overdue payment 체불 임금
- labor-management relations 노사관계

financial statement

n. 재무제표 (a record of a business's finances indicating earnings and expenses)
syn. financial reports

2 You should see the company's *financial statement* before you make a large investment.

accounting

[əkáuntiŋ]

n. 회계

3 Cindy works in the *accounting* department.

voca+
- accountant 회계사
- accounting book 회계 장부
- cook the books 장부를 조작하다
- financial audit 회계 감사
- income statement 손익계산서
- balance sheet 대차대조표

surplus

[sə́ːrpləs]

n. 흑자, 잉여금 ant. deficit

4 A budget *surplus* occurs when revenues exceed government expenditures.

voca+
- budget[trade] surplus 재정[무역] 흑자
- surplus finance 흑자 재정
- go into the black[red] 흑자[적자]를 내다

promote

[prəmóut]

v. 승진시키다 ant. demote

5 She works hard and will soon be *promoted* to vice president.

voca+
- shake-up 대규모 인사이동
- transfer 전근
- personnel[HR] management 인사 관리

1 노조는 투표 결과 파업에 돌입하기로 했다. **2** 큰 돈을 투자하기 전에 반드시 그 회사의 재무제표를 봐야 한다. **3** Cindy는 회계 부서에서 일한다. **4** 세입이 정부 지출을 초과할 때 재정 흑자가 발생한다. **5** 그녀는 열심히 일하고 있으며 곧 부사장으로 승진될 것이다.

subcontract
[sʌbkɑ́:ntrækt]

v. **하청을 주다** (한 회사가 따낸 계약건의 일부나 전부를 다시 제 3의 업체에게 맡기다)

1 The company is ***subcontracting*** most of the production.

n. **하청**

voca+
- subcontractor 하청업자, 도급업자
- outsourcing 아웃소싱(회사 자체에서 하던 일을 비용 절감과 효율성 증대를 목적으로 외부 인력으로 대체하는 것)
- OEM(original equipment manufacturing) 주문자 상표부착 생산

recruit
[rikrú:t]

v. **(주로 신입사원을) 채용하다**

2 The lab director ***recruited*** some assistants.

voca+
- recruiting (ad)/help wanted 구인 광고
- job opening[vacancy] 결원, 공석
- application form 입사지원서
- résumé/CV(curriculum vitae) 이력서
- headhunter (기업의) 인재 스카우트 담당자
- appoint sb on probation 임시로[수습사원으로] 채용하다

lay-off

n. **정리해고** (a situation where the employer ends a worker's employment temporarily because there's not enough work)

3 The company is in financial trouble. There may be a ***lay-off*** soon.

voca+
- lay off 정리해고하다
- be made redundant 정리해고 당하다
- severance[redundancy] pay (해고 시의) 퇴직금
- furlough (조업 단축 등에 의한) 일시해고

boycott
[bɔ́ikɑ:t]

n. **불매[거부] 운동, 보이콧, 배척** (an act of refusing to buy a product or take part in an activity as a way of protesting)

4 Dr. Martin Luther King led a ***boycott*** against the bus companies by asking blacks not to ride on the buses.

voca+
- economic boycott[blockade] 경제 봉쇄
- organize[stage] a boycott 불매 운동을 벌이다

v. **배척하다, 불매운동을 하다**

1 그 회사는 생산량의 대부분을 하청업체에 맡긴다. 2 연구소장은 몇 명의 조수를 채용했다. 3 회사가 재정난을 겪고 있다. 곧 정리해고를 할지도 모른다.
4 마틴 루터 킹 박사는 흑인들에게 버스를 타지 말 것을 종용하며 버스 회사들에 대한 거부 운동을 이끌었다.

exercise

정답 및 해설 p.388

A Match the words in the left column to the sentences in the right column.

ⓐ **retire**: to finish one's career; to stop working

ⓑ **promote**: to move someone to a higher level in an organization

ⓒ **recruit**: to attract future employees to a company

ⓓ **fraudulent accounting**: illegal accounting practices

ⓔ **supervisor**: one who oversees an operation and has authority over the people involved

1. His ________ warned him that if he arrived late to work again, he would be fired.
2. In recognition of his talent and hard work, the boss is going to ________ Jack to senior manager.
3. The soccer player had to ________ because of a leg injury.
4. The company was accused of ________.
5. Employers visited university campuses to ________ MBA students.

B Choose the option that best completes the sentence.

1. She is the CEO of a very successful ________________.
   ⓐ labor union ⓑ department ⓒ corporation ⓓ stock market

2. The company's budget ________________ resulted in an increase in its stock price.
   ⓐ boycott ⓑ account book
   ⓒ surplus ⓓ deficit

3. The ________________ is fighting for higher wages for its workers.
   ⓐ management ⓑ applicant ⓒ franchise ⓓ labor union

4. Most of the project will be ________________ to a smaller company to save time.
   ⓐ invested ⓑ subcontracted
   ⓒ discharged ⓓ designated

5. The CEO was forced to ________________ because of mismanagement.
   ⓐ promote ⓑ lay off ⓒ downsize ⓓ resign

day 39

Finance 금융

Finance 금융

financial institution 금융기관

- bank 은행
- insurance company 보험회사
- securities company 증권회사
- credit union 신용 조합
- investment trust company 투자신탁회사
- credit card company 신용카드회사
- installment financing company 할부금융회사

financial crisis 금융위기

- be in arrears 연체되다
- late fee 연체료
- liabilities 부채
- delinquent 체납한, 신용불량의
- go into insolvency 채무 불이행 상태에 빠지다
- bankruptcy 파산
- IMF(international monetary fund) 국제통화기금
- IMF bailout IMF 구제금융

financial instruments[products] 금융상품

savings 예금

- open a bank account 계좌를 개설하다
- deposit 예금하다
- principal 원금
- withdraw 인출하다
- ATM(automated teller machine) 현금인출기
- transfer 이체하다
- commission (은행)수수료
- (account) balance 잔고
- loan 융자, 대출
- mortgage 담보대출
- interest 이자
- warrant 보증, 담보

stocks 주식

- IPO(initial public offering) 주식상장, 기업공개
- listed company 상장사
- public offering 주식 공모
- stockholder 주주
- blue chip 우량주
- bull[bear] market 강세[약세]장
- buy[sell] order 매수[매도] 주문
- daily trading volume 일일 거래량
- dividend 배당(금)
- portfolio 유가증권 일람표
- ROI(return on investment) 투자 수익률

insurance 보험

- insurance policy 보험 상품
- life[casualty] insurance 생명[상해]보험
- annuity insurance 연금보험
- premium 보험료
- policy holder 보험 계약자
- insurance beneficiary 보험 수혜자
- uninsured 보험에 들지 않은

Voca Check

정답 p.388

Complete the English translation by referring to the page on the left.

❶ The company needs to balance its assets with its ___________.
회사는 자산과 부채의 균형을 맞출 필요가 있다.

❷ I have some extra money so I'm going to invest it in ___________ and bonds.
여유 자금이 약간 있어서 주식과 채권에 투자하려고 한다.

❸ The stock increased steeply during its ___________, but then it leveled off.
그 주식은 상장 기간 동안에는 주가가 엄청나게 올랐으나 그 뒤에는 안정되었다.

❹ I do my banking with a ___________ because profits are shared among members.
이윤을 조합원들이 나누어 받기 때문에 나는 신용 조합과 거래하고 있다.

❺ I'm going to have to dip into my ___________ in order to make ends meet this month.
이번 달 수지를 맞추기 위해서는 아무래도 예금을 조금 빼서 써야 할 것 같다.

❻ Before I can get my first paycheck, I need to ___________.
첫 월급을 받기 전에 은행 계좌를 개설해야 한다.

❼ If we don't do something soon, the company is going to ___________.
당장 무언가를 하지 않으면 회사가 채무 불이행 상태에 빠지게 될 것이다.

❽ The ___________s will be distributed at the end of the month.
배당금은 월말에 지급될 것이다.

More Words

stock price index 주가 지수
rally (증권 등이) 반등하다, 시세를 회복하다
turnover 총 증권액, 거래 총액
prime rate 우대금리
maturity 만기
bonds 채권
installment savings 적금
stand[go] surety 보증 서다, 보증인이 되다
mortgage lien 저당권
note/bill 어음
auction 경매
slush fund 비자금
broker 중개인
non-banking financial institution 제2금융권
hedge one's bets 분산투자하다
go under/go belly up (회사 등이) 파산하다

credit card

n. 신용카드 syn. plastic

1 Do you accept[take] *credit cards*?

voca+
- spending limit 사용한도
- annual fee 연회비
- (credit card) slip (신용카드) 전표
- in[by] installments 할부로
- in a lump sum/in one payment 일시불로
- debit card 직불카드
- cash advance service 현금서비스

delinquent

[dilíŋkwənt]

a. 체납한, 신용불량의 ant. creditworthy 신용 있는

2 The bank is calling him daily because he is a *delinquent* borrower.

voca+
- credit delinquent 신용불량자
- debtor[creditor] 채무[채권]자
- go bankrupt[broke/bust] 파산하다
- keep one's head above water 빚을 지지 않고 지내다
- credit scoring system 개인 신용 평가시스템

arrears

[əríərz]

n. (항상 복수로) 연체(금), 지체 syn. overdue debt

3 We're two months *in arrears* with the rent.

voca+
- pay off arrears 연체금을 갚다
- late fee 연체료
- fall[get] into arrears 연체되다

loan

[loun]

n. 융자(금), 대출(금)

4 I took out a *loan* from the bank.

voca+
- apply for a loan 대출을 신청하다
- repay[pay off] a loan 대출금을 갚다
- secured[unsecured] loan 담보[무담보] 대출
- home mortgage loan 주택 담보 대출
- loan term 대출 조건

1 신용카드로 계산해도 되나요? **2** 그는 체납 채무자이기 때문에 은행에서는 날마다 그에게 전화를 건다. **3** 우리는 임대료가 두 달째 밀려 있다. **4** 나는 은행에서 대출을 받았다.

transfer
[trænsfə́:r]

v. 이체하다

❶ With Internet banking, I can *transfer* money directly into his account.

voca+ • wire transfer 온라인 송금
• transfer[remittance] fee 송금 수수료

bank account

n. 은행계좌

❷ To open a *bank account*, you must bring your personal identification with you.

voca+ • bankbook 통장 • account number 계좌번호
• open[close] a bank account 은행계좌를 개설하다[해약하다]
• PIN(personal identification number) 비밀번호

deposit
[dipɑ́:zit]

n. 예금, 입금 ant. withdrawal v. 예금하다

❸ *Deposits* can be made at any branch.

voca+ • deposit rate 예금 금리 • deposit slip 예금 신청서
• ordinary deposit 보통예금 • time[term] deposit 정기예금

interest
[íntərest]

n. 이자

❹ How much *interest* do you pay on the loan?

voca+ • accrue (이자가) 붙다, 생기다
• interest rate 이자율 • prime rate 우대금리
• simple[compound] interest 단리[복리]

bailout
[béilàut]

n. 구제 금융, 긴급 융자 (money given to a person, company or foreign country that has very serious financial problems)

❺ The bank was forced to seek a government *bailout*.

voca+ • monetary crisis 통화 위기

❶ 인터넷 뱅킹을 이용해서 나는 그의 계좌에 바로 돈을 이체할 수 있다. ❷ 은행 계좌를 개설하려면 개인 신분증을 지참하셔야 합니다. ❸ 예금은 어느 지점에서나 할 수 있다. ❹ 대출금 이자를 얼마나 내고 있니? ❺ 그 은행은 어쩔 수 없이 정부의 구제 금융을 요청해야 했다.

stockholder

[stákhòuldər]

n. 주주 syn. shareholder

1 A *stockholder* actually owns a part of a company.

voca+
- major[largest] stockholder 대[최대] 주주
- minority stockholder 소액 주주
- daily trading volume 일일 거래량

portfolio

[pɔːrtfóuliòu]

n. 유가증권 일람표 (investments that are owned by a particular person or organization)

2 A financial institution conducts investment analysis with its own *portfolio*.

voca+
- investment portfolio 투자 포트폴리오
- portfolio management (금융) 자산 관리[운용]

listed company

n. 상장사 (a company whose shares can be traded on a stock market)

3 Fletcher Building is the third largest *listed company* in New Zealand.

voca+
- Nasdaq[Kosdaq]-listed 나스닥[코스닥]에 등록된

insurance policy

n. 보험 상품

4 This travel *insurance policy* covers terrorist attacks.

voca+
- insurance agent[broker] 보험 담당자[중개인]
- accident[health / endowment / life / annuity] insurance 사고[건강 / 양로 / 생명 / 연금] 보험

premium

[príːmiəm]

n. 보험료

5 I have to pay the *premium* by January 1st.

voca+
- loading 부가 보험료
- settlement option 보험금 지급 방법의 선택

1 주주는 실제로 한 회사의 일부를 소유한다. 2 금융기관은 자신의 유가증권 일람표를 가지고 투자 분석을 한다. 3 Fletcher Building은 뉴질랜드에서 세 번째로 큰 상장사이다. 4 이 여행 보험 상품은 테러리스트 공격에도 보상 적용된다. 5 나는 1월 1일까지 보험료를 내야 한다.

exercise

정답 및 해설 p.388

A Match the words in the left column to the sentences in the right column.

ⓐ **arrears**: a debt that is unpaid and overdue

ⓑ **interest**: the fee for borrowing money

ⓒ **listed company**: a company whose shares are bought and sold on a stock market

ⓓ **portfolio**: all of one's investments

ⓔ **delinquent**: failing to make payments on one's debt

1. To become a(n) ________, you must meet certain requirements.
2. This is a good time to take out a loan because the ________ rates are really low.
3. He never answers the phone because he's ________ on his loan and is avoiding the bank.
4. Can I borrow some money? I owe ________ on my rent.
5. Don't put all your eggs in one basket. Diversify your ________.

B Choose the option that best completes the sentence.

1. The company would have failed without the government ________________.
   ⓐ portfolio ⓑ bailout ⓒ commission ⓓ warrant

2. I need to ________________ this check in my bank account so that my balance will be sufficient.
   ⓐ invest ⓑ cash ⓒ withdraw ⓓ deposit

3. The insurance company is raising their ________________.
   ⓐ mortgage ⓑ arrears ⓒ premiums ⓓ principal

4. Instead of sending you a check in the mail, why don't I do a bank ________________?
   ⓐ dividend ⓑ deposit ⓒ loan ⓓ transfer

5. It's important to have a good ________________, just in case something awful happens.
   ⓐ insurance policy ⓑ account number
   ⓒ stock price index ⓓ daily trading volume

Newspaper & Broadcasting 신문과 방송

Newspaper 신문

contents 기사 항목
- flyer/flier 광고지
- editorial 사설, 논설
- column 칼럼, (기고)란
  - columnist 기고가, 칼럼니스트
- classified[want] ads 매매 광고(란)
- horoscope 별점 운세
- obituary 사망 기사, 부고(란)
- feature (article) 특집 기사, 연재물
- exclusive/scoop 특종
- caption 사진 설명
- headline 표제, 주요 뉴스
- cover story 1면 기사

journalist 언론인
- run/carry 게재하다, 보도하다
- on[off] the record 보도하는[하지 않는] 조건으로
- press ban 보도 금지
- embargo 보도 유보
- press conference 기자회견
- press briefing 언론 브리핑
- correspondent 특파원, 통신원
  - unbiased coverage 공정한 보도
  - cover 취재하다
- TV reporter 방송 기자

- circulation 판매부수
- issue 발행하다
- subscribe 구독하다
- periodical 정기간행물

Broadcasting 방송

program 프로그램
- program rescheduling 프로그램 개편
  - prime time 황금시간대
  - ratings 시청률
- educational program 교양 프로그램
- newscast 뉴스 방송
- documentary 다큐멘터리
- soap opera 연속극, 드라마
- entertainment program 오락 프로그램
- previously recorded program 녹화 방송
- bilingual broadcast 음성다중 방송
- rerun 재방송
- commercial break 광고시간

news 뉴스
- on (the) air 방송 중인
- news bulletin[flash] 속보, 긴급 뉴스
- footage 보도 화면
- news commentator 뉴스 해설자, 시사평론가
- tip off 제보하다
- foreign dispatch 외신

Voca Check

정답 p.388

Complete the English translation by referring to the page on the left.

❶ She always expresses a controversial opinion in her ___________.
그녀는 사설에서 항상 논쟁거리가 될 만한 의견을 제시한다.

❷ According to the ___________, the men in the picture are the defendant and his lawyer.
사진 설명에 따르면 사진 속 사람들은 피고와 그의 변호사이다.

❸ The president will answer all questions in a ___________ scheduled for noon.
대통령은 정오에 예정된 기자회견에서 모든 질문에 대답할 것이다.

❹ You have to ___________ to a newspaper in order to have it delivered.
배달을 받으려면 신문을 구독해야 한다.

❺ I appreciate the ___________ because I don't speak Korean very well.
나는 한국어를 능숙하게 하지 못하기 때문에 음성다중 방송을 잘 활용하고 있다.

❻ Can I look at the ___________? I want to buy some second-hand furniture.
매매 광고란을 볼 수 있을까요? 중고 가구를 좀 사고 싶어서요.

❼ The press ___________ the story for weeks before people eventually lost interest.
신문은 사람들이 완전히 흥미를 잃을 때까지 몇 주 동안 그 사건을 보도했다.

❽ I will look for bargains in the ___________s before I go shopping on Saturday.
토요일에 쇼핑을 가기 전에 전단지에서 할인 정보를 찾아봐야겠다.

More Words

make-up/layout (인쇄물의) 지면 구성
by courtesy of (자료나 사진 등을) ~가 제공한
press release[kit/material] 보도 자료
help wanted (ad) 구인광고
right to know 알 권리
yellow journalism 선정주의
PR(public relations) 홍보
indirect advertising 간접 광고
spin-off 시리즈 후속편
sitcom(situation comedy) 시트콤
reality show 리얼리티 쇼
continuity 방송대본, 콘티
poor reception 난시청
AM(Amplitude Modulation) 진폭 변조 방식
FM(Frequency Modulation) 주파수 변조 방식
couch potato 앉아서 TV만 보는 사람

scoop
[skuːp]

n. 특종, 독점기사 syn. exclusive, beat

1 A regional newspaper got the *scoop* first.

voca+
- exclusive interview[coverage] 독점 인터뷰[취재]
- in-depth reporting 심층 보도
- paparazzi 파파라치(유명인을 쫓아다니는 사진사)

column
[kɑ́ləm]

n. 칼럼, (특별) 기고란

2 Did you see her *column* in the Washington Post?

voca+
- agony[advice] column (신문의) 고민 상담란
- correspondence column 투고란
- fashion[sports] columnist 패션[스포츠] 칼럼니스트

press ban

n. 보도 금지

3 The public prosecutor issued a *press ban* during the ongoing corruption investigation.

voca+
- impose[lift] a press ban 보도 금지조치를 취하다[해제하다]
- censorship 검열
- news blackout 보도 관제, 보도[방송] 금지

obituary
[əbítʃuèri]

n. 사망기사, 부고 (a notice in the newspaper informing people of a death)

4 I was shocked when I read of his death in the *obituary*.

circulation
[səːrkjəléiʃən]

n. 판매[발행]부수

5 The newspaper has a daily *circulation* of more than 1 million.

voca+
- mass circulation 많은 발행부수(의)
- controlled[free] circulation (신문 · 잡지 등의) 무료배부 부수
- newsstand 신문 가판대
- news vendor 신문 판매원

1 한 지방 신문사가 그 특종을 처음으로 보도했다. 2 워싱턴 포스트지에서 그녀의 칼럼을 봤니? 3 그 검사는 부정 사건 조사가 진행되는 동안 관련 보도를 금지했다. 4 나는 부고란에서 그의 사망 기사를 읽고 충격을 받았다. 5 그 신문의 1일 발행부수는 1백만 부가 넘는다.

periodical
[pìriɑ́:dikəl]

n. 정기간행물

1 The company is the largest publisher of books and *periodicals* in the country.

voca+ • weekly[biweekly / monthly / quarterly / yearly] 주간[격주간 / 월간 / 계간 / 연간]지
• back issue[number] 과월호

ratings
[réitiŋz]

n. 시청률 (=audience rating)

2 The series will be canceled if it continues to drop in the *ratings*.

voca+ • audience measurement 시청률 조사
• prime time / peak hour 황금 시간대
• fringe ratings 주변시간대 시청률

subscribe
[səbskráib]

v. 구독하다

3 Which newspaper do you *subscribe to*, the Times or the Post?

voca+ • subscriber 구독자
• subscription (fee) 정기구독(료)

off the record

a. 비공개[비공식]의 ad. 보도하지 않는 조건으로

4 Her comments were *off the record*.

voca+ • (go) on the record 공식적으로[보도를 전제로] (말하다)
• tip off / leak ~에게 제보하다, (비밀을) 누설하다
• informant / informer 제보자
• anonymous 익명의
• whistle-blower 내부 고발자

coverage
[kʌ́vəridʒ]

n. 취재, 보도 (범위)

5 The issue has received massive media *coverage*.

voca+ • live coverage 생중계
• news source 취재원
• on the spot 현장에서
• quote sb as saying ~을 인용보도하다

1 그 회사는 국내 최대의 서적 및 정기간행물 출판사이다. 2 시청률이 계속 떨어진다면 그 시리즈는 조기 종영될 것이다. 3 너는 타임즈와 포스트 중에서 어느 것을 구독하니? 4 그녀의 발언에는 공개하지 않는다는 조건이 붙었다. 5 그 사안은 언론에 엄청나게 많이 보도되었다.

news bulletin

n. 속보, 긴급 뉴스 syn. newsflash

1 They just aired a *news bulletin* about the terrorist attack.

voca+ • spot news (프로그램 사이의) 짤막한 뉴스

commercial break

n. (프로그램 사이의) 광고 시간대

2 I don't usually pay much attention to the TV during the *commercial breaks*.

voca+ • sponsor/advertiser 광고주
• advertising revenue 광고수입
• advertising expenditure 광고비
• PPL(product placement) (광고를 목적으로) 프로그램의 소품으로 등장시키는 기법

feature

[fíːtʃər]

n. 특집기사 (a special article that deals with a particular subject)

3 The magazine has a *feature* on heart disease in women.

voca+ • Sunday feature 일요 특집판 • special number 특집호

correspondent

[kɔ̀ːrəspɑ́ːndənt]

n. 특파원, 통신원

4 She has been a White House *correspondent* for more than 10 years.

voca+ • war[foreign/parliamentary] correspondent 종군[외신/의회 담당] 기자

flier

[fláiər]

n. 광고지, 전단지 syn. leaflet

5 They mailed the *flier* to all their subscribers.

voca+ • booklet/pamphlet 소책자
• brochure 선전책자, 브로슈어

1 테러리스트 공격에 대한 속보가 방금 방송되었다. 2 나는 광고 시간에는 TV에 별로 주의를 기울이지 않는 편이다. 3 그 잡지에는 여성의 심장 질환에 대한 특집 기사가 실려 있다. 4 그녀는 10년 넘게 백악관 통신원으로 일하고 있다. 5 그들은 모든 구독자에게 광고 전단지를 보냈다.

exercise

정답 및 해설 p.388

A Match the words in the left column to the sentences in the right column.

ⓐ **circulation**: the usual number of copies of a newspaper or magazine sold

ⓑ **feature**: an article that concentrates on a particular subject

ⓒ **correspondent**: a reporter who deals with a particular subject or area

ⓓ **coverage**: the act of reporting news

ⓔ **off the record**: without permission to publish or report publicly

1. There will be a(n) ________ in Monday's paper about a new computer dating service.
2. The newspaper's ________ has been declining since it changed its format.
3. I'm watching live ________ of the war on TV.
4. The reporter couldn't print the information because it was ________.
5. Our ________ in Bangkok has sent this report.

B Choose the option that best completes the sentence.

1. The reporter wishes he had gotten the ________________ before his competitors.
   ⓐ caption ⓑ want ads ⓒ flier ⓓ scoop

2. I write a weekly ________________ in the local newspaper.
   ⓐ obituary ⓑ ratings ⓒ column ⓓ footage

3. The new soap opera had high ________________ right from the start.
   ⓐ circulation ⓑ subscription ⓒ coverage ⓓ ratings

4. I didn't know he had died until I read his ________________.
   ⓐ horoscope ⓑ feature article ⓒ obituary ⓓ editorial

5. We interrupt your regular programming to bring you this special ________________.
   ⓐ soap opera ⓑ news bulletin
   ⓒ press ban ⓓ commercial break

Popular Culture & Film 대중문화와 영화

Film 영화

film making 영화 제작

- producer 제작자
- (film) director 감독
- staff 제작진
- scenario/screenplay 각본
- star 주연(을 맡다)
- shoot 촬영하다
- edit 편집하다
  - censorship 검열
  - film rating 영화등급
  - director's cut 감독판
- subtitle 자막
- distributor 배급사
- trailer 예고편
- premiere 시사회
- box office 흥행성적
  - blockbuster 대작 영화
- sequel 후속편

film festival 영화제

- Academy Awards 아카데미상
- red carpet 레드 카펫, 예우
- nominee 수상 후보
- winner 수상자
- Best Actor[Actress] in a leading[supporting] role 남[여]우 주[조]연상
- Best Picture Award 작품상
- Best Director Award 감독상
- Best Cinematography Award 촬영상
- Best Screenplay Award 각본상
- Best Costume Design Award 의상상
- Best Visual Effects Award 특수효과상
- Honorary Award 공로상
- Cannes Film Festival 칸영화제
- Venice Film Festival 베니스영화제
- Berlin Film Festival 베를린영화제

Popular Culture 대중문화

characteristics 특징

- consumerism 소비주의
- commercialism 상업주의
- standardization 표준화, 획일화
- diversification 다양화

performance 공연

- audience 관객
- rehearsal 예행 연습(리허설)

theatrical genre 연극 장르

- play 희곡
- playwright 극작가
- lines 대사
- prompt 대사를 알려주다
- improvise/wing 즉흥 연기를 하다
- act 막
- intermission 중간 휴식, 막간

musical genre 음악 장르

- concert 콘서트, 연주회
- recital 독주[독창]회, 리사이틀
- musical band 밴드, 음악단체
- concert tour 순회 콘서트
- head-banging 헤드뱅잉
- crowd-surfing 관객이나 밴드 멤버가 관중석으로 몸을 날리는 행위
- moshing 모싱(락 공연장에서 과격하게 춤추는 행위)

Voca Check

정답 p.389

Complete the English translation by referring to the page on the left.

❶ That was such a great movie. I can't wait to see the ___________.
그 영화는 정말 재미있었어. 속편이 나오기를 손꼽아 기다리고 있어.

❷ I got to attend the ___________ because my boyfriend played a small role in the film.
남자친구가 그 영화에서 작은 역할을 맡았기 때문에 나는 시사회에 참석할 수 있었다.

❸ I prefer to watch movies in their original language with ___________s.
나는 자막과 함께 원어로 영화 보는 것을 더 좋아한다.

❹ The other ___________s for the award congratulated the winner.
그 상의 다른 후보자들은 수상자를 축하했다.

❺ They are going to ___________ the film on an island in the Pacific.
그들은 태평양의 한 섬에서 영화를 촬영할 것이다.

❻ I'm going to attend my daughter's piano ___________ tonight.
나는 오늘 밤 딸의 피아노 독주회에 참석할 것이다.

❼ Many people think that ___________ has ruined Christmas.
많은 사람들이 소비주의가 크리스마스를 망치고 있다고 생각한다.

❽ The band is going on a three-month ___________ to promote their new CD.
그 밴드는 새 CD를 홍보하기 위해서 3개월간 순회 콘서트를 할 것이다.

More Words

mainstream 주류
marginal culture 주변 문화
counter culture 저항 문화
subculture 하위 문화
avant-garde 전위의
fandom 팬덤, 팬층
enthusiast/buff 애호가, ~광
mogul (업계의) 거물
matinée 낮공연
commentary 논평, 해설
running time 상영 시간
advance ticket 예매권
dog tour 순회 공연
indie 독립적으로 제작하는

Academy Awards

n. 아카데미상, 아카데미 시상식

1 The *Academy Awards* have been held annually since 1927.

voca+
- Oscar 오스카상, 아카데미상(트로피)의 별칭
- Oscar winner 아카데미상 수상자[수상작]

staff

[stæf]

n. 제작진, 스태프 syn. crew

2 The problem with the Korean movie industry is the poor working conditions for production *staff*.

voca+
- (assistant) director (조)감독
- cinematographer 촬영감독
- art[stage] director 미술[무대] 감독
- gaffer 조명감독

star

[stɑːr]

v. 주연을 맡다, 주연으로 출연시키다 n. 주연

3 This is a funny and heart-warming film *starring* Drew Barrymore.

voca+
- cast(ing) 배역(을 정하는 것)
- protagonist/main character 주역
- villain 악역
- extra 단역
- stunt person 스턴트맨
- stand-in 대역

film rating

n. 영화 관객 연령 제한 등급

4 *Film rating* is related to offensive words, violence and sexual content.

voca+
- G(General) 일반용
- PG(Parental Guidance Suggested) 보호자 동반
- PG-13(Parental Guidance 13) 13세 미만 보호자 동반
- R(Restricted) 17세 미만 보호자 동반
- NC-17(No Children Under 17 Admitted) 17세 미만 관람불가
- X-rated 성인용

1 아카데미 시상식은 1927년부터 매년 개최되어 왔다. **2** 한국 영화 산업의 문제는 제작진의 열악한 노동 환경이다. **3** 이것은 Drew Barrymore 주연의 재미있고 감동적인 영화이다. **4** 영화의 관객 연령 제한 등급은 불쾌감을 주는 언어, 폭력, 성 묘사 장면과 관계 있다.

distributor
[distríbjətər]

n. 배급사

■1 He found it difficult to find a *distributor* of the film.

voca+ • film distribution agency 영화 배급사
• screen quota system 스크린 쿼터 제도(자국 영화를 일정 일수 이상 의무적으로 상영하도록 하는 제도)

screenplay
[skrí:nplèi]

n. 영화 각본, 대본 syn. script, scenario

■2 He wrote the *screenplay* for *Minority Report*; it was based on a novel by Philip K. Dick.

voca+ • plot 영화의 중심이 되는 이야기 • synopsis 대강의 줄거리, 시놉시스
• shooting script/conti(nuity) 촬영 대본, 콘티
• adaptation 각색

trailer
[tréilər]

n. 예고편

■3 I saw a *trailer* for the latest Spielberg film.

voca+ • teaser trailer 맛보기 예고편
• sneak preview/premiere 시사회
• (ending) credits 배우와 촬영 스태프 목록

nominee
[nɑ̀:məní:]

n. (상 등의) 후보자

■4 Not all of the *nominees* have prepared an acceptance speech.

voca+ • nominate A for B A를 B의 후보로 지명하다
• Oscar-nominated 아카데미상 후보에 오른

blockbuster
[blɑ́kbʌ̀stər]

n. 대작 영화, 흥행작 (a book or film that is very successful)

■5 Bruce Willis's new *blockbuster* took in $10.6 million in its first weekend.

voca+ • independent[low-budget] movie 독립[저예산] 영화

■1 그는 그 영화의 배급사를 찾기가 어렵다는 것을 알았다. ■2 그는 Minority Report의 각본을 썼다. 그것은 Philip K. Dick의 소설을 바탕으로 한 것이다. ■3 나는 Spielberg의 최신작 예고편을 보았다. ■4 모든 후보자들이 수상 소감을 준비하지는 않았다. ■5 Bruce Willis의 새로 나온 대작 영화가 개봉 첫 주에 1천 60만 달러를 벌어들였다.

box office

n. 매표소, 영화 흥행성적

1 The director was sure that his movie would be a ***box office*** hit.

voca+
- release a film 영화를 개봉하다
- box office hit[success] 흥행 성공
- break box office records 흥행 기록을 깨다
- long run 장기 상영
- early finish 조기 종영
- advance ticket 예매권
- admission fee 입장료

act

[ækt]

n. 막(幕)

2 The heroine dies in ***Act*** 4, Scene 2.

voca+
- prologue 서막
- epilogue 종막
- scene 장(場)
- intermission / interlude 중간 휴식

line

[lain]

n. (주로 복수로) 대사

3 I've memorized all my ***lines*** for the play.

voca+
- soliloquy 독백
- aside 방백
- dialogue 대화
- ad lib 애드립, 즉흥 대사
- stage direction 무대 지시, 지문
- learn[fluff] one's lines 대사를 외우다[틀리다]
- prompt 배우에게 다음 대사를 알려주다[알려주는 것]

consumerism

[kənsúːmərìzəm]

n. 소비주의 (the belief that it is good for the economy to buy and use a lot of goods)

4 Modern American culture is characterized by ***consumerism*** and standardization.

rehearsal

[rihə́ːrsəl]

n. 예행 연습, 리허설

5 Changes to the script are often made during ***rehearsal***.

voca+
- dress rehearsal 총연습

1 그 감독은 자신의 영화가 흥행작이 될 것으로 확신했다. 2 여주인공은 4막 2장에서 죽는다. 3 나는 연극의 내 대사를 모두 외웠다. 4 현대 미국 문화의 특징은 소비주의와 획일화이다. 5 대본 수정은 예행 연습 중에 종종 이루어진다.

exercise

정답 및 해설 p.389

A Match the words in the left column to the sentences in the right column.

ⓐ **rehearsal**: the act of practicing for a performance

ⓑ **blockbuster**: a film that is very popular and earns a lot of money

ⓒ **star**: to play an important role in a film

ⓓ **lines**: the words in a play or screenplay

ⓔ **censorship**: the act of removing content from a work because it is deemed unsuitable

1. She will ________ in a romantic comedy film next summer.
2. As the lead in this play, I have a lot of ________ to learn.
3. Because of ________ laws, foul language is removed from movies before being shown on TV.
4. The high-budget film is expected to be a ________.
5. The final ________ before opening night will be held on Monday.

B Choose the option that best completes the sentence.

1. The production ________________ complained of poor working conditions.
   ⓐ audience ⓑ staff ⓒ maniac ⓓ nominee

2. Her mother wouldn't let her see the movie because of its ________________.
   ⓐ censorship ⓑ budget ⓒ rehearsal ⓓ film rating

3. I really wanted to see the film after I saw the ________________.
   ⓐ trailer ⓑ premiere ⓒ scenery ⓓ prompt

4. After having completed the film, the independent director found it difficult to find a ________________.
   ⓐ distributor ⓑ sequel ⓒ screenplay ⓓ staff

5. The film earned millions at the ________________.
   ⓐ rehearsal ⓑ premiere ⓒ box office ⓓ commentary

Education 교육

Education 교육

school affairs 학사과정

- certificate 수료증
- transcript 성적 증명서
- diploma 학위 증명서
- degree 학위
  - doctor 박사
  - master 석사
  - bachelor 학사
- thesis 학위논문
- graduation 졸업
- graduate student 대학원생
- undergraduate 학부생
- scholarship 장학금
- tuition (fee) 수업료
- admission 입학허가
- application form 입학원서

examination 시험

- repeater 유급생
- flunk 낙제하다
- report card 성적표
  - credit 이수 단위
  - GPA(grade point average) 평점
- makeup exam 재시험
- cramming 벼락치기
- final (exam) 기말고사
- mid-term (exam) 중간고사
- placement test 배치고사
- entrance exam 입학시험
  - SAT (미국) 대학수학능력시험
  - GRE (미국) 대학원 입학자격시험

curriculum 교육과정

- syllabus 강의계획표
- compulsory[required] course 필수과목
- elective[optional] course 선택과목
- extracurricular activities 과외활동
- field day 운동회
- excursion 수학여행

education policy 교육정책

- compulsory education 의무교육
- holistic education 전인교육
- vocational education 직업교육
- gifted education 영재교육
- liberal education 일반교양교육
- distance learning 원격교육

school violence 학교폭력

- bullying 괴롭힘
- outcast 왕따
- juvenile delinquent 비행 청소년
  - truancy 무단결석
- corporal punishment 체벌
- suspend 정학시키다
- expel 퇴학시키다
- drop out 중퇴하다
- dropout 중퇴자

Voca Check

정답 p.389

Complete the English translation by referring to the page on the left.

❶ Many teachers don't believe __________ is an effective method for studying.
많은 교사들이 벼락치기는 효과적인 학습 방법이 아니라고 생각한다.

❷ He does very well in school. He has a __________ of 4.0.
그는 공부를 매우 잘 한다. 그의 평점은 4.0이다.

❸ She was afraid to show her parents her __________ because of her grade in math.
그녀는 자신의 수학 성적 때문에 부모님께 성적표를 보여드리기가 두려웠다.

❹ It is getting harder for young people to go to college because of increasing __________.
등록금 인상 때문에 젊은이들이 대학에 가는 것이 더욱 힘들어지고 있다.

❺ Last year I had to take out a student loan, but this year I have a __________.
작년에 나는 학자금 대출을 받아야 했지만, 올해는 장학금을 받게 되었다.

❻ Please attach your __________ to your résumé.
이력서에 성적 증명서를 첨부하시오.

❼ His parents are worried he is going to __________ because he has no interest in school.
그의 부모님은 그가 학업에 흥미가 없어서 중퇴할까 봐 걱정하고 있다.

❽ The Internet has made __________ a viable way to earn a degree.
인터넷 덕분에 원격교육이 학위 취득을 위한 실용적인 방편 중 하나가 될 수 있었다.

More Words

pedagogy 교육학, 교수법
formal education 정규교육
alternative education 대안교육
transfer 전학(가다)
coed 남녀공학의
prep(aratory) school *AmE.* 사립 고등학교 *BrE.* 사립 초등학교
PTA(Parent Teacher Association) (미국) 사친회, 학부모회
dissertation 학위 논문
treatise 학술 논문
freshman (대학) 1학년
sophomore (대학) 2학년
junior (대학) 3학년
senior (대학) 4학년
essay test 논술시험

degree
[digríː]

n. 학위

1 Mark has a ***degree*** in engineering.

voca+ • bachelor's[master's] degree 학사[석사] 학위
• doctorate/Ph.D. 박사 학위
• honorary degree 명예 학위
• Bachelor of Arts[Science] 문학사[이학사]

admission
[ədmíʃən]

n. 입학 (허가)

2 Private colleges set their own ***admission*** policy.

voca+ • admission procedures 입학 절차
• entrance quota 입학 정원
• contributions 기여 입학

transcript
[trǽnskript]

n. *AmE.* (대학) 성적 증명서

3 University ***transcripts*** are often printed on security paper to avoid forgery.

voca+ • certificate of enrollment 재학 증명서
• diploma 졸업장, 졸업증서

compulsory education

n. 의무교육

4 In Korea, we have 9 years of ***compulsory education***.

voca+ • elementary[secondary/higher] education 초등[중등/고등]교육

bullying
[búliŋ]

n. 왕따 시키기, 약자 괴롭히기

5 ***Bullying*** is a serious problem in many schools.

voca+ • bully (약자를) 괴롭히는 사람; 괴롭히다
• group bullying 집단 따돌림
• outcast/misfit 따돌림 당하는 사람

1 Mark는 공학 학위를 갖고 있다. **2** 사립 대학들은 저마다 고유의 입학 정책을 수립하고 있다. **3** 대학 성적 증명서는 위조 방지를 위해 주로 보안 용지에 인쇄된다. **4** 한국의 의무교육 기간은 9년이다. **5** 많은 학교에서 왕따 현상은 심각한 문제이다.

thesis
[θíːsis]

n. 학위 논문 (복수형 theses) syn. dissertation

1 She is writing her master's *thesis* on black holes.

voca+
- doctoral[master's/graduation] thesis 박사[석사/학사] 논문
- abstract 논문 초록 (a short written statement containing the main ideas of a document)
- bibliography 참고문헌
- source 출처

graduate student

n. 대학원생 syn. *BrE.* postgraduate

2 Mark is a *graduate student* majoring in physics.

voca+
- grad(uate) school 대학원
- graduate 학부 졸업생
- undergraduate 학부생 (a student at college who is studying for their first degree)

flunk
[flʌŋk]

v. 시험에 실패하다, 낙제점을 받다 syn. fail

3 Tom *flunked* chemistry last semester.

voca+
- flunk out (성적 불량으로) 퇴학당하다

SAT

n. 미국의 대학 수학 능력시험 (Scholastic Aptitude Test)

4 I guess the *SAT* is sort of like the Korean college entrance exam.

voca+
- GRE(Graduate Record Examination) 미국의 일반대학원 입학시험

syllabus
[síləbəs]

n. 강의계획(표) (outline or summary of the subjects to be covered in a course)

5 Our *syllabus* this semester includes a visit to a social service agency.

voca+
- on a syllabus 강의계획에 있는
- curriculum 교과과정 (the subjects that students study at a particular school or college)

1 그녀는 블랙홀을 주제로 한 석사 학위 논문을 쓰고 있다. 2 Mark는 물리학을 전공하는 대학원생이다. 3 Tom은 지난 학기에 화학에서 낙제했다. 4 SAT는 한국의 대입시험과 다소 비슷한 것 같다. 5 이번 학기 강의계획에는 사회복지기관 방문이 포함되어 있습니다.

corporal punishment

n. 체벌

1 Many teachers are opposed to *corporal punishment*.

voca+ • chastise 체벌하다

suspend

[səspénd]

v. 정학시키다

2 She was *suspended from* school for a week because she swore at her teacher.

voca+ • suspension 정학
• expulsion 퇴학
• suspension for an indefinite period 무기정학

truancy

[trúːənsi]

n. 무단결석, 등교 거부 (=truanting)

3 She has very good exam results and no *truancy*.

voca+ • truant 무단결석 학생; 무단결석하다
• play hooky 학교를 마음대로 빼먹다
• regular[perfect] attendance 개근

elective (course)

n. 선택 과목 syn. optional course

4 I am taking Spanish as an *elective course*.

voca+ • prerequisite 선행과목
• liberal arts (대학의) 교양과목 (college subjects that develop thinking ability and general knowledge rather than technical skills)

gifted education

n. 영재교육 (education for the gifted or talented)

5 He published books on *gifted education* for teachers and parents.

voca+ • gifted child 영재
• IQ(Intelligence Quotient) 지능지수
• early education 조기교육
• special education 특수교육
• elitist education system 영재교육 제도

1 많은 교사들이 체벌에 반대한다. **2** 그녀는 교사에게 욕설을 해서 일주일 간 정학 처분을 받았다. **3** 그녀는 시험 성적이 매우 좋고 무단결석 기록도 없다. **4** 나는 선택과목으로 스페인어를 수강하고 있다. **5** 그는 교사와 부모를 위한 영재교육 관련 도서를 출간했다.

exercise

정답 및 해설 p.389

A Match the words in the left column to the sentences in the right column.

ⓐ **flunk**: to fail to achieve a minimum grade

ⓑ **transcript**: an official document which contains the grades a person earned in school

ⓒ **truancy**: the act of missing class without permission

ⓓ **suspend**: to prevent someone from attending classes as a punishment

ⓔ **syllabus**: an outline or plan for a course of study

1. The teacher called the boy's mother to inform her of his ________.
2. According to the ________, we are starting a unit on World War II next.
3. She was ________(e)d for cheating on the test.
4. If you don't study, you're going to ________.
5. You have to have your ________ sent to the university as part of your application.

B Choose the option that best completes the sentence.

1. The bright boy was put in ____________ education because of his high IQ.
   ⓐ compulsory ⓑ gifted ⓒ holistic ⓓ vocational
2. I finally finished my ____________ so now I can graduate.
   ⓐ thesis ⓑ placement test
   ⓒ scholarship ⓓ entrance exam
3. I have a bachelor's ____________ in biology.
   ⓐ syllabus ⓑ elective ⓒ report card ⓓ degree
4. She worked hard and gained ____________ to Harvard.
   ⓐ curriculum ⓑ admission ⓒ excursion ⓓ bachelor
5. ____________ can make it difficult for some students to focus because they feel scared.
   ⓐ Cramming ⓑ Tuition ⓒ Bullying ⓓ Syllabus

day 43

Weather & Climate 날씨와 기후

Weather 날씨

weather conditions 기상 상태

- wind velocity 풍속
- tornado 회오리바람, 폭풍
- gust/blast/gale 돌풍
- breeze 미풍, 산들바람
- wind 바람

- heavy snowfall 폭설
- blizzard 눈보라
- sleet 진눈깨비
- snow 눈(오다)

- rain 비(오다)
- precipitation 강수량
- drizzle 이슬비, 가랑비
- shower 소나기
- downpour 폭우
- hail 우박

weather forecast 일기예보

- wind chill factor 체감 온도
- daily temperature range 일교차
- heavy rain warning 호우경보
- high[low] (atmospheric) pressure 고[저]기압
- misty 안개 낀
- overcast 잔뜩 흐린, 우중충한
- scorching 찌는 듯이 더운
  - tropical night 열대야
  - discomfort index 불쾌지수

Climate 기후

meteorological disasters 기상재해

- natural disasters 자연재해
- deluge 홍수, 범람
- drought 가뭄
- earthquake 지진
- landslide 산사태
- avalanche 눈사태
- yellow dust 황사
- typhoon 태풍
- tidal wave 해일

- weather anomaly 기상이변
- heat wave 폭염
- cold spell 한파
- El Niño 엘니뇨
- La Niña 라니냐

climate zone 기후대

- temperate zone 온대지역
- tropical zone 열대지역
- subtropical zone 아열대지역
- subpolar zone 냉대지역
- polar zone 한대지역

Voca Check

정답 p.390

Complete the English translation by referring to the page on the left.

❶ The ___________ is calculated by the relationship between temperature and relative humidity.
불쾌지수는 기온과 상대습도의 관계로 측정된다.

❷ The cool ___________ brought relief from the heat.
시원한 산들바람이 열을 식혀주었다.

❸ Our heating bill was really high after the ___________.
한파 후 난방비가 정말 많이 나왔다.

❹ The skiers narrowly escaped an ___________.
그 스키 선수들은 가까스로 눈사태를 피했다.

❺ Palm trees grow well in the ___________ because the climate is ideal.
야자나무는 열대 기후에 잘 맞아 그 곳에서 잘 자란다.

❻ The sudden ___________ resulted in flooding and landslides.
갑작스런 폭우로 인해 홍수와 산사태가 발생했다.

❼ The government is giving funds to farmers who have been affected by the ___________.
정부는 가뭄 피해를 입은 농부들에게 지원금을 지급하고 있다.

❽ The ___________ is a result of desertification.
황사는 사막화의 결과이다.

More Words

Fahrenheit 화씨
Centigrade / Celsius 섭씨
thermometer 온도계
hygrometer 습도계
maximum[minimum] temperature 최고[최저] 기온
meteorological phenomena 기상 현상
THI (temperature-humidity index) 온윤지수
seismic intensity 지진 강도
mudslide 진흙 사태
squall (눈 · 비를 동반한) 돌풍
haze 아지랑이
muggy / humid 후텁지근한, 덥고 습도 높은
sultry 찌는 듯이 더운
arid 건조한
bleak 살을 에는 듯한
Indian summer (늦가을의) 봄날 같은 날씨

wind velocity

n. 풍속 syn. wind speed

1 A tornado usually has a maximum *wind velocity* of 125 to 200 miles per hour.

voca+
- anemometer 풍속계
- anemoscope 풍향계
- wind direction[pressure] 풍향[풍압]

sleet

[sliːt]

n. 진눈깨비 v. 진눈깨비가 내리다

2 We couldn't see anything because of the *sleet* and snow.

voca+
- driving sleet[rain / snow] 휘몰아치는 진눈깨비[비 / 눈]
- ice pellets 우박, 싸락눈

precipitation

[prisìpitéiʃən]

n. (눈 · 비 등을 포함한) 강수(량)

3 The forecast is for dry, cloudy weather with no *precipitation* expected.

voca+
- heavy[light] precipitation 많은[적은] 강수량
- precipitation probability 강수 확률

deluge

[délju:dʒ]

n. 홍수, 범람 syn. flood(s), inundation

4 The central areas were submerged by the *deluge*.

voca+
- flood victims 수재민
- the Deluge [성서] 노아의 대홍수
- After me, the deluge. 나중에야 어찌되든 내 알 바 아니다.

tidal wave

n. (지진 · 강풍으로 인한) 높은 파도, 해일

5 The news report said a *tidal wave* hit the coast of Taiwan.

voca+
- tsunami 지진 해일, 쓰나미

1 토네이도의 최대 풍속은 보통 시속 125에서 200마일이다. **2** 진눈깨비와 눈 때문에 아무것도 보이지 않았다. **3** 눈비 없는 건조하고 흐린 날씨가 예상됩니다. **4** 중부 지방이 홍수에 의해 침수되었다. **5** 뉴스에서 해일이 대만 해안을 덮쳤다고 보도했다.

typhoon

[taifúːn]

n. 태풍

1 More than 1,000 people died or have been missing since a series of *typhoons* hit the area.

voca+
- hurricane 허리케인 (서인도제도의 열대성저기압)
- cyclone 사이클론 (인도양 등의 열대성저기압)
- tornado 토네이도 (서아프리카 · 미국 미시시피강 유역의 대선풍)
- issue[give] a typhoon warning 태풍 경보를 내리다
- the eye[center] of a typhoon 태풍의 눈

heat wave

n. 폭염, 혹서 syn. hot spell ant. cold spell[snap/wave]

2 Early in August a *heat wave* hit.

voca+
- heat stroke/sunstroke 일사병
- heat island effect 열섬현상 (급속한 도시화와 마구잡이 개발로 인해 도심의 기온이 외곽보다 높아지는 현상으로 이상고온 현상의 원인이다.)

El Niño

n. 엘니뇨 (a warm ocean current starting in South America that is able to affect weather in different parts of the world)

3 *El Niño* caused a drought in Indonesia last year.

voca+
- La Niña 라니냐 (해수의 온도가 지나치게 내려가는 현상으로 대기의 기온을 급격히 변화시켜 기상이변의 한 요인이 된다.)

scorching

[skɔ́ːrtʃiŋ]

a. 몹시 더운, 찌는 듯한

4 The *scorching* heat kept us indoors today.

voca+
- scorching[blazing/blistering] heat 찌는 듯한 무더위

wind chill factor

n. 체감 온도

5 It's two degrees outside, but with the *wind chill factor*, it feels like minus five.

1 태풍이 연속적으로 그 지역을 강타한 이후 천 명 이상이 사망하거나 실종되었다. 2 8월 초에 폭염이 기승을 부렸다. 3 지난 해 인도네시아는 엘니뇨 현상으로 인해 가뭄이 들었다. 4 찌는 듯한 무더위 때문에 오늘 우리는 실내에만 있었다. 5 바깥 온도는 2도이지만 체감 온도는 영하 5도이다.

temperate zone

n. 온대지역

1 The *temperate zone* is the most populated zone of the world.

voca+
- temperate arid[humid] climate 온대건조[습윤]기후
- temperate monsoon climate 온대계절풍기후
- temperate (rain) forest 온대(강우)림

polar zone

n. 한대지역 syn. frigid zone

2 The aurora is a glow observed in the night sky, usually in the *polar zone*.

voca+
- midnight sun / white night 백야
- tropical[torrid] zone 열대지역

overcast

[òuvərkǽst]

a. 잔뜩 흐린, 우중충한 syn. dull

3 It looks too *overcast* to have a picnic today.

voca+
- overcast sky 잔뜩 흐린 하늘

heavy snowfall

n. 폭설

4 *Heavy snowfall* continues to worsen road conditions.

voca+
- snow clearing 제설 작업
- snow plow 제설기
- grit (결빙된 도로에 뿌리는) 모래
- winter storm warning[advisory] 대설경보[주의보]

heavy rain warning

n. 호우 경보

5 The Korea Meteorological Administration issued a *heavy rain warning* yesterday afternoon.

voca+
- heavy rain advisory 호우주의보
- rain gauge 우량계
- torrential rain 억수 같이 쏟아지는 비

1 온대지역은 세계에서 인구가 가장 많은 지역이다. 2 오로라는 보통 한대지역의 밤하늘에서 관찰되는 빛이다. 3 오늘은 야유회를 하기에는 날이 너무 흐리다. 4 폭설로 도로 상태가 계속 악화되고 있다. 5 한국 기상청은 어제 오후에 호우 경보를 발령했다.

exercise

정답 및 해설 p.390

A Match the words in the left column to the sentences in the right column.

ⓐ **typhoon**: a heavy storm formed in the western Pacific Oceans

ⓑ **scorching**: extremely hot

ⓒ **polar zone**: the regions connected with, or near the North or South Pole

ⓓ **deluge**: a heavy flood

ⓔ **overcast**: clouded over

1. Few people live in the ________ because of the harsh climate.
2. Let's go swimming to get out of this ________ heat.
3. It was ________ this morning, but the sun came out in the afternoon.
4. We watched from the rooftop as our belongings floated away in the ________.
5. There are several ________(e)s every summer in Asia.

B Choose the option that best completes the sentence.

1. We were on the beach when all of a sudden we noticed a(n) ________________ coming towards us.
   ⓐ blizzard ⓑ avalanche ⓒ tidal wave ⓓ La Niña

2. Pilots need to consider ________________ every time they fly.
   ⓐ droughts ⓑ wind velocity ⓒ avalanches ⓓ heat waves

3. The ________________ made it difficult to drive.
   ⓐ sleet ⓑ drought ⓒ drizzle ⓓ breeze

4. You'd better take an umbrella. There's a 75% chance of ________________.
   ⓐ wind chill ⓑ tidal wave ⓒ cold spell ⓓ precipitation

5. The temperature is minus five, but with the ________________, it feels like it's minus twenty.
   ⓐ yellow dust ⓑ wind chill factor
   ⓒ heavy rain warning ⓓ daily temperature range

day 44 Cosmos 우주

Cosmos 우주

astronomical observation 천체 관측

- astronomy 천문학
  - planetarium 천문관
  - observatory 천문대
    - Hubble telescope 허블 망원경
  - astronomical telescope 천체 망원경
  - total[partial] eclipse 개기[부분]식
  - lunar[solar] eclipse 월식[일식]
  - crescent moon 초승달
- stellar 별의
  - constellation 별자리
  - zodiac signs 12궁도 별자리
  - horoscope 별자리 운세
  - astrology 점성술

celestial body 천체

- solar system 태양계
  - fixed[permanent] star 항성
  - planet 행성
    - Mercury 수성
    - Venus 금성
    - Earth 지구
    - Mars 화성
    - Jupiter 목성
    - Saturn 토성
    - Uranus 천왕성
    - Neptune 해왕성
    - Pluto 명왕성
  - satellite 위성
  - asteroid 소행성
  - meteorite 운석
  - meteor 유성
    - meteor shower 유성우(
  - comet 혜성
  - supernova 초신성
  - nebula 성운
  - galaxy 은하
- axis 지축
  - orbit 궤도
  - rotate 자전하다
  - revolve 공전하다

space exploration 우주 탐사

- alien 외계인, 외계의
  - extraterrestrial 외계인, 외계의
  - U.F.O. 미확인 비행 물체 (Unidentified Flying Object)
- spacecraft/space shuttle 우주선
  - blast-off/lift-off 발사
  - launch pad 발사대
  - booster 발사용[보조 추진] 로켓
  - astronaut/cosmonaut 우주비행사
  - zero-gravity/weightlessness 무중력 상태
  - manned mission 유인 탐사
  - space probe 우주 탐사기
  - mission control 우주 관제소
  - artificial satellite 인공 위성

cosmology 우주론

- Big Bang theory 빅뱅 이론
- general theory of relativity 일반 상대성 이론
- astrophysics 천체 물리학

Voca Check

정답 p.390

Complete the English translation by referring to the page on the left.

❶ Some people argue that Pluto is not really a __________, but just a large asteroid.
어떤 이들은 명왕성이 행성이 아니라 단지 커다란 소행성일 뿐이라고 주장한다.

❷ People used to think that the Earth was the center of the universe until it was proven that the Earth actually __________s around the Sun.
지구가 태양 주위를 공전한다는 것이 증명되기 전까지 사람들은 지구가 우주의 중심이라고 생각했다.

❸ I would like to study __________ because I'm interested in the stars.
나는 별에 대해 흥미를 느끼고 있기 때문에 천문학을 공부하고 싶다.

❹ The __________ consists of nine planets and their satellites going around the Sun.
태양계는 태양 주위를 공전하는 9개의 행성과 그 위성들로 구성되어 있다.

❺ Putting __________s in space has made a huge impact on communications here on Earth.
우주 공간에 위성을 쏘아 올린 것은 지상에서의 통신에 큰 영향을 미치고 있다.

❻ Neil Armstrong was part of the first __________ to the Moon.
Neil Armstrong은 최초의 달 유인 탐사의 일원이었다.

❼ Astronauts in space communicate with __________ on Earth.
우주 공간에 있는 우주 비행사들은 지상의 우주 관제소와 통신을 한다.

❽ A __________ is the base from which the rocket is launched.
발사대는 로켓이 발사되는 기지이다.

More Words

aerospace 항공 우주
splashdown/touchdown 우주선의 착수(바다로 떨어짐)
light year 광년
white dwarf 백색 왜성
sunspot 태양 흑점
interstellar matter 성간 물질
neutron star/pulsar 중성자별
black hole 블랙홀
white hole 화이트홀

planetarium
[plæ̀nətɛ́əriəm]

n. 천문관

■1 A *planetarium* is a building with a dome where lights in the ceiling represent the movement of planets and stars.

observatory
[əbzə́:rvətɔ̀:ri]

n. 천문대, 관측소

■2 The Cincinnati *Observatory* is the oldest professional observatory in the United States.

voca+
- the Royal Greenwich Observatory 그리니치 천문대
- orbiting solar observatory 태양 관측 위성
- meteorological observatory 기상대

eclipse
[iklíps]

n. (해 · 달의) 식

■3 On Wednesday there will be a total *eclipse* of the sun.

voca+
- solar[lunar] eclipse 일식[월식]
- total[partial/annular] eclipse 개기[부분/금환]식

crescent
[krésənt]

n. 초승달 (모양)

■4 The moon in the sky was a brightly shining *crescent*.

voca+
- waxing[increscent] moon 상현달
- waning[decrescent] moon 하현달
- full[half] moon 보름달[반달]
- phase (달의) 상(相)

constellation
[kɑ̀:nstəléiʃən]

n. 별자리

■5 Some *constellations* are named after animals, and others after ancient heroes or gods.

voca+
- the constellation of Orion 오리온 자리
- the Big Dipper 북두칠성
- Ursa Major[Minor] 큰곰자리[작은 곰자리]

■1 천문관은 돔(둥근 지붕)이 있는 건물로 천장의 빛들이 행성과 별들의 움직임을 보여준다. ■2 신시내티 천문대는 미국에서 가장 오래 된 전문 천문대이다. ■3 수요일에 개기 일식이 있을 것이다. ■4 하늘에 떠 있는 것은 밝게 빛나는 초승달이었다. ■5 어떤 별자리들의 이름은 동물에서 따왔고, 고대 영웅이나 신의 이름에서 따온 것도 있다.

zodiac signs

n. 12궁도 (별자리) syn. star[astrological/horoscope] signs

1 What is your *zodiac sign*?

voca+ • the 12 signs of the zodiac 12궁
(Aquarius 물병 Pisces 물고기 Aries 백양 Taurus 황소 Gemini 쌍둥이 Cancer 게 Leo 사자 Virgo 처녀 Libra 천칭 Scorpio 전갈 Sagittarius 궁수 Capricorn 염소)

astrology

[əstrɑ́:lədʒi]

n. 점성술

2 Sagittarius and Leo are compatible signs in *astrology*.

voca+ • astrologer 점성술사
• cast a horoscope 별점을 치다
• star divination 별점
• fortune teller 점쟁이

celestial

[səléstʃəl]

a. 천체의, 하늘의 syn. heavenly

3 Stars, planets and moons are all *celestial* bodies.

voca+ • celestial map 천체도
• celestial globe 천구의(천구상에 있는 항성의 위치를 표시한 구체)

asteroid

[ǽstərɔ̀id]

n. 소행성 syn. minor planet, planetoid

4 Some scientists believe an *asteroid* or comet may collide with Earth.

voca+ • asteroid belt 소행성대 • asteroid impact 소행성 충돌

extraterrestrial

[èkstrətəréstriəl]

n. 외계인 a. 외계의

5 Some believe that *extraterrestrial* beings regularly visit the Earth.

voca+ • SETI(Search for Extraterrestrial Intelligence)
외계 지적 생명체 탐사 프로젝트

1 너는 별자리가 무엇이니? 2 궁수자리와 사자자리는 점성술상 궁합이 잘 맞는 별자리이다. 3 항성, 행성, 위성은 모두 천체이다. 4 몇몇 과학자들은 소행성이나 혜성이 지구와 충돌할 수도 있다고 생각한다. 5 몇몇 사람들은 외계인이 주기적으로 지구에 왔다 간다고 믿고 있다.

nebula

[nébjulə]

n. 성운 (a very large cloud of dust and gas that exists in outer space)

1 In 1758, Charles Messier found the Crab *Nebula* while looking for comets.

voca+
- dark nebula 암흑 성운
- planetary nebula 행성형 성운
- emission nebula 발광 성운
- diffuse nebula 산광[확산] 성운
- spiral nebula 나선형 성운
- reflection nebula 반사 성운

galaxy

[gǽləksi]

n. 1. 은하(계) 2. (the G~) 태양과 지구가 속해 있는 우리 은하

2 Hubble discovered that distant *galaxies* are moving away from us.

voca+
- the Milky Way 은하수
- irregular galaxy 불규칙 은하
- spiral galaxy 나선 은하
- elliptical galaxy 타원 은하

space probe

n. 무인 우주 탐사기

3 *Space probes* have been sent to nearly every planet.

voca+
- lunar probe 무인 달 탐사기

mission control

n. (지상의) 우주 관제소

4 A *mission control* center is a unit that manages space exploration.

voca+
- NASA(National Aeronautics and Space Administration) 미 항공 우주국
- control tower 관제탑

axis

[ǽksis]

n. 축, 지축 syn. earth axis

5 It takes one day for the Earth to rotate on its *axis*.

1 1758년 Charles Messier는 혜성을 찾던 중 게 성운을 발견했다. 2 Hubble은 먼 거리에 있는 은하계들이 우리로부터 점점 멀어지고 있다는 것을 알아냈다.
3 무인 우주 탐사선은 거의 모든 행성에 보내졌다. 4 우주 관제소는 우주 탐사를 관리하는 곳이다. 5 지구가 축을 중심으로 자전하는 데는 하루가 걸린다.

exercise

정답 및 해설 p.390

A Match the words in the left column to the sentences in the right column.

ⓐ **astronaut**: someone who has been trained to travel in a spacecraft

ⓑ **constellation**: a group of stars that appear as a figure or picture

ⓒ **asteroid**: a large, planet-like chunk of rock moving through space

ⓓ **astrology**: the study of how the positioning of stars affects people's lives and their destinies

ⓔ **eclipse**: an occasion when the sun or moon disappears from view because of their positioning

1. If a(n) ________ collided with the Earth, it might be the end of the world.
2. The Little Dipper is actually part of the Ursa Minor ________, which looks like a small bear.
3. A total ________ of the sun is a spectacular event.
4. The first Korean ________ will stay at the International Space Station for 10 days.
5. I don't believe in ________, but I sometimes read my horoscope for fun.

B Choose the option that best completes the sentence.

1. The earth rotates on a(n) ______________ between the north and the south poles.
   ⓐ comet ⓑ axis ⓒ galaxy ⓓ zodiac
2. Some people claim to have seen a(n) ______________ in a UFO.
   ⓐ supernova ⓑ meteorite ⓒ extraterrestrial ⓓ astrologer
3. Planets, moons and meteors are all examples of ______________ bodies.
   ⓐ stellar ⓑ celestial ⓒ solar ⓓ alien
4. You can look at the sky through a telescope in a(n) ______________.
   ⓐ observatory ⓑ launch pad ⓒ constellation ⓓ asteroid
5. You cannot see the moon when there is a lunar ______________.
   ⓐ crescent ⓑ nebula ⓒ rotation ⓓ eclipse

Diseases 질병

Diseases 질병

infectious disease 전염병

- STD (sexually transmitted disease) 성병
- AIDS (acquired immune deficiency syndrome) 후천성면역결핍증
- typhoid fever 장티푸스
- tuberculosis 결핵
- influenza/flu 독감
- carrier 보균자
- quarantine 격리(기간), 검역
- transmit 전염시키다
- epidemic/plague 역병, 전염병

health conditions 건강 상태(질환)

- appendicitis 맹장염
- malnutrition 영양실조
- osteoporosis 골다공증
- arthritis 관절염
- anemia 빈혈(증)
- leukemia 백혈병
- stroke 뇌졸중
- diabetes 당뇨병
- asthma 천식
- pneumonia 폐렴

symptoms 증상

- dizziness 현기증
- fatigue 피로
- chill 오한
- sweat/perspiration 발한
- migraine 편두통
- insomnia 불면증
- paralysis 마비
- rash 발진
- indigestion 소화불량
- nausea 메스꺼움, 구역질
- runny nose 콧물
- coughing 기침
- fit/seizure 발작
- spasm/cramp 경련, 쥐

injury 부상

- sprain 삠, 접질림
- bruise 타박상
- abrasion 찰과상
- fracture 골절
- bleeding 출혈
- fester 곪다
- scar 상처 자국, 흉터
- choking 질식

types 유형

- malignant 악성의
- chronic 만성의
- acute 급성의
- latent 잠복성의
- intractable disease 난치병
- terminal illness 불치병
- inherent 선천적인
- acquired 후천적인
- relapse 재발(하다)

Voca Check

정답 p.390

Complete the English translation by referring to the page on the left.

❶ My grandmother used to play the piano well, but now she has ___________ so it's hard for her to play.
할머니는 예전에 피아노를 곧잘 연주하셨지만 지금은 관절염으로 인해 힘들어지셨다.

❷ Denise left work early because she had a ___________.
Denise는 편두통 대문에 일찍 퇴근했다.

❸ ___________ is cancer of the blood or bone marrow.
백혈병은 혈액이나 골수의 암이다.

❹ He has difficulty breathing because of his ___________.
그는 천식 때문에 호흡 곤란을 겪고 있다.

❺ The soldier's wounds began to ___________ in the heat and humidity.
그 군인의 상처는 덥고 습한 날씨에서 곪기 시작했다.

❻ This medicine may cause ___________, so after you take it you shouldn't drive for a while.
이 약은 피로감을 유발할 수 있으므로 복용 후에는 당분간 운전하지 마십시오.

❼ Shortness of breath, pressure on the chest, and pain in the arm are all ___________s of a heart attack.
호흡 곤란, 가슴의 압박감, 팔의 통증은 모두 심근경색의 징후이다.

❽ I don't eat that. It gives me ___________.
저는 그거 안 먹습니다. 그걸 먹으면 소화가 잘 안 되거든요.

More Words

complication 합병증
measles 홍역
amnesia 기억상실(증), 건망증
autism 자폐증
dementia 치매
hepatitis 간염
night blindness 야맹증
hypochondria 건강 염려증, 심기증
trauma 외상, 정신적 충격
SARS (severe acute respiratory syndrome)
사스(중증 급성 호흡기 질환)
sore 상처가 아픈, 쑤시는
hoarse (감기 등으로) 목소리가 쉰
vomit 토하다
disabled / crippled 장애가 있는

malignant
[məlígnənt]

a. 악성의 (getting worse and causing death eventually) ant. benign

1 Is the tumor *malignant* or benign?

voca+ • malignant tumor 악성 종양

dizziness
[dízinis]

n. 현기증, 어지럼증 syn. faintness, light-headedness

2 Some medications can cause *dizziness* as a side effect.

voca+ • faint 기절하다 • blackout 갑작스런 의식 상실
• (an attack of) vertigo 현기증

insomnia
[insάmniə]

n. 불면증

3 I suffered from *insomnia* and took sleeping pills to overcome it.

voca+ • insomniac 불면증 환자
• sleeping pills[tablets] 수면제
• sleep disturbance 수면 장애
• sleepwalking 몽유병
• hypersomnia 수면 과다증

malnutrition
[mæ̀lnu:tríʃən]

n. 영양실조, 영양 부족 ant. overnutrition

4 The most obvious sign of *malnutrition* is extreme weight loss.

voca+ • recommended daily allowance 일일 섭취 권장량
• eating disorder 섭식장애

chronic
[krάnik]

a. 만성의, 고질적인 ant. acute

5 She has suffered from *chronic* back pain for more than 12 years.

voca+ • chronic fatigue syndrome 만성 피로 증후군

1 그 종양은 악성인가요, 양성인가요? 2 어떤 약은 부작용으로 현기증을 일으킬 수 있다. 3 나는 불면증에 시달리다 그것에서 벗어나려고 수면제를 복용했다. 4 영양실조의 가장 뚜렷한 증상은 극심한 체중 감소이다. 5 그녀는 12년 넘도록 만성 요통을 앓고 있다.

stroke
[strouk]

n. **뇌졸중(의 발작)** (a medical condition in which a blood vessel in the brain bursts or becomes blocked, often causing death or loss of some ability)

1 He had a *stroke* that left him unable to speak.

voca+
- have[suffer] a stroke 뇌졸중으로 쓰러지다
- cerebral hemorrhage 뇌출혈
- hypertension 고혈압

relapse
[riːlǽps]

n. **재발** syn. recurrence v. **재발하다**

2 Doctors say that he runs little chance of a *relapse*.

voca+
- incidence 발병률
- have a relapse (병이) 도지다

paralysis
[pərǽləsis]

n. **마비** syn. palsy

3 Botox causes temporary *paralysis* of facial muscles.

voca+
- paralytic 중풍[마비] 환자
- numb 감각이 마비된
- cramp / spasm (근육의) 쥐, 경련
- infantile paralysis / polio 소아마비
- cerebral palsy 뇌성마비
- Parkinson's disease / paralysis agitans 파킨슨병, 진전마비

sprain
[sprein]

v. **(손목 · 발목 등을) 삐다** (to damage a joint in the body by suddenly twisting it)
syn. twist, wrench

4 I fell down the steps and *sprained* my ankle.

n. **삠, 접질림**

voca+
- tear a ligament 인대가 끊어지다
- (plaster) cast 깁스
- orthopedics 정형외과(학)

---

1 그는 뇌졸중으로 인해 말을 못하게 되었다. **2** 의사들은 그의 병이 재발할 가능성이 거의 없다고 말한다. **3** 보톡스 주사는 안면 근육의 일시적인 마비를 일으킨다. **4** 나는 계단에서 넘어져서 발목을 삐었다.

terminal illness

n. 불치병 syn. incurable[fatal] disease

1 His youngest daughter is battling a *terminal illness*.

voca+
- lethal / deadly / fatal 치명적인
- life-support system[machine] 생명 유지 장치
- vital signs (맥박 · 호흡 · 체온 등의) 생명 징후

fracture

[frǽktʃər]

n. 골절 v. 부러뜨리다, 부러지다

2 He suffered a compound *fracture* in his left leg.

voca+
- simple[compound] fracture 단순[복합] 골절
- stress fracture (운동선수 · 댄서 등에게 자주 나타나는) 피로로 인한 골절
- have a hairline fracture[crack] 뼈에 금이 가다

bleeding

[blíːdiŋ]

n. 출혈

3 Control the *bleeding* before trying to clean the wound.

voca+
- stanch / stop[arrest] the bleeding 지혈하다
- severe[heavy] bleeding 과다출혈
- internal bleeding 내출혈

choke

[tʃouk]

v. 숨이 막히다, 질식하다[시키다] syn. suffocate

4 The dog was *choking* on a small object, but he's okay now.

voca+
- artificial respiration 인공호흡

carrier

[kǽriər]

n. 보균자, 보인자, 병원균 매개체

5 Rats are known as disease *carriers*.

voca+
- incubation[latent] period 잠복기
- healthy carrier 잠복성 보균자

1 그의 막내딸은 불치병과 싸우고 있다. **2** 그는 왼쪽 다리에 복합 골절상을 입었다. **3** 상처 부위를 닦으려고 하기 전에 지혈부터 하라. **4** 그 개는 작은 물체가 목에 걸려 질식할 뻔했지만 지금은 괜찮다. **5** 쥐는 병균 매개체로 알려져 있다.

exercise

정답 및 해설 p.390

A Match the words in the left column to the sentences in the right column.

ⓐ **malignant**: developing in a way that is not normal and dangerous

ⓑ **insomnia**: a condition of having difficulty sleeping

ⓒ **terminal illness**: an incurable and fatal disease

ⓓ **paralysis**: inability to move

ⓔ **dizziness**: the state of being unable to stand steadily

1. He lost all hope when he was diagnosed with a(n) ________.
2. She went to the doctor because she was worried that her mole might be ________.
3. I'm worried she might fall in the shower because she's been experiencing ________.
4. Damage to the spine could result in ________.
5. When I'm really stressed out, I get ________.

B Choose the option that best completes the sentence.

1. I'm raising funds to buy food for children who suffer from ________________.
   ⓐ tuberculosis ⓑ nausea ⓒ malnutrition ⓓ leukemia

2. He's had ________________ stomach problems since he was a teenager.
   ⓐ acute ⓑ chronic ⓒ anemic ⓓ epidemic

3. She's unable to move the left side of her face as a result of her ________________.
   ⓐ stroke ⓑ asthma ⓒ diabetes ⓓ measles

4. The doctors thought he had beaten the cancer, but then he ________________.
   ⓐ relapsed ⓑ festered ⓒ bleeded ⓓ transmitted

5. You should keep small objects away from children so they don't ________________ on them.
   ⓐ bruise ⓑ scar ⓒ fracture ⓓ choke

day 46

Treatment & Prescription 치료와 처방

Treatment 치료

operation/surgery 수술
- anesthetize 마취하다
- anesthetic 마취제
- transplant 이식(하다)
- organ donor 장기 기증자
- organ recipient 장기 수용자
- rejection 거부반응
- transfusion 수혈
- staunch/stanch 지혈하다
- sterilize 소독[살균]하다
- injection 주사
- administer 투약하다, (치료를) 해주다
- relieve/soothe (고통을) 완화시키다
- euthanasia 안락사

therapy 요법, 치료법
- drug therapy 약물 요법
- kinesitherapy 운동 요법
- diet 식이 요법
- go on a diet 다이어트 하다
- dietary fiber 식이섬유
- regimen 섭생
- eating disorder 섭식장애
- folk remedy 민간 요법
- acupuncture 침술
- acupressure 지압

- first aid (treatment) 응급치료
- artificial respiration 인공호흡
- in a critical condition 위독한

Prescription 처방

medication 의약품
- pharmacy 약국
- pharmacist 약제사
- dispense 조제하다
- dispensary 조제실
- prescription 처방(전)
- over-the-counter(OTC) 의사의 처방 없이 판매할 수 있는
- dosage 복용량
- overdose 과잉투약
- ointment 연고
- disinfectant 소독약
- antibiotic 항생제
- antidote 해독제
- painkiller 진통제
- Tylenol 타이레놀
- antifebrile 해열제
- aspirin 아스피린
- sedative 진정제
- laxative 변비약

prevention 예방
- checkup (정기) 건강 검진
- diagnosis 진단
- vaccinate 백신 접종을 하다
- inoculate 예방 접종을 하다
- immunize 면역시키다
- immune system 면역체계
- antibody 항체
- antigen 항원

Voca Check

정답 p.391

Complete the English translation by referring to the page on the left.

❶ Pay close attention to the recommended ___________ so that you don't take too much.
과다 복용하지 않도록 권장량에 각별히 주의를 기울여라.

❷ I was bitten by a poisonous snake while trekking, but luckily the guide had an ___________ to snake venom.
트레킹을 하다가 독사에게 물렸으나 다행히도 안내인이 뱀 독의 해독제를 가지고 있었다.

❸ The nurse ___________d the needle before giving the injection.
간호사는 주사를 놓기 전에 바늘을 소독했다.

❹ The patient is waiting for a donor so that he can have a kidney ___________.
환자는 신장 이식을 받기 위해 기증자를 기다리고 있다.

❺ The nutritionist recommended I eat more fruits and grains to increase my intake of ___________.
영양사는 나에게 식이섬유 섭취량을 늘리기 위해 과일과 곡물을 더 많이 먹으라고 권했다.

❻ Whenever I had a cold, my grandmother would give me an old ___________: hot water with lemon and cayenne pepper.
감기에 걸릴 때마다 우리 할머니께서는 나에게 오래된 민간 요법인 레몬과 카옌 고추를 넣은 뜨거운 물을 주시곤 했다.

❼ You don't need a prescription. It's ___________ medicine.
처방전은 필요 없어요. 그것은 처방없이 판매할 수 있는 약이에요.

❽ She's been taking ___________s since the surgery.
그녀는 수술 후 줄곧 진통제를 복용해 왔다.

More Words

pathology 병리학
panacea/cure-all 만병통치약
infirmary 양호실
ICU(intensive care unit) 중환자실
inpatient 입원환자
outpatient 외래환자
invalid 병자, 지체 부자유자
CPR(cardiopulmonary resuscitation) 심폐소생술
side effect/ADR(adverse drug reaction) 부작용
physician 내과 의사
surgeon 외과 의사
plastic surgeon 성형외과 의사
pediatrician 소아과 의사
psychiatrist 정신과 의사
dermatologist 피부과 의사

therapy
[θérəpi]

n. (장기간의) 치료, 요법

1 He needs four weeks of *therapy* after the surgery.

voca+
- therapist 치료 전문가, 치료사
- alternative therapy 대체 요법
- radiotherapy 방사선 요법
- gene therapy 유전자 치료
- hypnotherapy 최면 요법
- psychotherapy 심리 치료

acupuncture
[ǽkjupʌ̀ŋktʃər]

n. 침술

2 She tried *acupuncture* in order to relieve the pain in her back.

voca+
- acupuncturist 침술가
- hand acupuncture 수지침
- acupuncture point 경혈

regimen
[rédʒimən]

n. 섭생 (a plan of food, exercise, etc. that is intended to improve health)

3 After his heart attack, the doctor put him on a strict *regimen*.

voca+
- vegetarian 채식주의자
- organic food 유기농 식품
- therapeutic regimen 최적 치료 계획, 최적 투약 방식

eating disorder

n. (신경성) 섭식 장애 (an emotional disorder that causes abnormal eating habits)

4 America's *eating disorder* rates continue to rise.

voca+
- anorexia 식욕부진증, 거식증
- bulimia 폭식증

diagnosis
[dàiəgnóusis]

n. 진단 (복수형 diagnoses)

5 Early *diagnosis* is important in treating cancer.

voca+
- diagnose 진단하다
- certificate of health 건강진단서
- initial[early] diagnosis 초기 진단
- misdiagnosis / wrong[erroneous] diagnosis 오진
- prognosis 예후, 향후 병의 진행 양상을 예상하는 것

1 그는 수술 후에 4주간의 치료가 필요하다. 2 그녀는 허리 통증을 완화하기 위해 침을 맞아 보았다. 3 심장마비가 있은 후 의사는 그에게 엄격하게 짜여진 운동 및 식생활을 따르도록 했다. 4 미국에서 섭식 장애를 겪는 사람들의 비율이 계속 높아지고 있다. 5 조기 진단은 암 치료에 있어 중요하다.

operation
[ɑ̀:pəréiʃən]

n. 수술 syn. surgery

❶ She underwent a minor *operation* on her elbow.

voca+
- major[minor] operation 큰[작은] 수술
- perform[have/undergo] an operation 수술을 하다[받다]
- operating room[table] 수술실[대]
- informed consent 환자의 수술 동의(수술 결과나 위험성 등에 대해 알고 난 후 동의하는 것)
- plastic[cosmetic] surgery 성형수술
- ward 병동, 병실

transfusion
[trænsfjú:ʒən]

n. 수혈

❷ She suffers from a rare disease that requires regular blood *transfusions*.

voca+
- blood donation 헌혈
- blood center 혈액원
- blood donor[recipient] 헌혈자[수혈자]
- (in)compatible 수혈에 (부)적합한
- universal donor 만능 공혈자, O형 혈액(을 가진 사람)

anesthetize
[ənésθətàiz]

v. 마취시키다

❸ Before the surgery, my eyes were *anesthetized* with eye drops.

voca+
- anesthesia 마취
- anesthetic 마취제
- anesthetics (병원의) 마취과
- anesthetist 마취 전문의
- local[general] anesthesia 국부[전신] 마취

sedative
[sédətiv]

n. (신경 · 정신) 진정제, 안정제 syn. tranquilizer

❹ The doctor gave me a *sedative* so I could sleep.

sterilize
[stérəlàiz]

v. 살균[소독]하다 syn. sanitize, disinfect

❺ All medical equipment must be *sterilized* before use.

voca+
- sterilizer 소독기, 살균장치
- chemical[radiation] sterilization 화학[방사선] 소독
- pathogen 병원균(체내에서 발병의 원인이 되는 박테리아나 세균)

❶ 그녀는 팔꿈치에 간단한 수술을 받았다. ❷ 그녀는 정기적인 수혈이 필요한 희귀병을 앓고 있다. ❸ 수술 전에 내 눈은 안약으로 마취된 상태였다. ❹ 의사는 내가 잠을 잘 수 있도록 진정제를 주었다. ❺ 모든 의료 장비는 사용 전에 소독해야 한다.

dosage
[dóusidʒ]

n. (1회분의) 복용[투약]량 syn. dose

1 You mustn't exceed the recommended *dosage*.

voca+
- designated dosage 처방된 복용량
- dispense 조제[투약]하다
- powdered medicine 가루약
- suppository 좌약
- lethal dose (약의) 치사량
- overdose 과다 복용
- tablet / pill 알약, 정제
- capsule 캡슐 형태의 약

antibiotic
[æ̀ntibaiɑ́:tik]

n. (주로 복수로) 항생제 (a drug that is used to kill bacteria that cause infections)

2 Taking *antibiotics* for too long will make the condition worse.

voca+
- penicillin 페니실린
- tolerance / resistance (약에 대한) 내성
- antibiotics misuse[overuse / abuse] 항생제 오용[남용]

injection
[indʒékʃən]

n. 주사 syn. shot

3 Daily insulin *injections* are necessary for some diabetics.

voca+
- intravenous[intramuscular] injection 정맥[근육] 주사
- disposable syringe 일회용 주사기
- Ringer's solution 링겔액

vaccinate
[vǽksənèit]

v. 백신 접종을 하다 (to protect from a disease by injecting a vaccine)

4 All children should be *vaccinated* against measles.

voca+
- inoculate 예방 접종을 하다(소량의 병원균을 주사하여 항체를 생성하게 하고 면역력을 키우는 방법)

transplant
[trænsplǽnt]

v. 이식하다 n. [trǽnsplænt] 이식

5 His kidney was successfully *transplanted* to his identical twin brother.

voca+
- organ[bone-marrow] transplant(ation) 장기[골수] 이식
- artificial organs 인공 장기

1 권장 복용량을 초과하면 안 됩니다. 2 항생제를 너무 오랫동안 복용하는 것은 상태를 더 악화시킬 것이다. 3 일부 당뇨병 환자에게는 매일 인슐린 주사가 필요하다. 4 모든 아이들은 홍역 예방 접종을 받아야 한다. 5 그의 신장은 그의 일란성 쌍둥이 형에게 무사히 이식되었다.

exercise

정답 및 해설 p.391

A Match the words in the left column to the sentences in the right column.

ⓐ **sedative**: a drug used to make a person calm down or sleep

ⓑ **euthanasia**: the intentional killing of a person in order to end suffering

ⓒ **anesthetize**: to give a patient a drug to make him or her lose feeling

ⓓ **vaccinate**: to protect from a disease by boosting their immune system

ⓔ **diagnose**: to identify an illness

1. Doctors ________ the patients before surgery so that they can't feel the pain.
2. He died just three months after being ________(e)d with cancer.
3. ________ is a controversial topic in the medical community.
4. The nurse gave the hysterical woman a(n) ________.
5. The nurse gave the baby a shot to ________ her against measles.

B Choose the option that best completes the sentence.

1. After years of physical ______________, she is finally able to walk again.
   ⓐ checkups ⓑ transplants ⓒ therapy ⓓ immunization
2. Western doctors are beginning to recognize the effectiveness of ______________.
   ⓐ acupuncture ⓑ antibiotics ⓒ ointment ⓓ laxatives
3. The doctor recommended a strict ______________ of diet and exercise.
   ⓐ antigen ⓑ regimen ⓒ dosage ⓓ prevention
4. Some people have contracted AIDS through a blood ______________.
   ⓐ transfusion ⓑ shortage ⓒ antigen ⓓ rejection
5. The doctor prescribed a(n) ______________ for an ear infection.
   ⓐ antibody ⓑ transfusion ⓒ antibiotic ⓓ first aid

day 47 Travel & Transportation 여행과 교통

Travel 여행

airport 공항
- check-in 탑승 수속
- check one's luggage 짐을 부치다
- departure[entry] card 출국[입국] 신고서
- customs 세관
- declare 세관 신고를 하다
- security checkpoint 보안 검문소
- metal detector 금속 탐지기
- inspect the baggage 수하물을 검사하다
- quarantine station 검역소
- boarding 탑승
- visa 비자, 입국허가(증)
- immigration 입국심사
- admission 입국허가

sightseeing 관광
- provisions 여행 준비물
- itinerary 여행 일정
- high[peak] season 성수기
- low[off] season 비수기
- currency exchange 환전
- traveler's check 여행자 수표
- tourist attraction 관광 명소
- accommodations/lodging facilities 숙박
  - (hotel) voucher (호텔) 숙박권
- amenity 편의시설
- souvenir 기념품
- overcharge/rip-off 바가지요금
- tip/gratuity 봉사료, 팁
- jet lag 시차 피로

Transportation 교통

air transportation 항공 교통
- domestic[international] flight 국내[국제]선
- one-way[round] trip 편도[왕복]행
- bound for ~행의
- connecting[connection] flight 연결항공편
- taxi along the runway 활주로를 따라 이동하다
- stopover/layover 중간 기착(지)
- boarding pass 탑승권
- (overhead) compartment 좌석 위 짐칸
- safety regulations 안전 수칙
- flight cancellation 결항

road transportation 도로 교통
- commute 통근하다
- transfer 갈아타다
- intersection 교차로
  - underpass 지하도
  - overpass 고가도로
- congestion 혼잡, 밀집
- detour 우회(하다)
- pull over 차를 길가에 대다
- pedestrian 보행자
- jaywalk 무단횡단하다
- be run over by a car 차에 치이다
- casualty 사상자

Voca Check

정답 p. 391

Complete the English translation by referring to the page on the left.

❶ It took me a few days to recover from my __________ when I flew from New York to Seoul.
뉴욕에서 서울까지 비행했을 때 시차로 인한 피로에서 회복되기까지 며칠이 걸렸다.

❷ These bags are heavy. Let's __________ and then get something to eat.
이 가방들은 무거우니 우선 짐을 부치고 나서 무언가를 먹으러 가자.

❸ You must __________ the jewel at customs.
그 보석은 세관에 신고해야 해.

❹ There are so many __________s in New York. Let's go to the Statue of Liberty first.
뉴욕에는 가볼 만한 관광 명소가 아주 많다. 먼저 자유의 여신상에 가보도록 하자.

❺ Europe is so expensive in the __________. Let's wait until November.
성수기 때 유럽은 매우 비싸다. 11월까지 기다려 보자.

❻ It's really foggy. We'd better call the airline and find out if there are any __________s.
안개가 정말 자욱하다. 항공사에 전화를 해서 결항된 항공편이 있는지 알아보는 게 좋겠다.

❼ I don't need my passport because it's a __________.
나는 국내선을 타기 때문에 여권이 필요하지 않다.

❽ Turn right at the next __________.
다음 교차로에서 우회전을 해라.

More Words

tourism 관광 (산업)
airport limousine 공항 리무진버스
ETA(estimated time of arrival) 도착 예정시간
ETD(estimated time of departure) 출발 예정시간
blackout period 탑승 제한 기간
cruise 선박여행
bus depot 버스 터미널
interchange (입체형) 교차로
speed camera 과속 단속 카메라
sobriety check 음주 단속
hit-and-run accident 뺑소니 (사고)
parking violation 주차 위반
one-way street 일방통행로
bus-only lane 버스 전용차선

visa
[víːzə]

n. **비자, 입국허가(증)** (an official mark put on your passport that allows you to enter or leave a foreign country)

1 Michelle applied for a tourist *visa*, but it was rejected.

voca+
- issue[renew/extend] a visa 비자를 발급[갱신/연장]하다
- visa exemption treaty 무비자협정
- work[student/tourist] visa 취업[학생/관광] 비자
- entry[exit] visa 입국[출국] 비자

quarantine

n. **검역** (an act or a system keeping a person or animal apart from others so that a disease cannot spread)

2 All animals entering the U.K. used to be put in *quarantine*.

voca+
- quarantine station 검역소

v. **(질병 때문에) 격리하다**

customs
[kʌ́stəmz]

n. **세관**

3 Did you declare anything on your *customs* form?

voca+
- customs (duty) 관세
- customs fee 통관료
- customs declaration form 세관 신고 양식
- duty-free shop 면세점
- clear customs 세관을 통과하다

baggage
[bǽgidʒ]

n. **수하물, 짐** syn. luggage

4 Go to the agent and check your *baggage*.

voca+
- baggage claim (area) 수하물 찾는 곳
- baggage claim check[tag] 수하물 표
- excess baggage charge 추가 수하물 운임
- carry-on (baggage) 기내 휴대용 수하물

souvenir
[sùːvəníər]

n. **기념품** syn. memento

5 Did you buy many *souvenirs* on your trip abroad?

voca+
- local specialty 특산품

1 Michelle은 관광 비자를 신청했지만 거부당했다. **2** 한때 영국에 들어오는 모든 동물들은 검역소를 거쳐야 했다. **3** 세관 신고서에 신고하신 것 있습니까? **4** 직원에게로 가서 짐을 부치세요. **5** 해외 여행 하면서 기념품 많이 샀니?

tourist attraction

n. 주요 관광지, 관광 명소 syn. tourist destination[magnet]

1 The Galapagos Islands are one of Ecuador's main *tourist attractions.*

voca+ • must-see 꼭 봐야 할 것
• city sightseeing 시내 관광
• package deal[tour] 패키지 관광, 여행사 단체여행
• land only (항공편이 제외된) 현지 여행상품
• tourist trap 관광객을 상대로 바가지를 씌우는 곳

itinerary
[aitínərèri]

n. 여행 일정 syn. route, path

2 Brussels was not on the *itinerary.*

voca+ • plan (out) an[one's] itinerary 여정을 짜다

amenity
[əménəti]

n. (주로 복수로) 편의시설 (options intended to make lodging more enjoyable)

3 The hotel *amenities* include health clubs, conference facilities, and banquet rooms.

stopover
[stɑ́pòuvər]

n. 중간 기착(지) (a stop during a trip, especially during a flight) syn. layover

4 I made a *stopover* in Hawaii on my way to Korea.

voca+ • via ~을 경유하여
• transit 통과 (비행기가 중간 기착지에 잠시 멈추나 입국은 하지 않음)
• transfer 환승 (중간 기착지에 내려 비행기를 갈아타는 것. 환승하는 시간이 길어 중간 기착지에서 8시간 이상 보내는 경우를 스톱오버라고 함)

taxi
[tǽksi]

v. (비행기가) 지상을 활주하다

5 Each plane has to *taxi* along the runway before takeoff.

voca+ • takeoff 이륙 • landing 착륙

---

1 갈라파고스 섬은 에콰도르의 주요 관광지 중 하나이다. 2 브뤼셀은 여행 일정에 없었다. 3 그 호텔은 헬스 클럽, 회의실, 연회장 등의 편의시설을 갖추고 있다. 4 비행기로 한국에 오는 길에 하와이에 잠시 들렀다. 5 비행기는 이륙 전에 활주로를 달려야 한다.

pedestrian
[pədéstriən]

n. 보행자 syn. passerby

1 The death rate for ***pedestrians*** hit by cars is unacceptably high.

voca+ • pavement 보도, 인도
• crosswalk 횡단보도
• road sign 도로 표지
• bicycle lane 자전거 전용도로

pull over

v. (차를) 길가에 대다

2 The police officer signaled to him to ***pull over***.

voca+ • tow (차를) 견인하다
• tow truck/wrecker 견인 차량
• turn[directional] signal 방향 지시등

congestion
[kəndʒéstʃən]

n. 혼잡, 밀집 syn. overcrowding

3 The traffic ***congestion*** in the city is getting worse.

voca+ • traffic jam/standstill 교통 정체
• congestion charge/road pricing 혼잡 통행료
• road rage 교통 체증이나 다른 운전자로 인해 치미는 분노
• bottle neck 병목현상(병의 목 부분처럼, 넓은 길이 갑자기 좁아짐으로써 생기는 교통 정체 현상)

commute
[kəmjú:t]

v. 통근[통학]하다

4 It's exhausting ***commuting*** between Daejeon to Seoul every day.

n. 통근 (거리)

voca+ • metropolitan area 대도시권
• reverse commuter 역방향 통근자 (도심에서 교외로 통근하는 사람)

detour
[dí:tuər]

n. 우회(로) v. 우회하다, 돌아서 가다

5 I often took ***detours*** to avoid construction sites.

voca+ • make[take] a detour 우회하다

1 차 사고로 인한 보행자 사망률이 심각한 수준으로 높다. **2** 경찰관이 그에게 차를 길가에 대라고 신호를 보냈다. **3** 도시의 교통 혼잡은 갈수록 악화되고 있다. **4** 대전과 서울 사이를 매일 통근하는 것은 무척 피곤한 일이다. **5** 나는 공사 지역을 피해 가려고 자주 우회를 했다.

exercise

정답 및 해설 p.391

A Match the words in the left column to the sentences in the right column.

ⓐ **souvenir**: an item that reminds you of a place you've visited

ⓑ **amenities**: things that make a place comfortable and easy to live in

ⓒ **taxi**: to drive a plane on a runway

ⓓ **commute**: to travel a long distance to work or school

ⓔ **detour**: an alternative route, often used to avoid something such as a traffic jam or construction site

1. It seemed like we ________(e)d for about half an hour before we finally took off.
2. Sorry, I'm late. I had to take a(n) ________.
3. This key chain is a(n) ________ of my trip to Hong Kong.
4. I turned down the job because I don't want to ________ to Seoul every day.
5. My wife likes camping, but I prefer to have all of the ________ of a hotel.

B Choose the option that best completes the sentence.

1. I need to get my ________________ processed for my trip to China next month.
   ⓐ tip ⓑ boarding pass ⓒ visa ⓓ departure card

2. She was kept in ________________ because she developed a fever while traveling during the SARS outbreak.
   ⓐ transit ⓑ quarantine ⓒ congestion ⓓ immigration

3. According to my ________________, I will arrive at 7:30 a.m.
   ⓐ reservation ⓑ departure card ⓒ traveler's check ⓓ itinerary

4. I had a ________________ in Tokyo on my way to Vancouver.
   ⓐ stopover ⓑ detour ⓒ domestic flight ⓓ commute

5. You won't be able to take fruits through ________________.
   ⓐ the overpass ⓑ the souvenir ⓒ customs ⓓ the metal detector

Sports 스포츠

Sports 스포츠

the Olympics 올림픽

- track and field/athletics 육상
  - marathon 마라톤
  - discus throw 원반던지기
  - javelin throw 창던지기
  - shot put 투포환
  - pole vault 장대높이뛰기
  - sprint race 단거리 달리기
- combat sports 격투기
  - martial arts (동양)무술
    - judo 유도
    - Kung Fu 쿵후
    - Taekwondo 태권도
  - boxing 권투
  - wrestling 레슬링
- equestrian events 승마
- gymnastics 체조
- weightlifting 역도
- biathlon 2종 경기
  - triathlon 3종 경기
  - pentathlon 5종 경기
  - decathlon 10종 경기
- archery 양궁
- aquatics 수상 스포츠
  - swimming 수영
    - freestyle 자유형
    - backstroke 배영
    - breaststroke 평영
    - butterfly 접영
  - water polo 수구
  - synchronized swimming 싱크로나이즈드 스위밍
  - diving 다이빙

football 축구

- forward 공격수
- defender 수비수
- sweeper 최종 수비수
- substitute 교체선수
- referee (축구 · 농구 · 권투) 심판
- root[cheer] for ~를 응원하다
- hooligan 훌리건(폭력적인 축구 광팬)
- preliminary round 예선전
- second round 16강전
- quarter finals 8강전
- first-half 전반전
- second-half 후반전
- injury time 추가 경기시간
- overtime 연장전

baseball 야구

- make a hit 안타 치다
- base on balls 포볼(4구)
- reliever 구원 투수
- umpire (야구 · 테니스) 심판
- battery 투수와 포수
- hit by pitch 데드볼, 사구(死球)
- designated hitter 지명 타자
- batting average 타율
- grand slam 만루 홈런
- top ~회초
- bottom ~회말
- extra inning 연장전

basketball 농구

- dunk shot 덩크 슛
- slam dunk 슬램덩크
- rim/hoop 골대의 둥근 고리
- buzzer beater 종료 순간의 득점
- traveling violation 워킹 바이얼레이션
- basket interference 바스켓 인터피어런스
- crossover 다리 사이로 공빼기
- sixth man 대체투입 1순위 선수
- turnover 실책(공격권 상실)
- feint 상대를 속이다, 속이는 동작
- beat the defender 수비수를 제치다

Voca Check

정답 p.392

Complete the English translation by referring to the page on the left.

❶ The basketball player was disappointed as he watched the ball bounce off the ___________.
그 농구 선수는 공이 골대를 맞고 튕겨 나오는 것을 보고 실망했다.

❷ I usually ___________ for the underdog unless my home team is playing.
내 홈 팀의 경기가 아니라면 나는 보통 약한 팀을 응원하는 편이다.

❸ The baseball fans were angry when the ___________ called a strike.
심판이 스트라이크를 외쳤을 때 야구팬들은 분노했다.

❹ You have to be able to jump pretty high to make a ___________.
슬램덩크를 하기 위해서는 매우 높이 점프할 수 있어야 한다.

❺ The referee gave the ___________ a yellow card for faking an injury.
부상당한 척 했다는 이유로 심판은 그 공격수에게 경고를 주었다.

❻ With the bases loaded the batter made a ___________ to win the game.
만루 상황에서 그 타자는 만루 홈런을 날려 경기를 승리로 이끌었다.

❼ Babe Ruth ended his career with a .342 ___________.
Babe Ruth는 타율 3할 4푼 2리로 야구 인생을 마감했다.

❽ ___________ is the sport of shooting arrows from a bow.
양궁은 활로 화살을 쏘는 운동이다.

More Words

IOC(International Olympic Committee) 국제 올림픽 위원회
FIFA 국제 축구 연맹
Olympic Flame[Torch] 올림픽 성화
Paralympic Games 장애인 올림픽
world record holder 세계기록 보유자
exhibition game 시범경기
friendly match[game] 친선경기
roster 선수 명단
draft (프로 팀의) 신인 선수 선발
rookie 신인 선수
throw-in 스로인(코트 안으로 공을 던지는 것)
neck-and-neck match 접전
M.V.P.(Most Valuable Player) 최우수 선수
canoe 카누(한쪽에만 날이 달린 노를 사용)
kayak 카약(양쪽에 날이 달린 노를 사용)

track and field

n. 육상 syn. *BrE.* athletics

1 She won the women's 400-meter run at her first *track and field* event.

voca+
- sprinter 단거리 육상선수
- hurdles 장애물 경주
- walkathon[walk/walking] 경보
- ultra-distance runner (30마일 이상) 초장거리 선수
- lap time 랩타임(트랙을 한 바퀴 도는 데 걸리는 시간)

gymnastics

[dʒimnǽstiks]

n. 체조

2 the U.S. women's *gymnastics* team

voca+
- gymnast 체조선수
- balance beam 평균대
- floor exercise 마루운동
- tumbling 텀블링
- parallel[uneven] bars [이단] 평행봉
- apparatus gymnastics 기계체조

aquatics

[əkwǽtiks]

n. 수상 스포츠 syn. aquatic[water] sports

3 One of the most popular summer programs is *aquatics*.

voca+
- water skiing 수상스키
- yachting 요트경기
- life jacket[vest] 구명조끼
- windsurfing 윈드서핑
- boat race 조정경기

equestrian events

n. 승마, 마술(馬術) 경기

4 *Equestrian events* were included in the Olympic Games for the first time in 1900.

voca+
- horse(back) riding 승마

triathlon

[traiǽθlɑn]

n. (철인) 3종 경기

5 The name *triathlon* is mostly applied to a combination of swimming, cycling, and running.

voca+
- ironman 3종 경기 선수, 철인
- modern pentathlon 근대 5종 경기(승마, 펜싱, 사격, 수영, 크로스컨트리)

1 그녀는 처음 출전한 육상 대회 여자 400미터 경기에서 우승했다. **2** 미국 여자 체조팀 **3** 가장 인기 있는 여름 프로그램 중 하나는 수상 스포츠이다. **4** 승마 경기는 1900년에 처음으로 올림픽 종목으로 채택되었다. **5** 철인 3종 경기라는 말은 대부분 수영, 사이클, 달리기 종목의 조합을 칭한다.

substitute
[sʌ́bstitjùːt]

n. 교체 선수

1 The 23-year-old *substitute* on France's national soccer team scored the "golden goal."

voca+
- call a foul 파울을 선언하다
- expulsion 퇴장
- bench warmer (야구) 후보선수

preliminary round

n. 예선전

2 There will be four matches in the *preliminary round*.

voca+
- warm-up match 평가전
- semi-finals 준결승
- finals 결승
- close game[match] 접전
- preliminary[final] draw 예선[본선] 조추첨

injury time

n. 추가 경기시간 (playing time added to the end of a game because of time lost dealing with injured players) syn. stoppage time, loss time

3 The winning goal was scored in *injury time*.

voca+
- end in a draw 무승부로 끝나다
- overtime/extra time 연장전

hooligan
[húːligən]

n. 훌리건, (폭력적인) 축구 광팬 (a soccer fan who is unruly and destructive in public places)

4 Football *hooligans* often cause damage in bars and restaurants near the stadium.

batting average

n. 타율

5 A season *batting average* higher than 0.3 is considered to be good.

voca+
- steal 도루하다
- beanball 위협구, 타자의 머리를 향한 투구
- hit 안타
- bunch (안타를) 몰아치다
- winning streak 연승
- grand slam 만루 홈런

1 프랑스 국가 대표팀 소속인 23세의 교체 선수가 골든골을 넣었다. 2 예선전에서는 네 경기가 있을 것이다. 3 결승골은 추가 경기시간에 나왔다. 4 축구 훌리건들은 경기장 근처의 술집과 식당에 자주 피해를 입힌다. 5 한 시즌 타율이 3할 이상이면 높은 것으로 여겨진다.

battery
[bǽtəri]

n. 투수와 포수(를 함께 일컫는 말)

1 The pitcher and catcher together are known as the *battery*.

voca+
- dugout 더그아웃, 선수 대기소
- bullpen 구원 투수(연습장)
- fastballer 속구 투수
- box 타자석
- mound (투수의) 마운드

buzzer beater

n. 종료 득점, 종료골, 버저비터

2 He released a three-point play in a *buzzer beater*.

voca+
- lay-up shot 레이업 슛
- three-point shot 3점 슛
- free throw 자유투

basket interference

n. 바스켓 인터피어런스(공이 하강 곡선이거나 림(rim)위에서 튕기고 있을 때 건드리는 반칙)
syn. goaltending

3 The official calls *basket interference* and awards 2 points to the team.

turnover
[tə́:rnòuvər]

n. 실책, 공격권 상실

4 A *turnover* can result from making mistakes or committing a violation or an offensive foul.

voca+
- possession 공을 가진 상태
- tip-off 점프볼로 공격권을 정함
- traveling / walking 워킹 파울(공을 가진 채 3보 이상 걷기)
- technical foul 신체 접촉이 아닌 항의나 비신사적인 행동에 대해 부과하는 파울
- loose ball 어느 쪽 팀에도 속해 있지 않은 공

martial arts

n. 무술

5 *Martial arts* have become popular in America and Europe.

voca+
- judo 유도
- karate 가라테(공수도)
- mixed martial arts 이종 격투기

1 투수와 포수를 함께 일컬어 '배터리'라고 한다. 2 그는 경기 종료와 동시에 3점 슛을 성공시켰다. 3 심판진은 바스켓 인터피어런스 판정을 내려 그 팀에게 2점을 주었다. 4 실책을 저지르거나 규칙을 위반하거나 공격자 파울을 했을 때 공격권을 넘겨주게 된다. 5 무술이 미국과 유럽에서 인기를 얻고 있다.

exercise

정답 및 해설 p. 392

A Match the words in the left column to the sentences in the right column.

ⓐ **aquatics**: sports or activities that take place in the water

ⓑ **triathlon**: a contest involving three successive sports

ⓒ **turnover**: the transfer of possession of the ball from one team to the other

ⓓ **substitute**: a player who replaces another player

ⓔ **injury time**: time added to a soccer game to make up for time lost when players are hurt

1. The foul resulted in a(n) ________ that cost the team the game.
2. I'm afraid of water, so I never got involved in ________.
3. The game was tied at the end of the second half, but Korea won it in ________.
4. When the athlete hurt his leg, a(n) ________ was sent in.
5. I like to watch the ________ because I get to see a variety of events.

B Choose the option that best completes the sentence.

1. ________________ consists of such games as sprints, the javelin throw and the pole vault.
   ⓐ Archery ⓑ Triathlon ⓒ Gymnastics ⓓ Track and field

2. You need extremely good balance, flexibility and grace to do ________________.
   ⓐ gymnastics ⓑ weightlifting ⓒ the backstroke ⓓ turnover

3. I love horses, so I like to watch the ________________.
   ⓐ aquatics ⓑ equestrian events ⓒ sprint race ⓓ water polo

4. Bruce Lee helped to make ________________ popular in the West.
   ⓐ Taekwondo ⓑ boxing ⓒ martial arts ⓓ athletics

5. We were very upset when we lost in the ________________ and didn't get to advance.
   ⓐ turnover ⓑ warm-up match ⓒ hooligan ⓓ preliminary round

day **49** # Music, Art & Literature 음악, 미술, 문학

Music, Art & Literature 음악, 미술, 문학

- **art** 미술
  - modern[contemporary] art 현대미술
    - post-modernism 포스트모더니즘
    - cubism 입체파
    - realism 사실주의
    - Impressionism 인상주의
    - surrealism 초현실주의
  - landscape 풍경화
    - portrait 초상화
    - still life 정물화
    - abstract 추상화
    - illustration 삽화
  - sculpture 조각(품)
    - statue 상
    - masterpiece 걸작
    - carve 조각하다, 새기다
    - engraving 조각술
    - etching 에칭, 부식 동판화
    - lithograph 석판화
    - woodcut 목판화
- **music** 음악
  - instrument 악기
    - wind instrument 관악기
    - brass (instrument) 금관악기
    - woodwind (instrument) 목관악기
    - stringed instrument 현악기
    - percussion (instrument) 타악기
    - accompany 반주하다
    - conduct 지휘하다
    - maestro/virtuoso 거장
  - solo 독주
    - duet 2중주
    - trio 3중주
    - quartet 4중주
    - quintet 5중주
- **literature** 문학
  - genre 장르
    - prose 산문
      - fiction 픽션, 소설
      - non-fiction 논픽션
      - sci-fi (SF, science fiction) 공상과학 소설
      - adventure novel 모험소설
      - saga novel 대하소설
      - satire novel 풍자소설
      - mystery 추리소설
    - poetry 운문
      - epic 서사시
      - lyric 서정시
      - dramatic poetry 극시
      - comedy 희극
      - tragedy 비극
  - metaphor 은유법
    - simile 직유법
    - allegory 풍유법
    - irony 반어법
    - paradox 역설법
    - satire 풍자법
    - hyperbole 과장법
    - personification 의인법
    - euphemism 완곡어법
    - writing skills 글쓰기 기법

Voca Check

정답 p.392

Complete the English translation by referring to the page on the left.

❶ The drummer did a two-minute ____________ that was really impressive.
그 드러머는 매우 감동적인 2분간의 독주를 보여주었다.

❷ Her vivid imagination was reflected in her works of ____________.
그녀의 생기 넘치는 상상력은 그녀의 소설 작품 속에 반영되었다.

❸ I don't think I have the lung capacity to play a ____________.
나는 관악기를 연주할 만한 폐활량을 갖고 있지 못한 것 같다.

❹ I like painting ____________s because I am a nature lover.
나는 자연을 사랑하기 때문에 풍경화 그리는 것을 좋아한다.

❺ I met a lot of fellow *Star Trek* fans at the ____________ convention.
공상과학 소설 동호회 모임에서 수많은 '스타트렉' 팬들을 만났다.

❻ The hero was memorialized with a ____________ in the park.
공원에 동상을 세워 그 영웅을 기렸다.

❼ My favorite ____________ of music is jazz.
내가 가장 좋아하는 음악 장르는 재즈이다.

❽ I really like the dreamlike quality of ____________.
나는 초현실주의의 꿈꾸는 듯한 기법을 매우 좋아한다.

More Words

classic 고전
pastoral poetry 목가시
symbolist poetry 상징시
cliché 클리셰, 진부한 표현
conceit 기발한 표현[착상]
climax 점층법, (희곡의) 절정
solo exhibition 개인전
retrospective 회고전
connoisseur (미술품 등의) 감정가
mural 벽화, 벽장식
perspective 원근법
handicraft 수공예
improvise (즉흥적으로) 작곡[연주]하다
variation 변주곡
irregular time 변박자
refrain 후렴구

carve
[kɑːrv]

v. 새기다, 조각하다 syn. engrave

1 He *carved* little tulips around the opening of the vase.

masterpiece
[mǽstərpìːs]

n. 걸작, 명작, 대표작 syn. masterwork

2 The Louvre in Paris contains many of the world's greatest *masterpieces*.

prose
[prouz]

n. 산문(체) a. 산문의 ant. verse

3 I've always preferred reading *prose* to poetry.

voca+ • purple prose 화려한 산문 • write in prose 산문으로 쓰다

paradox
[pǽrədɑ̀ːks]

n. 역설, 모순된 말[상황]

4 "More haste, less speed" is a well-known *paradox*.

realism
[ríːəlìzm]

n. 1. 사실주의, 리얼리즘 2. 현실성

5 His lifelike paintings are good examples of *realism*.

voca+ • surrealism 초현실주의 • hyperrealism 극사실주의
• gritty realism (혐오스러운 것도 그대로 보여주는) 대담한 현실주의

cubism
[kjúːbizm]

n. 입체파, 큐비즘 (물체의 모양을 분석하여 기하학적인 점과 선으로 표현하려고 했음)

6 Picasso was a pioneer of *cubism*.

voca+ • cubist 입체파 예술가; 입체파(식)의

sculpture
[skʌ́lptʃər]

n. 조각(술)

7 There's a lovely *sculpture* garden behind the museum.

voca+ • sculptor 조각가

1 그는 꽃병의 입구 주위에 작은 튤립 무늬들을 새겼다. 2 파리 루브르 박물관은 전 세계의 위대한 걸작들을 많이 보유하고 있다. 3 나는 언제나 시보다 산문 읽는 것을 더 좋아했다. 4 "서두를수록 속도는 느려진다"는 유명한 역설이다. 5 그 화가가 그린 실물과 꼭 닮은 그림들은 리얼리즘의 좋은 예이다. 6 Picasso는 입체파의 선구자였다. 7 그 박물관 뒤에는 예쁜 조각 공원이 있다.

fiction
[fíkʃən]

n. 소설, 지어낸 이야기 ant. non-fiction

1 This story is *fiction*, but some of it is based on fact.

voca+
- romantic[historical/crime] fiction 연애[역사/범죄] 소설
- airport novel 공항 판매용 소설 (기내에서 읽는 가벼운 소설)
- paperback (종이 표지로 된) 보급판 책
- hardcover/hardback 양장본

satire
[sǽtaiər]

n. 풍자, 비꼼

2 His latest book is a biting *satire* on pop culture.

voca+
- political[social] satire 정치적[사회적] 풍자

personification
[pərsɑ̀ːnifikéiʃən]

n. 의인화, 의인법

3 *Personification* is often used in animation where animals or objects talk like humans.

euphemism
[júːfəmìzm]

n. 완곡어법 (a word or expression used to avoid saying something unpleasant or offensive)

4 "Passing away" is a *euphemism* for "dying."

accompany
[əkʌ́mpəni]

v. 반주하다

5 Carla wants me to *accompany* her on the piano at church tomorrow.

voca+
- accompanist 반주자
- to the accompaniment of ~의 반주로
- sing unaccompanied 무반주로 노래하다

lyric
[lírik]

a. 서정시의, 서정적인

6 A sonnet is a *lyric* poem of 14 lines.

voca+
- lyric drama 가극

n. 1. 서정시 (a short poem that expresses feelings)
2. (복수로) 가사 syn. words

1 이 이야기는 소설이지만 일부분은 사실에 바탕을 두고 있다. 2 그의 최근 저서는 대중 문화에 대한 신랄한 풍자를 담고 있다. 3 의인화는 동물이나 사물이 사람처럼 말하는 만화영화에서 자주 사용된다. 4 '세상을 떠나다'는 '죽다'의 완곡한 표현이다. 5 Carla는 내일 교회에서 내가 그녀에게 피아노 반주를 해 주기를 바란다. 6 소네트는 14행으로 이루어진 서정시이다.

genre
[ʒɑ́:nrə]

n. (예술 작품의) 유형, 양식, 장르

1 What *genre* does the book fall into, comedy or tragedy?

voca+ • literary[musical/film] genre 문학[음악/영화] 장르
• classify by genre 장르에 따라 분류하다

Impressionism
[impréʃənìzm]

n. 인상파, 인상주의

2 Claude Monet is often known as the father of *Impressionism*.

voca+ • Impressionist painter 인상파 화가
• Post-Impressionism 후기 인상파[주의]

metaphor
[métəfɔ̀:r]

n. 은유, 비유

3 Saying the Internet is an information highway is a good example of a *metaphor*.

irony
[áirəni]

n. 1. (익살맞은) 반어법 2. 비꼬는 말 3. 예상 밖의 결말, 반전

4 Her writing contains much humor and *irony*.

voca+ • touch[hint/trace] of irony 빈정대는 투[기미]
• sarcasm 조롱이나 불쾌함을 나타내기 위한 반어법

conduct
[kəndʌ́kt]

v. 지휘하다

5 The composer *conducted* the orchestra himself.

voca+ • conductor 지휘자 • baton 지휘봉
• conduct a choir 성가대를 지휘하다

illustration
[ìləstréiʃən]

n. 삽화

6 This encyclopedia is full of color *illustrations* and photographs.

voca+ • full-color[black and white] illustration 총천연색[흑백] 삽화

1 그 책은 장르가 뭐니? 희극이니 비극이니? 2 Claude Monet는 인상파의 아버지로 많이 알려져 있다. 3 인터넷이 정보의 고속도로라는 말은 은유의 좋은 예이다. 4 그녀의 글에는 많은 유머와 반어적 표현이 담겨 있다. 5 작곡가가 관현악단을 직접 지휘했다. 6 이 백과사전에는 컬러 삽화와 사진이 많이 실려 있다.

day 49 exercise

정답 및 해설 p. 392

A Match the words in the left column to the sentences in the right column.

ⓐ **euphemism**: an indirect word or phrase to refer to something unpleasant

ⓑ **realism**: the practice of depicting objects in art exactly as they appear in life

ⓒ **personification**: the representation of a thing or a quality as a person

ⓓ **metaphor**: a word or phrase that includes an implicit comparison

ⓔ **illustration**: a drawing or picture appearing in a text to explain something

1. ________(e)s are used to clarify the meaning of a text.
2. Shakespeare used many ________(e)s such as, "all the world's a stage."
3. Picasso's distortions were rejection of the ________ of his predecessors.
4. I wrote a letter to her using ________(e)s not to offend her.
5. ________ of household items is used in *Beauty and the Beast*.

B Choose the option that best completes the sentence.

1. I have a reproduction of Van Gogh's ________________, "Sunflowers."
   ⓐ epic ⓑ masterpiece ⓒ solo ⓓ virtuoso
2. The artist ________________ the statue out of marble.
   ⓐ painted ⓑ wrote ⓒ illustrated ⓓ carved
3. He's known more for his ________________ than his poetry.
   ⓐ irony ⓑ simile ⓒ prose ⓓ perspective
4. Her use of ________________ was so comical and insightful I was laughing out loud.
   ⓐ satire ⓑ quintet ⓒ engraving ⓓ woodwind
5. His strong voice, combined with beautifully written ________________, made for a powerful song.
   ⓐ percussion ⓑ allegory ⓒ lyrics ⓓ tragedy

Religion 종교

Religion 종교

faith 신앙

- shamanism 무속 신앙
- Judaism 유대교
- Islam 이슬람
- Hinduism 힌두교
- Buddhism 불교
- Catholicism 천주교
  - (holy) trinity (성) 삼위 일체
  - godfather 대부
  - godmother 대모
- Christianity 기독교
- sect 교파
- orthodox 정통의, 공인된
- heterodox 이단의
- heathen 이교도
- convert 개종시키다
- persecution (종교적) 박해
- martyr 순교자

the Bible 성서

- the Ten Commandments 10계명
- the Old Testament 구약성서
- the New Testament 신약성서

religious person 종교인

- secular 세속적인
- pious 독실한, 경건한
- priest 성직자, (카톨릭) 신부
- minister/pastor 목사
- Pope 로마 교황
- cardinal 추기경
- bishop 주교
- monk 수도사
- nun 수녀
- Buddhist 불교도
- Muslim 이슬람교도
- Christian 기독교도
- Catholic 천주교도, 카톨릭교도
- Jew 유대교도
- Hindu 힌두교도
- missionary 선교사
- layperson 평신도

religious activities 종교 활동

- shrine 사당
- mosque 이슬람교 사원
- cathedral 대성당
- monastery 수도원
- abbey 대(大)수도원
- priory 소(小)수도원
- temple 사원, 절
- worship 예배하다, 숭배하다
  - mass 미사
- sermon 설교
  - preacher 설교자
- doctrine 교리
  - scripture 성서, 경전
- theology 신학
  - seminary 신학교
- ritual 의식, 예식
- mission 전도, 포교
- offering 헌금
  - consecrate 봉헌하다
- confession 고해성사
- benediction 축복(기도)
- pilgrimage 성지 순례
  - pilgrim 성지 순례자

Voca Check

정답 p.392

Complete the English translation by referring to the page on the left.

❶ __________ endorses a non-materialistic lifestyle.
불교는 정신적(비물질적)인 삶의 방식을 추구한다.

❷ The historic __________ of the Jewish people culminated in the Holocaust.
유태인들에 대한 역사적인 박해의 정점은 대학살이었다.

❸ The holy __________ consists of the Father, the Son, and the Holy Spirit.
성 삼위일체는 성부, 성자, 성령으로 이루어진다.

❹ Protestantism is a __________ of Christianity.
개신교는 기독교의 한 종파이다.

❺ The Muslim place of worship is called a __________.
이슬람교의 예배당은 모스크라고 불린다.

❻ Each year many Muslims walk miles and miles on a __________ to Mecca.
매년 많은 이슬람교도들이 수 마일을 걸어 메카로 성지 순례를 간다.

❼ Catholics are expected to attend __________ every Sunday.
카톨릭교도들은 매주 일요일 미사에 참석해야 한다.

❽ The first of the __________ states, "You shall have no other gods before me."
십계명의 첫 번째는 '나 이외에 다른 신을 섬기지 말라' 이다.

More Words

atheism 무신론
pantheism 범신론
evangelist 복음전도사
Puritanism 청교도주의
Presbyterian 장로교도
Methodist 감리교도
Baptist 침례교도
pseudo religion 사이비 종교
idolize 우상화하다
sanctity 신성
resurrection 부활
baptism 세례
emancipation 해탈
redeem 속죄하다

orthodox
[ɔ́:rθədɑ̀:ks]

a. 정통의, 공인된 ant. unorthodox

1 *Orthodox* Christianity teaches that Jesus is both the Creator God and a real human being.

voca+ • Eastern Orthodoxy[Orthodox church] 동방 정교회, 그리스 정교회

consecrate
[kɑ́:nsəkrèit]

v. 1. 봉헌하다, 신성하게 하다 syn. dedicate ant. desecrate 신성을 모독하다
2. 성직에 임명하다

2 This church was *consecrated* in 1853.
3 He was *consecrated* bishop two years ago.

voca+ • consecrated bread[wine/ground/church] 신성한 빵[포도주/땅/교회]

scripture
[skríptʃər]

n. 1. (S~) 성서 2. (기독교 외 종교의) 경전

4 According to the *Scripture*, God created the world in six days.

voca+ • the Holy Scriptures 성서(= the Bible)
• Hindu[Buddhist/Muslim] scriptures 힌두교[불교/이슬람교] 경전

shamanism
[ʃɑ́:mənìzəm]

n. 샤머니즘, 무속신앙 (the belief that the world is controlled by good and evil spirits, and these spirits can be directed by people with special powers)

voca+ • shaman 무당
• totemism 토테미즘 (자기 부족의 기원을 특정 동식물과 연결시켜 숭배하는 신앙)
• animism 애니미즘 (무생물계에도 영혼이 있다고 믿는 세계관)

martyr
[mɑ́:rtər]

n. 순교자

5 Saint Stephen was the first Christian *martyr* who chose to die for his faith.

v. (종교 · 신념 등을 이유로) ~를 죽이다, 순교자로 만들다

1 정통 기독교에서는 예수가 창조주 신이자 실존했던 인간이라고 가르친다. 2 이 교회는 1853년에 봉헌되었다. 3 그는 2년 전 주교직에 임명되었다. 4 성서에 따르면 신은 엿새만에 세상을 창조했다. 5 성도 Stephen은 그의 신앙을 위해 죽음을 선택한 최초의 기독교 순교자였다.

heathen
[hí:ðən]

n. 이교도 syn. infidel, pagan

1 She considered him a *heathen* for not going to church.

voca+ • heathenism 이단 • idolatry 우상 숭배
• freedom of religion 종교의 자유

a. 이교도의 syn. heretical

Buddhism
[bú:dizəm]

n. 불교

2 *Buddhism* emphasizes personal salvation through meditation.

voca+ • Buddha 부처 • Buddhist 불교의, 불교 신자
• karma 업보, 인연 • nirvana 열반, 지극한 행복의 경지
• reincarnation 환생 • transmigration 윤회

worship
[wə́:rʃip]

v. 숭배하다, 예배를 드리다 syn. revere

3 In the various regions of India, Hindus *worship* different gods.

voca+ • church service 예배 • mass 미사
• preach a sermon 설교하다 • prayer 기도
• hymn 찬송가 • chant 성가

n. 예배, 숭배

secular
[sékjələr]

a. 세속적인, 비종교적인 syn. mundane, worldly

4 Turkey, although predominantly Muslim, is a *secular* country.

voca+ • secularism 세속주의(the belief that religion is not allowed to interfere with the social and political affairs)
• secularist 세속주의자 • secularization 세속화

nun
[nʌ́n]

n. 수녀

5 As a *nun*, she worked for the poor in Africa.

voca+ • nunnery/convent 수녀원
• Sister 수녀에 대한 호칭

1 그녀는 그가 교회에 다니지 않기 때문에 이교도라고 생각했다. 2 불교에서는 명상을 통한 개인의 구제를 강조한다. 3 인도의 여러 지역에서 힌두교도들은 각기 다른 신을 섬긴다. 4 터키는 이슬람교도들이 대부분이지만 세속 국가이다. 5 수녀로서 그녀는 아프리카의 가난한 사람들을 위해 일했다.

Pope
[poup]

n. 로마 교황 syn. pontiff, Holy Father

1 Thousands of people gathered to hear the *Pope* speak.

voca+
- the papacy 교황의 직위[임기]
- the Vatican 바티칸 궁전, 로마 교황청
- Pope John Paul Ⅱ 교황 요한 바오로 2세
- Pope Benedict XVI 현(現) 교황 베네딕토 16세

confession
[kənféʃən]

n. 고해, 참회

2 The priest heard his *confession*.

voca+
- go to confession 고해를 하러 가다
- (the sacrament of) confession 고해성사
- confession of faith 신앙 고백
- original sin 원죄

theology
[θiːɑ́ːlədʒi]

n. 신학 (the study of religion) syn. divinity

3 This is a new article on *theology* and Christian history.

voca+
- theologian 신학자
- theological[divinity] school 신학교
- priory school 수도원 학교

layperson
[léipə̀ːrsn]

n. 평신도, 속인(俗人) syn. layman ant. cleric

4 His father is a pastor, but he is a *layperson*.

voca+
- laity (집합적) 성직자가 아닌 평신도
- clergy (집합적) 성직자
- congregation (집합적) 종교 회중(會衆)
- religious fanatic[zealot] 광신도

convert
[kənvə́ːrt]

v. 개종하다, 개종시키다

5 He *converted to* Catholicism when he got married.

n. [kɑ́ːnvəːrt] 개종자

voca+
- conversion 개종

1 수천 명이 교황의 말을 듣기 위해 모였다. 2 신부는 그의 고해를 들었다. 3 이것은 신학과 기독교 역사에 대한 새로운 글이다. 4 그의 아버지는 목사이지만 그는 평신도이다. 5 그는 결혼할 때 카톨릭으로 개종했다.

exercise

정답 및 해설 p.392

A Match the words in the left column to the sentences in the right column.

ⓐ **secular**: not having any connection with religion

ⓑ **scripture**: written text that is considered sacred or holy by a religion

ⓒ **theology**: the study of religion and religious faith

ⓓ **heathen**: someone who is not connected with established religions such as Christianity

ⓔ **orthodox**: following closely the traditional beliefs of a religion

1. The priest read from the ________.
2. I learned a great deal about different religions in ________ class.
3. ________ Christians are opposed to divorce.
4. My mother sent me to a religious private school because she thought the public school teachers were ________(e)s.
5. Although my parents were religious, I went to public school and received a(n) ________ education.

B Choose the option that best completes the sentence.

1. Missionaries travel the world trying to ________________ people to their religion.
   ⓐ confess ⓑ convert ⓒ preach ⓓ resurrect

2. The priest ________________ the altar by sprinkling holy water on it.
   ⓐ martyred ⓑ persecuted ⓒ worshiped ⓓ consecrated

3. The ________________ is the head of the Catholic Church.
   ⓐ priest ⓑ rabbi ⓒ Pope ⓓ Jew

4. Catholics believe that God will forgive their sins if a priest hears their ________________.
   ⓐ confessions ⓑ sermons ⓒ hymns ⓓ ritual

5. A ________________ might attend church once a week, but a priest commits his whole life to his faith.
   ⓐ monk ⓑ missionary ⓒ pagan ⓓ layperson

JOCKEY
1500
maxell

정답 및 해설

day 01 exercise

A.

1 ⓑ 2 ⓔ 3 ⓓ 4 ⓐ 5 ⓒ

1 탐욕은 자본주의에 내재된 특성이다. **2** 뉴스 속보는 사람들에게 재난이 임박했다는 것을 알려 주었다. **3** 나는 예금 계좌에 이자가 붙게 둘 것이다. **4** 그녀가 워크숍의 모든 면을 총괄할 것이다. **5** 그는 그 계획에 대해 암묵적 승인을 했다.

• occur 생기다 • imply 내포[함축]하다 • capitalism 자본주의

B.

1 ⓑ 2 ⓐ 3 ⓒ 4 ⓐ 5 ⓒ

1 만일 당신이 어떤 것을 긍정하면 당신은 그것에 동의하는 것이다. **2** 만일 당신이 후퇴한다면 당신은 도망가는 것이다. **3** 당신이 사람들을 비웃는다면 당신은 그들을 조롱하는 것이다. **4** 도발을 받으면 당신은 아마도 싸울 것이다. **5** 당신에게 충실함이 없다면 당신은 성실하지 않은 것이다.

• dispense with ~ 없이 지내다 • come along 나타나다 • fire 해고하다 • ridicule 비웃다 • applaud 박수를 보내다 • unfaithful 불성실한 • defensive 방어적인

C.

1 ⓑ 2 ⓑ 3 ⓓ

1 획기적인 과학적 발견 **2** 초보 운전자 **3** 진실을 왜곡하다

• setback 장애 • veteran 경험이 풍부한 사람 • request 요청하다 • twist 비틀다

D.

1 ⓑ 2 ⓓ 3 ⓐ

1 그 모든 소란 **2** 공공연한 적개심 **3** 미묘한 차이

• labor 노동 • mess 엉망진창 • apparent 명백한 • unfounded 사실무근의 • problematic 문제가 되는 • fundamental 근본적인

E.

1 ⓑ 2 ⓒ 3 ⓓ 4 ⓒ

1 취임식에서 가장 중요한 사람은 누구인가? **2** 다음 중 익명일 가능성이 가장 높은 것은? **3** 다음 중 어느 것을 감정하겠는가? **4** 당신과 가까운 사람이 죽었을 때 당신은 애도한다.

• master of ceremonies 사회자(MC) • president-elect 대통령 당선자 • would-be 예비의, ~이 될 예정의 • charitable 자선의 • donation 기부 • viewpoint 견해 • antique 골동품

day 02 exercise

A.

1 ⓐ 2 ⓓ 3 ⓔ 4 ⓑ 5 ⓒ

1 의사는 죽어가는 남자의 심장을 심장 질환을 겪고 있는 남자에게 이식할 것이다. **2** 현직 시장이 선거에서 패배했다. **3** 같은 주제가 그 작가의 여러 작품에 스며들어 있다. **4** 엄마는 다정한 말로 우는 아이를 달랬다. **5** 소유지의 외곽에 울타리가 쳐져 있다.

• calm 진정시키다 • soothe 달래다 • outline 윤곽을 그리다

B.

1 ⓒ 2 ⓓ 3 ⓐ 4 ⓐ 5 ⓒ

1 만일 어떤 결정이 만장일치라면 모두가 동의하는 것이다. **2** 만일 어떤 단체가 더 큰 단체와 제휴하고 있다면 그것과 연관되어 있는 것이다. **3** 만일 당신이 일을 위임하면 당신은 다른 사람을 지명해 그 일을 시키는 것이다. **4** 도로가 한데 모아지면 그것들은 하나가 된다. **5** 취하지 않은 사람은 술을 마시지 않은 것이다.

• appoint 임명[지명]하다 • pave (도로 등을) 포장하다 • separate 분리하다 • deadline 마감(기한)

C.

1 ⓑ 2 ⓓ 3 ⓐ

1 노골적인 무시 **2** 토박이들 **3** 과학의 영역

• subtle 미묘한 • obvious 명백한 • flavory 풍미 있는 • unintentional 고의가 아닌 • industrious 근면한 • native 토박이의

D.

1 ⓒ 2 ⓑ 3 ⓓ

1 유연한 물질 **2** 의상을 칭찬하다 **3** 드문드문 일어나는 일들

• durable 내구성이 있는 • rigid 딱딱한, 유연하지 않은 • soil 더럽히다 • brief 짧은

E.

1 ⓐ 2 ⓒ 3 ⓐ 4 ⓒ

1 다음 중 어느 것을 퇴치하려고 애쓰겠는가? **2** 다음 중 '유가족'으로 불릴 가능성이 가장 높은 사람은? **3** 다음 중 어느 것이 증류될 수 있는가? **4** 만일 당신이 낮은 임금을 받는다면 당신은 임금 인상을 요구할 것이다.

• gambler 도박꾼 • widow 과부 • bride 신부 • wheat 밀 • degree 학위 • raise (임금) 인상 • retire 은퇴하다

day 03 exercise

A.

1 ⓓ 2 ⓒ 3 ⓔ 4 ⓐ 5 ⓑ

1 그 환자는 피를 많이 흘렸다. 그는 살아남기 위해 수혈이 필요하다. **2** 그 도시에는 무단횡단에 관한 엄격한 법률이 있다. **3** 야구를 하려던 그들의 계획은 폭풍우 때문에 분명히 이루어지지 못할 것이다. **4** 그녀의 아버지는 그녀의 남자친구의 미심쩍은 과거에 대해 물었다. **5** 그 은둔자는 숲 속에서 혼자 살았다.

• arouse 불러일으키다 • suspicion 의심 • withdraw 물러나다 • inflexible (규칙 등이) 변경할 수 없는 • transfer 이동 • jaywalking 무단 횡단

B.

1 ⓒ 2 ⓓ 3 ⓐ 4 ⓑ 5 ⓑ

1 냉정한 사람은 감정적이지 않다. **2** 당신이 어떤 사람을 혐오한다면 당신은 그 사람을 몹시 싫어하는 것이다. **3** 위생을 염려하는 사람은 청결함에 주의를 기울인다. **4** 어떤 것이 과잉이라면 그것은 불필요한 것이다. **5** 당신이 어떤 주장에 논박을 한다면 당신은 그것을 반박하는 것이다.

• passionate 열정적인 • detest 몹시 싫어하다 • moral 도덕 • genetics 유전학 • contradict 반박하다

C.

1 ⓒ 2 ⓑ 3 ⓓ

1 계속 남아 있는 의문 **2** 지명된 운전사 **3** 너무 비싼 가격

• pressing 절박한 • remaining 남아 있는 • intoxicated 술에 취한 • expert 전문가인 • negotiable 협상할 수 있는 • reasonable 합리적인

D.

1 ⓐ 2 ⓓ 3 ⓒ

1 숲 속에서의 캠핑을 싫어하다 **2** 고르지 않은 이발[머리 모양] **3** 불 속에서 소멸되다[죽다]

• delight in ~을 즐기다 • crooked 굽은 • awful 끔찍한 • extinguish (불을) 끄다

E.

1 ⓓ 2 ⓑ 3 ⓒ 4 ⓑ

1 당신은 누구에게 가장 비밀을 털어놓기 쉽겠는가? **2** 다음 중 주식인 것은 어느 것인가? **3** 심장 과학을 공부하는 사람들은 심장에 관심이 있다. **4** 그는 운전을 해야 했기 때문에 식사할 때 와인을 마시지 않기로 했다.

• acquaintance 아는 사람[사이] • criminal 범죄자 • kidney 신장

day 04 exercise

A.

1 ⓐ 2 ⓒ 3 ⓔ 4 ⓑ 5 ⓓ

1 장엄한 음악이 교회에 울려퍼졌다. **2** 그 소년들은 자신들의 문제를 어떻게 해결해야 할지 몰랐다. **3** 이 새로운 크림은 정말로 당신의 피부를 생기있게 해줄 것이다. **4** 새 놀이공원 때문에 많은 방문객들이 그 도시로 몰려들 것으로 기대된다. **5** 그 약은 단지 위약 정도의 효과밖에 없었다.

• majestic 장엄한 • awe-inspiring 경외심을 일으키는 • incoming 유입 • proportion 분량 • dilemma 진퇴양난(의 상태) • restore 회복하다

B.

1 ⓓ 2 ⓒ 3 ⓑ 4 ⓑ 5 ⓐ

1 만만찮은 상대는 도전적이다. **2** 당신이 능력을 발휘할 때 당신은 그것을 활용하는 것이다. **3** 이기적인 사람들은 주로 자기 자신에 대해 생각한다. **4** 당신이 누군가를 따돌릴 때 당신은 그들을 제외시키는 것이다. **5** 전례가 없는 것은 결코 일어난 적이 없는 것이다.

• humble 겸손한 • utilize 활용하다 • property 재산 • reward 보상하다 • exclude 배제하다 • accuse 고소하다 • legalize 합법화하다

C.

1 ⓓ 2 ⓑ 3 ⓐ

1 폐위된 왕 **2** 기가 질리는 업무 **3** 신성한 결혼을 하다

• respected 존경받는 • assassinated 암살당한 • ridiculous 엉뚱한 • discord 불일치

D.

1 ⓑ 2 ⓒ 3 ⓐ

1 황무지 **2** 서 있는 자전거 **3** 현재의 가정을 반박하다

• sandy 모래의 • fertile 비옥한 • plowed 경작한 • folded 접힌 • mobile 이동성의 • affirm 긍정[확언]하다 • impede 방해하다

E.

1 ⓒ 2 ⓐ 3 ⓓ 4 ⓑ

1 누가 반란을 일으킬 가능성이 높은가? **2** 다음 중 어느 것이 난독증의 영향을 받는가? **3** 조사 보고서를 쓸 때 당신은 전문 잡지를 참조할 것이다. **4** 위선자는 실제로는 갖고 있지 않은 신념을 가진 척한다.

• recipe 요리법 • soap opera TV연속극 • journal 학술지

day 05 exercise

A.
1 ⓓ 2 ⓐ 3 ⓑ 4 ⓔ 5 ⓒ

1 사냥을 허용하면 우리의 보존 노력이 수포로 돌아갈 것이다. **2** 바다는 폭풍 전에 잔잔했다. **3** 나는 딸의 자전거에서 보조 바퀴를 뗄 것이다. **4** 나는 늘 동물 권리 옹호자였다. **5** 해일은 재난을 일으킬 수 있다.

• attach 붙이다 • catastrophic 재해를 가져오는 • outcome 결과 • invalid 유효하지 않은 • advocate 옹호하다 • conservation 보호, 보존 • tidal wave 해일

B.
1 ⓒ 2 ⓑ 3 ⓐ 4 ⓒ 5 ⓓ

1 그저 그런 음악가는 2류이다. **2** 살균한 도구는 소독이 된 것이다. **3** 당신이 어떤 대의에 충성심을 갖고 있을 때 당신은 그것을 지지하는 것이다. **4** 사람들이 만장일치에 이르면 그들 모두가 동의하는 것이다. **5** 뉴스 보도가 어느 TV 쇼를 대체한다면 그것이 쇼를 대신해서 TV에 나오는 것이다.

• second-rate 2류의 • disinfected 살균된, 소독된 • inspiring 자극하는 • take part in ~에 참가하다 • survey 조사 • bump (TV 프로그램 등을) 다른 시간대로 옮기다

C.
1 ⓒ 2 ⓒ 3 ⓐ

1 기념비를 훼손하다 **2** 화를 억누르다 **3** 제멋대로인 아이들

• dedicate 바치다 • submit 제출하다 • suppress 억누르다 • attentive 주의를 기울이는 • enthusiastic 열렬한

D.
1 ⓒ 2 ⓐ 3 ⓒ

1 대단한 용기를 보이다 **2** 실행 가능한 계획 **3** 완곡한 질문

• generosity 관용 • cowardice 겁 • stupidity 어리석음 • affordable 감당할 수 있는 • awkward 어색한, 곤란한

E.
1 ⓑ 2 ⓓ 3 ⓐ 4 ⓐ

1 누가 기사도를 발휘하겠는가? **2** 다음 중 어느 것이 세련됨의 표시인가? **3** 다음 중 어느 것이 칭찬할 만한가? **4** 휴가를 가기에 좋은 때라면 당신은 휴가를 떠나야 한다.

• knight 기사 • peasant 소작농 • criminal record 전과 기록 • performance 공연 • gossip 가십, 흉보기 • postpone 미루다

day 06 exercise

A.
1 ⓓ 2 ⓔ 3 ⓑ 4 ⓒ 5 ⓐ

1 그 일은 너무 많은 시간이 걸렸다. **2** 그녀는 대입 시험에 떨어지자 낙심했다. **3** 그녀는 하찮은 물건에 돈을 낭비했다. **4** 독자들을 헷갈리게 할 수 있는 불필요한 정보는 삭제해라. **5** 그것은 내가 지금까지 본 것 중에서 가장 훌륭한 Hamlet 공연이었다.

• trivial 하찮은 • excessive 과도한 • depressed 우울한

B.
1 ⓑ 2 ⓓ 3 ⓒ 4 ⓐ 5 ⓑ

1 당신이 은둔한다면 당신은 사람들로부터 떨어져 지낸다. **2** 괴상한 어떤 것은 별난 것이다. **3** 변덕스런 사람은 예측할 수가 없다. **4** 당신의 명예가 훼손되면 당신의 평판이 손상된 것이다. **5** 당신이 어떤 것을 강화하면 당신은 그것을 보다 강하게 하는 것이다.

• bizarre 별난, 기괴한 • diseased 병든 • reputation 명성, 평판 • ruin 파괴하다

C.
1 ⓓ 2 ⓒ 3 ⓓ

1 뒤늦은 생일 파티 **2** 계속되는 기침 **3** 올챙이에서 개구리로의 변태

• heartfelt 진심에서 우러난 • unexpected 느닷없는 • overdue 기한이 지난, 늦은 • occasional 이따금씩의 • tadpole 올챙이 • coloration 채색 • lifespan 수명 • transformation 변형

D.
1 ⓑ 2 ⓓ 3 ⓑ

1 마냥 행복한 젊은이 **2** 꾸밈없는 태도 **3** 상당한 변화들

• miserable 불행한 • hostile 적대적인

E.
1 ⓒ 2 ⓓ 3 ⓒ 4 ⓑ

1 이 샌드위치는 당신의 배고픔을 덜어 주는 데 도움이 될 것이다. **2** 보호 관찰을 받을 가능성이 가장 높은 사람은 누구인가? **3** 다음 중 어느 것이 해독될 필요가 있는가? **4** 영화가 호평을 받으면 그것은 아마도 상을 받을 것이다.

• retiree 은퇴자 • ban 금지하다

day 07 exercise

A.

1 ⓑ 2 ⓓ 3 ⓔ 4 ⓐ 5 ⓒ

1 나는 네가 그 무뢰한과 교제하지 않았으면 좋겠다. 그는 나쁜 본보기다. **2** 구체적으로 언급하지 않았지만, 그는 그 거래를 넌지시 암시했다. **3** 그는 나를 교묘히 조종하여 협약에 서명하게 하려 했다. **4** 과학자들은 실험을 할 때 아주 꼼꼼해야 한다. **5** Linda는 간신히 하품을 참았다.

• refer to ~을 언급하다 • yawn 하품

B.

1 ⓓ 2 ⓐ 3 ⓒ 4 ⓐ 5 ⓒ

1 당신이 캐묻기를 좋아한다면 당신은 질문을 한다. **2** 마지못해 하는 사람은 어떤 일을 하는 것을 내키지 않아 한다. **3** 당신이 보수적이라면 당신은 아마 전통에 따를 것이다. **4** 당신이 옆길로 샌다면 당신은 주제에서 벗어나는 것이다. **5** 당신이 답을 추론하면 당신은 그것을 알아내는 것이다.

• doomed 운명지어진 • rebellious 반항적인 • accuracy 정확성 • figure out ~을 알아내다 • double-check 재확인하다

C.

1 ⓒ 2 ⓓ 3 ⓓ

1 상냥한 소년 **2** 곤경에 빠진 **3** 당신 자신의 의지로

• naughty 장난꾸러기의 • deliberation 숙고, 신중함 • investigation 조사, 취조 • problematic 문제가 있는 • free will 자유의지, 자의

D.

1 ⓑ 2 ⓒ 3 ⓒ

1 돈을 아껴 쓰는 **2** 움트고 있는 꽃 **3** 계약을 파기하다

• stingy 인색한 • budding 피어나려 하는 • fragrant 향기로운 • modify 수정하다 • validate 유효하게 하다

E.

1 ⓑ 2 ⓓ 3 ⓑ 4 ⓑ

1 다음 중 땀이 나게 하는 것은 어느 것인가? **2** 다음 중 당신은 어느 것을 철회하겠는가? **3** 은밀한 작전은 아마 불법일 것이다. **4** 범인이 당국을 교묘히 피해 갔다.

• statement 진술 • overt 공공연한 • urgent 긴급한 • authorities 당국 • witness 목격자, 증인

day 08 exercise

A.

1 ⓒ 2 ⓓ 3 ⓑ 4 ⓔ 5 ⓐ

1 그는 계약서의 조건을 지킬 의무가 있었다. **2** 두 당은 쌍방 협약을 맺었다. **3** 그가 그런 완곡어구를 쓰지 말고 솔직히 말했으면 좋겠다. **4** 그 쟁점으로 인해 국민 여론이 분열될 것이다. **5** 고여 있는 연못에는 많은 세균들이 있다.

• inoffensive 불쾌감을 주지 않는 • refer to 가리키다, 지시하다 • requirement 요구 • term 조건 • conflict 충돌하다 • obligate 의무를 지우다

B.

1 ⓓ 2 ⓑ 3 ⓑ 4 ⓒ 5 ⓐ

1 만일 당신이 경찰을 빠져나간다면 당신은 그들을 피하는 것이다. **2** 만일 당신이 어떤 것의 복제품을 만든다면 당신은 그것을 복사하는 것이다. **3** 만일 정부가 과세한다면 그것을 부과하는 것이다. **4** 만일 논쟁이 격렬하다면 그것은 신랄한 것이다. **5** 만일 어떤 여자가 당신의 상대편이라면 그녀는 당신과 비슷한 일을 하는 것이다.

• aid 돕다 • impose 부과하다 • refund 환불하다 • function 기능, 역할 • superior 우월한 • competition 경쟁

C.

1 ⓑ 2 ⓒ 3 ⓒ

1 열정적인 화가 **2** 사건을 유발하다 **3** 총 수익

• passionate 열렬한 • unique 독특한 • projected 예상된

D.

1 ⓓ 2 ⓑ 3 ⓐ

1 자만심을 보이다 **2** 소용없는 시도 **3** 정보를 누설하다

• grace 우아함 • modesty 겸손함 • admirable 훌륭한 • pointless 무의미한, 쓸데없는 • analyze 분석하다

E.

1 ⓓ 2 ⓐ 3 ⓓ 4 ⓒ

1 다음 중 어느 것의 등받이 각도를 조절하겠는가? **2** 다음 중 어느 것을 풀겠는가? **3** 누가 당신의 유산을 물려받을 것인가? **4** 백내장이 있는 사람은 눈에 문제가 있다.

• fishing rod 낚싯대 • knot 매듭

day 09 exercise

A.

1 ⓒ 2 ⓐ 3 ⓓ 4 ⓑ 5 ⓔ

1 시끄러운 술집에서 여러 해 동안 일한다면 당신의 청각이 손상될 것이다. **2** 그는 질 좋은 포도주에 대해 전문가이다. **3** 해양법에 따르면 이곳은 국제 수역이다. **4** 우리는 그 변덕스런 젊은이가 앞으로 무엇을 할지 전혀 알 수가 없었다. **5** 당신의 의도를 분명히 해주세요.

• specialized 전문적인 • relate to ~와 관련되어 있다

B.

1 ⓑ 2 ⓒ 3 ⓐ 4 ⓓ 5 ⓒ

1 당신이 연애를 하고 있다면 당신은 사랑에 빠져 있는 것이다. **2** 당신이 도움을 주고 있다면 당신은 도움을 제공하고 있는 것이다. **3** 당신이 기금을 모으고 있다면 당신은 돈을 걷고 있는 것이다. **4** 당신이 누군가에게 사기를 친다면 당신은 그들을 속여 돈을 빼앗는 것이다. **5** 당신이 무언가를 쪼갠다면, 그것을 나누는 것이다.

• humiliated 모욕당한 • broken-hearted 실연당한 • reveal 드러내다 • split 쪼개다

C.

1 ⓑ 2 ⓓ 3 ⓓ

1 가장 두드러진 특징 **2** 특권을 부여하다 **3** 불필요한 과잉 정보

• subtle 미묘한 • noticeable 눈에 띄는 • disturbing 교란시키는 • deserve ~을 받을 만하다 • thrive on ~을 잘해내다 • grant 주다, 부여하다 • secretive 비밀스런 • organized 정리된

D.

1 ⓒ 2 ⓐ 3 ⓓ

1 갑자기 사라지다 **2** 몹시 마른 체격 **3** 버릇없는 아이

• flee 달아나다 • evaporate 증발하다 • physique 체격, 체형 • chubby 통통한 • slender 날씬한 • awkward 어색한 • spoiled 버릇없는

E.

1 ⓒ 2 ⓐ 3 ⓓ 4 ⓒ

1 누가 가장 규칙에 집착하기 쉬운가? **2** 당신은 어떤 것을 시작하겠는가? **3** 다음 중 어느 것이 잔물결치는가? **4** 당신이 나태하게 느껴진다면 당신은 십중팔구 침대에 있을 것이다.

• rebel 반역자 • conformist (체제 · 관례의) 순응자 • radical 급진주의자 • statue 상, 조각상 • ice cube (냉동실의) 조각 얼음 • flagpole 깃대 • pond 연못

day 10 exercise

A.

1 ⓓ 2 ⓑ 3 ⓔ 4 ⓐ 5 ⓒ

1 그는 지역의 저명한 인사이다. **2** 나는 앉아서 하는 일은 싫다. 활동적인 일이 더 좋다. **3** 내가 부자라면 자선 활동에 참여할 것이다. **4** 이 음료에는 설탕이 섞여 있다. **5** 나는 생명 보험을 들려고 하는데, 수혜자를 아들로 하고 싶다.

• pollute 오염시키다 • impure 순수하지 않은 • fund 자금 • charitable 자비로운 • life insurance 생명보험

B.

1 ⓐ 2 ⓒ 3 ⓑ 4 ⓑ 5 ⓓ

1 당신이 많은 영향력을 지니고 있다면 당신은 사람들에게 영향을 미칠 수 있다. **2** 행상인은 물건을 파는 사람이다. **3** 그 집과 인접해 있는 어떤 것은 그 옆에 있다. **4** 당신이 죄를 뉘우친다면 당신은 죄책감을 느끼는 것이다. **5** 당신이 징집되었다면 당신은 군에 입대해야 한다.

• offend 성나게 하다 • deceive 속이다 • voluntarily 자발적으로 • discharge 제대시키다

C.

1 ⓒ 2 ⓐ 3 ⓑ

1 새 자동차를 자랑하다 **2** 건장한 체격 **3** 나이가 들어 퇴화하다

• purchase 구입하다 • boast of ~을 자랑하다 • insure 보험에 들다 • frail 연약한 • ripen 익다 • shift 바뀌다, 바꾸다

D.

1 ⓐ 2 ⓒ 3 ⓑ

1 핵무기를 확산시키다 **2** 분쟁의 시대 **3** 공정한 중재자

• eliminate 제거하다 • protest 항의[저항]하다 • recession 후퇴, 퇴거 • mediator 중재자 • biased 편견을 지닌 • compassionate 동정심이 있는

E.

1 ⓓ 2 ⓑ 3 ⓓ 4 ⓓ

1 완고한 사람은 항상 자신이 원하는 대로 하며 마음을 바꾸려고 하지 않는다. **2** 바다에서 수영을 하는 사람은 무엇을 조심해야 하는가? **3** 당신은 갑작스런 통증을 느낄 때 찌푸린다. **4** 누가 출산 휴가를 받아 일을 쉬는가?

• sunscreen 자외선 차단제 • on a business trip 출장 중인 • stressed out 스트레스를 받는

day 11 exercise

A.

1 ⓓ 2 ⓒ 3 ⓑ 4 ⓔ 5 ⓐ

1 그는 자신의 얼마 안 되는 급여에 만족하지 못했다. **2** 정부를 전복하려는 음모는 성공하지 못했다. **3** 그들은 호사스런 결혼식을 올렸다. 그것은 마치 동화 같았다. **4** 들어오기 전에 구두의 진흙을 닦아내세요. **5** 내가 그에게 진실을 말하게끔 강요해 보겠다.

• urge 촉구하다 • plot 음모 • insufficient 충분하지 않은 • dirt 진흙; 먼지 • overthrow 전복하다, 뒤집어엎다 • fairytale 동화

B.

1 ⓑ 2 ⓐ 3 ⓒ 4 ⓐ 5 ⓒ

1 당신이 어리둥절해 있다면 당신은 혼란스러운 것이다. **2** 두 가지 사이에 불일치가 있다면 차이가 있는 것이다. **3** 요행으로 이긴다면 당신은 운이 좋은 것이다. **4** 당신이 병에 잘 걸리는 편이라면 당신은 병의 진단을 받을 확률이 높다. **5** 불만이 많다면 당신은 많은 것에 대해 불평한다.

• confident 자신감 있는 • perceptive 지각력 있는, 예민한 • be diagnosed with ~라고 진단을 받다 • be immune to ~에 면역성이 있다 • take pleasure in ~을 즐기다

C.

1 ⓑ 2 ⓐ 3 ⓒ

1 처음부터 단호하다 **2** 전자 기기를 보내다 **3** 질서를 어지럽히는 행동

• uneasy 불안한 • determined 단호한 • disorganized 질서가 없는 • modest 겸손한 • troublesome 성가신, 귀찮은

D.

1 ⓐ 2 ⓒ 3 ⓓ

1 우호적인 분위기 **2** 간헐적인 전투 **3** 기초 테스트

• hostile 적대적인 • courteous 예의바른 • straightforward 솔직한, 직접적인 • strict 엄격한 • compulsory 강제적인 • advanced 상급의

E.

1 ⓒ 2 ⓐ 3 ⓑ 4 ⓓ

1 다음 중 어떤 것을 꾸며내겠는가? **2** 당신은 다음 중 어느 것을 입증하겠는가? **3** 다음 중 어느 것이 구식인가? **4** 대리모는 다른 사람을 위해 아이를 갖고 낳는다.

• excuse 변명 • findings 조사 결과 • light bulb 전구 • adopt 입양하다 • carry (아이를) 배다 • deliver 분만하다

day 12 exercise

A.

1 ⓒ 2 ⓐ 3 ⓔ 4 ⓑ 5 ⓓ

1 나는 더 많은 구어체 표현을 배우려고 노력하고 있다. **2** 폐렴은 아주 심각할 수 있으며 치료하지 않으면 사망에 이를 수도 있다. **3** 군사 집단이 그 나라의 통치권을 장악하여 소수 독재 정치를 실시했다. **4** 지나친 음주는 위험한 악습이다. **5** 그 선동가에게는 많은 추종자들이 있었다.

• immoral 비도덕적인 • consequence 결과 • passionately 열정적으로 • concern ~와 관계있다

B.

1 ⓐ 2 ⓓ 3 ⓒ 4 ⓐ 5 ⓓ

1 당신이 누군가를 현혹시키면 당신은 그들을 속이는 것이다. **2** 어떤 것이 수출입 금지 품목이라면 그것은 불법이다. **3** 어떤 것이 강제적이면 당신은 그것을 하지 않으면 안 된다. **4** 당신이 감시하에 있다면 당신은 관찰되고 있는 것이다. **5** 당신이 염세가라면 당신은 혼자 있는 편을 좋아할 것이다.

• valuable 귀중한 • be willing to-v 기꺼이 ~하다 • be obliged to-v ~해야 한다 • pretend to-v ~하는 체하다 • promotion 승진

C.

1 ⓑ 2 ⓓ 3 ⓐ

1 그의 오랜 숙적 **2** 해방된 노예 **3** 증상을 완화하다

• colleague 동료 • mistreat 학대하다 • capture 붙잡다 • liberate 해방시키다

D.

1 ⓒ 2 ⓐ 3 ⓑ

1 대의의 옹호자 **2** 규칙에 대한 경멸 **3** 머리카락을 헝클어뜨리다

• author 창시자, 입안자 • validity 타당성 • violation 위반 • rinse ~을 헹구다 • mess up ~을 엉망진창으로 만들다

E.

1 ⓐ 2 ⓒ 3 ⓑ 4 ⓑ

1 다음 중 어느 것이 변장의 일부인가? **2** 다음 중 수면 부족으로 인해 발생할 결과로 가장 알맞은 것은? **3** 당신은 다음 중 어느 것에 수를 놓겠는가? **4** 심문 중에는 많은 질문이 던져진다.

• wig 가발 • sore 뻐근한 • impaired 손상된 • pillow 베개 • chore 잡일, 허드렛일 • picture frame 액자 • suspect 용의자 • jail 수감하다

day 13 exercise

A.

1 ⓐ 2 ⓓ 3 ⓑ 4 ⓔ 5 ⓒ

1 당신의 결론은 잘못된 생각을 바탕으로 하고 있다. **2** 그녀는 쉽게 병에 걸린다. **3** 물 풍선이 땅에 닿자 터졌다. **4** 그 사무실은 토요일에 운영되지 않았다. **5** 나는 그 외로운 소녀가 불쌍하게 느껴졌다.

• reasoning 추론 • burst 파열하다 • abandon 버리다

B.

1 ⓐ 2 ⓓ 3 ⓒ 4 ⓑ 5 ⓒ

1 당신이 누군가를 낙담시키면 당신은 그 사람을 실망시키는 것이다. **2** 경험적 조사 결과는 관찰 가능하다. **3** 당신이 간계를 이용해 행동하면 당신은 교활한 것이다. **4** 당신이 단기 체류 상태에 있다면 당신은 일시적으로 머무르는 것이다. **5** 당신이 누군가에게 종속되어 있다면 당신은 그들이 시키는 대로 한다.

• forsake 버리다 • appreciate 감사해하다 • theoretical 이론적인 • unmistakable 틀림없는 • suspicious 의심스러운 • observable 관찰할 수 있는 • unstable 불안정한 • sly 교활한, 음흉한 • conventional 진부한, 인습의 • for good 영원히 • wander 헤매다, 떠돌다 • equal 대등한 사람

C.

1 ⓒ 2 ⓑ 3 ⓓ

1 실수를 하다 **2** 모의 재판 **3** 서서히 진행되는 파멸

• fake 가짜의 • lengthy 긴, 장황한 • recovery 회복

D.

1 ⓑ 2 ⓐ 3 ⓑ

1 불리한 결과 **2** 격렬한 운동 **3** 비정상적인 행동

• trivial 사소한 • favorable 유리한 • foreseeable 예측할 수 있는 • brisk 재빠른 • excessive 과도한 • vulnerable 약한, 상처받기 쉬운

E.

1 ⓐ 2 ⓓ 3 ⓒ 4 ⓑ

1 경쟁하는 자는 무엇이 되기를 바라는가? **2** 다음 중 어느 것이 꽃가루를 만들어 내는가? **3** 당신은 장을 이용하여 음식을 소화시킨다. **4** 당신은 기념식을 거행함으로써 누군가를 기념한다.

• cooperator 협력자 • competitor 경쟁자 • judge 심판 • reproduce 번식시키다 • digest 소화시키다 • process 처리하다 • in one's honor ~을 기념하여

day 14 exercise

A.

1 ⓑ 2 ⓔ 3 ⓓ 4 ⓐ 5 ⓒ

1 폭풍이 공사 계획에 지장을 줄지도 모른다. **2** 나는 그 일자리를 수락해야 할지 확신이 안 선다. 좀더 생각해 봐야 할 것 같다. **3** 아파트가 철거되고 쇼핑 센터가 지어질 것이다. **4** 우리는 더이상 천연자원을 낭비하지 말고 환경 친화적인 삶을 추구해야 할 필요가 있다. **5** 그 무자비한 독재자는 자신의 정책에 반대하는 모든 시민을 체포하라고 명령했다.

• construction 공사, 건설 • aim 추구하다 • dictator 독재자

B.

1 ⓓ 2 ⓐ 3 ⓑ 4 ⓓ 5 ⓑ

1 만일 당신이 누군가를 얕잡아 보면 당신은 그들이 중요하지 않다고 느끼게 만들 것이다. **2** 어떤 것이 개시되면 그것은 시작되는 것이다. **3** 당신이 저지된다면 당신은 행동을 못하게 된 것이다. **4** 만일 당신이 큰 문제에 빠져 있다면 당신에게는 풀어야 할 문제가 있는 것이다. **5** 논쟁이 교착 상태에 빠지게 되었다면 아무 결론 없이 끝난 것이다.

• renowned 유명한 • explode 폭발하다 • wear down 닳다 • congratulate 축하하다 • reputation 명성 • resolve 해결하다 • convince 설득하다

C.

1 ⓒ 2 ⓑ 3 ⓓ

1 부상을 가장하다 **2** 부담되는 일 **3** 덕망있는 지도자

• fake 속이다, 꾸며내다 • additional 부가적인 • honorable 존경할 만한

D.

1 ⓒ 2 ⓐ 3 ⓓ

1 효능이 강한 약 **2** 논점을 흐리게 하다 **3** 모순적인 충고

• clarify 분명하게 하다 • bring up ~을 제기하다 • well-intended 선의로 행한 • consistent 모순되지 않는

E.

1 ⓒ 2 ⓐ 3 ⓓ 4 ⓓ

1 다음 중 좌우로 움직이는 것은 어느 것인가? **2** 다음 중 어느 것이 당신을 취하게 하는가? **3** 당신이 어떤 사람을 기소할 때 당신은 그들이 유죄라는 것을 입증하려고 하는 것이다. **4** 당신은 연설을 할 때 목소리를 크게 해야 한다.

• doormat 현관 깔개 • decaffeinate 카페인을 제거하다 • praiseworthy 칭찬할 만한 • competent 유능한

day 15 exercise

A.

1 ⓒ 2 ⓔ 3 ⓑ 4 ⓐ 5 ⓓ

1 뒷좌석이 너무 비좁아서 여행길이 더 긴 것 같았다. **2** 그는 격앙된 발언을 한 것을 후회했다. **3** 우리는 사탕이 나오는 기계를 설치할 것이다. **4** 우리는 빨간 스티커를 이용하여 판매 가격을 표시할 것이다. **5** 그 수다스러운 청년은 모두의 주목을 받았다.

• signify 나타내다 • give out 나누어주다 • overly 지나치게 • arouse 불러일으키다

B.

1 ⓐ 2 ⓒ 3 ⓑ 4 ⓑ 5 ⓑ

1 만일 어떤 것이 변칙적인 것이라면 그것은 특이한 것이다. **2** 만일 누군가에게 생기가 있다면 그 사람은 활기찬 것이다. **3** 만일 당신이 어떤 것에 마음을 빼앗겼다면 당신은 매혹된 것이다. **4** 만일 어떤 것이 계속 보존되고 있다면 그것은 유지된 것이다. **5** 누군가가 당신을 사취한다면 당신은 돈을 잃게 된다.

• unnamed 이름 없는, 무명의 • detached 초연한 • indifferent 냉담한 • furious 격노한 • jail 교도소

C.

1 ⓑ 2 ⓐ 3 ⓓ

1 땅을 척박하게 하다 **2** 부차적인 계획 **3** 대파괴를 야기하다

• enrich 비옥하게 하다 • deplete 고갈시키다 • plow (밭 등을) 갈다 • backup 예비의, 보조의 • argument 논쟁, 다툼

D.

1 ⓒ 2 ⓐ 3 ⓓ

1 실행 가능한 해결책 **2** 사람들을 예속시키다 **3** 꾸며낸 이야기

• ambitious 야심찬 • long-term 장기간의 • inspire 격려하다 • irritate 짜증나게 하다 • absurd 어리석은, 터무니 없는 • authentic 진짜의

E.

1 ⓐ 2 ⓓ 3 ⓒ 4 ⓓ

1 누가 미학과 가장 관련이 많겠는가? **2** 다음 중 어느 것이 골다공증의 영향을 받는가? **3** 장식물은 장식하는 데 쓰인다. **4** 당신은 어디에서 상품권을 사용할 가능성이 가장 높은가?

• priest 성직자 • mathematician 수학자 • gardening 원예 • department store 백화점

day 16 exercise

A.

1 ⓑ 2 ⓓ 3 ⓔ 4 ⓐ 5 ⓒ

1 그들 부부는 딸의 결혼 지참금을 위해 저축을 하고 있었다. **2** 우리 어머니는 내가 친구들을 집에 데려오면 항상 대접을 정말 잘 해주신다. **3** 그 환경 운동가는 사람들이 쓰레기를 재활용하도록 설득하기 위해 열정적인 연설을 했다. **4** 범인은 훔친 물건을 가지고 달아났다. **5** 아이들은 부상으로부터 회복이 상당히 빠르다.

• commit a crime 범죄를 저지르다 • groom 신랑 • bride 신부 • feel at home 편안하게 느끼다 • induce 야기하다 • by means of ~에 의해, ~으로 • appeal 호소 • passionate 열정적인

B.

1 ⓐ 2 ⓒ 3 ⓑ 4 ⓓ 5 ⓑ

1 당신이 어떤 사람을 비난한다면 당신은 그를 비판하는 것이다. **2** 당신이 후세를 위해 어떤 것을 보존한다면 당신은 후손을 위해 그렇게 하는 것이다. **3** 당신이 어느 나라에서 추방되었다면 당신은 멀리 보내어진 것이다. **4** 어떤 것이 법령에 근거한 것이라면 그것은 법에 의해 규제된다. **5** 당신이 추정한다면 당신은 추론을 하는 것이다.

• advocate 옹호하다, 주장하다 • conserve 보존하다 • antiquity 오래됨 • acquaintance 아는 사람[사이] • hierarchy 계급, 계층 • dissect 해부하다 • inference 추론

C.

1 ⓑ 2 ⓐ 3 ⓓ

1 논쟁을 부추기다 **2** 모든 권리를 포기하다 **3** 그의 명성이 손상되었다.

• incite 불러일으키다 • renounce 포기하다 • enhance 강화하다 • exaggerate 과장하다

D.

1 ⓓ 2 ⓑ 3 ⓒ

1 은밀한 작전 **2** 천연자원을 고갈시키다 **3** 위험한 여행

• risky 위험한

E.

1 ⓑ 2 ⓓ 3 ⓐ 4 ⓒ

1 다음 중 발굴되는 것은 어느 것인가? **2** 우리가 허점을 발견할 수 있는 곳은 어디인가? **3** 다음 중 어느 것이 가장 개탄할 만한 것인가? **4** 그 부부는 그들 간의 차이를 조정할 수 없었다.

• ruins 잔재, 옛터 • contract 계약(서) • mortgage 저당

day 17 exercise

A.

1 ⓒ 2 ⓐ 3 ⓓ 4 ⓔ 5 ⓑ

1 그의 동생이 왕위를 찬탈하려 했다. **2** 그 영화는 그녀의 끔찍했던 삶에 대한 가슴 아픈 기억을 떠올리게 했다. **3** 그녀에게 청혼할 때 그의 손은 떨리기 시작했다. **4** 그는 매우 박식하고 견문이 넓다. **5** 마약 단속반이 두 용의자를 체포했다.

• specific 특정의 • extensive 광범위한 • throne 왕위
• well-informed 박식한

B.

1 ⓓ 2 ⓑ 3 ⓐ 4 ⓓ 5 ⓑ

1 만일 당신이 누군가의 견해를 받아들인다면 그것을 인정하는 것이다. **2** 만일 당신이 누군가의 충고에 주의를 기울인다면 그것을 주의깊게 듣는 것이다. **3** 만일 무언가가 어떤 일의 전조라면 그것은 그 일이 있기 전에 벌어진다. **4** 만일 어느 지역이 주권을 가지고 있다면 그곳은 독립해 있는 것이다. **5** 발암성 물질은 암을 일으킨다.

• thriving 번성하는 • acne 여드름 • obesity 비만

C.

1 ⓑ 2 ⓐ 3 ⓓ

1 기억 상실 **2** 라벨을 붙이다 **3** 사람들을 교화하다

• token 표시, 상징 • flashback 플래시백 (과거의 회상 장면으로의 전환)
• attach 붙이다 • liberate 자유롭게 하다 • brainwash 세뇌하다

D.

1 ⓓ 2 ⓑ 3 ⓒ

1 유순한 학생 **2** 가연성 의류 **3** 무기력하게 느끼다

• industrious 부지런한 • fireproof 내화의, 불연성의 • dizzy 어지러운

E.

1 ⓐ 2 ⓓ 3 ⓑ 4 ⓒ

1 다음 중 어느 것이 유형 자산인가? **2** 다음 중 어느 것이 시간이 흐르면서 침식되는가? **3** 다음 중 어느 것이 부식의 결과로 생기는가? **4** 만일 당신이 돈벌이가 잘 되는 직업을 갖고 있다면 당신은 많은 돈을 벌게 된다.

• patent 특허 • copyright 저작권 • reputation 평판 • species (생물의) 종 • rust 녹

day 18 exercise

A.

1 ⓑ 2 ⓐ 3 ⓒ 4 ⓔ 5 ⓓ

1 저 음악 짜증나! 꺼 버려! **2** 나는 Smith씨와 의견이 일치하는 편이다. **3** 그는 식욕이 왕성하다. **4** 정부는 죄수들의 석방을 인가할 것이다. **5** 그 말 수 적은 여자는 나를 불편하게 만들었다.

• reserved 말없는 • approval 승인 • release 석방

B.

1 ⓐ 2 ⓑ 3 ⓑ 4 ⓑ 5 ⓓ

1 당신이 기소되었다면 당신은 어떤 죄에 대해 고발당한 것이다. **2** 당신이 교통을 방해하고 있다면 당신은 그것을 막고 있는 것이다. **3** 당신의 지원서가 늦었다면 기한이 지난 것이다. **4** 당신이 누군가의 관심을 돌려놓았다면 당신은 그 사람의 주의를 딴 데로 돌린 것이다. **5** 당신이 누군가를 호출한다면 당신은 그 사람이 당신에게 오기를 바라는 것이다.

• be accused of ~혐의로 고발당하다 • testify 증언하다 • hearing 청문회 • be convicted of ~으로 유죄 선고를 받다 • endure 참다
• overdue 기한이 지난 • distract (정신을) 딴 데로 돌리다

C.

1 ⓑ 2 ⓓ 3 ⓓ

1 대량으로 사다 **2** 추악한 마녀 **3** 역삼각형

• bargain price 할인가 • second hand 중고(품) • capable 능력 있는 • genuine 진짜의 • tiny 아주 작은 • massive 대량의

D.

1 ⓐ 2 ⓒ 3 ⓓ

1 예비 청문회 **2** 모욕적인 발언 **3** 혐오감으로 가득 차다

• mandatory 강제적인 • complimentary 칭찬의 • regrettable 유감스런 • rage 격노, 분노 • sincerity 성실, 성의 • humiliation 굴욕, 수치
• admiration 존경

E.

1 ⓓ 2 ⓐ 3 ⓐ 4 ⓓ

1 다음 중 어느 것에 대하여 아이를 체벌하겠는가? **2** 다음 중 어느 것이 정부 수입원인가? **3** 농업 사회는 농작물 생산과 연관되어 있다. **4** 잘 속는 사람은 거짓말을 쉽게 믿는 경향이 있다.

• tax 세금 • process 가공하다 • dispute 논쟁하다 • detect 탐지하다

day 19 exercise

A.

1 ⓑ 2 ⓔ 3 ⓓ 4 ⓒ 5 ⓐ

1 그는 학교의 열악한 상태를 보고 슬퍼졌다. **2** 그의 거짓말은 내 평판을 나쁘게 할 것이다. **3** 그 어부는 그 기간 내 자신의 할당량에 도달했다. **4** 나는 계급 제도의 하층에 속해 있으나, 위로 올라가기를 희망한다. **5** 밀크쉐이크의 재료는 우유와 아이스크림이다.

• as to ~에 관하여 • permit 허가하다 • admirable 존경할 만한

B.

1 ⓑ 2 ⓓ 3 ⓐ 4 ⓒ 5 ⓐ

1 만일 어떤 것이 잘못되었다면 그것은 틀린 것이다. **2** 만일 상황이 몹시 나쁘다면 끔찍한 것이다. **3** 만일 당신이 누군가에게 아첨한다면 당신은 그를 칭찬하는 것이다. **4** 식사가 훌륭하다면 그것은 매우 좋은 것이다. **5** 당신이 어떤 것에 대해 서두를 제시한다면 당신은 그것을 소개하는 것이다.

• offensive 불쾌한 • stable 안정적인 • chastise 체벌하다 • abuse 학대하다 • abundant 풍부한 • interrupt 방해하다 • analyze 분석하다

C.

1 ⓒ 2 ⓐ 3 ⓓ

1 괴짜인 남자 **2** 시작 전제 **3** 특권을 빼앗다

• conservative 보수적인 • remark 발언, 말 • pass up ~을 거절하다 • come by ~을 손에 넣다

D.

1 ⓒ 2 ⓒ 3 ⓐ

1 가난한 아이들 **2** 충동 구매 **3** 걱정을 누그러뜨리다

• spoiled 버릇없는 • needy 가난한

E.

1 ⓓ 2 ⓒ 3 ⓒ 4 ⓒ

1 다음 중 어느 것이 가장 좋은 분위기를 갖고 있겠는가? **2** 방탕함에 빠진 여자는 과음을 할지도 모른다. **3** 대부분의 사람들은 정부 기관이 매우 관료적이라고 생각한다. **4** 아이들이 장난이 심하면 우리는 그들을 혼낼지도 모른다.

• work out 운동을 하다 • convenience store 편의점 • chore (일상의) 허드렛일 • punish 벌주다

day 20 exercise

A.

1 ⓒ 2 ⓔ 3 ⓓ 4 ⓐ 5 ⓑ

1 아들이 많이 아파서 소아과 의사에게 진료 예약을 해야 한다. **2** 뇌졸중은 언어 능력을 손상시킬 수 있다. **3** 그 남자는 부주의로 인해 목숨을 잃었다. **4** 그 여자는 면허가 일시 정지된 상태라 운전할 수 없다. **5** 흡연은 건강에 아주 해롭다.

• temporarily 일시적으로 • withhold 허락하지 않다, 억제하다 • privilege 특권 • severely 심하게 • impact 충격, 영향 • specialize in ~을 전문으로 하다

B.

1 ⓒ 2 ⓓ 3 ⓑ 4 ⓐ 5 ⓑ

1 만약 돈이 위조되었다면 그것은 가짜이다. **2** 만일 어떤 것이 필수불가결하다면 그것은 필요한 것이다. **3** 만일 당신이 심기증 환자라면 늘 자신이 병에 걸려 있다고 생각한다. **4** 당신이 기금을 할당한다면 그것들을 분배하는 것이다. **5** 당신이 어떤 것을 끌어올린다면 당신은 그것을 들어올리는 것이다.

• tax 과세하다 • problematic 문제가 있는, 골치아픈 • unattractive 매력 없는 • victimize 희생시키다 • invest 투자하다 • unload 짐을 내리다

C.

1 ⓐ 2 ⓒ 3 ⓐ

1 습기찬 환경에서 잘 자라다 **2** 직원을 질책하다 **3** 온갖 편의시설을 다 갖추다

• seed 씨뿌리다 • adapt 적응하다 • promote 승진시키다 • fire 해고하다 • convenience 편의(시설)

D.

1 ⓒ 2 ⓐ 3 ⓒ

1 경솔한 결정 **2** 무아지경에 빠져 있다 **3** 혹독한 훈련

• risky 위험한 • misery 불행 • confusion 혼동 • athletic 운동의, 강건한 • tiresome 성가신, 귀찮은

E.

1 ⓒ 2 ⓑ 3 ⓒ 4 ⓐ

1 다음 중 어느 것을 짜겠는가? **2** 관개는 땅에 물을 공급하는 일이다. **3** 다음 중 어느 것을 휘갈겨 쓰겠는가? **4** 다음 중 어느 것이 금세 사라지는가?

• insecticide 살충제 • fertilizer 비료 • application 지원서 • chronic 만성의

day 21 exercise

A.

1 ⓐ 2 ⓓ 3 ⓔ 4 ⓑ 5 ⓒ

1 나는 네 등에 자외선 차단 크림을 발라 주고 나서 손을 씻으러 갈 것이다. **2** 이 편리한 기구는 당신이 감자를 금방 깎을 수 있도록 도와준다. **3** 그녀는 동료 직원들을 설득하는 데 계속적으로 노력을 기울였다. **4** 영양 결핍은 많은 개발도상국들의 심각한 문제이다. **5** 그 남자는 경찰을 맞닥뜨리게 되자 공격적으로 변했다.

• sticky 끈적거리는 • greasy 기름진 • substance 물질 • nutrient 영양분 • hostile 적대적인 • device 장치 • persistent 끊임없는

B.

1 ⓒ 2 ⓑ 3 ⓒ 4 ⓓ 5 ⓐ

1 만일 어떤 것이 어떤 것에 의해 중단되었다면 그것에 의해 방해된 것이다. **2** 만일 커튼이 비친다면 그것은 안이 들여다보이는 것이다. **3** 만일 당신이 어떤 것을 타고났다면 좋은 자질을 갖고 있는 것이다. **4** 당신이 눈에 띈다면 당신은 돋보이는 것이다. **5** 만일 어떤 일이 우연의 일치라면 그것은 우연히 일어난다.

• deceive 속이다 • handsewn 손으로 꿰맨 • see-through 속이 비치는 • favorable 좋은 • stand out 두드러지다 • interfere with ~을 방해하다 • take place 발생하다 • ahead of schedule 예정보다 일찍

C.

1 ⓐ 2 ⓓ 3 ⓑ

1 일에 전념하다 **2** 고통을 완화시키다 **3** 단기적인 이익

• devote 바치다 • inflict 가하다 • soothe 진정시키다 • contradictory 모순된 • short-term 단기적인 • mutual 상호의, 서로 간의

D.

1 ⓒ 2 ⓒ 3 ⓑ

1 공연을 즐기다 **2** 방탕한 소비 **3** 온전한 구조물

• applaud 박수갈채를 보내다 • decorative 장식의

E.

1 ⓐ 2 ⓒ 3 ⓐ 4 ⓓ

1 다음 중 어느 것이 나이가 들면서 뒤로 물러나는가? **2** 당신 집에서 문지방은 어디에 있는가? **3** 다음 중 어느 것이 확대되는가? **4** 당신은 죄를 지었을 경우 면죄받기를 원할지도 모른다.

• hairline (앞이마의) 머리털이 난 선 • wrinkle 주름 • pupil 동공 • earlobe 귓불 • sin 죄를 짓다

day 22 exercise

A.

1 ⓑ 2 ⓓ 3 ⓔ 4 ⓐ 5 ⓒ

1 흡연은 당신의 병을 악화시킬 뿐이다. **2** 그녀는 (직무) 태만으로 인해 해고되었다. **3** 알코올 중독에서 벗어나기 위한 유일한 방법은 절제이다. **4** 한 문화의 언어를 모르면 그 문화에 융화되기 어렵다. **5** 램프 위에 불투명한 자주색 필름을 씌우면 방 전체가 자주색으로 보일 것이다.

• transparent 투명한 • alcoholism 알코올 중독

B.

1 ⓑ 2 ⓐ 3 ⓒ 4 ⓓ 5 ⓑ

1 당신이 어떤 것에 대해 냉철한 경우 당신은 편견이 없는 것이다. **2** 당신이 추억에 잠겨 있을 때, 당신은 어떤 것을 회상하는 것이다. **3** 만일 소년이 버릇없다면 그는 무례한 것이다. **4** 만일 어떤 것이 끊임없다면 그것은 결코 멈추지 않는다. **5** 만일 당신이 공동 작업의 일원이라면 당신은 다른 사람들과 협력하고 있는 것이다.

• unbiased 편견이 없는 • unaware 알지 못하는 • messy 엉망진창의 • motivate 동기 부여를 하다 • volunteer 자진하여 제공하다 • promotion 승진

C.

1 ⓑ 2 ⓒ 3 ⓐ

1 재미없는 책 **2** 터무니없는 계획 **3** 엄격한 교사

• attainable 달성할 수 있는 • inventive 창의적인

D.

1 ⓓ 2 ⓓ 3 ⓐ

1 열광적인 팬 **2** 친구를 달래다 **3** 조화로운 생각들

• crazed 미친 • unenthusiastic 열광적이지 않은 • flatter 아첨하다 • provoke 성나게 하다 • incompatible 조화되지 않는 • innovative 혁신적인

E.

1 ⓑ 2 ⓐ 3 ⓓ 4 ⓒ

1 당신은 무기고에서 무엇을 발견하겠는가? **2** 다음 동물 중 어느 것이 풀 뜯어 먹는 것을 좋아하는가? **3** 다음 중 어느 것이 가장 은은하게 빛나겠는가? **4** 사망 원인을 모를 때 의사들은 부검을 실시한다.

• treasure 보물 • weapon 무기 • criminal 범인 • cattle 소 • tumor 종양 • stroke 뇌졸중 • heart attack 심장 마비

day 23 exercise

A.

1 ⓒ 2 ⓐ 3 ⓔ 4 ⓓ 5 ⓑ

1 파이프에서 열이 방출되었다. **2** 만일 그들이 선거에서 이기면 그 지역은 자치구가 될 것이다. **3** 바람이 꽃의 씨앗을 퍼뜨릴 것이다. **4** 그 낡은 집은 살기에 적합하지 않다. **5** 남자는 회의 석상에서 날카로운 발언을 했다.

• give off ~을 방출하다 • worn out 닳아빠진 • distribute 분배하다

B.

1 ⓐ 2 ⓐ 3 ⓓ 4 ⓓ 5 ⓒ

1 만일 당신이 어떤 것을 향상시킨다면 더 좋게 만드는 것이다. **2** 행동이 위축되었다면 행동이 제한된 것이다. **3** 당신이 배반을 한다면 누군가를 배신하는 것이다. **4** 신성모독을 하는 사람은 신을 모욕하는 것이다. **5** 만일 당신이 어떤 사람에게 복수를 한다면 그가 당신에게 해를 끼친 것에 대해 벌주는 것이다.

• restrict 제한하다 • overlook 무시하다 • legalize 합법화하다 • cure 치료하다 • abduct 유괴하다 • betray 배반하다 • quote 인용하다 • insult 모욕하다 • scold 꾸짖다 • wrongdoing 잘못

C.

1 ⓐ 2 ⓓ 3 ⓒ

1 세밀한 디자인 **2** 잔잔한 시냇물 **3** 침착함을 보이다

• detailed 상세한 • courtesy 공손함 • contempt 경멸 • stability 안정(성)

D.

1 ⓒ 2 ⓑ 3 ⓐ

1 우호적인 대화 **2** 그 소식에 크게 기뻐하다 **3** 암울한 전망

• grieve 슬퍼하다 • exaggerate 과장하다

E.

1 ⓑ 2 ⓒ 3 ⓑ 4 ⓐ

1 다음 중 어느 것이 가전 제품의 가장 좋은 예인가? **2** 누가 당신의 형제자매가 되겠는가? **3** 다음 중 어느 것이 매운 냄새가 나겠는가? **4** 당신에게 임무가 주어졌다면 당신은 그것을 우선 순위로 둬야 한다.

• flowerpot 화분 • rug 깔개 • cosmetics 화장품 • priority 우선 순위 • handle 다루다, 조정하다 • complaint 불만 • compromise 타협하다

day 24 exercise

A.

1 ⓑ 2 ⓒ 3 ⓓ 4 ⓔ 5 ⓐ

1 문신은 바늘이 피부 상피를 뚫고 들어가므로 영구적이다. **2** 그들은 도둑으로부터 자전거를 되찾아 올 방법을 짜냈다. **3** 그는 한국 군대에 입대하기 위해 미국 시민권을 포기했다. **4** 그녀는 다작을 하는 작가이다. 그녀는 30권이 넘는 소설을 썼다. **5** 많은 아이들이 선천성 심장병을 앓는다.

• layer 층 • abundance 풍부(함) • permanent 영구적인 • citizenship 시민권

B.

1 ⓓ 2 ⓐ 3 ⓒ 4 ⓑ 5 ⓓ

1 만일 어떤 것이 수수께끼라면 그것은 영문을 알 수 없는 것이다. **2** 당신이 어떤 사람에게 원한을 품고 있다면 그에게 분노를 느끼는 것이다. **3** 어떤 사람이 유행병에 걸렸다면, 그는 전염병에 걸린 것이다. **4** 만일 당신이 어떤 것에 대해 반감을 갖고 있다면 그것을 싫어하는 것이다. **5** 만일 어떤 이야기가 연대순이면 사건들이 시간 순서대로 나타나는 것이다.

• enlighten 계몽하다 • compassion 연민 • infectious 전염성의 • disorganized 무질서한

C.

1 ⓑ 2 ⓓ 3 ⓐ

1 결정을 미루다 **2** 집회를 열다 **3** 비만 아동

• playful 쾌활한 • studious 학구적인

D.

1 ⓐ 2 ⓒ 3 ⓑ

1 임시적인 계획 **2** 아이를 나무라다 **3** 진부한 책

• abuse 학대하다 • second-hand 중고의, 헌

E.

1 ⓑ 2 ⓑ 3 ⓐ 4 ⓒ

1 충치가 있다면 당신은 누구를 찾겠는가? **2** 누가 판매용으로 동물을 도살하는가? **3** 다음 중 어느 것을 퍼뜨리겠는가? **4** 모계 사회에서는 누가 권력을 쥐고 있는가?

• surgeon 외과의사 • carpenter 목수 • butcher 정육점 주인, 도축업자 • vet 수의사 • willpower 의지력 • wound 상처 • royalty 왕족

day 25 exercise

A.

1 ⓓ 2 ⓑ 3 ⓐ 4 ⓔ 5 ⓒ

1 나는 그의 갑작스러운 키스에 매우 당황했다. 2 그는 괴벽으로 유명했다. 3 그녀는 자신이 제일 좋아하는 TV 프로그램을 보지 못한 것에 대해 하루 종일 투덜댔다. 4 교사는 학생의 노력을 부당하게 비난했다. 5 그 소설은 전쟁 시기의 혼란을 그리고 있다.

- disapproval 반감, 비난

B.

1 ⓒ 2 ⓑ 3 ⓑ 4 ⓐ 5 ⓐ

1 만일 당신이 누군가를 빈정대면 당신은 경멸감을 나타내는 것이다. 2 사람들이 반목하고 있다면 그들은 싸우고 있는 것이다. 3 만일 누군가가 이단아라면, 그는 독특한 생각을 가지고 있는 것이다. 4 만일 어떤 것이 유해하다면 그것은 해로운 것이다. 5 만일 중역들이 모였다면 그들은 회의를 갖는 것이다.

- contempt 경멸 - considerate 사려 깊은 - tedious 싫증나는

C.

1 ⓒ 2 ⓐ 3 ⓓ

1 물건을 물물교환하다 2 부러지기 쉬운 뼈 3 그럴듯한 변명

- trade 거래하다 - tiny 아주 작은 - aching 아픈 - pitiful 불쌍한
- impulsive 충동적인

D.

1 ⓐ 2 ⓒ 3 ⓑ

1 용의자를 붙잡다 2 누군가를 단념시키다 3 부족한 기금

- release 풀어주다 - chase 쫓다 - identify (신원 등을) 확인하다
- confine 가두다 - adequate 충분한

E.

1 ⓑ 2 ⓑ 3 ⓐ 4 ⓓ

1 당신은 누구에게 구애하겠는가? 2 어디에서 대량 학살을 볼 수 있겠는가? 3 다음 중 어느 것을 거절하겠는가? 4 나무를 다루다 보면 나무조각이 생긴다.

- battlefield 전쟁터 - issue 논점 - mud 진흙

day 26 exercise

A.

1 ⓒ 2 ⓐ 3 ⓔ 4 ⓓ 5 ⓑ

1 나는 철두철미한 인권 옹호자이다. 2 나는 오늘 오후에 투표를 했다. 3 굶주린 동물들이 사체를 갈기갈기 물어 뜯었다. 4 그 증인이 피고의 모든 혐의를 벗겨 줄 것이다. 5 그는 불법 행위들로 인해 그 나라에서 추방당했다.

- with regards to ~에 관하여 - accusation 혐의
- cast a ballot[vote] 투표하다 - rip apart 갈기갈기 찢다
- defendant 피고

B.

1 ⓐ 2 ⓓ 3 ⓒ 4 ⓑ 5 ⓑ

1 어떤 것이 재발한다면 그것이 다시 발생하는 것이다. 2 당신이 활보할 때 당신은 자신감 있게 걷는 것이다. 3 당신이 어떤 것을 회피할 때 당신은 그것을 피하는 것이다. 4 어떤 생각이 터무니없다면 그것은 불합리한 것이다. 5 여왕이 왕좌를 버릴 때 그녀는 그것을 포기한 것이다.

- absurd 불합리한 - claim 요구하다, 주장하다

C.

1 ⓐ 2 ⓓ 3 ⓒ

1 인류의 기원 2 공원에서 유괴된 아이 3 많은 돈이 걸린 카드놀이를 하다

- origin 기원 - rescue 구조하다 - kidnap 유괴하다

D.

1 ⓑ 2 ⓓ 3 ⓐ

1 서툰 동작 2 환희의 감정 3 울적한 날

- clumsy 서툰 - sympathy 동정, 공감 - misery 불행 - chilly 쌀쌀한

E.

1 ⓐ 2 ⓓ 3 ⓑ 4 ⓒ

1 다음 중 몰수될 수 없는 것은 어느 것인가? 2 다음 단체들 중 시 당국이 관할하는 것은 어느 것인가? 3 적대적인 사람은 다음 중 어떤 행동을 취하기 쉬운가? 4 재판장님, 제 의뢰인이 증언을 철회하고 싶어합니다.

- preside over ~을 관장하다 - testimony 증언

day 27 exercise

A.

1 ⓒ 2 ⓓ 3 ⓔ 4 ⓐ 5 ⓑ

1 네가 한 짓을 아시면 네 어머니가 너를 나무라실 것이다. **2** 나는 네가 행동으로 옮기기 전에 네 결정에 뒤따르는 결과를 고려해 보기를 바란다. **3** 집념이 강한 이 젊은 여성은 좀체 포기하지 않는다. **4** 이 크림은 햇볕에 탄 피부를 진정시켜 줄 것이다. **5** 우리는 가난한 사람들의 어려운 처지에 도움이 되도록 약간의 돈을 주었다.

• additional 부가적인 • stubbornly 완강하게 • determined 단호한 • unyielding 굽히지 않는

B.

1 ⓒ 2 ⓐ 3 ⓑ 4 ⓓ 5 ⓒ

1 만일 결정이 자의적이라면 그것은 아마도 임의적인 것이다. **2** 만일 당신이 마비되었다면 당신은 움직일 수 없을 것이다. **3** 만일 당신이 어떤 것에 대해 호감을 갖고 있다면 당신은 그것을 좋아하는 것이다. **4** 만일 당신이 어떤 것에 굴하지 않는다면 당신은 낙심하지 않은 것이다. **5** 만일 어떤 과정이 필수적이라면 당신은 그것을 수강해야 한다.

• controversial 논란의 여지가 있는 • random 임의의 • unconfirmed 확정되지 않은 • notice 알아차리다 • distressed 괴로워하는

C.

1 ⓐ 2 ⓒ 3 ⓑ

1 어떤 문제에 간섭하다 **2** 어떤 상황을 바로잡다 **3** 원유(가공하지 않은 석유)

• interfere 간섭하다 • unrefined 정제되지 않은 • soiled 더러워진

D.

1 ⓑ 2 ⓑ 3 ⓐ

1 고의적인 행위 **2** 이론을 입증하다 **3** 변덕스런 행동

• accidental 우발적인 • significant 중대한 • intentional 의도적인 • contradict 반박하다 • predictable 예측 가능한 • abnormal 비정상적인

E.

1 ⓑ 2 ⓓ 3 ⓐ 4 ⓐ

1 다음 중 어느 나라가 적도상에 위치해 있는가? **2** 다음 중 어느 것이 집에 출몰하겠는가? **3** 다음 중 어느 것에 대해 애도하겠는가? **4** 분개하는 사람은 어떤 것이 부당하다고 생각한다.

• tenant 세입자 • triumph 승리, 의기양양함 • detour 우회 • brilliant 멋진, 좋은

day 28 exercise

A.

1 ⓔ 2 ⓓ 3 ⓐ 4 ⓒ 5 ⓑ

1 사교적인 그 사람은 파티를 좋아했고 혼자 있는 것을 싫어했다. **2** 테이블 위에 맛있는 디저트가 각양각색으로 있으니 골라 먹어라. **3** 연구 결과에 의하면 교육 정도와 소득 수준에는 상관관계가 있다. **4** 자동차에 손대지 마라. 넌 망가뜨리기만 할 거야. 내가 정비소에 맡길게. **5** 그 젊은이는 의학을 공부하길 원하는 부모님의 바람을 따랐다.

• mixture 혼합물 • sociable 사교적인 • company 친구, 일행

B.

1 ⓒ 2 ⓒ 3 ⓑ 4 ⓐ 5 ⓓ

1 만일 모든 것이 평형을 이루고 있다면 그것들은 균형이 잡혀 있는 것이다. **2** 당신이 중얼거린다면 당신은 명료하게 말하는 게 아니다. **3** 만일 당신이 유약한 사람이라면 당신은 상처받기 쉽다. **4** 당신이 회고를 하고 있다면 당신은 과거에 대해 생각하고 있는 것이다. **5** 당신이 비난할 만하다면 당신은 비난받아야 한다.

• exhausted 기진맥진한 • defensive 방어의 • blameworthy 비난받을 만한

C.

1 ⓐ 2 ⓒ 3 ⓑ

1 활기찬 움직임 **2** 부유한 사업가 **3** 폭동을 부추기다

• cruel 잔인한 • greedy 욕심 많은 • suppress 진압하다 • survive 살아남다 • relate 관련시키다

D.

1 ⓑ 2 ⓓ 3 ⓒ

1 주요한 특징 **2** 우울한 분위기 **3** 예술의 거장

• minor 사소한 • noticeable 눈에 띄는 • specialist 전문가 • critic 비평가

E.

1 ⓒ 2 ⓑ 3 ⓑ 4 ⓓ

1 다음 중 어느 것이 고동치는가? **2** 누군가가 화가 났을 때 당신은 달래려고 노력한다. **3** 다음 중 어느 것을 박멸하겠는가? **4** 신중한 사람은 주의 깊은 결정을 내리는 사람이다.

• cockroach 바퀴벌레

day 29 exercise

A.

1 ⓑ 2 ⓒ 3 ⓔ 4 ⓓ 5 ⓐ

1 존경심을 갖고 부모를 대하라. **2** 잘못을 저지른 아이들은 벌을 받았다. **3** 그의 사업 수완이 그를 성공하게 만든 것이다. **4** 비위에 거슬리는 냄새가 냉장고에서 풍겼다. **5** 소녀는 원하는 것을 얻지 못하자 시무룩해졌다.

• gloomy 우울한 • esteem 존중 • disgusting 메스껍게 하는 • offensive 불쾌하게 하는

B.

1 ⓑ 2 ⓑ 3 ⓒ 4 ⓒ 5 ⓐ

1 나는 죄책감이 느껴질 때 후회한다. **2** 살충제는 벌레를 죽이는 데 쓰인다. **3** 당신이 내성적이라면 당신은 아마 수줍음을 탈 것이다. **4** 당신이 요구에 순응하면 당신은 그것에 굴복하는 것이다. **5** 어떤 것이 안중에 없다면 당신은 그것을 알아채지 못하는 것이다.

• fertilize 비료를 주다 • predator 육식동물; 포식자 • enhance 향상시키다 • flavor 풍미 • talkative 수다스러운 • outgoing 외향적인 • give in 항복하다 • unaware 알지 못하는 • supporter 지지자 • denial 부정

C.

1 ⓐ 2 ⓒ 3 ⓓ

1 양성 종양 **2** 종교적 열정 **3** 자신감을 발산하다

• terminal 말기의, 치명적인 • faith 신념 • enthusiasm 열성, 열정 • discrimination 차별 • fake 위조하다; 속이다

D.

1 ⓒ 2 ⓐ 3 ⓒ

1 순종하는 파트너 **2** 설득력 있는 주장 **3** 위협을 완화하다

• compliant 고분고분한 • passive 수동적인 • domineering 권력을 휘두르는 • imply 내포하다 • lessen 줄이다 • intensify 강화하다 • surrender 항복하다

E.

1 ⓒ 2 ⓑ 3 ⓓ 4 ⓓ

1 다음 중 어느 것이 만기가 되는가? **2** 다음 중 어느 것에 비명(碑銘)을 싣는가? **3** 부부는 결혼 서약을 했다. **4** 당신에게 밀실 공포증이 있다면 당신은 어디에 있을 때 마음이 불편하겠는가?

• funeral 장례식 • gravestone 묘비 • candidate 후보 • vow 서약, 맹세

day 30 exercise

A.

1 ⓑ 2 ⓒ 3 ⓔ 4 ⓐ 5 ⓓ

1 신문 편집자의 주장이 거짓인 것으로 드러나서 명예 훼손 혐의가 인정되었다. **2** 욕조에 목욕용 오일 찌꺼기가 남아 있었다. **3** 증인의 증언은 그 사건과 아무런 관련성이 없으므로 고려의 대상이 되어서는 안 된다. **4** 유성이 지구의 대기권을 뚫고 들어왔다. **5** 증인은 피고인의 무죄를 증명해 주었다.

• substance 물질 • suitability 적합성 • applicability 적용 가능성 • testimony 증언 • disregard 무시하다 • meteor 유성

B.

1 ⓑ 2 ⓑ 3 ⓓ 4 ⓓ 5 ⓒ

1 만일 당신이 동료에게 동의한다면 당신은 그와 의견이 같은 것이다. **2** 만일 어떤 것이 오르내린다면 그것은 변동하는 것이다. **3** 만일 한 남자가 건방지다면 그는 거만한 것이다. **4** 만일 당신이 어떤 것을 묘사한다면 당신은 그것을 설명하는 것이다. **5** 음울한 시는 사람을 우울하게 만든다.

• socialize with ~와 교제하다 • flee 달아나다 • arrogant 거만한 • inspect 조사하다 • uplifting 기분을 북돋워 주는

C.

1 ⓒ 2 ⓐ 3 ⓑ

1 치명적인 독 **2** 택배원으로 일하다 **3** 사람을 비난하다

• fatal 치명적인 • promote 승진시키다

D.

1 ⓐ 2 ⓒ 3 ⓑ

1 공감을 불러일으키다 **2** 자연스레 벌어진 파티 **3** 직원을 비방하다

• undergo 겪다 • flatter 추켜세우다

E.

1 ⓑ 2 ⓓ 3 ⓐ 4 ⓑ

1 다음 중 어느 것이 산수와 관련되어 있는가? **2** 다음 중 어느 것에 교파가 있는가? **3** 대부분의 사람들은 불쾌한 사람을 피하려고 한다. **4** 누가 가장 허세를 부리겠는가?

• meditation 명상 • division 나눗셈 • athletics 운동경기 • virtue 덕목 • imitate 모방하다 • gorgeous 멋진

day 31

Voca Check

1 Deforestation 2 fossil fuel 3 environmental policy
4 Nuclear fusion energy 5 Tidal power plant
6 environment(ally)-friendly 7 depletion of the ozone layer 8 hydrogen vehicle

exercise

A.

1 ⓒ 2 ⓐ 3 ⓔ 4 ⓓ 5 ⓑ

ⓐ disposable : 쓰고 버리도록 만들어진
ⓑ biodegradable : 자연적으로 분해될 수 있는
ⓒ landfill : 쓰레기 처리 방식 또는 쓰레기가 매립된 장소
ⓓ sustainable development : 지구의 자원을 고갈시키지 않는 수준으로 개발하는 방식
ⓔ desertification : 비옥한 토지를 사막으로 변화시키는 과정

1 쓰레기 매립지들이 가득 채워져 가고 있어서 쓰레기를 버릴 새로운 장소를 찾는 일이 어렵다. **2** 1970년대에 천 기저귀가 일회용 기저귀로 대체되었다. **3** 최근 황사의 증가는 사막화의 결과이다. **4** 우리는 미래 세대가 편안하게 살 수 있도록 지속가능한 개발을 추구해야 한다. **5** 많은 패스트푸드 체인점들이 스티로폼 포장재를 자연분해가 되는 포장재로 바꾸었다.

• decompose 분해시키다, 썩게 하다 • disposal 처리 • bury 묻다
• deplete 고갈시키다 • fertile 비옥한

B.

1 ⓒ 2 ⓓ 3 ⓐ 4 ⓑ 5 ⓒ

1 물속의 오염 물질들 때문에 어류가 죽어가고 있었다. **2** 처리되지 않은 하수 오물들이 강물로 버려지고 있다. **3** 소각 시 발생하는 연기는 건강을 위협하는 요소이다. **4** 우리는 앞으로 예상되는 에너지 위기에 대비하여 대체 에너지원을 개발해야 한다. **5** 온실효과가 기온 상승을 유발하고 있다.

• exhaust fumes 배기 가스 • particulates 미세먼지 • sewage 하수 오물 • incineration 소각 • reclaimed land 간척지 • devastating 황폐화시키는 • natural restoration 자연 정화 • synthetic detergent 합성세제

day 32

Voca Check

1 Amphibian 2 photosynthesis 3 survival of the fittest 4 omnivore 5 stem cell 6 reptile 7 Mammal 8 food chain

exercise

A.

1 ⓒ 2 ⓓ 3 ⓐ 4 ⓑ 5 ⓔ

ⓐ species : 다른 동식물들과 구별되는 특징을 공통으로 가진 동식물의 무리
ⓑ respiratory : 숨을 들이쉬고 내쉬는 과정과 관계된
ⓒ gene : 유전성이 있는 형질을 자손에게 전달해주는 하나의 DNA 개체
ⓓ in vitro fertilization : 실험실에서 난자를 수정시켜 자궁에 착상시키는 행위
ⓔ interbreed : 다른 종의 동물과 교배시키다

1 과학자들은 비만과 관련된 유전자가 있을지도 모른다고 생각한다. **2** 시험관 수정은 많은 부부들이 아이를 가질 수 있도록 도왔다. **3** 아마존 열대 우림에는 수많은 종의 나비들이 있다. **4** 천식은 숨쉬기를 어렵게 하는 호흡기 계통의 질병이다. **5** 사자와 호랑이의 이종교배를 통해 라이거를 만들어 낼 수 있다.

• distinguish A from B A와 B를 구별하다 • heritable 유전되는
• trait 특성 • offspring 후손 • fertilize 수정하다 • womb 자궁
• obesity 비만

B.

1 ⓐ 2 ⓒ 3 ⓓ 4 ⓑ 5 ⓐ

1 갈색 눈은 우성이고 파란 눈은 열성이다. **2** 원숭이, 유인원, 인간은 모두 영장류이다. **3** 소화란 우리가 먹은 음식을 분해하기 위해 우리의 몸이 거치는 과정이다. **4** 아기의 성(性)은 2개의 성염색체에 의해 결정된다. 2개의 X는 여자를 의미하고 1개의 X와 1개의 Y는 남자를 의미한다. **5** 어떤 사람들은 우리가 생물체를 복제해서는 안 되기 때문에 생물 복제는 잘못된 것이라고 생각한다.

• variant 다른, 상이한 • manipulated 조작된 • predator 포식자
• rodent 설치류 • respiration 호흡 (작용) • mutation 돌연변이
• transpiration 증산(작용) • enzyme 효소 • photosynthesis 광합성

day 33

Voca Check

1 broadband 2 Telecommuting 3 compatible
4 ISP(internet service provider) 5 blog(web log)
6 search engine 7 netiquette 8 anonymity

exercise

A.

1 ⓒ 2 ⓔ 3 ⓑ 4 ⓐ 5 ⓓ

ⓐ peripheral : 컴퓨터와 연결하여 사용되는 장비
ⓑ ubiquitous : 어느 곳에나 존재하는

ⓒ web browser : 사용자가 인터넷을 이용할 수 있도록 해주는 프로그램
ⓓ digital divide : 컴퓨터와 인터넷에의 접근성과 관련된 사회 · 경제적 격차
ⓔ copyright infringement : 어떤 저작물을 인가받지 않고 불법적으로 베끼는 행위

1 나는 예전에는 웹브라우저로 Netscape를 썼는데 지금은 Explorer를 쓴다. **2** 한국 음반업계는 무료 온라인 음악으로 인한 저작권 침해 문제로 진통을 겪어 왔다. **3** 유비쿼터스 컴퓨팅으로 컴퓨터가 우리 일상 생활의 모든 면에서 필수 요소가 될 것이다. **4** 컴퓨터 한 대를 샀으므로 이제는 웹캠이나 프린터 같은 주변 기기만 몇 개 사면 된다. **5** 정보 격차의 희생자는 인터넷 접속이 제한적이거나 불가능한 사람들이다.

• access 접근(하다) • unauthorized 인가받지 않은 • essential 필수적인

B.

1 ⓒ 2 ⓓ 3 ⓑ 4 ⓐ 5 ⓑ

1 나는 Windows XP를 사용하는데, 너는 어떤 운영 체제를 사용해? **2** 대부분의 공항은 노트북으로 인터넷에 접속할 수 있도록 무선랜을 갖추고 있다. **3** 새 프로그램이 내 운영 체제와 호환되지 않는다. 그래서 그것을 설치할 수가 없다. **4** 증가하는 PC와 인터넷 보급률은 정보 격차를 해소하는 데 도움을 줄 수 있다. **5** 안전하지 않은 사이트에서 신용카드를 사용하면 당신은 사이버 범죄의 희생자가 될 수 있다.

• install 설치하다 • anonymous 익명의 • cyberporn 사이버 포르노, 인터넷 음란 외설물 • censorship 검열

day 34

Voca Check

1 embargo 2 (military) coup 3 refugee 4 armistice 5 ambassador

exercise

A.

1 ⓒ 2 ⓑ 3 ⓔ 4 ⓐ 5 ⓓ

ⓐ protocol : 두 개 이상의 나라 간의 국제 협약
ⓑ talks : 정부 간 혹은 조직 간의 공식적인 논의
ⓒ coup : 군부에 의해 이루어지는 정부의 통치권 장악을 위한 시도
ⓓ multilateralism : 여러 나라 간의 무역이나 외교적 협상
ⓔ Free Trade Agreement : 두 개 이상의 나라 간의 수입과 수출에 관한 규제를 제한하는 협약

1 6월에 쿠데타가 일어난 후로 그 나라의 정치적, 사회적 긴장이 고조되고 있다. **2** 한국, 중국, 일본, 러시아, 미국, 북한은 핵무기에 관한 회담을 할 것이다. **3** 자유 무역 협정은 무역 상대국 간의 세금과 할당제를 없애는 것이다. **4** 교토 의정서의 목적은 이산화탄소 배출량을 줄이는 것이었다. **5** UN과 NATO는 다국간 공동 정책과 관련된 조직의 예이다.

• negotiation 협상 • restriction 제한 • tension 긴장 • soar 치솟다 • emission 배출

B.

1 ⓒ 2 ⓐ 3 ⓑ 4 ⓓ 5 ⓓ

1 두 나라는 결국 2003년에 조약에 합의하고 서명했다. **2** 나는 아버지가 외교관이어서 어렸을 때 여러 나라에 살았다. **3** 그 협정이 시행되기 위해서는 45개국의 비준이 필요하다. **4** 북한은 미국이 경제 제재를 철회하기를 촉구하고 있다. **5** 미국과 소련 간의 냉전은 핵무기 경쟁을 수반했다.

• embargo 통상금지(령) • sanction 제재(조치) • monarch 군주 • ratification 비준 • disarmament 군축 • abolition 폐지 • summit talks 정상 회담 • radiation 방사능

day 35

Voca Check

1 abolish 2 president-elect 3 inauguration 4 referendum 5 voter turnout 6 Prime Minister 7 the Supreme Court 8 legislature

exercise

A.

1 ⓓ 2 ⓐ 3 ⓔ 4 ⓒ 5 ⓑ

ⓐ exit poll : 유권자들이 투표를 한 직후에 하는 조사
ⓑ by-election : 공석을 채우기 위해 실시하는 특별 선거
ⓒ ruling party : 정부 내에 가장 큰 세력을 가진 정당
ⓓ lawmaker : 입법부의 일원; 법률을 만드는 사람
ⓔ election campaign : 유권자들이 특정한 쪽으로 투표를 하도록 설득하는 것을 목적으로 하는 행위

1 국회의원들이 그 안건을 논의 중이다. **2** 출구 조사를 지표로 한다면 현직 대통령이 재임할 것이다. **3** 그녀의 선거 운동에는 매우 성공적으로 이루어진 연설과 토론이 포함되어 있었다. **4** 여당이 오랫동안 집권해왔다. **5** 그 상원의원이 사임한 후 그의 후임자를 찾기 위해 보궐 선거가 실시되었다.

• vacancy 공석 • legislature 입법부 • authority 권한 • indication 지시, 징후 • term 임기; (일정한) 기간 • senator 상원의원

B.

1 ⓓ 2 ⓑ 3 ⓒ 4 ⓑ 5 ⓐ

1 Susan B. Anthony는 여성의 목소리가 힘을 얻을 수 있도록 여성 참정권을 위해 싸웠다. **2** 나는 선거일에 투표를 함으로써 우리 나라의 정치 과정에 참여하는 것이 중요하다고 생각한다. **3** 대통령이 법안에 거부권을 행사한다면 그것이 통과되지 못하도록 할 수 있다. **4** 이 후보는 만일 당신이 그를 뽑

아준다면 많은 변화를 이루겠다는 공약을 걸고 있다. **5** 우리 아버지께서는 전통을 고수하며 변화를 싫어하신다. 그는 아주 보수적인 견해를 갖고 계시다.

• inauguration 취임(식) • immunity 면책 • suffrage 참정권 • enact 제정하다 • submit 제출하다 • impeach 탄핵하다 • nominate 지명하다 • veto 거부권을 행사하다 • moderate 온건한, 중도의 • spokesperson 대변인

day 36

Voca Check

1 prosecutor **2** witness **3** suspect **4** death penalty **5** verdict **6** assassinate **7** forensic evidence **8** Constitution

exercise

A.

1 ⓓ 2 ⓒ 3 ⓐ 4 ⓔ 5 ⓑ

ⓐ detective : 범죄를 조사하는 사람
ⓑ fraud : 돈을 얻기 위해 사람들을 속이는 범죄 행위
ⓒ plagiarism : 의도적으로 다른 사람의 생각이나 저작물을 모방하는 것
ⓓ sexual harassment : 원치 않는 상대에게 가하는 성적인 행동
ⓔ plea bargain : 피고인이 덜 무거운 처벌을 받기 위하여 덜 심각한 혐의에 대해 유죄를 인정하기로 합의하는 것

1. 그는 여성 직원을 대하는 방식 때문에 성희롱으로 기소되었다. **2.** 그 교수의 최근 논문에서 표절의 증거가 발견되었다. **3.** 형사는 피해자의 아파트에서 중요한 단서를 많이 발견했다. **4.** 그녀의 변호사는 배심원들이 아마도 유죄 판결을 내릴 것 같으니 유죄 답변 거래를 받아들이라고 조언했다. **5.** 그는 사람들에게서 그들이 평생 저축한 돈을 사취한 후 결국 사기죄로 기소되었다.

• investigate 조사하다 • deception 사기, 속임 • at the expense of ~에게 해를 끼치고, ~를 희생시켜서 • intentionally 의도적으로 • take credit for ~을 자신의 공로로 삼다 • accused 고발된 • plead guilty (피고가) 죄를 인정하다 • charge 혐의

B.

1 ⓒ 2 ⓑ 3 ⓓ 4 ⓐ 5 ⓒ

1 그는 그 나라로 마약을 밀반입하려 했지만 국경에서 자동차 검문을 당했다. **2** 불과 4시간의 심의 끝에 배심원들은 그녀에게 유죄 평결을 내렸다. **3** 판사는 그의 체포 영장을 발부했다. **4** 그 용의자는 재판 때까지 구금되어 있었다. **5** 그는 집행유예 상태에 있었기 때문에 그 나라를 떠날 수 없었다.

• prescribe 처방하다 • ban 금지하다 • fraud 사기(꾼) • plea (피고의) 진술 • warrant 영장 • custody 구금, 구류 • felony 중죄 • breach 위반, 침해 • bribery 뇌물수수 • sentence 판결 • probation 집행유예, 보호관찰 • hostage 인질

day 37

Voca Check

1 competitive edge **2** plummet **3** privatize **4** inflation rate **5** economic boom **6** income disparity **7** soar/skyrocket **8** real estate

exercise

A.

1 ⓐ 2 ⓒ 3 ⓔ 4 ⓑ 5 ⓓ

ⓐ nationalize : 민영 기업을 정부가 운영하는 기업으로 바꾸다
ⓑ appreciation : 가치 상승
ⓒ dumping : 쓸모없는 제품을 국내 시장에서 팔리는 것보다 낮은 가격으로 수출하는 행위
ⓓ multilateral trade: 셋 이상의 나라들 사이에서 이루어지는 무역
ⓔ speculate : 큰 이익을 얻기 위해서 위험을 감수하다

1 이란 국회는 투표를 통해 석유 산업을 국영화하기로 결정했다. **2** 선진국들은 개발도상국으로의 농산물 덤핑을 그만두어야 한다. **3** 나는 안전한 투자를 선호하지만 남편은 투기를 좋아한다. **4** 그 부부는 부동산 가격이 많이 올라 있을 때 집을 팔았기 때문에 많은 돈을 벌었다. **5** 그 5개국은 다자간 무역을 하고 있었다.

• domestic 국내의 • investment 투자 • engage in 참여하다

B.

1 ⓒ 2 ⓐ 3 ⓓ 4 ⓒ 5 ⓓ

1 정부는 섬유 산업에 보조금을 제공하기로 결정했다. **2** GDP(국내 총생산)는 한 나라의 국경 내에서 생산되는 모든 재화의 가치를 측정한 것이다. **3** 미국 제조업자의 관점에서 달러 가치의 하락은 같은 액수의 돈으로 살 수 있는 수입품의 양을 감소시켜, 결국 수입량의 감소를 가져온다. **4** 1970년대에는 경제 성장률이 2% 이하였던 경기침체기가 있었다. **5** 기름값이 치솟음에 따라 운전을 해서 출근하는 사람이 줄어들었다.

• inflation 인플레이션, 물가폭등 • monopoly 독과점 • CPI(consumer price index) 소비자 물가지수 • NTB(non-tariff barriers to trade) 비관세장벽 • retaliation 보복 • depreciation 가치 하락 • speculation 투기 • stagnation 침체, 불경기 • stabilize 안정되다 • soar 폭등하다

day 38

Voca Check

1 franchise 2 employee[fringe] benefits 3 performance evaluation 4 downsizing 5 Bankruptcy 6 liquidation 7 lay-off 8 consortium

exercise

A.

1 ⓔ 2 ⓑ 3 ⓐ 4 ⓓ 5 ⓒ

ⓐ retire : 경력을 끝내다; 일하기를 그만두다
ⓑ promote : 조직 내에서 더 높은 지위로 이동시키다
ⓒ recruit : 미래의 직원을 회사로 유치하다
ⓓ fraudulent accounting : 불법적인 회계 관행
ⓔ supervisor : 작업 공정을 감독하고 관계자들에 대한 권한을 가진 사람

1. 그의 주임은 그에게 또다시 회사에 지각을 하면 해고 당할 것이라고 경고했다. **2** 사장은 Jack의 재능과 성실함을 인정하여 그를 부장으로 승진시킬 것이다. **3** 그 축구선수는 다리 부상으로 인해 은퇴해야만 했다. **4** 그 회사는 분식회계로 고소당했다. **5** 고용주들이 MBA 학생들을 모집하기 위해 대학 캠퍼스를 방문했다.

• accounting 회계 • oversee 감독하다 • authority 권한 • involve 관련시키다 • in recognition of ~을 인정하여

B.

1 ⓒ 2 ⓒ 3 ⓓ 4 ⓑ 5 ⓓ

1 그녀는 아주 성공한 기업의 최고 경영자이다. **2** 그 회사의 재정 흑자는 주가 상승으로 이어졌다. **3** 노조가 근로자의 임금 인상을 위해 투쟁 중이다. **4** 시간 절약을 위해 대부분의 사업이 소규모 회사에 하청 계약될 것이다. **5** 그 최고 경영자는 부실 경영 때문에 사퇴를 강요받았다.

• applicant 신청자 • subcontract 하청을 주다 • discharge 해임하다 • designate 임명하다 • lay off 일시 해고하다 • downsize (조직을) 축소하다

day 39

Voca Check

1 liabilities 2 stocks 3 IPO(initial public offering) 4 credit union 5 savings 6 open a bank account 7 go into insolvency 8 dividend

exercise

A.

1 ⓒ 2 ⓑ 3 ⓔ 4 ⓐ 5 ⓓ

ⓐ arrears : 지불 기한이 지난 빚
ⓑ interest : 돈을 빌리는 것에 대한 수수료
ⓒ listed company : 자사 주식이 주식 시장에서 매매되는 회사
ⓓ portfolio : 한 사람의 전체 투자 내역
ⓔ delinquent : 빚을 갚지 못하는

1 상장 회사가 되기 위해서는 특정 조건을 갖춰야 한다. **2** 지금은 이자율이 아주 낮기 때문에 대출을 받기에 좋은 때이다. **3** 그는 대출 체납 상태라 은행을 피하고 있어 절대 전화를 안 받는다. **4** 돈 좀 빌릴 수 있을까요? 집세를 못 내고 있어서요. **5** 계란 전부를 한 바구니에 넣지 마세요. 투자 종목을 분산하세요.

• debt 빚 • overdue 체납된 • share 주식 • stock market 주식 시장 • investment 투자 • collectively 집합적으로, 총체적으로 • owe 빚지다 • diversify 다양화하다

B.

1 ⓑ 2 ⓓ 3 ⓒ 4 ⓓ 5 ⓐ

1 만일 정부의 기업 구제 조처가 없었다면 그 회사는 파산했을 것이다. **2** 내 계좌의 잔액이 충분하도록 이 수표를 입금해야 한다. **3** 그 보험사는 보험료를 인상하고 있다. **4** 수표를 우편으로 보내지 않고 계좌 이체를 해드리는 건 어때요? **5** 위급한 일이 일어날 경우를 대비하여 좋은 보험 상품에 가입해 두는 게 중요하다.

• bailout 기업 구제 (조처) • commission 수수료 • warrant 보증, 담보 • withdraw 인출하다 • mortgage 담보 대출 • premium (1회분의) 보험료 • principal 원금 • dividend 배당금 • index 지표, 지수

day 40

Voca Check

1 editorial 2 caption 3 press conference 4 subscribe 5 bilingual broadcast 6 classified[want] ads 7 ran/carried 8 flier/flyer

exercise

A.

1 ⓑ 2 ⓐ 3 ⓓ 4 ⓔ 5 ⓒ

ⓐ circulation : 한 신문 또는 잡지가 팔리는 평균 부수
ⓑ feature : 특정 주제를 집중적으로 다룬 기사
ⓒ correspondent : 특정 주제나 분야를 다루는 기자
ⓓ coverage : 뉴스를 보도하는 행위

ⓔ off the record : 공개적으로 출판하거나 보도해도 된다는 허락을 얻지 않은

1 월요일 신문에 새로운 컴퓨터 데이트 서비스에 대한 특집 기사가 실릴 것이다. **2** 그 신문은 체제를 바꾼 이후로 판매부수가 줄어들고 있다. **3** TV 생방송으로 전쟁 보도를 보고 있다. **4** 그 기자는 비공개를 전제로 그 정보를 취재한 것이므로 실을 수 없었다. **5** 방콕에 있는 우리 통신원이 이 취재 내용을 보내왔다.

• concentrate on ~에 집중하다 • permission 허가, 허락 • format 포맷, 인쇄물의 판형 및 디자인

B.

1 ⓓ 2 ⓒ 3 ⓓ 4 ⓒ 5 ⓑ

1 그 기자는 경쟁지들보다 앞서 특종을 따내지 못한 것을 아쉬워했다. **2** 나는 지역 신문에 일주일에 한 번씩 칼럼을 쓴다. **3** 그 새 드라마는 첫회부터 높은 시청률을 기록했다. **4** 나는 그의 부고를 읽고 나서야 그가 사망했다는 것을 알았다. **5** 잠시 정규 방송을 중단하고 속보를 말씀드리겠습니다.

• flier 광고 쪽지, 전단 • scoop 특종 • footage 보도 화면 • subscription 구독 • horoscope 별자리(표의 일종) • article 기사 • editorial 사설 • soap opera 연속극 • press ban 보도 금지

day 41

Voca Check

1 sequel 2 premiere 3 subtitle 4 nominee 5 shoot 6 recital 7 consumerism 8 concert tour

exercise

A.

1 ⓒ 2 ⓓ 3 ⓔ 4 ⓑ 5 ⓐ

ⓐ rehearsal : 공연을 위해 연습하는 행위
ⓑ blockbuster : 크게 인기를 얻어 많은 돈을 벌어들이는 영화
ⓒ star : 영화에서 중요한 배역을 연기하다
ⓓ lines : 희곡이나 영화 각본의 대사
ⓔ censorship : 부적합하다고 여겨 작품의 내용을 제거하는 행위

1 그녀는 내년 여름에 로맨틱 코미디 영화에 주연으로 출연할 것이다. **2** 나는 이 연극의 주인공이라 암기해야 할 대사가 많다. **3** 검열법에 따라 TV에서 방영되기 전에 영화 속 비속어는 삭제된다. **4** 예산이 많이 투입된 영화는 블록버스터가 될 것으로 기대된다. **5** 개막 전의 최종 리허설이 월요일에 있을 것이다.

• screenplay 영화 대본, 시나리오 • content 내용 • deem 여기다, 간주하다 • foul language 비속어

B.

1 ⓑ 2 ⓓ 3 ⓐ 4 ⓐ 5 ⓒ

1 제작진은 열악한 근무 조건에 대한 불만을 토로했다. **2** 그녀의 엄마는 그 영화의 등급 때문에 그녀에게 영화를 보지 못하게 했다. **3** 예고편을 보고 나서 그 영화가 정말 보고 싶어졌다. **4** 영화를 완성하고 난 뒤 그 독립 영화 감독은 배급사 찾는 일이 어렵다는 것을 알았다. **5** 그 영화는 수백만 (달러)의 흥행 수익을 올렸다.

• nominee 후보 • film rating 영화 등급 (표시) • trailer 예고편 • premiere 시사회 • prompt (배우가 대사를 잊었을 때) 숨어서 대사를 일러줌 • distributor 배급사 • sequel 속편 • box office 매표소; (흥행) 수익 • commentary 논평, 해설

day 42

Voca Check

1 cramming 2 GPA(grade point average) 3 report card 4 tuition (fees) 5 scholarship 6 transcript 7 drop out 8 distance learning

exercise

A.

1 ⓒ 2 ⓔ 3 ⓓ 4 ⓐ 5 ⓑ

ⓐ flunk : 최소한의 성적을 받는 데 실패하다
ⓑ transcript : 개인이 학교에서 받은 성적이 기록되어 있는 공식적인 문서
ⓒ truancy : 허락 없이 수업을 빠지는 행위
ⓓ suspend : 처벌로서 수업에 참여하지 못하게 하다
ⓔ syllabus : 학습 과정에 대한 개요나 계획

1 그 교사는 소년의 어머니에게 그의 무단 결석에 대해 알리려고 전화했다. **2** 강의 계획서에 따르면 다음 시간에는 2차 세계 대전에 대한 단원을 시작할 것이다. **3** 그녀는 시험 시간에 부정 행위를 하여 정학을 당했다. **4** 공부를 하지 않으면 낙제 할 것이다. **5** 지원서의 일부로 대학에 성적 증명서를 보내야 한다.

• minimum 최소의 • punishment 처벌

B.

1 ⓑ 2 ⓐ 3 ⓓ 4 ⓑ 5 ⓒ

1 그 총명한 남자아이는 IQ가 높아 영재교육을 받았다. **2** 나는 드디어 논문을 끝냈고 이제 졸업할 수 있다. **3** 나는 생물학 학사 학위를 소지하고 있다. **4** 그녀는 열심히 공부해서 하버드대의 입학 허가를 받았다. **5** 왕따 행위는 일부 학생들로 하여금 두려움 때문에 집중력이 떨어지게 만들 수 있다.

• compulsory 의무적인 • holistic 전인적인 • vocational 직업의 • placement test 배치고사 • elective 선택과목 • cramming 벼락 공부 • bullying 왕따시키기

day 43

Voca Check

1 discomfort index 2 breeze 3 cold spell 4 avalanche 5 tropical zone 6 downpour 7 drought 8 yellow dust

exercise

A.

1 ⓒ 2 ⓑ 3 ⓔ 4 ⓓ 5 ⓐ

ⓐ typhoon : 서태평양에서 발생하는 강한 폭풍우
ⓑ scorching : 극도로 더운
ⓒ polar zone : 북극이나 남극 지역과 연결되어 있거나 가까이 있는 지역
ⓓ deluge : 대홍수
ⓔ overcast : 구름이 잔뜩 낀

1 혹독한 기후 때문에 한대(寒帶)지역에는 사람이 거의 살지 않는다. **2** 이 무더위를 피해 수영하러 가자. **3** 오늘 오전에는 날이 흐렸으나 오후에 해가 났다. **4** 우리는 대홍수에 우리의 물건들이 둥둥 떠내려가는 것을 지붕에서 지켜보았다. **5** 매년 여름 아시아에는 여러 개의 태풍이 지나간다.

• North[South] Pole 북극[남극] • harsh 혹독한 • float 떠돌다, 둥둥 뜨다

B.

1 ⓒ 2 ⓑ 3 ⓐ 4 ⓓ 5 ⓑ

1 해변에 있던 우리는 불현듯 우리 쪽으로 해일이 몰려오고 있음을 알아챘다. **2** 비행기 조종사들은 비행할 때마다 풍속을 고려해야 한다. **3** 진눈깨비 때문에 운전하기가 어려웠다. **4** 우산을 갖고 가는 게 좋을 거야. 강수 확률이 75%야. **5** 기온이 영하 5도이지만 체감 온도로는 영하 20도 같이 느껴진다.

• blizzard 강한 눈보라 • avalanche 눈사태 • velocity 속도 • drought 가뭄 • drizzle 이슬비 • cold spell 한파 • precipitation 강수량 • daily temperature range 일교차

day 44

Voca Check

1 planet 2 revolve 3 astronomy 4 solar system 5 satellite 6 manned mission 7 mission control 8 launch pad

exercise

A.

1 ⓒ 2 ⓑ 3 ⓔ 4 ⓐ 5 ⓓ

ⓐ astronaut : 우주선을 타고 탐사하도록 훈련받은 사람
ⓑ constellation : 어떤 형상이나 그림으로 보이는 한 무리의 별들
ⓒ asteroid : 우주를 떠돌아다니는 행성과 비슷한 커다란 암석 덩어리
ⓓ astrology : 별들의 위치가 사람들의 삶이나 운명에 어떤 영향을 미치는지 연구하는 학문
ⓔ eclipse : 태양이나 달이 그 위치에 의해 시야에서 사라지는 현상

1 만일 소행성이 지구와 충돌한다면 그것이 지구의 종말이 될 것이다. **2** 소북두칠성은 사실 작은 곰처럼 생긴 작은곰자리의 일부분이다. **3** 개기일식은 아름다운 광경이다. **4** 최초의 한국인 우주비행사는 국제 우주 정거장에 열흘간 머물 것이다. **5** 나는 점성술을 믿지 않지만 가끔은 별점을 재미삼아 읽는다.

• chunk 덩어리 • destiny 운명 • position 위치시키다 • collide 충돌하다 • spectacular 볼 만한, 장관의

B.

1 ⓑ 2 ⓒ 3 ⓑ 4 ⓐ 5 ⓓ

1 지구는 남극과 북극 사이의 지축을 중심으로 자전한다. **2** UFO를 타고 온 우주인을 보았다고 하는 사람들이 있다. **3** 행성과 위성, 유성은 모두 천체의 예이다. **4** 관측소의 망원경으로 하늘을 볼 수 있다. **5** 월식 때는 달을 볼 수 없다.

• supernova 초신성 (별의 진화 과정에서 마지막으로 대폭발을 일으켜 태양의 천만 배에서 수억 배까지 밝아지는 별) • extraterrestrial 외계의, 외계인 • stellar 별의 • nebula 성운 • rotation 자전

day 45

Voca Check

1 arthritis 2 migraine 3 Leukemia 4 asthma 5 fester 6 fatigue 7 symptom 8 indigestion

exercise

A.

1 ⓒ 2 ⓐ 3 ⓔ 4 ⓓ 5 ⓑ

ⓐ malignant : 비정상적이고 위험한 방식으로 (병이) 진행되는
ⓑ insomnia : 수면에 어려움을 겪고 있는 상태
ⓒ terminal illness : 치료가 불가능하고 치명적인 질병
ⓓ paralysis : 움직일 수 없음
ⓔ dizziness : 안정적으로 계속 서 있을 수 없는 상태

1 그는 불치병 진단을 받고 모든 희망을 잃었다. **2** 그녀는 자신의 사마귀가 악성일까봐 걱정되어 의사를 찾았다. **3** 그녀가 어지럼증이 있기 때문에 샤워하다가 쓰러질까봐 걱정된다. **4** 척추 손상을 입으면 마비가 올 수 있다. **5** 나는 스트레스를 많이 받으면 불면증에 걸린다.

• incurable 고칠 수 없는 • fatal 치명적인 • inability 할 수 없음 • diagnose 진단하다 • mole 점, 사마귀 • spine 척추

B.

1 ⓒ 2 ⓑ 3 ⓐ 4 ⓐ 5 ⓓ

1 나는 영양실조로 고통받는 아이들에게 줄 식량을 구입하기 위해 기금을 모금 중이다. **2** 그는 십대 때부터 만성 위장병을 앓고 있다. **3** 그녀는 뇌졸중의 후유증으로 왼쪽 얼굴을 움직이지 못한다. **4** 의사들은 그가 암에서 완치되었다고 생각했으나 그 후 암이 재발했다. **5** 아이들이 삼켜서 질식하는 일이 없도록 작은 물건들을 아이들 손이 닿지 않게 둬야 한다.

• tuberculosis 결핵 • nausea 메스꺼움 • malnutrition 영양 실조 • leukemia 백혈병 • acute 급성의 • chronic 만성의 • anemic 빈혈(증)의; 무기력한 • epidemic 전염성의 • asthma 천식 • measles 홍역 • relapse 재발하다 • fester (상처가) 곪다 • transmit 전염시키다 • bruise 멍이 들다 • scar 상처[흉터]를 남기다 • fracture 부러지다 • choke 질식하다

day 46

Voca Check

1 dosage **2** antidote **3** sterilize **4** transplant(ation) **5** dietary fiber **6** folk remedy **7** over-the-counter **8** painkiller

exercise

A.

1 ⓒ 2 ⓔ 3 ⓑ 4 ⓐ 5 ⓓ

ⓐ sedative : 사람을 진정시키거나 잠들게 하는 약
ⓑ euthanasia : 고통 받는 것을 끝내주기 위해 의도적으로 사람을 죽이는 것
ⓒ anesthetize : 환자가 감각을 잃도록 약을 투여하다
ⓓ vaccinate : 면역 체계를 강화시켜 병으로부터 보호하다
ⓔ diagnose : 병을 알아내다

1 의사들은 환자들이 고통을 느끼지 않도록 수술 전에 환자를 마취시킨다. **2** 그는 암 진단을 받고 불과 3개월 후에 사망했다. **3** 안락사는 의학계에서 논란이 많은 주제이다. **4** 간호사는 병적으로 흥분한 상태의 여자에게 진정제를 주었다. **5** 간호사는 아기에게 홍역 예방 주사를 놓았다.

• intentional 의도적인 • suffering 고통 • boost 끌어올리다; 증가시키다 • immune system 면역 체계 • identify 확인하다 • controversial 논란이 많은 • hysterical 병적으로 흥분한, 히스테리의

B.

1 ⓒ 2 ⓐ 3 ⓑ 4 ⓐ 5 ⓒ

1 수년간의 물리 치료 끝에 그녀는 드디어 다시 걸을 수 있게 되었다. **2** 서양 의사들이 침술의 효과를 인정하기 시작했다. **3** 의사는 식이 요법과 운동을 병행한 엄격한 섭생을 권했다. **4** 어떤 사람들은 수혈을 통해 에이즈에 감염되었다. **5** 의사는 귀의 염증에 대해 항생제를 처방했다.

• transplant 이식 • immunization 면역 조치 • acupuncture 침술 • antibiotic 항생제 • ointment 연고 • laxative 변비약 • antigen 항원 • regimen (식사 · 운동 조절에 의한) 섭생 • dosage 복용량 • transfusion 수혈 • antibody 항체

day 47

Voca Check

1 jet lag **2** check our luggage **3** declare **4** tourist attraction **5** high[peak] season **6** flight cancellation **7** domestic flight **8** intersection

exercise

A.

1 ⓒ 2 ⓔ 3 ⓐ 4 ⓓ 5 ⓑ

ⓐ souvenir : 다녀온 곳을 생각나게 해주는 물건
ⓑ amenities : 어떤 곳을 편안하고 지내기 편리하도록 해주는 것
ⓒ taxi : 활주로에서 비행기를 몰다
ⓓ commute : 장거리 출근 또는 통학을 하다
ⓔ detour : 보통 교통 정체 혹은 공사장 등을 피하기 위해 사용되는 다른 길

1 마침내 이륙하기까지 약 30분간 활주로를 달린 것 같았다. **2** 늦어서 죄송해요. 우회 도로로 와야 했어요. **3** 이 열쇠 고리는 나의 홍콩 여행 기념품이다. **4** 나는 서울까지 매일 통근하는 게 싫어서 그 일자리를 거절했다. **5** 내 아내는 야영을 좋아하지만, 나는 호텔의 온갖 쾌적한 시설을 즐기는 것이 더 좋다.

• runway 활주로 • alternative 대안의 • construction site 공사장 • take off 이륙하다 • turn down 거절하다

B.

1 ⓒ 2 ⓑ 3 ⓓ 4 ⓐ 5 ⓒ

1 나는 다음 달에 중국 여행을 하기 위해 비자를 받아야 한다. **2** 그녀는 사스가 발생한 시기에 여행을 하다가 열이 나는 바람에 검역소에 격리되었다. **3** 여행 일정표에 따르면 나는 오전 7시 30분에 도착한다. **4** 나는 밴쿠버에 가는 도중에 도쿄에 잠깐 들렀다. **5** 과일은 세관을 통과하지 못할 것이다.

• outbreak 발발, 발생 • transit 통과, 통행 • quarantine 검역 • congestion 혼잡 • itinerary 여행 일정(표) • stopover 중간 기착

• overpass 고가도로 • detector 탐지기

day 48

Voca Check

1 rim/hoop **2** root/cheer **3** umpire **4** slam dunk
5 forward **6** grand slam **7** batting average **8** Archery

exercise

A.

1 ⓒ **2** ⓐ **3** ⓔ **4** ⓓ **5** ⓑ

ⓐ aquatics : 수중에서 이루어지는 스포츠나 활동
ⓑ triathlon : 3종목의 운동 경기에 연속으로 참가하는 대회
ⓒ turnover : 한 팀에서 다른 팀으로 공의 소유권이 이동하는 것
ⓓ substitute : 다른 선수를 대신하는 선수
ⓔ injury time : 축구 경기 도중 선수들의 부상으로 손실된 시간을 보충하기 위해 추가한 시간

1 그 파울은 공격권 상실을 가져왔고 그 때문에 그 팀은 경기에서 졌다. **2** 나는 물을 무서워하기 때문에 한번도 수상 스포츠를 하지 않았다. **3** 동점으로 후반전이 종료되었으나, 추가 경기시간에 한국이 이겼다. **4** 그 선수가 다리를 다쳐 교체 선수가 투입되었다. **5** 나는 다양한 경기를 볼 수 있기 때문에 3종 경기 보는 것을 좋아한다.

• successive 연속적인 • transfer 이전, 이동 • possession 소유(권)
• make up for ~을 벌충하다, 보충하다

B.

1 ⓓ **2** ⓐ **3** ⓑ **4** ⓒ **5** ⓓ

1 육상 경기는 단거리 달리기, 창던지기, 장대높이뛰기 같은 경기들로 구성되어 있다. **2** 체조를 하기 위해서는 균형 감각, 유연성, 동작의 우아함이 특히 뛰어나야 한다. **3** 나는 말을 아주 좋아하기 때문에 승마 경기 보는 것을 좋아한다. **4** 이소룡은 무술이 서방 세계에서 인기를 끌도록 하는 데 도움을 주었다. **5** 예선전에서 지고 본선에 진출하지 못하여 우리들의 희망이 꺾였다.

• archery 양궁 • weightlifting 역도 • equestrian 마술(馬術)의, 승마의 • martial arts 무술 • sweeper 축구 최종 수비수 • preliminary round 예선전

day 49

Voca Check

1 solo **2** fiction **3** wind instrument **4** landscape
5 sci-fi(SF, science fiction) **6** statue **7** genre
8 surrealism

exercise

A.

1 ⓔ **2** ⓓ **3** ⓑ **4** ⓐ **5** ⓒ

ⓐ euphemism : 불쾌한 것을 가리키는 간접적인 단어 또는 어구
ⓑ realism : 미술에서 사물을 실제로 보이는 모습 그대로 묘사하는 기법
ⓒ personification : 사물 또는 특징을 사람처럼 나타내는 것
ⓓ metaphor : 암시적인 비유를 담고 있는 단어 또는 어구
ⓔ illustration : 텍스트에서 무언가를 설명하기 위해 등장하는 그림 또는 사진

1 삽화는 글의 내용을 명확히 하기 위해 사용된다. **2** Shakespeare는 "온 세상은 무대이다"와 같은 은유적 표현을 많이 사용했다. **3** Picasso의 왜곡된 이미지들은 선대들의 사실주의에 대한 거부 표현이었다. **4** 나는 그녀를 불쾌하게 하지 않으려고 완곡한 표현을 사용해서 편지를 썼다. **5** '미녀와 야수'에서는 가재 도구들의 의인화가 사용되었다.

• depict 묘사하다 • implicit 암시적인 • distortion 왜곡
• predecessor 전임자, 선대

B.

1 ⓑ **2** ⓓ **3** ⓒ **4** ⓐ **5** ⓒ

1 나에게는 Van Gogh의 걸작인 '해바라기'의 복제품이 있다. **2** 그 예술가는 대리석으로 조각상을 만들었다. **3** 그는 시보다는 산문으로 더 많이 알려져 있다. **4** 그녀의 풍자가 너무나 재미있으면서도 통찰력이 있어서 나는 큰 소리로 웃었다. **5** 그의 우렁찬 목소리는 멋진 가사와 함께 강렬한 노래를 만들어 냈다.

• epic 서사시 • virtuoso 거장 • carve 조각하다 • perspective 원근법 • prose 산문 • simile 직유 • satire 풍자 • quintet 5중주[중창]
• percussion 타악기 • allegory 풍유법

day 50

Voca Check

1 Buddhism **2** persecution **3** trinity **4** sect **5** mosque
6 pilgrimage **7** mass **8** Ten Commandments

exercise

A.

1 ⓑ **2** ⓒ **3** ⓔ **4** ⓓ **5** ⓐ

ⓐ secular : 종교와 관계없는
ⓑ scripture : 어떤 종교 내에서 신성시되는 글
ⓒ theology : 종교와 신앙에 관한 학문

ⓓ heathen : 기독교 등의 기성 종교와 연관되어 있지 않은 사람
ⓔ orthodox : 어떤 종교의 전통적인 믿음을 철저하게 따르는

1 목사가 성경을 읽었다. **2** 나는 신학 시간에 여러 종교에 대해 많은 것을 배웠다. **3** 정통파 기독교인들은 이혼에 반대한다. **4** 어머니는 공립 학교 교사들은 이교도라 생각했기 때문에 나를 사립 종교학교에 보냈다. **5** 비록 부모님은 종교를 갖고 계시지만, 나는 공립 학교에 가서 세속적인 교육을 받았다.

• sacred 신성한 • holy 신성한, 거룩한 • faith 신앙 • established religion (기성) 종교

B.

1 ⓑ **2** ⓓ **3** ⓒ **4** ⓐ **5** ⓓ

1 선교사들은 세계를 돌아다니며 사람들을 자신의 종교로 개종시키기 위해 노력한다. **2** 신부는 성수를 뿌려 제단을 축성하였다. **3** 교황은 천주교의 가장 높은 지도자이다. **4** 천주교인들은 신부님께 죄를 고백하면 하나님께서 죄를 용서해 주실 거라고 믿는다. **5** 평신도는 일주일에 한 번씩 예배를 드리지만, 목사는 평생을 신앙에 바친다.

• confess 고백하다 • convert 개종시키다 • preach 설교하다
• resurrect 부활시키다 • martyr 순교시키다 • persecute 박해하다
• consecrate 축성(祝聖)하다; 신성하게 하다 • sermon 설교 • hymn 찬송가 • ritual 예식 • pagan 이교도 • layperson 평신도

Index

d

e

f

g

h

i

j

n

o

p

q

r

S

t

u

v

w

y

z

지은이

NE능률 영어교육연구소

NE능률 영어교육연구소는 혁신적이며 효율적인 영어 교재를 개발하고
영어 학습의 질을 한 단계 높이고자 노력하는 NE능률의 연구조직입니다.

능률 VOCA 〈고난도〉

펴 낸 이 주민홍
펴 낸 곳 서울특별시 마포구 월드컵북로 396(상암동) 누리꿈스퀘어 비즈니스타워 10층
(주)NE능률 (우편번호 03925)
펴 낸 날 2023년 1월 5일 개정판 제1쇄 발행
2023년 4월 15일 제2쇄
전 화 02 2014 7114
팩 스 02 3142 0356
홈페이지 www.neungyule.com
등록번호 제1-68호
I S B N 979-11-253-4102-4 53740
정 가 15,000원

NE 능률

고객센터

교재 내용 문의: contact.nebooks.co.kr (별도의 가입 절차 없이 작성 가능)
제품 구매, 교환, 불량, 반품 문의: 02-2014-7114 ☎ 전화문의는 본사 업무시간 중에만 가능합니다.

NE능률 교재 MAP

어휘

아래 교재 MAP을 참고하여 본인의 현재 혹은 목표 수준에 따라 교재를 선택하세요.

NE능률 교재들과 함께 영어실력을 쑥쑥~ 올려보세요!

MP3 파일 등 교재 부가 학습 서비스 및 자세한 교재 정보는 www.nebooks.co.kr 에서 확인하세요.

초1-2	초3	초3-4	초4-5	초5-6
	초등영어 단어가 된다 1	초등영어 단어가 된다 2 주니어 능률VOCA Starter 1	초등영어 단어가 된다 3 주니어 능률VOCA Starter 2	초등영어 단어가 된다 4

초6-예비중	중1	중1-2	중2-3	중3
주니어 능률VOCA 입문		주니어 능률VOCA 기본 능률VOCA 어원편 Lite	주니어 능률VOCA 실력	주니어 능률VOCA 숙어

중3-예비고	고1	고1-2	고2-3	고3
	능률VOCA 어원편 능률VOCA 고교기본 능률VOCA 숙어 TEPS BY STEP L+V Basic	능률VOCA 고교필수 2000	능률VOCA 수능완성 2200 특급 수능·EBS 기출 VOCA TEPS BY STEP L+V 1	

수능 이상/ 토플 80-89· 텝스 327-384점	수능 이상/ 토플 90-99· 텝스 385-451점	수능 이상/ 토플 100· 텝스 452점 이상		
TEPS BY STEP L+V 2	능률VOCA 고난도	TEPS BY STEP L+V 3		